More Than Two

MORE THAN TWO

A practical guide to ethical polyamory

FRANKLIN VEAUX

EVE RICKERT

FOREWORD BY JANET W. HARDY

Thorntree Press

More Than Two
A practical guide to ethical polyamory
Text copyright © 2014 by Franklin Veaux and Eve Rickert
Illustrations copyright © 2014 by Paul Mendoza (cover) and Tatiana Gill (interior)

Thorntree Press
P.O. Box 301231
Portland, OR 97294
press@thorntreepress.com

Cover illustration by Paul Mendoza
Interior illustrations by Tatiana Gill
Cover design by Vanessa Rossi
Interior design and typesetting by Mari Chijiiwa
Substantive editing by Alan M. MacRobert
Copy-editing by Naomi Pauls, Paper Trail Publishing
Proofreading by Roma Ilnyckyj
Indexing by Krista Smith

Publisher's Cataloging-In-Publication Data
(Prepared by The Donohue Group, Inc.)

Veaux, Franklin.
    More than two : a practical guide to ethical polyamory / Franklin Veaux, Eve Rickert ; foreword by Janet W. Hardy.

        pages : illustrations ; cm

    Issued also as an ebook.
    Includes bibliographical references and index.
    ISBN: 978-0-9913997-0-3 (paperback)
    ISBN: 978-0-9913997-1-0 (hardcover)

    1. Non-monogamous relationships. 2. Sexual ethics. 3. Intimacy (Psychology) I. Rickert, Eve. II. Hardy, Janet W. III. Title.

HQ980 .V43 2014
306.84/23   2014938252

ISBN (paperback): 978-0-9913997-0-3
ISBN (hardcover): 978-0-9913997-1-0

Digital print edition v1.0

Printed in the United States of America on acid-free paper.

To R.

Love is the extremely difficult realisation
that something other than oneself is real.

IRIS MURDOCH

CONTENTS

FOREWORD

It was around twenty years ago that my co-author Dossie Easton and I spoke to a roomful of Mensa members about what was then generally called S/M. We'd already written and published *The Bottoming Book* and *The Topping Book*, and taught a bunch of workshops and done a bunch of public scenes, so we were used to being outrageous in front of audiences. We had fun.

But afterward, a friend told me about a conversation she'd overheard. "Did you hear about that S and M presentation this afternoon?" she mimicked, in a voice high-pitched with shock. "There were these two women giving it...and they were talking about stuff they'd done *together*...and one of their boyfriends was *right in the room!*"

That's how unaware the world was of polyamory, and other monogamy alternatives, back then. And that's when we knew we needed to write a book about poly. The first edition of *The Ethical Slut* was published in 1997, and we were both pretty startled by the virulent reaction it got—far more virulent, much to our surprise, than we'd gotten for our BDSM titles. As we made the circuit of morning-drive radio shows and local-access cable television, we heard from the woman who said she'd "go upside his head with a frying pan" if her husband ever dared propose such a thing. Another woman told us we were the cause of the decline of Western civilization, and that our book should be banned, and we should be tied up and whipped. (We were able to restrain our giggles until the commercial break.)

When you're writing in a context like that, most of your job has to do with gently prying open your reader's mind, casting a bit of light on unexamined prejudices and making space for new ways of thinking. Even if we'd wanted to suggest some practical guidelines for how to make poly relationships work better, we had a relatively small database of experience and wisdom to work from—basically our own lives, and those of our circle of queerish, kinkyish, San Francisco-ish friends, whose needs and circumstances were quite different from those of the average American reader. So we stuck, for the most part, to first principles, and left the nuts and bolts for other writers.

We had no idea, way back then, that we and our little book were about to climb a gigantic wave of interest in polyamorous lifestyles. *Slut* has outsold all our other books put together, by a handy margin. It went on, a decade and a half later, into a larger, more slickly published edition from a major publisher, with exercises and practical information in addition to the basic principles.

But we're still only two writers, with our own backgrounds and prejudices. We're proud to have helped create a world, the world of polyamory, that's big enough and various enough to *need* different opinions, ideas and approaches from ours.

I've traveled the world teaching Ethical Slut workshops. When I ask my attendees about the biggest problem they've encountered doing polyamory, they've usually responded by naming something to do with logistics (time, space, attention) or something to do with jealousy. And these are indeed thorny issues...but I'd argue that they're really symptoms of a deeper problem. Imagine that you're a monogamous person, having the kinds of relationship problems that monogamous people have: jealousy (yes, they feel it too), boredom, "bed death," whatever. What do you do? You call a therapist, you ask your friends, you watch *Dr. Phil*, you go to the bookstore and pick one of the dozens of titles aimed at teaching monogamous people how to be better at monogamy.

But if you're a poly person? Where do we poly people get our answers? If we're lucky, we may live in a major city *and* be Internet-savvy *and* know the word *polyamory* so that we know what term to search on *and* have life circumstances that enable us to go to a poly munch or meetup. For the rest of the world, though, there are websites and books. And not nearly enough of either.

Many people, sad to say, attempt polyamory without knowing anyone who has done it successfully and is willing to talk about it in public. Many have little or no access to the small but growing body of wisdom that successful polyamorists have accumulated and shared. Which is why it's past time for *More Than Two*.

I've e-known (if that's the word for someone you know on the Internet but have never met) Franklin Veaux for a long time now; his co-author Eve is new to me. They are both experienced and articulate polyamorists—Franklin's poly website xeromag.com (now morethantwo.com) dates back to 1997, the same year that the first edition of *Slut* was published.

I am pleased to say that I disagree with Franklin and Eve on a few points (if you want to know which, you'll have to read both of our books). But, honestly, I'd be worried if I didn't. There are as many ways to do poly as there are people doing it, and beyond the basics of disclosure and consent, there's no "right" or "wrong" way—there are only things that have worked for some people and other things that haven't worked for others. Monogamous people get to decide whether to listen to advice from Dr. Phil or Dr. Laura or any of the other relationship "doctors" that fill our radio waves and TV screens; poly people should have the same opportunities to listen to different advice and make their own choices.

Different authors have different styles. Dossie and I have been described as "big sisters" (if your big sister is a slutty kinky aging hippie); Franklin and Eve are more like "wise neighbors"—think of the guy on the other side of the fence on *Home Improvement*, calm and wise and funny. Dossie and I write primarily about the sexual aspects of poly; Franklin and Eve are more interested in the day-to-day living part. Dossie and I like to indulge ourselves, just a little, in high-flown realms of abstraction and idealism; Franklin and Eve like to keep their feet on the ground.

You'll probably find yourself relating more to one style than the other, and that's just exactly the way it should be. The more people who open their minds to the infinite possibilities of poly, the more space there will be for new books (can *Polyamory for Dummies* be far in the future?), new opinions, specialized publications, personal gatherings and more.

Someday, perhaps, there will be as many resources and role models for poly people as there are today for monogamists. I'd like to live in a world where my grandchildren-to-be can watch *The Bill and Joan and Pat Show* as matter-of-factly as I watched *The Brady Bunch*. Well, my great-grandchildren, anyway.

And books like *More Than Two* are one of the ways that will happen. I hope you enjoy reading it as much as I did.

JANET W. HARDY

ACKNOWLEDGMENTS

Successful polyamory is a group effort. So perhaps it's fitting that the efforts of a great many people went into creating this book. Without their help and support, *More Than Two* would not exist. Writing this book was a long road, and a lot changed between the first draft and what you're reading now. Substantive editing was done by Alan M. MacRobert, who not only worked very hard to turn our draft into lucid prose, but filled in gaps, contributed ideas, and challenged us to address ideas and constituencies we'd overlooked.

Shelly DeForte contributed her wisdom and insight through written contributions to chapters 3, 7, 9 and 15, among others. Pepper Mint provided important contributions to the section on LBGTQ communities in chapter 25, as well as valuable feedback on an early draft. Sophia Kelly, Aggie Sez and two anonymous reviewers also provided feedback on several key chapters. The members of the poly women's discussion group in Vancouver, B.C., provided valuable feedback and discussion of ideas. We're also grateful to Janet Hardy, co-author of *The Ethical Slut* and poly pioneer, for supporting the book by contributing the foreword.

You'll find many stories throughout this book, both ours and other people's. These stories help illustrate the many lessons we've learned on our journey. The names you'll see other than ours are pseudonyms, and we have changed or removed some identifying details to maintain anonymity. We have taken care to choose stories we were involved in directly, stories that at least one participant has given us permission to use, or stories that were disclosed to us more than ten years ago and were not disclosed in a confidential setting.

We're grateful to Paul Mendoza for the beautiful cover illustration, and to Tatiana Gill for the interior illustrations. We're also tremendously lucky to have had a first-rate production team, who provided fantastic work on a very tight production schedule: Naomi Pauls, who copy-edited the manuscript; Vanessa Rossi, who designed the cover; Mari Chijiiwa, who designed and typeset the interior; Roma Ilnyckyj, who proofread the book; and Krista

Smith, who prepared the index and provided detailed research and fact-checking for chapter 20. Any errors that remain in the book are our sole responsibility.

We received generous sponsorships for writing and production from Kenneth R. Haslam, MD, curator of the polyamory collection for the Kinsey Institute for Research in Sex, Gender and Reproduction, and from Alan M. MacRobert and Ola Rozenfeld. The balance of the project was funded by a crowdfunding campaign, made successful by the support of many people who provided either material support in the form of rewards, or publicity in the form of a platform for our ideas. These people included Greta Christina, Abzu Emporium, Kendra Holliday, Louisa Leontiades, Alan MacRobert, Cunning Minx, Christopher Ryan, Aggie Sez and Elisabeth Sheff. Of course, we could not have completed this project without the 455 people who contributed to our campaign; those who contributed $100 or more are listed on the next page, and the rest are credited at morethantwo.com/supporters.

Franklin would also like to thank his other partners, referred to in the book as Vera, Amy, Amber and Sylvia—not only for their support on the book but also for filling his life with love and awesomeness. Eve is thankful to her husband, Peter, and her girlfriend, Paloma, for their emotional support and ideas, and for tolerating her long physical and emotional absences during the writing and editing. We'd both like to thank our mothers for being amazing.

Though they may not know it, this book wouldn't exist without a peculiar chain of events involving U.S. NASA, the Mars Curiosity mission, Phil Plait, Paul Fenwick and Twitter.

The first draft of *More Than Two* was written in a log cabin deep in the remote wilderness of rural Washington, where Kay and Harry Hibler—and their cat—graciously let us stay (and collect mushrooms!) for six weeks. We are immensely grateful for the opportunity they provided us, and the book would not be what it is without their generosity and hospitality. The stunning, handcrafted cabin, affectionately known as Hibler Hill, is an inspiring monument to loving, creative partnerships, making it an especially fitting place to have created this book.

OUR SUPPORTERS

The following people generously contributed $100 or more to the Indiegogo campaign that funded production of this book. A full list of all backers can be found at www.morethantwo.com/book.

Alan M. MacRobert
Alex Blue
Allison Frame
Andrea Longo
Annalisa Castaldo
Anonymous B. Shylock
Brittainy Shaw
Brodie Kristensen
C. Karl Neitzert
Carl de Malmanche
Coralie Gill
Dan Mahoney and M.K. Williams
Danjite
David Wheeler
Deborah Wallach
Edward Martin III
Elise West
Eric Côté
Ewen McNeill
Feygon Willow
Fritz Neumann
Gabrielle Lamoureux
Gwyneth
Hannah "Er00" Fordham
Ian Darson

Isa Pdx
Jan & Brian
Jared Pinkham
Jessica D.
Joachim Brackx
Kenneth R. Haslam MD
Louisa Leontiades
Luca Boschetto, Poliamore.org
Luca Pellanda
Luís Miguel Viterbo
Lynne Everett
Marilou Rickert
Mark Staudt
Matt Jones
Matthew Sheahan
Maxine Green
Michael Charboneau
Ola Rozenfeld
Rebekka K. Steg
Rob Igo
Stuart Cheshire
Suni
The Atlanta Fraggle Rock Community
The Graham Joys
Winston

INTRODUCTION

Will is married to Rachel. They own a beautiful house. Will (not his real name) is a successful businessman who runs a prosperous company. Every day, he comes home to Rachel and to her boyfriend Arnold, who also shares their home. Will and Arnold are good friends who often spend time together. The three of them plan vacations and go hiking together. Sometimes Arnold's girlfriend Leila joins them.

Santiago and Winona are engaged. They're both dating another woman, Helen. Santiago and Winona have been together for more than six years. He started dating Helen three years ago, and about a year after that, Helen and Winona started dating each other. Santiago and Winona live together. Helen lives nearby.

Eliza likes her independence. She doesn't fancy being tied down in a conventional relationship. She lives on her own, and she prefers it that way. She's been dating Kyle for about five years, and they're madly in love. Kyle is a long-distance partner; he lives in another state with his girlfriend Melody. When Eliza visits Kyle, she stays with them both. Eliza is also dating Stacie, who lives nearby with her husband, Seth. Eliza and Stacie have been dating for four years. Seth and Eliza are friends, though they aren't romantic partners. We know all of these people.

Yes, it is possible to live this way. Hundreds of thousands of people are doing it right now. It's called *polyamory*, which literally means "many loves." The crucial point: It's done with the full knowledge and consent of everyone who is affected.

Polyamorous relationships can be joyous, brimming with laughter and love. But they rarely just happen. They take work, and they require trust, communication and kindness. It's easier to build healthy, vibrant poly relationships and avoid disaster when you can see others doing it and learn from them. This is easier now than it used to be. In the past thirty years, the growing worldwide community of polyamorous people has built a treasure vault of hard-won wisdom. Much of it has been achieved at a bitter price, through many, many people's trials, errors, crashes and hard-won insights. We know far more than we did a generation ago about what is likely to work, and why, and how...and also what has a consistent track record of failure.

The authors of this book have been through a combined forty years of poly life. In addition to living it daily, we have observed literally thousands of poly relationships. For twenty years, Franklin has run probably the most linked-to polyamory information site on the Web.

Franklin started living polyamorously in the early 1980s, long before people were using the word. He had no language for what he felt, no community support, no role models, no one to talk to or learn from. He had to find his own way, and so he got to make all the mistakes on his own. That included marrying a monogamous woman and living for nearly two decades in a hierarchical, veto-based relationship that was never really happy for anyone. In 1997—the same year *The Ethical Slut* was published—he launched a website, then at Xeromag.com (now morethantwo.com), filled with introductory polyamory resources. His goal was to provide all the information that he wished he'd had when he first started out.

That website grew and changed, transforming over the years along with Franklin's relationships and his thinking about polyamory. It is now one of the first Google hits for "polyamory." Over the years, he's received thousands of emails from people thanking him for helping or even saving their relationships. His work is sometimes controversial, but the fact is, it helps people.

Eve first learned about polyamory when she was twelve, from a Sunday-school teacher who challenged her assumptions about monogamous relationships and introduced her to the concepts of "primary" and "secondary" partners. In high school, her social group flirted with polyamorous ideas and practices but didn't have a framework for exploring them under that name. After high school Eve's own relationships were monogamous, though she had friends who were poly. In her thirties she and her husband-to-be opened their monogamous relationship. She has embraced polyamory since 2008.

We tell our personal stories throughout this book. We're not experts on polyamory. We believe there are no experts. Polyamory is still too new for that. We wrote this book because we've spent a lot of time exploring this nearly trackless space, and along the way we've made plenty of mistakes we'd like to help you avoid. If what you find here serves you, use it. If it doesn't, that's okay too. Look at some of the other wonderful resources listed in the back of this book to find what meets your needs.

POLY JARGON

As polyamory has grown as a relationship model, it has developed its own vocabulary. Folks in poly relationships will talk about "compersion," a feeling of joy at the happiness of a partner in a new relationship, and "new relationship energy" or NRE, the giddy, honeymoon phase of a newfound love. You might hear someone talk about "wibbles," or minor twinges of jealousy. An OSO is a person's "other significant other."

All this lingo can create a certain amount of confusion. After all, the idea of non-monogamous relationships isn't new; people have been stepping out, swapping wives and generally fooling around since the dawn of time. So why all these new words?

New terminology arises where old terminology doesn't fit. These terms evolved to give polyamorous people a way to discuss the joys, challenges and situations they encounter that might not have direct corollaries in monogamy or in the most common forms of non-monogamy, which aren't polyamorous. The new jargon is a way to talk about what polyamory is (ethical, open, consensual long-term romantic relationships) without using the language of cheating or of swinging, casual wife-swapping, and other forms of traditional non-monogamy. We have tried to be careful not to overload this book with jargon, but if you get lost, there's a glossary in the back.

THEMES IN THIS BOOK

As you read this book, you will see several ideas we return to again and again. We have observed that happy, strong relationships of any kind have certain things in common, and we talk about them many times.

The first idea is *trust*. Many problems in any relationship, but especially in poly relationships, come down to "How much do I trust my partner?" Having such trust is often more difficult than it sounds, because internal emotions such as insecurity or low self-esteem can affect how much confidence we place in a partner's love for us.

The second theme is *courage*. We suggest many approaches to relationship that require confronting socially imposed norms and our own fears, and that takes courage. When many people think of "courage," they think of a firefighter charging into a burning building or a person facing down a hungry leopard—extraordinary acts of bravery in the face of danger. The kind of courage we mean is a more personal, ordinary thing: talking about our feelings even when we're afraid; giving a partner the freedom to explore new relationships even when we fear being abandoned; challenging ourselves to step outside our comfort zones even when we aren't sure there will be someone there to catch us.

The third theme is *abundance*. Looked at one way, polyamory might seem hopeless: we're seeking people who also want this unconventional way of life, which limits our potential dating pool; who have a compatible sexual orientation and gender identity, which narrows it further; who are available for new romantic connections, which narrows it still more; whose style of poly is compatible with ours; who we have chemistry with...how can we expect to find anyone? Looked at another way, we share this world with more than seven billion other people, so even 10 percent of 10 percent of 10 percent of 10 percent is over 700,000 potential partners—surely an embarrassment of riches. How we think about potential relationships, whether we view them as scarce or abundant, will make a huge difference in our romantic lives.

The fourth idea is *ethics*. We strongly believe there are ethical and unethical ways to treat other people, and we talk about them throughout this book. Treating people with compassion, integrity and respect, no matter what role they play in our lives, is something we believe to be of paramount importance in happy, healthy relationships.

The last theme we will often return to is *empowerment*. We believe that relationships work best when all the people involved feel empowered to help shape and guide their relationships, to advocate for their needs, and to feel that they have a hand in the outcomes.

Polyamory, like any worthwhile endeavor, is a journey. We hope to give you some signposts to help you along the way, but nobody can make the journey for you. It is up to you to navigate your way toward happy, ethical, compassionate relationships.

PART 1

What Is Polyamory?

STARTING
THE JOURNEY

The most successful people in life recognize,
that in life they create their own love,
they manufacture their own meaning,
they generate their own motivation.

NEIL DEGRASSE TYSON

It's a story as old as time: Boy meets girl (or perhaps boy meets boy, or girl meets girl), they date, they fall in love. They pledge sexual and emotional fidelity, start a family and settle down to live happily ever after, the end. But the story often proves to be a fairy tale. All too often it continues on into misery, breakdown, separation, divorce, boy meets new girl. Lather, rinse, repeat.

In one common variant, boy meets girl, they settle down, one of them meets someone new, things get messy, dishes are thrown, hearts are broken. Or perhaps you've heard this version: Girl meets two boys, or vice versa. A tragic choice must be made. Someone is left heartbroken, and everybody is left wondering what might have been.

We propose that there is a different way to write this story. Boy meets girl, they fall in love, girl meets another boy, they fall in love, girl and boy meet another boy, girl meets girl, girl meets boy, and they all live happily ever after.

The word *polyamory* was coined in the early 1990s from the Greek *poly*, meaning "many," and the Latin *amor*, meaning "love." It means having multiple loving, often committed, relationships at the same time by mutual agreement, with honesty and clarity. We know what you're thinking: "Who does the laundry?" We'll get to that in a bit.

Polyamory *isn't* about sneaking off and getting some action on the sly when your girlfriend is out of town. Nor is it about dating three people and keeping everyone in the dark. It's not about joining a religious cult and marrying a dozen teenage girls, or about having recreational sex while maintaining only one "real" relationship, or going to parties where you drop your keys in a hat.

Poly relationships come in an astonishing variety of shapes, sizes and flavors, just like the human heart. There are "vee" relationships, where one person has two partners who aren't romantically involved with each other; "triad" relationships, where three are mutually involved; and "quad" relationships of four people, who may or may not all be romantically involved with one another. A relationship might be "polyfidelitous," which means the people agree not to pursue additional partners. Or it may be open to members starting new relationships. A poly person might have one or more "primary" partners and one or more "secondary" partners, or recognize no rankings. They might have a "group marriage," sharing finances, a home and maybe children as a single family.

Some people imagine that polyamory involves a fear of commitment. The truth is, commitment in polyamory doesn't mean commitment to sexual exclusivity. Instead, it means commitment to a romantic relationship, with everything that goes along with that: commitment to being there when your partners need you, to investing in their happiness, to building a life with them, to creating happy and healthy relationships that meet everyone's needs, and to supporting one another when life gets hard. Unfortunately, society has taught us to view commitment only through the lens of sexual exclusivity; this diminishes all the other important ways that we commit to one another. People who can't commit to one person sure as hell can't commit to more than one!

Polyamory isn't the same thing as *polygamy*, which means having multiple spouses (most often in the form of *polygyny*, or multiple wives; sometimes in the form of *polyandry*, or multiple husbands). It's not about keeping a harem, though we know some of you there in the back row were kind of hoping we'd go that way. It's not the same as swinging, though some poly people also swing (as we discuss in chapter 17, on opening from a couple). And finally, it's not about rampant promiscuity. Polyamorous relationships are *relationships*—with good times, bad times, problem-solving, communication...and, yes, laundry.

DOWN WITH THE FAIRY TALE

The prelude to lifelong monogamy echoes through our culture in fairy tales we all hear: A beautiful, charming young woman toils alone in an unhappy life, friendless and beset on all sides. She endures hardships and trauma until one day along comes her handsome prince, who swoops down and lifts her into his arms. They fall in love; the chorus swells, the curtains close.

Stories like this resonate with us because they offer a comforting view of relationships: True love conquers all. Everyone has a soulmate, just waiting to be found. Once we've found our soulmate, we will live happily ever after. Love is all you need. There's no need to work hard at understanding yourself or your needs, no need to keep working on happiness once you've found it.

Forget the fairy tale. "Happily ever after" is a myth because people, unlike characters in fairy tales, are not static. We live, we grow, we change. Happy, healthy romantic lives require not just continual reinvestment but constant awareness of the changes in our partners, our situations and ourselves. Our partners do not owe us a guarantee that they will never change, nor do *we* owe anyone such a guarantee. And as we change, so do the things that make us happy.

Polyamory can feel threatening because it upsets our fairy-tale assumption that the right partner will keep us safe from change. Polyamory introduces the prospect of chaos and uncertainty into what's supposed to be a straightforward progression to bliss. But a healthy relationship must first of all be resilient, able to respond to the changes and complexity life brings. Nor is happiness actually a state of being. It is a process, a side effect of doing other things. The fairy tale tells us that with the right partner, happiness just happens. But happiness is something we re-create every day. And it comes more from our outlook than from the things around us.

The relationship fairy tale carries other hidden falsehoods. For instance, it promises that one person will always be able to meet our needs. The idea that polyamory addresses this situation has its own problems (as we talk about in chapter 4), but it's still unreasonable to expect one person to be everything.

If we accept the fairy tale, we may feel shaky and insecure whenever reality doesn't live up to our expectations. We may imagine that if we are attracted to someone else, something is wrong. (Actor Johnny Depp, whose ongoing relationship turmoil is the stuff of tabloid legend, famously remarked, "If you love two people at the same time, choose the second. Because if you really loved the first one, you wouldn't have fallen for the second." Cue poly eye-roll.) On the other hand, if our one true love is attracted to someone else, we may feel like a failure. After all, if we do everything we're supposed to do, then we should be enough, right? And if a partner loves someone else, that means our love isn't good enough, right?

The idea of The One, the "love of your life," is seductive. In reality, it's perfectly possible to have more than one love of your life. The two of us know many people who do, and each of us has several loves of our lives—and we're not even romantically involved with all of them. Even though all of our loves have other loves, we feel secure, because we have many people who will always be there for us.

WHY BE POLY?

The best way to understand why someone might be polyamorous is to ask, "What do people get out of relationships in the first place?" Romance is a fiddly business even in the best of circumstances; why not just give it all a miss and be done with it? A quick answer might be "We are happier when we're in relationships than when we're not." Humans are social animals. We do better when we share our lives intimately with others. We're built for it. As complicated and messy and unpredictable as romance is, its rewards are fantastic. Indeed, most of us feel driven to seek out people who see us for what we are, who share themselves with us, who love us.

For many people, establishing a romantic relationship switches off this drive. The task is done, the race is won; there's no need to find new partners. But for some, being in a relationship doesn't flip off that switch. We remain open to the idea of new connections and more love. We engage in multiple romantic relationships, and love others who do the same, because doing so enriches the lives of everyone involved. Loving more than one person at the same time is not an escape from intimacy; it is an enthusiastic embrace of intimacy.

Polyamorous relationships have practical benefits. More adults in a family often provides greater financial freedom and security. Some poly folk combine living spaces, incomes and expenses, which increases everyone's financial flexibility. Even poly people who don't cohabit or share expenses gain many things from mutual support among multiple partners. If you're having a bad day, there are more people to comfort and help you. If you're having a problem, you get more perspectives. You have more of everything you get from romantic relationships—more companionship, more advice, more joy, more love.

Being poly can also be fantastic for your sex life. Sex is a learned skill, and the human sexual horizon is vast. Whatever your tastes, however ingenious your imagination, the range of sexual experience is so great that someone, somewhere, is doing something you'd love to do that would never occur to you. Each time you invite another lover into your life, you have the opportunity to learn things you might never otherwise have learned...often, things you can bring into your existing relationships. Nobody is so creative that she has nothing to learn from someone else.

Conversely, there is a community saying: "Some people go into poly to have more sex; some go into poly to have less sex." A monogamous couple with mismatched sex drives has a major problem. Constant frustration on one side, and constant unwanted demands on the other, kill marriages routinely. But when the couple is part of a larger network of lovers, everyone can more easily find their own level, and the pressure is off.

ARE YOU POLYAMOROUS?

For some of us, whether we're polyamorous or monogamous is obvious; for others, it isn't. Many poly people feel it's an intrinsic part of who they are, like hair color or sexual orientation. A person who feels inherently non-monogamous can identify as poly even if she has only one relationship, or none.

Others embrace polyamory because they see it as inherently more honest than monogamy, which often requires denying attractions to other people. Still other folks see polyamory as a way to shed the assumptions about property and control that have long gone hand in hand with monogamy.

Deciding whether poly is a good fit requires not only deciding whether you're non-monogamous but also whether the things you want from life, and the personal ethics you bring to the world, align well with having multiple honest romantic relationships. For instance, a desire for sexual variety without romantic attachments might point to swinging as a better fit. A desire for multiple romantic relationships without openness or transparency might mean some self-work is in order.

Polyamory is not right for everyone. Polyamory is not the next wave in human evolution. Nor is it more enlightened, more spiritual, more progressive or more advanced than monogamy. Polyamorous people are not automatically less jealous, more compassionate or better at communicating than monogamists.

We believe relationships that are deliberately, intentionally constructed are more satisfying, and more likely to lead to happiness, than relationships whose shape is determined by default social expectations. It is absolutely possible for a monogamous relationship to be built by careful, deliberate choice. Many people are content in monogamous relationships, and that's fine. Monogamy doesn't necessarily mean simply following a social norm. If you decide that polyamory is not a good fit for your life, that's okay. Don't do it or let anyone push you into it.

It's useful to think of polyamory as an outgrowth of a certain set of relationship ideas. Rather than asking, "Am I polyamorous?" you could ask yourself, "Are the tools and ideas of polyamory useful to me?" Even if you don't desire multiple relationships, the things we talk about in this book may be valuable to you.

MISCONCEPTIONS ABOUT POLYAMORY

At this point, some of you may still be thinking "Woohoo! Endless orgies!", and others of you are likely thinking "What a load of horse manure! This is just a fancy way of saying your partner lets you cheat." For anyone who imagines that being poly means sleeping with whomever you like, whenever you like, without having to consider others' feelings, we have some bad news. A polyamorous relationship does not mean that anything goes. It means far more listening, discussing and self-analyzing than you may be used to.

You might end up with one partner (if you're on one end of a vee or an N or a W), or you might even be single (it's possible to be poly and have no partners at present). You might have fewer partners over your lifetime than someone who has many monogamous relationships in a row, like, say, Johnny Depp. Promiscuity suggests a lack of discernment; polyamorous people may be very picky indeed.

Of course you can, if you want to, run around shagging everyone you can...as long as you accept the consequences. If you disregard the needs and feelings of people you're sleeping with, you don't get to sleep with them anymore. And in the poly world, word gets around. Acting without thought for your partners is a poor long-term relationship strategy.

For those of you who imagine that *polyamory* is a fancy word to excuse your cheating, we have bad news for you as well. "Cheating" is violating trust by breaking the rules of a relationship. If taking multiple lovers does not violate trust, then it's not cheating by definition. Betrayal, not sex, is cheating's defining element. (A person can move from cheating to polyamory, though it's a road fraught with peril; we get into that in chapter 17.)

You may be tempted to think that a relationship allowing multiple partners has no rules at all, but think again. Many kinds of poly relationships exist; each has its own agreements. But all require trust, respect and compassionate behavior.

Despite the images of free-love compounds that might be dancing in your head, polyamory does not necessarily meaning living in a commune or an intentional community. Not all poly people live with multiple partners, or with any partners, for that matter. Nor is polyamory all about couples seeking thirds.

Polyamory doesn't necessarily suggest a taste for kinky sex. You can be polyamorous without mounting a trapeze in the bedroom. Many people in polyamorous relationships have straightforward tastes. Poly families spend their time balancing checkbooks, watching Netflix, doing laundry, all the ordinary things a family does. If you're interested in polyamory because you imagine nonstop kinky orgies, you may be disappointed.

Don't get us wrong; we're not knocking wild sex parties or kinky orgies. Some poly folks (Franklin, for example) are quite fond of these things. Others (like Eve), not so much. Many poly people dislike group sex, don't identify as bisexual or pansexual, and don't even own a vibrator, much less a trapeze.

When the poly community first took shape, many of the most visible activists and organizers were commune-oriented pagan or New Age spiritualists. Today polyamory attracts a much broader range of people. We've met poly folks from all walks of life: political liberals and conservatives, evangelical Christians, fundamentalist Muslims, rationalist skeptics, working single parents, college students, you name it.

DOWNSIDES OF POLYAMORY

The people in the modern poly community are, by and large, groundbreakers. We are ahead of the curve in a lot of ways; many of us embraced an unconventional approach to relationships decades before the word "polyamory" existed. Because of that, many of us are activists, cheerleaders and salespeople for polyamory. That means much of what you will hear about polyamory focuses on the benefits rather than the costs. We do not want to provide that one-sided view in this book. Polyamory is not Nirvana. Every silver lining has a cloud around it. Only you can decide whether the benefits are worth the costs.

Polyamory is complicated. When you have more than two people involved in your romantic life, things get complicated fast. Keeping many simultaneous relationships going is not for the faint of heart. Problems can occur in any relationship. Personality conflicts can arise, and all sorts of things can go wrong. In a polyamorous relationship, there are more opinions being offered, more people's feelings to get hurt, more personalities to clash, more egos to bruise. Navigating a disagreement or problem in a poly relationship requires outstanding communication skills and good problem-solving tools, which is kind of the point of this book.

For some people, the fact that polyamorous relationships are more complicated than traditional ones is "proof" that polyamory is wrong. This argument is nonsense; many relationships are complicated, such as those with stepchildren, or between people of different religious faiths or cultural backgrounds. Would any reasonable person say these relationships are also "wrong"? At the end of the day, the best measure of a relationship isn't how complicated it is, but rather how much joy, hope, delight, support and love it brings. Sure, polyamory can be complicated—but where's the virtue in a simple life?

You will grow—whether you want to or not. A polyamorous relationship offers many opportunities for growth, some easier than others. Whether that belongs in "good things" or "bad things" depends a lot on how you feel about personal growth. You may hear some poly people sighing about AFLE or AFOG: "another fucking learning experience" or "another fucking opportunity for growth."

Polyamory is not safe. When you give your heart to someone, it might get broken. Vulnerability can be painful. Many people try to protect themselves by placing strict controls on the form their relationships may take, or on the level to which they may grow. We have never seen this approach succeed; it merely replaces one kind of pain with another. Polyamory takes guts. It increases love and joy, but it also increases the odds that you'll be hurt. That's how it goes with romantic relationships.

Polyamory means giving things up. When your lover has another lover, there will be times when you will lose something, even if it's just time and attention. Any relationship needs attention in order to thrive, and no matter how close you may be to your partner's other lover—indeed, even if you and a partner share a lover—there will be times when the relationship requires one-on-one focus. It is not always possible to schedule that time so it never takes anything away from you.

Polyamory changes things. We talk more about this throughout the book, but especially in chapters 14 and 17. The short version is you cannot open your heart to other people and expect your life to be unchanged. There will be disruptions, and you will not always be able to anticipate or control them. All relationships are subject to change. Even seemingly idyllic polyamorous relationships don't necessarily last forever, any more than perfect-seeming traditional marriages do.

People don't always get along. Just because someone loves your partner doesn't necessarily mean she will mesh well with you. It's easy to say "I will only date people who like my current partners" (or in extreme cases, "I will only date people who are romantically involved with my current partners"), but in the real world that's not always practical. You can't coerce people to like one another, and we argue that in consensual relationships, it may not even be ethical to make your love contingent on how the person you love interacts with someone else. Sometimes, the best we can do is to agree to be civil toward one another. Biological families on occasion have members who don't particularly like one another, but still have to be reasonable at family dinners. Polyamory is no different.

QUESTIONS TO ASK YOURSELF

We find it's not very useful to tell you what you should do. It's far more effective to pose questions when you're contemplating a course of action. We will do this throughout the book. To start with, here are some questions that can help you determine whether polyamory might be a good match for you:

- *Have I ever felt romantic love for more than one person at the same time?*

- *Do I feel there can be only one "true" love or one "real" soulmate?*

- *How important is my desire for multiple romantic relationships?*

- *What do I want from my romantic life? Am I open to multiple sexual relationships, romantic relationships, or both? If I want more than one lover, what degree of closeness and intimacy do I expect, and what do I offer?*

- *How important is transparency to me? If I have more than one lover, am I happy with them knowing about each other? If they have other lovers, am I happy knowing them?*

- *How do I define commitment? Is it possible for me to commit to more than one person at a time, and if so, what would those commitments look like?*

- *If I am already in a relationship, does my desire for others come from dissatisfaction or unhappiness with my current relationship? If I were in a relationship that met my needs, would I still want multiple partners?*

THE MANY FORMS OF LOVE

Nature never repeats herself,
and the possibilities of
one human soul will never
be found in another.

ELIZABETH CADY STANTON

Imagine yourself as a tree. Your roots go deep into the soil; it nourishes and supports you. They're fed by the rain, which keeps your sap flowing. Your leaves are bathed in sunlight, which provides energy. The wind brings pollen from other trees, so you can produce seeds and fruit. Maybe there's even a bird that builds a nest in your branches, raises a brood and is gone by fall. Each one of these things—soil, rain, sun, wind—does something different for you. None are interchangeable. Lacking one, you might wither and die, or at least fail to flourish. With too much of one, you might suffocate.

This is a metaphor for your relationships. Some people—the people we might call anchor partners, but also perhaps our parents or siblings or best friends—ground us, stabilize us, support us. They are the ones we know we can always turn to. They're the soil. Others may be more variable, but no less crucial: the energizing, joy-bringing sunlight. The cooling, cleansing rain. The winds that bring you new ideas and draw forth your creative force.

How do you meet your own needs? Growing up in a monogamous society, we're shown only a handful of paths that love, particularly romantic love, can take. Relationships are expected to follow a specific trajectory, what we call the "relationship escalator." If a relationship doesn't follow that path, it's not "real." This cookie-cutter way of looking at relationships is so ingrained that we often try to hang onto it even when we discover polyamory. Sometimes we limit the shapes of our relationships: "My boyfriend can only ever be my boyfriend because I already have a husband." Sometimes we try to follow the standard relationship trajectory with multiple people: We start by searching for two or three live-in fidelitous partners before we even know what they want.

Polyamory allows us to let go of monogamy's predefined structures. One of the amazing things polyamory offers is the freedom to negotiate relationships that work for you and your partners. The possibilities are not always obvious, even for people who have lived polyamorously for years. For example, there's often no need to "break up" a relationship if something (or someone) changes. Maybe we can keep a connection and reshape it in another way. We can build relationships that are free to develop however they naturally want to flow.

It helps to recognize that love itself is malleable and ever-changing. Its intensity and nature varies, and this influences its flow, its mutable forms. Monogamy tells us that successful, "real" relationships all look about the same. Relationships that last a long time are called successes, without regard to misery, and those that end are called failures, without regard to happiness. Anything that is not sexually exclusive, we are told, invites chaos, anarchy, the breakdown of the family.

Monogamy tells us what to expect. Polyamory does not. There are no rigid templates, only nuance and shades of gray. This is both a blessing and a curse. Polyamory embraces the idea that relationships are, first and foremost, individual affairs, closely tailored to the specific needs of all the people involved. At the same time, it doesn't give us a clear path to follow, no royal road to "a good relationship." Abandoning the benchmarks of monogamy can be scary. Without them, how will we know what to do?

THE DNA OF RELATIONSHIPS

The moment we move from cookie-cutter relationships to custom-built ones, we have to start thinking about what is and is not possible. The vast potential in polyamorous relationships can be misleading. A relationship can be many things, but it also has built-in constraints. It's constrained by what you want—but also by what each of your partners wants, and what their partners want, and the inherent range of potential intimacy between you and your partner. Each relationship contains a range of possibilities. These possibilities are what you get to choose from.

That inherent set of possibilities is the DNA of a relationship. High-school science textbooks refer to DNA as a "blueprint," but this is inaccurate. You use a blueprint to build a house. It maps what the house will look like: every dimension, every detail. Sure, you get control over superficial things like paint and curtains, but basically you know what you're going to get. And once the house is built, it pretty much stays the same.

On the other hand, the DNA of every different creature *looks* pretty much the same. It's long chains of millions or billions of repeating elements, the "letters" that make the "words" that are our genes. A blueprint is a map, but DNA is more like a recipe: a set of instructions that tells cells step-by-step how to grow an organism. Under a microscope, a creature's DNA looks nothing like what the creature will, just as a written recipe doesn't look like a cake.

So imagine, then, that you pick up a new seed. It contains the DNA for a whole plant, but it's not obvious what it will grow to be: big or small? annual or perennial? weedy and tenacious, or delicate and high-maintenance? You have a lot of influence over how that seed grows, or whether it sprouts at all, based on the care you give it. But you're never going to get a watermelon from an onion seed. At best, you'll just get a bigger onion. And some plants seem downright determined to live: you can plant them in shade and forget to water them, and they'll keep right on growing.

Relationships—like living things, but unlike buildings—grow, change, and go through cycles. Some offer fruit and others flowers, and there might even be times when it seems like they're providing nothing at all. They have seasons, and they can die.

So when we say relationships have DNA, not blueprints, what we mean is that relationships, unlike houses, are alive. Society gives us a *blueprint* for what relationships are supposed to look like—one man, one woman, 2.4 kids, a yard, PTA meetings, apple pie. We propose relationships that don't fit a blueprint, relationships that are as individual as the people in them. Relationships don't need to be mass-produced to factory specifications; we can grow them to meet our needs.

That's why we like to compare the work that goes into growing your relationships to the work of tending a garden. Your garden will thrive, or not, based on the time and skill that goes into watering, weeding, fertilizing, and selecting and placing your plants (your relationship efforts), as well as on the health of the soil and exposure to the sun (your own self-work). But the things in your garden have lives of their own—things they can and cannot become, things they can and cannot give, things they need and things that don't affect them at all.

And sometimes they may not turn out the way you expect. Relationships will seek their own true expressions, no matter how much you try to contain or control them. Just as you can't look at a strange seed and tell what it will be, you can't start a new relationship and tell how it will grow. If you insist on planting the next seed you find in the shade no matter what, or if you insist on forcing a new relationship to fit a certain mold, and this approach works... coincidence has entered the picture.

Remain mindful of the needs of the things you choose to grow in your garden. Make sure there's space for the things you want to add to it, and that you have the time and energy to care for them. Remember, too, that the purpose of the garden is ultimately to nourish the gardener. If you've filled your garden with potatoes and you want some vitamins, it's okay to make room for some kale and carrots. If the big shady oak tree that you've loved for decades is shading your entire garden so that nothing else can take root, you might need to gently prune some of the tree's branches to let in light. And if something you're growing is no longer nurturing you, if it's taking up time and resources from you and the other things in your garden and not giving anything back, then it does not have an inherent right to be in your garden. And if it turns out to be toxic to you or those you care about, it's okay to pull it out.

BEING FLEXIBLE

A core value that we promote in this book is the idea of flexibility. Polyamorous relationships come in an enormous variety of flavors, so they encourage flexibility in ways that most other relationship structures don't. Flexibility does not come naturally; it can be difficult to cast off a lifetime of ideas about how relationships "should" look. Because we're steeped in a limited number of relationship models, it's sometimes overwhelming to try to understand just how many ways relationships *can* work.

We mentioned several different personal approaches to polyamory in chapter 1. These different approaches result, as you might imagine, in very different kinds of relationships. Since polyamory invites us to build relationships tailored to the needs of everyone involved, it demands that we think carefully about our relationships and craft them accordingly.

Poly relationships span the gamut from structured, living-together families to loose networks of people who don't cohabit, with all sorts of configurations in between. These relationship forms reflect their members' varying needs for structure or flexibility, for cohesion or independence, for touch and contact or private space.

If you're making a garden, you can buy the seeds that will grow into the plants you want. With poly relationships, it's tempting to plan out how you want your life to look and then search for people who fit the plan. But unlike seeds, people don't come from a store neatly labeled. You can't look at a person and predict what a relationship will grow into; relationships have a tricky way of zigging when you expect them to zag. Sure, it's important to communicate what you want in your relationships up front—but it's also important to remember you're not ordering a relationship from a catalog. Leave space for them to grow, and don't freak out if they grow in ways you didn't expect.

APPROACHES TO RELATIONSHIPS

Hidden within different types of polyamorous relationship structures are some very different ideas about relationships in general: about autonomy, community, entwinement, romance, sex and partnership. Poly people tend to speak of these different approaches as existing on two axes. One axis runs from "free agent" to "community-oriented." The other runs from "solo" to "entwined." They sound alike, but they are not.

Some poly people consider themselves free agents. That is, they value personal autonomy highly, place importance on the ability to make their own decisions, and present to the world as able to act without requiring permission from others. The model of free-agent poly can be difficult at first to understand. It's easy to make the mistake of thinking that free agents don't commit, or don't consider the needs of their lovers (a.k.a. metamours), or don't care about community. This isn't true. In reality, the free-agent model places responsibility for decision-making, and for bearing the consequences, on each person individually.

For instance, your partners may tell you how they feel about your desire to start a new relationship, and you may listen to them and decide not to go ahead with it based on what they say; but the choice is yours, not theirs. You evaluate their concerns, and then you choose. The extreme end of free agency is called "relationship anarchy," or RA. It's an approach that rejects the need to categorize and rank relationships at all ("Joe is my friend; Mark is my boyfriend; Keyser is my husband") or to create rules or define roles. In particular, RA does not privilege sexual or romantic relationships over others.

On the opposite end of the scale is what some call a community-oriented model of polyamory. People who adopt this model focus on the interconnectedness of their relationships and their community. You might think the difference between free agents and community-oriented polyamorists is about independent action vs. consensus, but that's overly simplistic. Free agents, and particularly relationship anarchists, emphasize the need for negotiation and mutual benefit over the idea that there's a "normal" or "right" way to have relationships. It might be more accurate to say the difference is in the priority that's given to different factors in the decision-making process; community-minded poly folks tend to prioritize the impact of a decision on the entire group over the needs of the individuals in the group. This doesn't necessarily mean that community-oriented people must have their partners' permission to start a relationship. However, decisions are made with an eye toward how, say, a potential new partner might fit with the others.

The other axis, from solo polyamory to entwined poly, looks similar on the surface but reflects a completely different underlying set of values. People who embrace solo poly present to the world as single at first glance. They are off the "relationship escalator": the assumption that relationships follow a defined course. You meet, fall in love, move in together, share property, have children and grow old together. Solo poly folks may not want to live with any partner, or if they do, they may not choose to share finances or property.

By contrast, other people prefer relationships that are more entwined: practically, financially or both. These people value sharing living space, spending time in close proximity, sharing financial or household obligations, and so on. They may see themselves as part of a unit, a single family that shares responsibilities together and approaches life together.

So the scale from free agency to community, then, is about decision-making within a relationship, whereas the scale from solo poly to entwined poly is about the form that the relationships will take.

Few are on the extreme ends of these scales. It's more common to en-counter people in the middle—for instance, who like living with a lover but still prefer to think of themselves as autonomous individuals, or people who pay close attention to how well potential partners fit together but still make relationship decisions themselves.

POLYAMOROUS RELATIONSHIP STRUCTURES

On the surface, the simplest-seeming poly configuration is a triad (three people who are all deeply involved with one another) or a vee (one person, called the "pivot," with two romantic partners). Triads and vees may or may not live together, and may or may not be open to new partners. In many—perhaps most—cases, triads start out as vees, and then a companionship or a romance develops between the two partners of the pivot person.

A quad is a poly relationship involving four people. Quads often, but not always, form when two couples come together. They might also form when one person has three partners, when the members of a couple each start an independent relationship with a new person who's single, or even when four previously unpartnered people start a relationship. The connections within a quad can vary all over the map. There are quads in which every member is in-timate with all three others; there are Ns, which often form when two couples come together with only one intimate relationship between the couples; and asterisks, where one person has three (or more!) partners not involved with each other. Like triads, quads may or may not live together, and they may or may not be open to new romantic connections.

An interesting pattern we have both seen with quads that form from two couples is that after a time, the two couples may swap partners, and the quad breaks up. Sometimes people in a couple know they have problems, but rather than deal with them directly, they try to start new relationships in a structure that is "safe." If, for example, the wife in one couple dates the hus-band in the other, while his wife dates the husband from the first couple, they may believe that nobody will ever feel left out and the other couple will have no reason to threaten them (because, presumably, the other couple wants to preserve their present setup too). In practice, the new relationships can highlight problems and unmet needs in both couples, with the result being a repartnering and breakup.

Larger configurations exist as well. Quite common are open networks, where each person may have several partners—some of whom may be involved with one another and others not. Relationship networks tend to be loosely structured and often don't have a defining hierarchy.

Members of some poly groups consider themselves married to one another. Plural marriage is not legally recognized in Western countries, but some people in poly relationships call each other husbands or wives, hold commitment ceremonies, exchange rings, or do other things that symbolize their serious relationship with each other. Franklin, for example, has exchanged rings with two of his current partners. Other polyamorous groupings don't consider themselves a single family.

Some groups have an internal hierarchy, in which certain relationships (often between a married couple) take precedence over others. This version of poly is often called "primary/secondary," and we talk about it in chapter 11. Other groups have no assumption of a power hierarchy. That does not necessarily suggest each person is treated the same as every other, but that no one relationship always takes precedence. Each is allowed to seek its own level, and new relationships are not necessarily expected to be subordinate. We talk about these in chapter 13.

Different groups have different expectations about agreements and rules. Some polyamorous relationships are rules-based, with detailed prescriptions on behavior, including sexual behavior, between different partners. Others don't impose rules on their members. Some include a "veto clause," which permits one person to tell another to end a relationship with a third person... though as we discuss in chapter 12, these agreements can be difficult to implement and dangerous to use. Other relationships have no veto provisions, preferring negotiation and discussion instead. We discuss some common poly structures, with their pitfalls and benefits, in Part 3.

CONFRONTING ASSUMPTIONS ABOUT SEX

Polyamory makes few assumptions about sexual connections. In monogamy, a romantic partner and a sexual partner are, almost by definition, the same person. Emotional intimacy and physical intimacy are so tightly entwined that some self-help books speak of "emotional infidelity" and encourage married couples not to permit each other to become too close to their friends. Advice columnists and television personalities will speak gravely of the dangers that "emotional affairs" pose to a monogamous marriage and ask, "Is emotional infidelity worse than sexual infidelity?" Monogamy can leave surprisingly little room for close friendships, much less nonsexual romances. Your intimate friend and your sexual partner are presumed to be one and the same.

This creates problems when the couple are no longer sexually attracted to one another or have mismatched libidos. It also creates problems for people who identify as asexual. If our romantic partner is also expected to be our only sexual partner, what happens when sexual compatibility isn't there? What do we do when one person is unwilling or unable to be sexual with the other? In cases like this, monogamy struggles. It seems on the face of it absurd to tell another person "I forbid you to have your sexual needs met by anyone but me, and I won't meet your sexual needs," but that's precisely what happens. The person with unmet sexual needs faces a choice: pressuring, coercion, cheating on the sly or celibacy.

Even when a good monogamous relationship is nonsexual through mutual choice, it is often treated dismissively, if not derisively. "You and your wife haven't had sex in two years? Oh, I'm so sorry. That must be awful! What's wrong?"

One of the advantages of polyamory is that it does not mean hitching all your sexual wagons to a single star. It allows room for change that would threaten the existence of many monogamous relationships. An emotionally satisfying, deeply committed, loving open relationship between two people who are, or have become, sexually incompatible can flourish without being sexually thwarted for the rest of their lives.

Now, of course, needs aren't necessarily transitive. What you need from one partner can't necessarily be given by someone else. We're not saying polyamory is an easy solution for mismatched or missing desire. For some people, sexuality is an expression of romance and love; such people may need to be sexual with all their romantic partners, and if that sexual expression isn't available, it may damage the relationship.

Many polyamorous people, including both of us, have deeply connected romantic relationships in which sexuality plays little or no role. We have also both spoken to people who self-identify as asexual who find polyamory attractive because it allows them to form intimate, loving bonds without the fear that they are depriving their partners of the opportunity for a happy sex life.

EVE'S STORY   Peter and I had been together for over ten years when we married. On our wedding day, we hadn't had sex in close to a year and a half.

We started out like most couples do, horny as hell, experimenting and fucking like rabbits. And like many couples, our sex life declined over time—though our decline may have been quicker than many, due to stress, my poor body image, medications I was on, and several long separations due to my graduate program. It was, in fact, a need for more sexual variety—and more sex—that initially prompted our choice to explore first swinging, and later polyamory.

When I became lovers with Ray, my sex life with Peter improved dramatically for a while, then plummeted again. After he had been with Clio and Gwen for about a year, we finally sat down and had The Talk. I had realized that I no longer felt any sexual interest in Peter and hadn't for a long time. The guilt from not being able to give him the intimacy I thought he deserved, and his frustrations when I rebuffed his advances, were too much for me to carry. If we were to stay together, I needed a formal, mutual recognition that the sexual component of our relationship had ended. I realized, I told him, that he might not want to remain my partner, and I would accept his decision.

The conversation hurt, for both of us. Peter had to take some time to think my proposal over. Eventually, he came back to me and told me he still wanted to be my partner. The transition wasn't easy—but it was much easier than trying to maintain or revive a sexual relationship that wasn't working anymore, or for me to continue carrying the guilt of not providing what I thought Peter deserved. Ultimately, the conversation did not actually institute a new change: it made what was already happening transparent and consensual. It was *after* this agreement that we decided to get married.

To come to terms with their new agreement and forge a relationship that was loving, mutually supportive and happy, Eve and Peter had to confront a number of deeply ingrained, toxic beliefs about sex and relationships:

- You owe sex to someone you're in a relationship with.
- Sexual desire is something that can be offered or withheld at will.
- A lack of sexual desire is, at best, a sign of something wrong in the relationship. At worst, it's a sign of malice.

Desire isn't a button you can push. No matter how much you may care for someone, no matter how much you may want to meet their needs, if sexual desire is not there, it's not there. Yes, some people can work on it, and many couples can work through reduced desire—but many can't, and there's nothing wrong with them. Sometimes you just don't want it—and sometimes you just don't want the person you're supposed to want.

You should never have to have sex when you don't want to. We don't think it's something you should have to do to save a relationship, to show you care, or to get any of your other needs met—financial, emotional or social. Not desiring someone physically isn't a sign that you don't love them. Or that you want to hurt them. Or that there's something wrong with you. It's not even a sign that you're not a compatible partner with them. It just means that, for whatever reason, your body isn't responding to them. And if you don't want it, for heaven's sake, don't do it.

Many deeply loving, lifetime relationships eventually become platonic. When we went looking for statistics, we found that between 20 and 30 percent of relationships are "sexless," with partners having sex less than ten times per year. Around 5 percent of married men under forty are completely celibate; by age fifty that increases to 20 percent, and that percentage keeps going up with age.

We found statistics about "sexless marriages" in papers and books with titles that make it quite clear how such relationships are viewed: "The Decision to Remain in an Involuntarily Celibate Relationship," *Rekindling Desire, A Tired Woman's Guide to Passionate Sex,* "Couple Therapy and the Treatment of Sexual Dysfunction." It's unfortunate that we pathologize something that is so normal, and that we assume nonsexual relationships must be broken. Polyamory allows for the possibility that we can remain in relationships that matter to us and have sex when (and only when) we want to, because we want to, and not because we have to because we fear losing someone we care for.

Eve and Peter have faced judgment and misunderstandings over their agreement, even from their closest friends. Peter is, by any objective measure, an absolutely wonderful human being, and Eve has more than once felt subtly shamed by mutual friends for denying him sexual access. She has been made to feel ungrateful or broken for not desiring him. She has even been told that their marriage isn't "real." (One well-meaning friend once commented, "It's so sweet that you still wear your wedding ring.") If that's the case, then millions of married couples are "not really married."

The only thing unusual about Eve and Peter is that their situation was mutually agreed to and they've chosen to talk about it openly. They want to share their story so that others in the same situation know there's nothing wrong with them, they are not alone and their relationships are still legitimate and "real."

DEFINING PARTNERSHIP

What is a "romantic relationship"? What separates a nonsexual romantic relationship from an ordinary friendship? Can asexual people have romantic relationships? (Don't laugh; that last one is a question Eve and Franklin have both heard.)

Wikipedia says that romantic relationships are characterized by emotions of love, intimacy, compassion, appreciation and affinity. That definition is not very helpful, because many of us feel these same emotions, though perhaps to a different extent, for non-romantic friends. The idea that relationships are characterized by these emotions is a good starting point, but ultimately, we believe the definition of a romantic relationship is up to the people involved.

FRANKLIN'S STORY   I have been in a relationship with my partner Amber for more than a decade. In the beginning, it looked pretty conventional: we lived together, shared a bed, sat down for dinner together at the end of the workday.

A few years later, she moved to a different town to pursue a graduate degree in neurobiology. Our relationship went from live-in to long-distance, but still kept many conventional markers of a romantic relationship. We visited often, sat down together when we could, and remained lovers.

Less than a year after that, I moved even farther away. Amber and I continued a long-distance relationship, but it became harder and harder. She was working on her master's thesis in bioinformatics and minoring in pure mathematics, so more and more of her attention became focused on her academic work, and less space was available for maintaining any romantic relationship, much less a long-distance one. I became accustomed to seeing her less often—twice a month, then once a month, then every six weeks.

Eventually, Amber came to me and said she didn't believe the sexual part of our relationship could continue. Her academic work was consuming her life, and her libido was feeling the effects of the stress. She said she was afraid that being open with me might be the end of our relationship, but she felt she needed to take sex off the table.

I really enjoyed being Amber's lover, and what she told me stung. But in truth, it didn't hurt as much as I expected it to. I have always admired Amber, and I believe very strongly in the work she's doing. I also believe just as strongly that sexuality must be consensual, and I don't want to have a lover who does not have the space or desire to be enthusiastic about being with me.

Most of our relationship changed surprisingly little. We still shared a bed when we visited each other, but just for snuggling and sleeping. We were, and are, still physically affectionate with one another. We still love each other greatly.

When I moved to Portland, the relationship became very long-distance indeed. It is still a romantic relationship, though. We still love one another, and we are still involved in one another's lives multidimensionally, to the degree we can be. We have exchanged rings. We still share intimacy. When she encountered turbulence in one of her other relationships, she was able to call on me for support, and I flew across the country to be with her. We share our hopes and dreams, joys and sorrows. We continue to be absolutely committed to each other's happiness. In all the ways that matter, Amber is still my partner. Our relationship does not look like conventional romantic relationships, at least not since the Victorian era, but one of the amazing things about polyamory is that we can chart our own course, defining our relationship to fit us rather than a cultural norm.

Franklin and Amber's experience shows that judging relationship success based on some arbitrary criteria makes less sense than judging success based on whether the people involved think the relationship is a success.

HOW MANY PARTNERS?

It's possible to be single and poly. It's possible to have only one partner and be poly. If your intention is to remain open to the possibility of multiple romantic relationships, you are polyamorous regardless of your current relationship status. Indeed, if polyamory is part of your identity (for some people, it is; for others, it isn't), you might be in a monogamous relationship and still be poly.

Is there a "right" number of partners to have to be poly? No. Is there a "right" number for *you* to have? Maybe. There is certainly some maximum. There's a saying among poly people: "Love is infinite; time and attention are not." It's debatable whether love is infinite; in practical terms, it probably isn't.* Time and attention definitely aren't. Different people have different constraints on the time and attention they can offer, and different relationships require different amounts, so some people can maintain more romantic relationships than others before they become, as the term goes, "polysaturated."

The number of partners you have room for can change. Some situations, such as starting a new job or caring for a baby or toddler, consume tremendous amounts of time and emotional space; it's normal to feel that you don't want to start a new relationship until more space opens up (though, hopefully, you will continue to nurture the ones you have). On the other hand, game changers happen; you may meet someone so amazing, so fantastic, that you are willing to rearrange parts of your life to create space for them. Game changers are disruptive, as we discuss in chapter 14.

FRANKENPOLY

Because different people have different needs, and polyamory allows us to distribute our need eggs into more than one relationship basket, it is possible to maintain a relationship in a poly setting that otherwise might not survive. We've talked about how happy poly relationships can exist between people with mismatched sex drives or no sex at all. The same thing can happen when one partner is more sexually adventurous than another, and wants to explore being tied up, spanked, or some other kink that leaves the other cold. Maybe one person really likes ballroom dancing, but the other has two left feet. (Two of

---

* Cognitive scientists place a limit, determined by the size of our brains, on the number of individuals an animal is capable of having stable social relationships with: that is, remembering who each person is and how they connect to us and others. For humans this number, called "Dunbar's number" after the researcher who proposed this idea, seems to be somewhere around 150.

Franklin's partners love ballroom dancing, but he's never felt the bug.) One person may have a deep religious conviction not shared by the other. Polyamory offers an opportunity for different relationships to provide for different needs.

The danger here is seeing other people as need-fulfillment machines. When a need isn't being met, that need can feel bottomless, and it can be tempting to go out searching for a person to fill it. One of Franklin's partners calls this "Frankenpoly"—stitching together the perfect need-providing romantic partner out of bits and pieces of other people. We've also heard it called "Pokémon poly," after the idea that you need to collect a complete set of different kinds of partners.

When we begin to look at people in terms of what needs they can meet rather than as whole people in their own right, we start down the road toward treating people as things. A person you're with only because you get some need filled when you insert time-and-attention tokens is not a full romantic partner joining you on the journey of life. Which is not to say that any attempt to have different needs met from different people leads this way. A friend of Franklin's has a need for specific sexual kinks that aren't met by her husband, and she has had success in seeking other lovers who share this need. But those other lovers are romantic partners in their own right, valued for reasons beyond helping meet that need.

Some needs, though, don't lend themselves well to outsourcing. Needs for intimacy, for understanding or for companionship are often attached to the *people* we are in a relationship with; if we have those needs met by Alice, we may still need those things from Bob too.

RELATIONSHIPS THAT BLOSSOM

Because there is no standardized template for polyamory, it's rare to see two poly relationships that look the same. We have observed, however, that strong, successful relationships do tend to have some things in common. Returning to our garden metaphor, no two gardens look the same, but all gardens need certain things to thrive: sunlight, air, soil, the right amount of water. What do poly relationships need to grow and thrive?

Something we've both heard often is "When I started exploring polyamory, the things I thought would be important and the things that turned out to be important were very different." We have found that poly relationships thrive most readily when they are free to change and adapt. When the people in the relationship are more important than the structure of the relationship—when they are free to advocate for their needs, to grow even in unexpected ways, when they feel a sense of personal empowerment over their relationships—the relationships themselves tend to be strong, resilient and happy.

As we discuss in chapters 4 and 8, it can be tempting, especially if you are new to polyamory, to try to script what your relationships will look like—to decide in advance what kinds of people you will place into what roles. People often do this to avoid dealing with issues like insecurity or fear of being left out. This approach treats people as interchangeable parts rather than as human beings with their own needs and desires. When we treat people as components to fit roles we have scripted for them, they are likely to feel disempowered, which plants the seeds for all kinds of trouble.

What almost invariably *does* work is to remain open to relationships in a wide variety of configurations, and develop tools for open communication, for advocating for your needs, and for acting ethically and compassionately no matter what form those relationships may take. As Eliezer Yudkowsky says, "You are personally responsible for becoming more ethical than the society you grew up in."

QUESTIONS TO ASK YOURSELF

A great tool for finding, growing and maintaining good relationships is to think about the relationship that you want from the perspective of the people you'd like to attract. The flip side is asking yourself questions about what you're offering them. Some questions that might help:

- *What are my needs in relationships? Are they attached to specific people? That is, do I need these things generally, or do I need them just from certain people?*

- *What configurations am I open to? Am I looking for a particular configuration because I'm afraid that others might be more scary or more threatening?*

- *Am I flexible in what I'm looking for?*

- *If my relationship changes, is that okay? Can I accommodate change, even unexpected change or change I don't like?*

- *When I visualize the kind of relationship I want, how much space does it leave for new partners to shape the relationship to their needs?*

- *Am I focusing on an idealized fantasy more than on making organic connections with real people?*

- *What happens if I connect with someone in a way that differs from how I want my poly relationship to look? What message does that send to someone who doesn't fit neatly into my dreams?*

ETHICAL POLYAMORY

*The most vital right is
the right to love and be loved.*

EMMA GOLDMAN

We're not going to teach you the easy way to be poly. The tools we recommend will seem hard, because they are—at first. Like starting anything new, practicing polyamory comes with a steep learning curve, and requires a lot of hard work, as you build new skills and challenge old ways of thinking. Our goal is to equip you with the tools you'll need to grow strong, loving relationships.

Ethics are crucial to polyamorous relationships, and we believe it is worth developing an explicit ethical compass to guide us. That shouldn't be a controversial statement, but it is: many people believe that ethics do not exist in any absolute sense, that they are all culturally determined. Even if that's the case, well then, with polyamory, we're building a new culture. What kind of culture do we want to build? Those are our ethics. The ethics of nontraditional relationships are such a huge topic that we can only touch on them here. But this entire book is about conducting polyamorous relationships ethically, so we must explain what we mean by that.

RIGHT AND WRONG POLY?

One of the things you'll hear a lot from poly people is that "there's no one right way to do poly." This is true. There are many ways to "do poly" (live polyamorously) that give you a decent chance of having joyful, fulfilling, meaningful relationships with low conflict. But when people say "There's no one right way," it sometimes seems they mean there are no bad ways to do poly. We disagree. There are plenty of choices likely to lead you into pain, stress, drama and tears. There are ways to do poly that shift most of the emotional risk that comes with any intimate relationship onto one person. There are ways to do poly that reliably cause suffering.

It seems pretty fair to say that approaches that are likely to cause pain to you and those you love probably aren't very good strategies. We are even comfortable calling such approaches "bad" ways of doing poly—though we are wary of the word "wrong," which tends to make people unnecessarily defensive. After all, we're all ultimately trying to do the best we can. Choosing a flawed strategy doesn't make someone a bad person; the two of us have gone down some of those roads ourselves. We are all struggling to meet the same basic human needs. People make mistakes because they're trying to solve a problem, and many of the less successful approaches to poly tend to promise quick relief—but come with insidious, hidden costs.

All of us have done some very bad things. We've all hurt other people when we thought we were doing the right thing, or at least not a bad thing. We were probably trying to get our own needs met—blinded, perhaps, by those needs. The two of us are no exception: in fact, it is our many mistakes, and what we have learned from them, that qualify us to write this book.

So what does it mean to be ethically polyamorous, given that we're all going to make mistakes, hurt others, be buffeted by our emotions and fall down sometimes? Being ethical means that you're willing to look at your actions and their effects on other people. If you're presented with evidence that you're causing harm, or that what you're doing won't achieve what you and your partner(s) want, you will look for ways to change this. In making decisions, you will consider the well-being of *everyone* involved, not just some. Being ethical also means that you're willing to have the kinds of discussions that would permit an honest analysis of the way you're choosing to do poly, without getting defensive or accusatory.

Because after all, we're all learning. We are pioneers, and unless we're willing to assess the path we're on and whether it's taking us where we want to go, we're likely to end up in some pretty messed-up places.

EVIDENCE-BASED POLYAMORY

We wrote the first draft of this book from a cabin deep in the temperate rain forest of the Pacific Northwest. On a half-hour walk from our front door, we passed a couple dozen varieties of wild mushrooms. Some made delicious additions to our nightly dinners. Others would sicken or kill us. Luckily, we had a book telling us which was which, and what poisonous look-alikes are most easily mixed up with safe and tasty edibles. After identifying a mushroom in the book, we might make a spore print, just to be sure. And then we would take a little piece of the mushroom, sauté it, eat it and wait a few hours, just to be sure neither of us got an upset tummy or started seeing the garden gnomes (oh God, so many garden gnomes!) climbing up the walls. Only then would we cook up a nice big batch into mushroom stew. Obviously, because you're reading this book, this strategy worked for us.

So let's imagine that we, as polyamorous people living in a mononormative society, are intrepid mushroom hunters discovering exotic, tasty treats by venturing into the forest. But here's the thing: we're new to this. Few are doing it; it's not part of our culture. There's no illustrated field guide, no cultural background to help us know what is poisonous, what's tasty, or what might give us the hallucinogenic trip of our lives.

So what do we do? We might look for other people—people already living off the land we're foraging on, say—and ask them what mushrooms they eat and which they avoid. We might watch what happens to others when they eat certain mushrooms. And if we can't find that kind of information—or maybe even if we could—we wouldn't wolf down a batch of some new mushroom all in one go. Probably we'd try a little piece, wait awhile, then try a little more.

And once we've determined that we can eat something with no ill effects, would we have a big dinner party and feed it to everyone else? If a dinner guest or two begins convulsing after consuming our delectable meal, would we shrug, say "Well, it works for me," and continue to feed it to others? No.

What we have just described is the process of collecting data. We like to do this as we explore new ways of relating too. We can observe, as we and others try out new relationship patterns, which choices tend to lead to pain and conflict and which tend to lead to harmony. Eventually, gradually, these patterns become evidence of what actions are most likely to promote the well-being of everyone in a relationship network. These might not be "right" ways to do poly—like there are no "right" foods—we might call them "good" ways.

Call this evidence-based polyamory, if you will.* That's what we're striving to give you in this book. Everything we suggest you do comes from what we have observed to work most often. The things we recommend you avoid are things we have observed, over and over, to cause strife. We're not criticizing the people doing the "bad" things, unless they act with malice, and we're not holding up the people doing the things that work as perfect poly role models that would be a good idea to emulate (though sometimes, maybe, you should). All we're saying is, if you want to choose strategies to help you get where you want to go, these are the ones we've observed to be most successful in the long term.

Polyamory is still new. We are not "experts," because there are no experts. At times, we present questions that don't have answers yet. In joining us in this big experiment, you will be helping to forge a path that others can follow, contributing to the body of knowledge on polyamory that is taking shape. In this book, we lay our own experiences—and, especially, our mistakes—open to view, in hopes that you can learn from them and avoid the same mistakes. We invite you to go out and explore the vast, fertile fields of new, undiscovered mistakes yet to be made! And then, perhaps, to share your experiences through your own blogs or comments on ours (at morethantwo.com), in poly forums and with one another—so we can all keep learning together.

A MORAL COMPASS

Think of this book as a compass, not a map. There is no magic road to poly happiness. That said, as we emphasize over and over, the compass directions we've seen that lead to strong, vibrant, happy relationships are courage, communication, willingness to accept responsibility for your own emotions, respect for the autonomy of others, compassion and empathy.

---

* We use the term evidence cautiously. The formal study of multi-partnered relationships is in its infancy, and genuine scientific evidence is sparse. Where we can back up our claims with peer-reviewed research, we will, but such instances will be rare. We look forward to a day when the state of knowledge has advanced to where it's possible to give genuinely evidence-based advice, but for now it is more accurate to refer to the cases in this book as "anecdote-based poly."

For each person, the "right" way to do poly is to talk about your needs, fears and insecurities; to talk about the ways your partner can support you; and to honor your commitments—without being controlling or placing rules on other people to protect you from your own emotional triggers. Above all else, trust that you don't have to control your partner, because your partner, given the freedom to do anything, will want to cherish and support you. And always, always move in the direction of greatest courage, toward the best possible version of yourself.

Strong, ethical polyamorous relationships are not a destination, they are a journey. Nurturing such relationships is like walking toward a point on the horizon: you move toward it or away from it with each choice you make, but you never actually arrive. Sometimes you'll make a choice that takes you farther away, but that's okay, because you can always make another choice and start moving again in the direction you want to go.

Before we can talk about things like nurturing healthy relationships and maximizing well-being, we need to make some assumptions about the kinds of relationships you want—what we mean when we use the word *healthy*. We know that poly people are a diverse bunch, and we can't speak to the full range of backgrounds, choices, needs and expectations of our readers. Even so, we think that if we *don't* make the following assumptions, our advice would be pretty much rubbish. We assume that you:

- seek, like most people, to engage in relationships because you value love, connection and belonging
- want your partners to engage in a relationship, and specifically a polyamorous relationship, of their own free will
- want your partners to feel loved, cared for and secure in their relationships with you, and want to feel loved, cared for and secure in your relationships with them
- value honesty in your relationships, which we define as, at minimum, everyone involved with you being aware of the other people you're involved with**

** *Some polyamorous people engage in a structure called "Don't ask, don't tell," in which the people involved don't talk about their other relationships or even mention they exist. This approach often causes problems (as we discuss in chapters 10, 14 and 18).*

- accept that all long-term relationships will contain some conflict, but do not want conflict, anxiety or pain to be a norm, and certainly not more frequent than joy, connection or comfort

Accepting and honoring these assumptions will lead in a natural way to caring, supportive, open relationships. When we talk about "good" ways to do poly, we're talking about strategies that, in our experience, seem most often to lead people toward these kinds of relationships. When we talk about "healthy" relationships, we are talking about relationships that move toward these values more often than they move away from them.

ON THE SUBJECT OF RIGHTS

We've talk about the idea of "right" (as opposed to "wrong"), but what about *rights*? Rights are a cornerstone of many systems of ethics, including ours. In fact, we believe that choices that maximize well-being are not ethical if they infringe on another person's rights. For example, a decision that improves the well-being of a group of people by violating the consent of one—say, telling a woman that she must bear a child that she doesn't want but the rest of her family does—is unethical, because bodily autonomy is a right whose defense supersedes group well-being.

It's common to hear the word "rights" used when the speaker actually means "things I really want." In relationships, a right often means "something I expect" or "something I feel entitled to," such as "I'm the wife, therefore I have a right to end your other relationships if they make me uncomfortable." Or "She and I have children together, so I have the right to decide who she can become involved with."

We have the right to want what we want. We do not, however, have the right to *get* what we want. For rights, a higher bar needs to be set. So what *is* a right? Many people believe in the idea of "natural rights": so-called inalienable rights we are all born with, such as life, liberty, and so on. Often people believe that such rights come from things like human nature or the edicts of a deity. That's one morass we're not going to wade into (at least not in this book). Instead, we will discuss "rights" that are more like legal rights: rights a person has by law or custom. Often, they must be fought for before they are granted—as with all of the "rights" enshrined in modern constitutional democracies, for example.

In proposing rights for relationships, we claim no natural authority for them, and we do not claim them as inalienable. Rather, we propose them as rights we think are essential to uphold if we are to build relationships based on the values we discussed on pages 39–40. Such rights underpin ethical relationships. We suggest that these rights should be taken as a given for ethical polyamorous relationships; that individuals should embrace and defend them for themselves; and that polyamorous communities should uphold them.

The rights we talk about here derive from two axioms, which together are a lens through which any relationship choice should be viewed. These principles are:

- The people in a relationship are more important than the relationship.
- Don't treat people as things.

These are simple, but not necessarily easy. We will be returning to them often.

Axiom 1, of course, does not mean that relationships aren't important. And it doesn't mean that you should never make personal sacrifices for the benefit of a relationship. But while it is often necessary to make sacrifices of time, short-term gratification or non-essential desires for the long-term benefit of a relationship (or a partner), it is never desirable to sacrifice your *self* for a relationship. We discuss this further in chapters 4 and 5. And while individual wishes do sometimes need to be subsumed to collective well-being, it's important to remember that relationships exist *to serve the people in them*. If a relationship stops serving the people in it, it's not doing its job. It may not even have a reason to exist anymore. Thus, axiom 1 is, like axiom 2, *always* true (that's why it's an axiom). Even though the people and the relationship need to serve each other, the people are always more important. Always.

In practice, these axioms mean that relationships are consensual, and people are not need-fulfillment machines. People cannot and should not be obligated to remain in any relationship: if a relationship ceases to meet the needs of the people in it, that relationship can end. People are not commodities; ethical relationships recognize the humanity, needs and desires of each individual involved.

A RELATIONSHIP BILL OF RIGHTS

In 2003 Franklin posted a "Secondary's Bill of Rights" on his growing polyamory website. It rapidly became both the most popular and most controversial page on the site. Many people at the time objected to the idea that secondary partners should have rights at all. Here we expand the Secondary's Bill of Rights to a Relationship Bill of Rights. To develop this list, we examined other documents that defined "rights," from United Nations documents to rules from domestic abuse organizations. We think a pretty high bar needs to be met before something can be called a right. Here's what passed the test. You have the right, without shame, blame or guilt:

In all intimate relationships:
- to be free from coercion, violence and intimidation
- to choose the level of involvement and intimacy you want
- to revoke consent to any form of intimacy at any time
- to be told the truth
- to say no to requests
- to hold and express differing points of view
- to feel all your emotions
- to feel and communicate your emotions and needs
- to set boundaries concerning your privacy needs
- to set clear limits on the obligations you will make
- to seek balance between what you give to the relationship and what is given back to you
- to know that your partner will work with you to resolve problems that arise
- to choose whether you want a monogamous or polyamorous relationship
- to grow and change
- to make mistakes
- to end a relationship

In poly relationships:
- to decide how many partners you want
- to choose your own partners

- to have an equal say with each of your partners in deciding the form your relationship with that partner will take
- to choose the level of time and investment you will offer to each partner
- to understand clearly any rules that will apply to your relationship before entering into it
- to discuss with your partners decisions that affect you
- to have time alone with each of your partners
- to enjoy passion and special moments with each of your partners

In a poly network:
- to choose the level of involvement and intimacy you want with your partners' other partners
- to be treated with courtesy
- to seek compromise
- to have relationships with *people*, not with relationships
- to have plans made with your partner be respected; for instance, not changed at the last minute for trivial reasons
- to be treated as a peer of every other person, not as a subordinate, even when differing levels of commitment or responsibility exist

CONSENT, HONESTY AND AGENCY

This Relationship Bill of Rights contains three important, intertwined ideas that need a bit more elaboration, because they are fundamental to the kind of ethical polyamory we are espousing: *consent, honesty* and *agency.*

Consent is about *you*: your body, your mind and your choices. Your consent is required to access what is yours. The people around you have *agency*: they do not need your consent to act, because you do not own their bodies, minds or choices. But if their behavior crosses into your personal space, then they need your consent.

Most of us will, over the course of our lives, encounter situations—perhaps at work, in our families of origin or on the streets—where we have to put up emotional walls and accept a loss of control over our lives, our minds or even our bodies. But we should never have to do that in our loving relationships. This may seem obvious, but make no mistake: it's a radical idea.

Honesty is an indispensable part of consent. Being able to share, to the best of your ability, who you are in a relationship is critical for that relationship to be consensual. You must give your partner the opportunity to make an informed decision to be in a relationship with you. If you lie or withhold critical information, you remove your partner's ability to consent to be in the relationship. If a partner of yours has sex with a dozen casual hookups, he may be breaking an agreement, but he has not (yet) violated your *consent*. If he then has sex with you—or engages in other forms of intimacy, including emotional intimacy—without telling you about his actions, he has violated your consent, because he has deprived you of the ability to make an informed choice.

It's especially important to communicate things that might be dealbreakers, or might be threatening to your partner's emotional or physical health. Your partner deserves to have a choice about how they want to participate in a relationship with you given the new information. Examples might be sexual activity with others, drug use, acquisition or use of weapons, and violent impulses or behavior. Anything you know or suspect might be a dealbreaker should be disclosed. You cannot force someone to make the choice you want them to make, and if you lie or withhold information, you deny them the ability to know there was a choice to be made.

When people talk about dishonesty, often it's in the context of uttering falsehoods. By the simplest definition, a lie is a statement that is factually untrue. But there are other kinds of lies. For example, Franklin has spoken to a married woman cheating on her husband who said, "I'm not lying to him, because I'm not telling him that I'm being faithful!" In truth, she was lying: she was concealing information that, if he knew about it, would have changed his assessment of their relationship. When we talk about honesty in this book, we will do so from the position that a lie of omission is still a lie.

Sometimes, when confronted with the notion of a lie of omission, people say, "Not mentioning something isn't a lie. I don't tell my partner every time I use the bathroom, and that's not lying!" That brings us to the idea of relevance. An omission is a lie when it is calculated to conceal information that, were it known to the other party, would be materially relevant to her. Failing to tell your partner how long it took to brush your teeth isn't a lie of omission. Failing to tell your partner you're having sex with the pool man is.

Agency is also intertwined with consent. Many people have been taught that if we are empowered to make our own choices—to have agency—we will become monsters, so we must surrender some of our decision-making power to external authority (which is somehow magically proof against becoming monstrous). This idea permeates society, but also seems to inform how we build our own intimate relationships. Without engaging in a debate about whether people are fundamentally good or bad (or option C), we ask you to look at your partners and ask yourself if you respect their ability to choose—even if a choice hurts you, even if it's not what you would choose—because we cannot consent if we do not have a choice.

Empowering people to make their own choices is actually the best way to have our own needs met. People who feel disempowered can become dangerous. Communicating our needs, and equipping others to meet them, succeeds more often than attempting to restrict or coerce another into meeting them. (We talk more in chapter 13 about what we mean by "empowerment.")

WHEN IT'S HARD TO ACT ETHICALLY

Embracing polyamory may well expose you to a great deal more uncertainty and change than people in monogamous relationships experience. Every new relationship is a potential game changer (see chapter 14, page 248). Every new relationship might change your life. And that's a good thing, right? Picture your best relationships. Can you think of any truly awesome relationship that didn't change your life in some important way? The first time you had a long-term partner, did it change things for you? The first time you fell in love, and had that love reciprocated, did it change things for you? Every person you become involved with stands a good chance of changing your life in a big or small way. If that weren't the case, well, what would be the point? The same goes for your partners and the new people they become involved with—and when their lives change, so will yours.

Change is scary for a lot of people, and so preparing for poly relationships in many ways is about assessing and improving your ability to handle change. Even just *thinking* about it, taking a deep breath and saying, "Yep, I know my life is about to change" is a huge step toward preparing yourself to live polyamorously.

In some cases, for some people, circumstances may make change even harder than usual. For example, if you've just had another big change—a new job, say, or a big move, or a marriage or divorce, or a new baby—additional changes might cause you a lot more stress than they otherwise would. In these situations, it's common for people to look at polyamory and how it could change their lives, and then try to limit the amount of change that can happen. In our experience, this tactic doesn't work very well and has a host of negative consequences, which we discuss in chapters 10 and 11.

A very common example is couples with young children. One real example we know of involved a couple with two very small children, one just a few months old. The mom was under intense stress, as often happens in such situations, and was emotionally volatile. As a result, the couple had a lot of restrictions in place to control each other's relationships. These restrictions were causing a lot of pain for the father's girlfriend, who was deeply in love with him but found her relationship with him unable to grow, while she was obliged to perform services such as babysitting for the couple in order to continue to have access to him.

In situations like this, it's easy to fall back on the idea of "putting the children first." Clearly, parents need to be able to live their lives in a way that allows them to care for their children's needs and provide loving, stable homes. (More on this later.) But too often, this need is used as an all-purpose shield to deflect any analysis of how a couple's behavior might be affecting other partners, or how it might be damaging their other relationships. Anything that looks like criticism can be framed as attacking the couple's right to care for their children.

Make no mistake, kids change things. They did not choose to come into the world, or choose the people who care for and make decisions for them. Only slowly and painfully, over many years, are children nurtured into agency and personal capability: with the ability to think and plan, to learn and make rational choices, to develop judgment and individual responsibility, and to consent or withhold consent.

When children come into a home, for the first time there are truly immature people present, making childish and selfish demands that have real moral legitimacy and must be dealt with. You have a choice how to deal with the issues, but you can't ignore them. Children add a categorically different new dynamic to the mix and, especially when they are very young, significantly subtract time and attention from adult matters. But that still doesn't mean you can use their needs as emotional blackmail or to excuse unethical behavior in the adults around them.

Being an ethical person means being ethical to everyone—partners and children. Children are not an ethical Get Out of Jail Free card: it's possible to be both a responsible parent and an ethical partner. We discuss ethical approaches to polyamory with children, with real-life poly parenting stories, in chapters 13, 15, 17 and 24.

Remember that not every time in your life will be a good time to add new partners. If you have young children and you simply can't stand the idea of your partner having other partners without, say, instituting a hierarchy, you might wait until your children are a little older before you start new relationships. If you (or a partner) are struggling with anxiety, insecurity, depression or other issues that leave you (or them) sobbing under the covers when the partner is with someone else, you could get into therapy and learn some coping strategies, or avoid polyamory altogether, instead of bringing someone into your life but surrounding them with metaphorical barbed-wire fences to keep them from getting too close. If you are dealing with a recent betrayal, you might want to work with your partners on building trust before testing that trust by investing in someone new.

If a particular relationship decision, such as placing a partner under a veto (see chapter 12) is unethical, don't make excuses for it by saying, "But I have to because..." Try reframing the situation. Instead of looking for partners who will let you treat them unethically, who will let you compromise their agency or keep them at arm's length, ask yourself if you are in a position to seek new partners at all. Put another way: It is not ethical to hurt one person to protect another. It's better to look at yourself and the relationships you have and ask what you need to do, individually and collectively, to enable you to have relationships that will let you treat everyone well.

MAKING ETHICAL CHOICES

Ethical decision-making is not always easy. That's fitting, because the measure of a person's ethics lies in what she does when things are difficult. We believe every decision that affects other people should be examined from an ethical perspective. Ethical relationships are something we *do*, not something we *have*. Being an ethical person means looking at the consequences of our choices on others. To make ethical choices and treat others with compassion, you need to have a strong internal foundation. Building this foundation is the subject of the next chapter, which begins Part 2: A Poly Toolkit.

QUESTIONS TO ASK YOURSELF

Here are some questions we can ask when making decisions that affect other people, to help guide us toward ethical relationships:

- *Have I disclosed all relevant information to everyone affected by my decision?*

- *Have I sought input from everyone affected? Have I obtained their consent where my decision overlaps their personal boundaries?*

- *Does my decision impose obligations or expectations on others without their input or consent?*

- *Am I seeking to have my needs met at the expense of the well-being of others?*

- *Am I imposing consequences that will make others feel unsafe saying no to me?*

- *Am I offering others the same consideration that I expect from them?*

PART 2

A Poly Toolkit

TENDING
YOUR SELF

To be a good person,
you have to always want to be
better than yourself right now.

P. Z. MYERS

Polyamory is awesome. But as you read this book, you might wonder why anyone would walk down this road. We're asking a lot of you, dear reader. We tell you what can go wrong and illustrate our lessons with messy examples from our own lives. So you might be tempted to throw up your hands and say, "Polyamory sounds hard!"

But polyamory *is* awesome. By opening ourselves to multiple romantic connections, the two of us have built amazing lives, filled with love and brilliance. Every person we have invited into our lives has made them better. Despite all the hard parts, neither of us would consider for even half a second going to a life of monogamy. We are nourished by the people who love and cherish us. Every partner we have had, all the relationships we have built, have made us stronger, taught us, supported us, made us better human beings.

We keep hearing that polyamory is hard work. We don't agree—at least not for the reasons that people say. But developing the *skills* to be successful in poly relationships? That's a different story. Learning to understand and express your needs, learning to take responsibility for your emotions...that's hard work. Once you've developed those skills, poly relationships aren't hard. The skills we're talking about aren't all unique to polyamory; they'll benefit any relationship. But poly will be really, really challenging without them. These skills have to be *learned*. And, alas, they aren't often taught.

Think of it like tilling the ground before planting a garden, so that things will more easily grow. You're learning a way of approaching relationships that helps them run smoothly. What skills are we talking about? Communication. Jealousy management. Being honest, compassionate, understanding. These are not easy to master. Relationship skills are *emergent phenomena*; they come from developing ways of thinking about relationships and about yourself. Once you've developed those ways of thinking, practicing these skills in your relationships starts to feel natural. If you get a handle on communication, compassion and self-awareness; if honesty and jealousy management become a part of your approach to life, then managing multiple romantic relationships become easy.

These attitudes and skills will express themselves outside of your relationships too. For instance, jealousy is the bugaboo we hear people mention most often. It is beaten most effectively by developing a strong sense of self-confidence and by confronting your personal demons of insecurity. Determine for yourself what you actually want and need from a relationship, and learn the communication tools to ask for those things. Construct a sense of what is and is not acceptable to you. All of these skills strengthen you in other ways as well. They're *life* skills, and they'll help when you're looking for a new job, or negotiating a raise, or buying a car.

The same is true for things like communication and honesty in a relationship. Develop the habits of being open and honest with the people around you, and you'll likely find that communicating with a lover does not take work; it's automatic. Develop the habit of behaving with integrity, and all of your life will become simpler and smoother. Developing these traits is work, sure, but it's not *relationship* work—it's work you do on *yourself*. It benefits you in ways beyond your relationship. In fact, this is work that's beneficial to do even if you have no relationships at all!

We discuss some big concepts in this chapter and the next. Things like integrity, courage, worthiness, compassion. Don't get scared off. These are not *states* you need to attain, and there's no magic bar you need to cross before you'll be "good enough" to be poly. These principles are meant as guides, as stars to navigate by. They are not innate character traits but practices you can cultivate, skills you can learn.

Of course, two chapters in one book can barely scratch the surface of the self-work that's involved in learning to practice ethical polyamory. What we're presenting is not a set of instructions, but a collection of principles that we believe are most important in building robust, ethical open relationships. These principles are only a jumping-off point; you will need additional resources. Books that we consider must-reads for anyone who still has work to do on building a strong sense of self, setting good boundaries and creating healthy intimate relationships are those by Harriet Lerner and Brené Brown listed in the resources section on page pages 469–72, particularly *The Dance of Intimacy* and *The Gifts of Imperfection*.

And if the things we discuss are linked for you to genuine mental health issues, such as serious anxiety, depression or low self-worth, always consider professional help to work through those issues. We make this recommendation as people who have spent time in the therapist's office and have seen the transformative power of really good psychological help. Some problems can't be solved with self-help books. When you confront one of them, we urge you to get the help you need without shame or self-judgment. See pages 446–47 for information on finding a poly-friendly mental health professional.

NOSCE TE IPSUM

"Know thyself." You can't have what you want if you don't know what you want. You can't build a relationship that's satisfying without first understanding yourself and your needs. A willingness to question yourself, to challenge yourself, and to explore without fear the hidden parts of you are the best tools to gain that self-knowledge. A quote often attributed to Francis Bacon reads, "Your true self can be known only by systematic experimentation, and controlled only by being known." Understanding and programming your own mind is your responsibility; if you fail to do this, the world will program it for you, and you'll end up in the relationship other people think you should have, not the relationship you want.

Poly preparedness starts with taking responsibility for the work you need to do. It's not easy. We are very good at hiding the truth about ourselves from ourselves. Some of us are very good at making everything seem like someone else's problem. Others of us are too good at taking on other people's problems as our own. No one's self-awareness is perfect. But it starts with the simple act of looking inward, of asking yourself, "Is this my problem? What is the issue?" Self-awareness starts with awareness, period.

One of our readers recently said, "You can come with baggage, but you're responsible for knowing what's in the suitcases." This is often described as "owning your own shit." So what do you need to know? First, your needs. Most of us are never taught how to figure out what we need, let alone communicate it effectively. We are usually really good at feeling our feelings, but we tend to react to the *feeling* rather than the actual need. For example, we tend to think that when we feel angry, it's because someone else did something bad to us, so we react to that person, tell them how much they hurt us, and perhaps demand they stop. Sometimes anger really is about the thing you think it's about. But often, particularly in intimate relationships, the anger is about something else. It's about a need that's not being acknowledged or expressed, or even known.

Getting in touch with those needs can be really hard. So working to understand the needs driving strong emotions is a valuable practice. Then there's understanding your needs as they pertain to relationships. Do you need to be polyamorous? Do you need to be monogamous? Do you need at least the possibility of eventually moving in with a partner—or are you entirely closed to living together? Is sex an indispensable part of an intimate relationship for you? Are you open to nonsexual intimate connections? Are you willing to be involved in hierarchical relationships, where you are a secondary partner or subject to a veto? Or do you need to have a larger hand in the course your relationship takes?

You may find it helps to reframe some of what you are calling needs as things that feed you, things that give you joy. There's a dangerous side to focusing on needs, though, which we discuss more later. This is the risk of treating people as need-fulfillment machines. For example, it's not uncommon to see people create detailed descriptions of what their future partners will have to look like, be like and want: what role they should play. That's dangerous.

One way to think about (and seek) the kind of relationships you want without objectifying others is to think about what you have to offer (or not). Examples might be: I can offer life-partnering relationships. I can offer intimate relationships that don't include sex. I am interested in supporting a family. I am interested in caring for a family. I am not willing to move from my home for a partner. I have only two nights a week available for relationships. And so on.

This exercise can be useful in setting boundaries and helping clarify the kind of relationships you're looking for and can sustain. It also plays an important role in partner selection, something we'll talk about later. It's not going to be very satisfying, for example, for you to end up in a closed triad if what you really need is an open network with the potential to date other people. If you are looking for life partners, you may choose to be long-term friends, rather than romantic partners, with people who are looking for other types of relationships.

MINDING THE GAP

Lots of polyamorous people we know, ourselves included, tend to be idealists. We have lofty goals for our relationships and how we want to conduct ourselves within them. But becoming the kind of person who can live those ideals is a never-ending process. Not only doing the work is important. Understanding where you are *right now* is just as important. That includes understanding whether you are ready to share a partner or to be shared. The problem with being idealists about polyamory is that we risk putting ourselves into situations we're not ready for. If we do that, we risk hurting other people.

Although self-awareness is important, so is self-compassion. We don't look inward so that we can pass judgment on all our flaws. We do it so we can be aware of how our behavior is aligning with our values, what effect we're having on other people, how we may be sabotaging ourselves and our relationships. Understand where you are, yes, but also understand that it's okay to be there, at least for now.

In the book *Daring Greatly*, shame researcher Brené Brown introduces the idea of "minding the gap." She's talking about the values gap: the space between who we are now and who we want to be. Minding the gap is part of walking toward the horizon we talked about in the previous chapter. There will always be times when we are imperfect, when we fall short of the best possible versions of ourselves. Minding the gap is being *aware* of where we are now and striving to move in the direction we want to go. That's part of living with integrity.

EVE'S STORY When my husband, Peter, and I opened up from monogamy, the first few months of my relationship with Ray were difficult for Peter, and for his relationship with me. He did a lot of work in those months to reach a place where he could come to terms with the connection between me and Ray—which flourished quite quickly—and give it space to grow.

When, about six months into that relationship, Peter started what would become a four-year long-distance relationship with Clio, I wanted to show him the same grace he had shown me—all at once. He'd done all that work, I reasoned; I wanted to show him I could do the same. But I neglected to give myself the time and space he had taken. I wanted to start out at the same place it had taken him six months to reach.

So I failed to set boundaries, and I failed to take care of myself. During Clio's first overnight visit with us, we were walking down the street toward the party the three of us were attending together. I wasn't prepared when he put his arm around her and I felt my throat constrict and the ground drop out from under me. I wasn't prepared when, surrounded by people in a packed room that allowed very little movement, I got separated from them and watched from across the room while they sat together and flirted and I felt the walls closing in. And I wasn't prepared to lie awake the entire night while he spent the night with her in the guest room, or for my emotional meltdown the next day.

There were some basic things Peter and Clio could have given me that would have helped me ease into the situation and feel safe—we talk about those in chapter 9—but I didn't know to ask for them. In fact, I actively avoided asking for them, because I wanted to be the strong, noble poly person who never felt jealous or insecure. I was looking at where I wanted to be standing instead of where I was standing, at what I wanted to offer instead of what I actually could at the time.

As Eve's story illustrates, none of us are perfect. Our lives are filled with struggles and mistakes. The effort to be perfect only drives us away from one another and damages our self-worth.

The reason you need to understand where you are right now is so that you can understand your limitations. Your relationships will benefit if you can examine what your triggers are—not so that you can instruct everyone to tiptoe around them, but so you can be aware, when you're triggered, of what is going on. Knowing where you stand now will help you remember that there's not something wrong with you when you feel jealous, when the ground drops out from beneath your feet when you see your husband holding hands with his girlfriend for the first time.

You can't control how your partners' other relationships develop, but you can control how you allow them to intersect with and affect your life. You are allowed to set boundaries on your personal space and time. You don't have to make the first time you hang out with your husband and his girlfriend be a public appearance at a crowded party. You don't have to be okay with hearing them have sex, now or ever. Take care of yourself so you can take care of those around you.

When you make mistakes, think in terms of "I am a person who values integrity" rather than "I am a super-together person." Think of compassion and free will as values you strive for, not attributes you have. That way, you can more easily realign your actions with your values if things go wrong. For example, if you think of yourself as a person who values free will, you can respond constructively when someone points out that you appear to be trying to control someone. Minding the gap is about being able to see these things.

Very few of us make it to adulthood without getting a little broken on the way. None of us can see each other's wounds; none of us can really know what other people's struggles look like from the inside. But one thing's for sure: we all have them. Polyamory can push on our broken bits in ways few other things do. We may be able to build walls around deep-rooted fears, insecurities and triggers in monogamous relationships—walls that poly relationships will often raze to the ground. And because so many more people are involved, more people stand to suffer. We *all* have things we need to work on. Expect it.

WORTHINESS

Polyamory will challenge your emotional resiliency. Instead of building walls around painful feelings like fear and jealousy, you'll need to find a way through them. You may experience more loss: more relationships means more possibilities for heartbreak. And you may encounter judgment: slut-shaming, trivialization of your relationships, and claims that you're treating your partners badly or neglecting your kids are some of the most common forms. We discuss these more in chapter 25, but what's important here is developing a sense of self-worth that protects you from *internalizing* these corrosive messages.

You'll sometimes hear poly people say things like "Don't give other people power to hurt you." But that ignores the very healthy impulse to seek feedback on our perceptions of the world. Even the healthiest person, when persistently rejected, will be hurt. Rejection may erode your mental boundaries or your ability to engage in intimacy. The only way to maintain good mental boundaries, to counteract social rejection and to assess when to disengage is to have self-knowledge and self-confidence and to engage in self-compassion and self-care. In other words, to commit to behaviors that will help you develop a strong sense of worthiness. And yes, feeling worthy is a practice too.

EVE'S STORY   The first time in my adult life I remember feeling worthy was when I was thirty-six years old. I was with my poly women's group. We were talking about worthiness and how it connects to our sense of belonging, which we get when we allow ourselves to be vulnerable and are accepted as we are. But being able to allow that vulnerability requires—gotcha!—a sense of worthiness. To connect with others, we must take a leap of faith and believe we are worthy of connection.

Inside I was growing more and more distraught. *I don't know how to feel worthy.* Finally I asked, "How do we begin to believe we are worthy?" My group members said, "Well, maybe *imagine* what it feels like to feel worthy, and focus on that. Over time, it will begin to feel real." I took a deep breath and made a very scary and vulnerable admission: "I don't know what it feels like to feel worthy." I was surprised at how much it hurt to say those words—to admit that the concept of "worthiness" was so far outside my realm of personal experience that I couldn't even *imagine* it.

Unfortunately, because I'm not entirely sure *how* I learned how to imagine worthiness, I find it difficult to advise others. I know that I worked at it. I read, I blogged, I took risks with my friends by sharing more with them. I started keeping a daily journal of things I was grateful for. I had recently completed several months of intense therapy, and the work I had done there seemed to finally start to take hold. But the truth is, I don't know what the pivot was. One day I just...felt worthy.

Since feeling worthy does *not* come naturally to me, if I do not work at reminding myself the feeling fades, and then I slip back into a miasma of fear and self-doubt. Then I remember to start practicing again, and I work my way back out.

The good news is that once you know what worthiness feels like, only once, you know that you *can* experience it—even if you aren't experiencing it right now. A sense of worth is critical to counteracting the *scarcity model* of love and life. If we do not believe in our worth, we become disempowered, unable to advocate for our needs. We do not see or embrace the love that is actually around us in our lives. It becomes harder to treat our partners well, because we do not see what we bring to their lives. And if we don't understand our value to them, we are more likely to feed our jealousy and fear of loss. Notice that institutions built on the scarcity model—too many workplaces, too many families—*always* inculcate a sense of low self-worth.

Worthiness is not the same as validation. A sense of self-worth comes from within, not from someone else. It can be tempting to look to the outside for validation—to look to your partner and say, "She loves me, therefore I am worthy." That creates fear rather than reducing fear, because when we rely on outside things in order to feel worthy, we fear losing them all the more. In the end, we can't wait until we see evidence that we are worthy before we allow ourselves to believe it. We start by taking that leap of faith and believing we are worthy.

Our sense of self—what psychologists might term self-differentiation—has a huge impact on relationships. If we make mistakes that hurt people, we can say, "I did something bad" rather than "I am bad." And if something is our fault, that means it is within our power to change the outcome.

Low self-worth will try to protect itself, sometimes in sneaky ways. It can tell us that if we have a high sense of self-worth we might not get our partner's time and attention, because we're not in crisis. Emotional crisis can become a way to get our partners to give us what we need. The solution to this problem is tricky, but one place to start is to look at people who do have a strong sense of self-worth, and see if their needs are being met.

If you are struggling with worthiness, you'll find resources at the back of this book. If you are seriously struggling, professional help can be of huge benefit—not just in your intimate relationships but in all parts of your life.

SELF-EFFICACY

Let's say you, as our intrepid mushroom hunter, get lost in the woods. Do you know a few wild plants you can collect to feed yourself? Do you know how to find water? How to make a shelter and stay warm? If not, how confident are you in your ability to figure these things out? Will you begin to panic? Will you think, *Oh, my God, I'm going to die—I don't know how to survive in the forest!* Or will you take a deep breath and say, "Well, I've never done this before, but here I am and I'd better get on with it. Let's see, it's getting dark. I guess the first thing is to look for some shelter and figure out if there's something I can eat."

There's a kind of calm that comes from believing you can handle a situation, even one you haven't faced before, and that calm increases your competence. This effect is called *self-efficacy*. Trying new things—like writing a book, or exploring polyamory—involves learning new skills, and research shows that key to learning new skills is simply believing you can learn them. Self-efficacy in poly relationships is the feeling that you can make it through your wife's first date. That you'll figure out a way to manage your jealousy, even if you don't know how yet. That if you have to sleep alone some night, even if it's been years and you don't remember what it feels like, you'll get through it and be okay.

All this may seem to have a flavor of New Age power-of-intention pop psychology, but the study of self-efficacy goes back four decades, and there's solid evidence supporting it. Whether or not someone believes they can do something has important effects on whether they can. This has proven true for everything from learning new skills to quitting smoking.

As to developing this calming competence, research has identified strategies for improving self-efficacy. Here are two simple ones.

Small successes. Step outside your comfort zone. Find something you can succeed at: something that seems hard to you, but not so hard that it will land you quivering under the covers in tears. Stay home while your wife is on a date. Talk to your partner about your insecurity or jealousy. Each small step will build on the last, giving you a stronger sense of your ability to tackle the next challenge. They won't necessarily become easier. But the key is to develop your belief that *I can do this.*

The flip side of that is to address how you cope with "failure," if it turns out you weren't quite as strong (yet) as you'd hoped. People with high self-efficacy tend to be resilient in the face of failure; they know that often you have to fail many times before you succeed.

Role models. An important factor contributing to a person's idea of whether they can do something is whether they see other people doing it. We can't stress enough the usefulness of having polyamorous role models, ideally people in your social network who you can talk to and get feedback from. Find your local poly discussion and support group, or start one. As polyamorous people we are surrounded by a culture that tells us, "You can't do this," "That's not possible," or even "That's morally wrong." It can be hard to maintain a belief in yourself and your abilities in the face of this social censure, especially when things get hard. That's why it's critical to establish a poly-friendly support system and find people you consider to be good examples. We discuss this more in chapter 25, on social and community support.

Building self-efficacy in other areas of your life also builds success in poly relationships. It takes the bite out of two scary monsters: "failure" and being alone. For many of us, for example, our first breakup is the scariest, because it's our first taste of romantic "failure." Will we find love again? What if the person we just broke up with was The One? Believing that you can be alone and thrive, that you can survive the end of something and rebuild, are important elements of self-efficacy.

A SPECIAL KIND OF COMMITMENT

An essential aspect of successful poly relationships, in our experience, is a commitment to *being poly*. Sometimes learning the skills is hard. We have to practice and muddle through painful situations when they befall us. At some point, poly may just feel too damn hard.

EVE'S STORY   Despite all our preparation, Peter and I didn't really know what to expect when Ray and I became lovers. I got caught up in a full-on flood of new relationship energy, and Peter, with whom

I had settled into a low-key, eight-year-relationship groove, struggled with the intensity of it all. One day, when Ray and I had been lovers for about a month, Peter sat me down and said, "You're falling in love with Ray." He was right. Surprisingly, perhaps, we had never talked before about the possibility of falling in love. And there we were, and we weren't ready.

My growing relationship with Ray forced me and Peter to confront a long-buried structural problem in our relationship, one we had been able to sweep under the rug for years. One day, the day before I was scheduled to go visit Ray, Peter told me he wasn't sure he wanted to be with me anymore. I panicked. I said I wanted to cancel my trip so I could stay home and work on things with Peter, but Peter said no, he wanted me to go. And he wanted me to stay with Ray until he had decided he was ready for me to come back.

I drove the next day to see Ray, and that afternoon, we made love, and then I lay there sobbing in his arms, torn apart by conflicting emotions: fear and grief at the thought of losing Peter, joy at the new connection with Ray. And then, suddenly, I accepted the situation. I imagined myself without Peter, was able to picture my life without him, and I realized that even without him or Ray, even alone, I would be okay. I would mourn, but my life would go on, and I would rebuild. I wrote in my journal that day, "After a few days of feeling in free-fall, it's like I suddenly looked behind me and realized...Oh. I have wings."

A couple of days later, Peter called and said it was okay for me to come home. The ground beneath our relationship had shifted dramatically—as it would continue to over the next few years, as we found our new normal. But coming face-to-face with the reality of losing Peter inoculated me against some of the fear that accompanies the biggest changes and greatest uncertainties. Having looked the worst-case scenario in the eye, I found it no longer so scary.

Eve has called this kind of time the "dark night of the soul" moment. Unless you are truly exceptional, you will experience it at some point, usually early on. Maybe your partners are struggling. Maybe you're tired of fighting your inner demons. And *this* is when it really matters whether you've committed, with all your heart and soul, to being poly. If you don't commit, if you aren't ready for that dark night of the soul, and you back away in fear when it comes, then you and people you love are going to get very hurt.

So be ready. Because if you step into it and keep walking, you will get through it. It ends. Know that you're not alone: thousands of people before you have walked this path—not exactly yours, of course, but just as dark and scary. *It ends.* And it's better on the other side. Getting through that dark night removes its power over you, and that's what it takes to get you (and your partners, and their partners) onto a solid footing that will lead you to happiness, a place where you can make clear-headed decisions focused on the good of everyone.

The longer people avoid confronting that dark night of the soul, the more power it has over them and their relationships. Some people elaborately construct their entire lives to avoid confronting fear. Many people use the hearts of their lovers or their metamours as sacrifices to the unknown beasts they think live within the darkness they're not willing to explore.

We urge you, if you are going to explore polyamory, don't just dip a toe in. One, that's not going to give you the strength and tools to succeed. Two, you'll be treating people as things.

Of the people who do decide to make that commitment, to live polyamorously and treat their partners ethically even when it means confronting those heart-shaking fears, no one makes quite the same trip. Everyone charts a different path through that dark night. But it begins with commitment: knowing you are going to do this, and that you can.

COURAGE

When many of us think of courage, we think of heroics, of facing down a tank in Tiananmen Square. But everyday, ordinary courage is the courage it takes to confess a crush. The courage it takes to say, "Yes, I am going to open my heart to this person, even though I don't know what the outcome will be." The courage to love a partner who loves another person even though you do not have the trappings of security that monogamy promises. The courage to sleep alone. The courage to begin a relationship with someone who's already partnered, trusting that person to carve out the space for you that you're going to need.

This kind of moral courage comes from a willingness to be vulnerable, and to accept that you will be okay even though you don't know what will happen. And you know what? Courage is required because sometimes what we're trying doesn't work. The tank rolls over us. Our vulnerability is rejected, or worse, mocked.

That's the whole thing about courage. It can't promise a happy outcome. We can't say, "Just be brave and vulnerable and you will obtain love and master happy poly relationships ever after." It wouldn't be courage if there were any guarantees.

You may feel like saying, "Well, I'm just not that brave." But we're not talking about something you are or are not. We all have times when we act with courage and times when we don't. In fact, it's something that we and our partners struggle with all the time. Like everything else we talk about, courage is not a destination. Courage is a verb, grammarians be damned: it's not something you *have*, it's something you do. You practice a bit every day. And if you fall down, if your courage fails you, you always get another chance. Always. Courage happens in increments.

You'll need courage because polyamorous relationships can be scary. Loving other people without a script is scary. Allowing the people you love to make their own choices without controlling them is scary. The kind of courage we're talking about involves being willing to let go of guarantees—and love and trust your partners anyway.

So how do you learn to have courage, to develop this practice? Imagine you want to learn how to swim. You sign up for swim lessons, you get yourself a swimsuit and goggles, and on the day your lessons are to begin, you show up at the pool, nervous and eager. Imagine if, to your surprise, the swim coach takes you out onto a boat. What, maybe you'll learn to swim off the side of the boat? But instead, he spends the entire day teaching the basics of sailing—how to tie knots, how to tack against the wind, how to work the sails. "When you have mastered the art of sailing," the swim coach intones, "you will know how to swim."

You would know that that's daft. Yet often, that's exactly how we try to learn skills like trust and courage. We try to build the skills that can help us face our fears by doing things that are completely unrelated to courage—things like avoiding the triggers for our fears, or creating structures that shelter us from the things we're afraid of, waiting until we feel brave. If we fear that a partner might want to leave us, we lay down regulations telling her not to. If we fear being replaced by someone sexier than we are, we are tempted to create prohibitions that restrict certain kinds of sex.

We do not learn courage, or trust, by avoiding the things that trigger our fears any more than we learn to swim by trimming the sails on a boat. In fact, the time and effort we spend doing this is time and effort we are not spending learning to swim.

As you well know, you learn to swim by getting in the water. Maybe you start with kicks at the shallow end of the pool, but you need to get wet. We learn courage by taking a deep breath, steadying ourselves, and then choosing the difficult, scary path over the easy way out. As the theologian Mary Daly said, we "learn courage by couraging." The path of greatest courage also seems like the hardest: it takes us right past the places where our fears live. But just as we cannot put off learning to swim until the day we magically know the butterfly stroke, we cannot put off learning courage until the day we magically become courageous. This is work we must do, now, to create fertile ground within our relationships that allows us to move with integrity and compassion.

QUESTIONS TO ASK YOURSELF

To become more self-aware and identify your personal strengths, weaknesses and fears—especially as they relate to relationships—here are some questions to consider:

- *Why do I have romantic relationships? What do I get out of them?*

- *What do I consider essential, indispensable elements of a relationship?*

- *Are there specific kinds of relationships that I know I am looking for? Kinds that I know I don't want?*

- *What do I bring to the table for others?*

- *What makes me feel cherished, loved and secure?*

- *What makes me afraid in relationships? Why?*

- *In what ways do I protect myself from being hurt? Do those strategies help or hinder my search for connection?*

NURTURING YOUR RELATIONSHIPS

*Everyone who tries to create love
with an emotionally unaware partner suffers.*

BELL HOOKS

When you start down the path of polyamory, your relationships may grow in all kinds of different directions. Shaking off the template of monogamy means you're free to build your life to your specifications, consistent with compassionate treatment of the people close to you. We can't tell you what your life will look like. We can tell you one thing, though, particularly if there are two of you starting from an existing relationship: it will change.

Quite likely, it will change in ways you don't expect. If there are weaknesses in your existing relationship, polyamory has a way of finding them. Trying to buffer these changes with rules probably won't work very well, for reasons we talk about in chapter 10. The things you think will be important might not be, and things you don't think about at all might be the ones that challenge you. We've spoken to countless couples who have come to polyamory, and the one thing we've heard over and over is, "When we talked about this, the things we thought would be the most important weren't, and things we hadn't thought about were."

The first part of laying the groundwork for polyamory concerns yourself—things like developing security, self-confidence and flexibility. The second involves creating fertile soil for growth in your existing relationship, if you have one. The tools for doing these two different things will be very similar. Those of you who are currently single or solo poly don't necessarily get to skip over this chapter, because past relationship experience, and the assumptions we carry with us, can still surprise us in unexpected and unpleasant ways.

THE ISSUE OF SECURITY

Why do we seek romantic relationships? For many of us, relationships are a way to feel loved and treasured and to share some part of our life with people who support and nurture us. When we've found a relationship, or two, we want to feel safe there: to feel like we can relax into the security of our partners' love.

In poly relationships, the need for security tends to play out in two ways. First, we can be tempted to seek security by placing controls on our partners. Whether it's limiting a partner's access to other people to build our sense of security against being replaced, or restricting our partner's range of action with others to make ourselves feel safe, we can be lured by a feeling that if we can just get our partners to do what we want, we will feel secure.

Conversely, if we are at all compassionate, we want to help our partners feel safe. So we might be tempted to accept their restrictions, in the hopes that we can make our partners feel more secure. Security is a tricky thing. On the one hand, our choices do affect our partners' security a lot. On the other, genuine security has to be built from within. Security that rests on another person's actions is fragile, and easily lost.

Four principles about personal security seem to be true:

- It's impossible to "make" another person be secure. We can provide a compassionate and supportive environment by providing reassurance, by listening, by acting in thoughtful ways, but these actions cannot *make* someone else secure. Internal work is required for a sense of security and confidence.
- It's almost impossible to build a strong relationship of any kind amid insecurity. This seems especially true in polyamory.

- Insecurity invents its own evidence and supports its own premises. No amount of someone else's time and effort is enough to make an insecure person see the light and realize that the insecurity is unfounded. He or she must intentionally and deliberately challenge, understand and then choose to move past the insecurity.
- Intentionally and deliberately challenging, understanding, and choosing to move past insecurity is frightening, uncomfortable work. Staring our inner demons in the face is so uncomfortable that it can make crawling through broken glass dipped in alcohol and rattlesnake venom seem like a cakewalk. It is the rare person who's willing to do this without being prodded into it. And this principle has a corollary.
- Trying to avoid upsetting a partner by giving in to their insecurity, or steering around their sensitivities and triggers, can become enabling: reinforcing rather than alleviating the problem. The very things we do to try to make a partner feel more secure can make the insecurity worse.

Another point we've learned: As counterintuitive as it may seem, sometimes a lasting sense of security comes more from knowing a partner is free to go but chooses to stay than from attempting to obligate that partner to stay.

PRACTICING SECURITY

Insecurity is toxic. You can't trust what you're always afraid of losing. You can never become a full partner in a relationship you do not believe you "deserve." You can never embrace happiness if you do not believe you are good enough for it. When we feel insecure, it can blind us to the love our partners offer, which can make us feel alienated, which makes us more insecure, which further blinds us to the love we're offered.

EVE'S STORY   I have always been pretty profoundly insecure. Not long ago, I had an epiphany: it's as though I imagine that each person casts a circle of light around them. That light is their affection. People bring you closer in, into brighter light, depending on how much they like you. In all my relationships—personal and professional, romantic or friendship—I have always felt I was standing just outside that circle of light, always hesitant to take a step forward, always petitioning for entry. And always a bit sheepish about that petitioning, never sure I would be welcome.

Even in my closest relationships I never pictured myself included in the circle, so I could never simply feel calm and confident that the relationship *existed* and would continue. To say it another way, I always felt I was the one asking, never the one offering—as though time spent with people I cared about was something I took from them, not something I gave to them. This perception caused the end of at least a couple of my relationships, because it caused me to pull away, to stop investing: I felt that investing in relationships with the people I cared about was a burden on them.

I had a close friend in university who, for about a year, I spent most of my social time with. One weekend we spent three days backpacking together in the Olympic Mountains. I remember sitting by the fire with him, feeling insecure (of course), worried that I might be getting on his nerves. The thought crossed my mind, *I hope he doesn't hate me.* Then the absurdity of the thought struck me: *If he hates you, why would he be spending three days in the mountains with you?*

It took another, oh, decade and a half for this kind of realization to become normal. When I had the epiphany about the circles of light, I realized that in most of my relationships, I had been standing in the light *all along.* All it took for me to be inside it was to realize that I already was. I found that simply imagining that circle, and that it contained me, changed my interactions with the people close to me. That visualization is now an ongoing practice.

Franklin has talked to many people who say things like "I'm just an insecure person," as if feeling insecure is something they're born with. In reality, it is something you can control. "Insecure" is something you can, if you want to, choose not to be. We are big believers in the affirmative power of choice, and we believe that people are often insecure because they make choices, dozens of times a day, that confirm and reinforce their own insecurity.

Changing the way you feel about yourself is painful and uncomfortable. For that reason many people choose, without necessarily even being aware that it is a choice, to hang onto destructive ideas about themselves rather than face the discomfort and fear of changing those ideas.

Self-image, like playing the piano, is something you become good at by practice. If you practice being insecure—if you accept thoughts and ideas that tear down your sense of self, if you lie in bed at night and think about the reasons you are not worthy or good enough—then you become highly skilled at being insecure. On the other hand, if you practice security—if you reject thoughts and ideas that tear down your sense of self and accept ideas that build it up, if you lie in bed at night and think about the qualities that make you special and give the people in your life value—then you become skilled at being self-confident and secure.

On his website, Franklin's "guide to becoming a secure person" is one of the most popular essays he's ever written. Here's a three-step exercise that he has found incredibly valuable for building internal security:

Step 1. Understand that you have a choice. You did not choose your past experiences, of course (the people who made fun of you in fifth grade, or a past partner who told you you weren't good enough), but right now you have a choice about continuing to believe them, or changing the things you believe about yourself. The single hardest thing to do to change your self-image is to realize that you have the choice. The rest gets easier.

Step 2. Act like someone who is self-confident, even if you aren't. "Fake it 'til you make it" is a great personal development strategy. You might not control your feelings, but you do control your actions. You control your body; you can choose to act self-confident even if you don't feel it. When faced with something that scares you or makes you feel threatened, think what choice you'd make if you were confident and secure...and then do that. Even if it scares the hell out of you. No one will know. Do you feel insecure when you see your partner kiss his other partner in front of you? Take a deep breath, say "I feel insecure when I see this, but I want you to do it anyway," and let it happen. Acting self-confident will feel phony and forced at first, but gradually it will become normal.

Step 3. Practice. You become good at what you practice. A person who is insecure becomes very good at being insecure because he practices all the time. You practice being insecure by thinking about those old insults you heard in fifth grade and telling yourself they are true. You practice being insecure by going over in your mind all the reasons you are not good enough to be with your partner.

People who are secure practice being secure. Stop thinking about those old insults; when they come to mind, tell yourself, "No, these are false, and I choose not to believe them anymore." When you find yourself thinking about all the things that are wrong with you, stop and say "No, these are wrong. Here is a list of things that are good and sexy about me instead." (Corny as it sounds, writing a list of things you like about yourself and keeping it in your pocket helps.) When you find yourself thinking about why your partner doesn't or shouldn't really want you, stop yourself and say "No, this is not true."

Practicing security means continually turning toward the best version of yourself. Each belief about yourself that you choose to hold onto, in each moment, is a step toward or away from the person you want to be. As Canadian entrepreneur Lynn Robinson says, "Our beliefs about ourselves are all made up. So it's a good idea to make up some good ones."

FEAR OF LOSS

We love our partners. Hopefully, we are with our partners because they bring us joy. And allowing that joy inside makes us vulnerable, because life is uncertain. With joy comes the fear of losing the thing that makes us joyful. For many of us, the kind of vulnerability that comes with letting in deep, heartfelt joy is a little scary. For some of us, it's terrifying. Some of us protect ourselves from that fear by never allowing ourselves to fully open up, or numbing ourselves by imagining worst-case scenarios. Others of us protect ourselves by trying to control the people around us, to keep the possibility of loss at bay.

Our distress may be compounded by the cultural script that says if you aren't torn apart by the thought of losing a partner, it means you don't really love them. In reality, commitment and fear of loss are only indirectly related. Often the fear of loss is more closely linked to a fear of being alone than commitment to a partner; in monogamous relationships, losing a partner means being alone. And, paradoxically, if you want something too badly, the fear of losing it can become greater than the joy of having it. When that happens, we hold onto things not because they make us happy, but because the thought of losing them makes us suffer. Both having them and not having them become sources of pain.

This is all a bit ironic, because the truth is that we *will* lose everything. Every one of our partners, friends, family members, everything that brings us joy will one day leave our lives—either through life's normal uncertainty and change, or through the inevitability of death. So we have two choices: embrace and love what we have and feel joy as deeply and fully as we can, and eventually lose everything—or shield ourselves, be miserable...and eventually lose everything. Living in fear won't stop us from losing what we love, it will only stop us from enjoying it.

What's the antidote to that fear? Gratitude. Welcome the people who care for you and the experiences you have together. Take joy in them, be thankful for them. Eve has found a gratitude journal to be incredibly helpful. Making an active practice out of gratitude creates constant reminders of what you have in your life. Know that you are lucky to have people in your life with the power to break your heart, because it means you have love.

THE INEVITABILITY OF CHANGE

We know our readers are approaching polyamory from a lot of different places. Some of you have never had a monogamous relationship. Others will be exploring polyamory after decades of monogamy. Some of you will be venturing into polyamory single, while others will be opening a previously monogamous partnership.

Eve's experience fell into the latter category. Like many couples venturing into poly, she and Peter initially tried to change as little as possible—*especially* their existing relationship. And like many, they gravitated toward rules and structures to try to preserve the relationship as it had been to create a feeling of security and stability. They agreed that the marriage was primary, and they had rules: things like "We will never spend more time with another partner than with each other," and "No one else is allowed to try to come between us." In fact, Eve's first online dating profile said (she shudders to recall), "Try to come between me and my primary and you'll be out of my life faster than you can say 'polyamory.'"

It's easy to understand why Eve and Peter wanted rules like these. Security, some basic predictability: these are fundamental human needs. At the same time, autonomy, independence and self-reliance are also fundamental values for many people, including both of us. We've seen how a focus on these latter values alone can lead to some pretty poor treatment of partners. It's important to build relationships in such a way that the people within them *can* feel secure, can feel a sense of belonging, and can have some basic expectations they can rely on. But it's also essential that people have agency in their relationships, that relationships be built on a foundation of choice and free will. These are not mutually exclusive goals.

Here's an uncomfortable truth, though. If you decide to do this, if you decide to open your heart and your life to loving more than one person and letting your partners love others too, your life will change. You will change. If you started this journey with a partner, your partner will change. *Every* new person you let into your heart will disrupt your life—sometimes in small ways, sometimes in big ones.

Disruption is a fact of life. And that's okay. After all, almost everything else you do in life risks disruption to your relationships. Taking a new job. Losing a job. (Couples counselors say that financial stress is more likely to ruin a marriage than any other single factor, including infidelity.) Having a baby. Moving to another city. Getting sick or injured. Having problems in your family of origin. Taking up new hobbies. Experiencing a death in the family. Hell, every time you walk outside your door or step into a car, you're risking serious injury or death, and that'll disrupt a relationship real quick!

We don't live in fear of disruption when we're offered a new job or decide to have a child. We accept that these choices will change our lives. Ethical polyamory is similar: you accept that changes in your romantic life will affect your relationship, you resolve to act with integrity and honesty to cherish your partners to the best of your ability, and you trust that your partners will do the same for you.

Many problems we encounter in polyamory, particularly when we're in a relationship that was previously monogamous, come from attempts to explore new relationships without having anything change. Sometimes those changes involve coming face-to-face with our deepest fears: abandonment, fear of loss, fear of being replaced, fear of no longer being special. Relationship change is scary. Sometimes it comes on us in jarring ways.

MELISSA'S STORY   Melissa, a friend of Franklin's, loves sushi. She tried for months to get her husband, Niko, to try sushi with her, with no success whatsoever. He expressed in no uncertain terms that he was not interested in raw fish strapped to rice with electrical tape.

Long after she gave up trying to take him to the sushi house, he started dating a new partner, Naveen, who also loved sushi. One day Naveen suggested they go out for sushi, and this time he said, "Okay!" Unsurprisingly, he discovered he loved it.

Rather than think, *Hey, this is awesome, now I can finally share my love of sushi with him!* Melissa was less than thrilled. It hurt her to, as she said, make a request of her partner, get a no, and then see him doing it with another.

Melissa's story illustrates one of the hidden assumptions we often make about relationships: we can feel entitled to have our partners experience new things with us first, and become hurt if a partner chooses to experience these things with someone else. For a single person starting a relationship with someone who's partnered, this hidden expectation can plant land mines everywhere. Something as innocuous as an invitation to go out for sushi might trigger an unexpected blowup.

Poly readiness involves not only examining the expectation that our partners will never change, but also examining expectations about how and when they change. People don't always change in the ways or on the timetable we want them to. New partners bring new experiences, and these experiences will change our relationships. Good relationships always change us; it's one of the best things about them!

One of the standard tropes of monogamy is that we can prevent infidelity by limiting our partner's access to members of the opposite sex. Opportunity creates infidelity, or so we're told, so we limit opportunity. In polyamorous relationships this trope can manifest in more subtle ways, such as by trying to limit the depth of a connection or the time a partner spends with another lover. As we discuss in chapter 11, it's common for people in a relationship to seek to use the power they have to constrict, limit or regulate a partner's other relationships, in the hopes that this will make those other relationships less disruptive or threatening. People try all kinds of structures to do this: enforced power hierarchies, limitations on how much a partner is permitted to experience emotional or sexual intimacy with others, rules that an established couple will only have sex with a third person if both are there for it (often on the assumption that this will prevent jealousy), and so on.

Of course, not everyone will have such feelings. If the idea of controlling your partner's other romantic connections to protect your relationship seems strange to you, you probably won't run into the problems we describe in this chapter. An important skill in creating happy poly relationships involves learning to see other lovers, particularly a partner's other lovers, as people who make life better for both of you rather than a hazard to be managed.

If such a perspective does not come naturally to you, though, it can be learned. Doing so requires investing in communication, overcoming fear and rejecting some of the pathological things we're taught about romance. It means accepting that you and your partners *will* grow and change, and the secret to maintaining relationships in the face of change is to be resilient and flexible. It also means cultivating a strong sense of security, accepting that we'll all make mistakes, building relationships robust enough to weather the mistakes, and making peace with change.

BEING ALONE

Humans are social animals. We function best when we're surrounded by people who care about us. The fear of being alone is part of being human. But if we're driven by that fear, if we're so afraid of being alone that we think losing a partner will destroy us, it's almost impossible to have a healthy relationship. It's okay to dislike being alone, but when we believe we *can't* be alone, things run off the rails.

When that fear drives us, we can't easily set good boundaries or make reasoned choices. And if we don't feel like we've fully consented to a relationship but instead are there because being alone is worse, then it's easy to feel like the relationship is something that's done to us rather than something that enriches our lives. From here, it's very easy to become resentful of our partners—especially when they do anything that reminds us of our fear of being alone.

This fear and resentment can create a self-reinforcing cycle. When we're afraid of being alone, we get angry and resentful much more easily. This drives people away, which triggers the fear of being alone, which makes us angry and resentful. How do we break that cycle? By building relationships that move toward something rather than away from something. Relationships make us much happier when we move toward intimacy with people who bring out the best in us, rather than away from loneliness.

In polyamory it becomes especially vital to come to terms with the fear of being alone, first because you *are* likely to be alone from time to time, and second because more than one relationship is on the line. One of the core ingredients of a successful polyamorous relationship is the ability to treat all the folks involved, including not only our partners but their partners as well, with compassion and empathy. It's almost impossible to be compassionate when all we feel is fear of loss.

SCARCITY VS. ABUNDANCE

When they approach romantic relationships, people often fall into one of two patterns. Some follow a starvation model, and some follow an abundance model.

In the starvation model, opportunities for love seem scarce. Potential partners are thin on the ground, and finding them is difficult. Because most people you meet expect monogamy, finding poly partners is particularly difficult. Every additional requirement you have narrows the pool still more. Since relationship opportunities are so rare, you'd better seize whatever opportunity comes by and hang on with both hands—after all, who knows when another chance will come along?

The abundance model says that relationship opportunities are all around us. Sure, only a small percentage of the population might meet our criteria, but in a world of more than seven billion people, opportunities abound. Even if we exclude everyone who isn't open to polyamory, and everyone of the "wrong" sex or orientation, and everyone who doesn't have whatever other traits we want, we're still left with tens of thousands of potential partners, which is surely enough to keep even the most ambitious person busy.

The sneaky thing about both models is they're both right: the model we hold tends to become self-fulfilling. If we have a starvation model of relationships, we may tend to dwell on the times we've been rejected, which may lower our self-esteem, which decreases our confidence...and that makes it harder to find partners, because confidence is sexy. We may start feeling desperate to find a relationship, which decreases our attractiveness further. So we end up with less success, which reinforces the idea that relationships are scarce.

When we hold an abundance model of relationships, it's easier to just go do the things that bring us joy, without worrying about searching for a partner. That tends to make us more attractive, because happy, confident people are desirable. If we're off doing the things that bring us joy, we meet other people there who are doing the same. Cool! The ease with which we find potential partners, even when we aren't looking for them, reinforces the idea that opportunities for love are abundant, which makes it easier for us to go about doing what makes us happy, without worrying overmuch about finding a partner...and 'round it goes. We think our perceptions are shaped by reality, but the truth is, the reality we get is often shaped by our perceptions.*

These ideas will also influence how willing we are to stay in relationships that aren't working for us, both directly and indirectly. If we believe relationships are rare and difficult to find, we may not give up a relationship even when it's damaging to us. Likewise, if we believe that relationships are hard to find, that may increase our fear of being alone, which can cause us to remain in relationships that aren't working for us.

Naturally, there's a fly in the ointment. Sometimes the things we're looking for, or the way we look for them, create artificial scarcity. This might be because we're doing something that puts other people off, or because we're

---

* Cognitive scientists talk about confirmation bias—the tendency to notice things that confirm our ideas, and to discount, discredit or not notice things that don't.

looking for something unrealistic. If you're looking for a Nobel Prize–winning Canadian supermodel with a net worth of $20 million, you might find potential partners few and far between. Similarly, if you give people the impression that you've created a slot for them to fit into that they won't be able to grow out of, opportunities for relationships might not be abundant either.

FACING DISCOMFORT

Flexibility promotes resilience. It helps create relationships that can adapt to the winds of change without breaking. It has a cost, though. Being flexible means being willing to face discomfort, because change is often uncomfortable. Accepting change, welcoming the idea that there might be many ways to have our needs met, letting go of the desire to hide from our fears by controlling the structures of our relationships...at some point, these will almost certainly bring us nose to claw with uncomfortable feelings.

There is a trope in some circles, often applied to relationships: "Don't do anything you're not comfortable with." When it concerns access to your body, your space or your mind, it's good advice. We can always choose what we consent to. Often, though, it really means "Don't *let your partner* do anything you're not comfortable with," or "Don't explore unknown situations if they make you uncomfortable." In such cases, we think "Don't do anything you're not comfortable with" is terrible advice. There is more to life than avoiding discomfort. Sometimes discomfort is an inevitable part of learning and growth. Remember the first time you tried to ride a bike, or swim, or play a musical instrument? Remember how awkward and uncomfortable it felt? Having a brilliant life means going outside your comfort zone. And sometimes discomfort shows us ways we can improve.

We would like to suggest the radical notion that being uncomfortable is not, by itself, a reason not to do something, nor to forbid someone else from doing something. There is more to life than going from cradle to grave by the path of least discomfort. Furthermore, refusing to face discomfort can, if we are not careful, lead to unethical behavior. When avoidance of discomfort comes at the cost of placing controls on other people, we disempower those people.

The status quo in almost any relationship is usually less scary than change, no matter how beneficial the change. When new people come into our lives, they bring new challenges and new delights. When relationships grow, they change. We can be tempted to try to maintain as much of the status quo as possible by limiting what the people around us can do: "You may come into my life, but only this far. You may grow, but only to this level."

In our experience, building walls around each other's freedom is more damaging in the long run than trusting in our partners' desire to do what's right by us—and trusting in ourselves to be able to adapt, find happiness and feel cherished even when things change. Discomfort and change will find us, sooner or later, no matter how much we try to hide from them. Meeting these things on our own terms, believing that we can be happy even in the face of change—all go a long way to building security and stability that endures.

LIVING WITH INTEGRITY

Throughout this book, we position trust as an alternative to control in poly relationships. Fundamental to *building* trust is living with integrity. You build trust when you keep your promises—when you "walk your talk." Trust decays when you break agreements, violate boundaries and act in ways that are not in accordance with your professed values. Living with integrity can be the thing that holds you together when nothing else can. When you have no easy choices, and the effects of those choices on people you care about are impossible to predict, what serves as your guide? When you fail, or make mistakes, are you able to look back and say, "I upheld the values that are most important to me"?

Times can come in polyamorous relationships when there are no good choices, when you can't win and no one else can either. Maybe it's just a question of where everyone is going to spend Christmas. Maybe it's where the kids go after a breakup. Maybe it's what to do when two partners whom you cherish with all your heart can't stand being in the same room together. We can talk about negotiation and compromise and finding win-win solutions, but sometimes the happy medium doesn't exist. The more people you put in the mix, the more likely conflicts are to arise, and sometimes there are no easy solutions.

We've talked about the need for an ethical framework that maximizes the well-being of everyone involved. But sometimes you are stuck minimizing losses rather than maximizing gains, and no matter how you reason your way through a situation, it feels like crap to make choices that you know are going to hurt people. And sometimes you genuinely can't tell. Sometimes you're faced with choices that feel lousy in the short term and whose long-term effects can't be predicted. So when that happens—when you can't make a move without hurting yourself or someone else—how do you make your choices?

When we've come to those places, that's when we try to center back on integrity. But even that can be slippery. What does it mean to act with integrity? Some people define integrity as essentially the same thing as honesty. Others see it as consistency of action, or consistency of action with belief. But the root of the word integrity means "whole." Focusing on integrity, for us, means intense examination of the present moment: *What am I doing right now, and is it in alignment with my most authentic self? If I look back at myself in ten years, would I like the person I see?*

COMPASSION

Before we talk about compassion, it's worth repeating the two axioms that underpin the ethics of this book:

- The people in the relationship are more important than the relationship.
- Don't treat people as things.

Following an ethical system that relies on not treating people as things means, well, treating people as people. And that means practicing compassion.

The word *compassion* is all over the place these days. But what does it mean? It's easy to throw it out as a glib admonishment, and ironically, it can sometimes include a shaming undertone. As in, "I am a compassionate person and you are not. Look how good I am because I am compassionate." If your social set intersects at all with New Age circles, you probably know someone who likes to play the "more compassionate than thou" Olympics. In fact, many of the ideas in this book can be used that way. Please don't do that.

Compassion is—again—not something you *are*, not something you *feel*, but something you *practice*. Compassion is putting ourselves in another's shoes. We can sit with a person in whatever they are feeling, bear witness to their pain while still loving who they are. Sometimes that person is ourselves.

Compassion is not politeness, and isn't even the same as kindness. It's not doing good deeds for someone while quietly judging them! Compassion engages your whole person, and it requires vulnerability, which is part of what makes it so hard. We have to be able to allow ourselves to be present as an equal with another person, recognize the darkness in them and accept it—and that forces us to embrace, as well, the darkness within ourselves.

A lack of boundaries is not the same thing as compassion, nor is letting someone walk all over us, or overlooking poor behavior or mistreatment of others. Real compassion requires strong boundaries, because if we are letting someone take advantage of us, it becomes very hard to be authentically vulnerable to them. Compassion requires a willingness to hold other people accountable for the things they *do*, while accepting them for who they *are*.

How do we practice compassion? The cornerstone of compassion is simple, but emotionally difficult to achieve. It means, first and foremost, assuming good intent from others. In other words, looking for the most charitable interpretation of someone else's deepest motives.

Until we all have magic mind-reading rubies in our foreheads, assuming another person's motives is always going to be dangerous. That's why we need compassion. When someone has done something we don't like, or that hurts us, or has failed to do what we want them to do, it's too easy to assume the worst motivations from them: "He doesn't care about my needs." "She completely disregards my feelings."

Compassion means coming from a place of understanding that others have needs of their own, which might be different than ours, and extending to them the same understanding, the same willingness to appreciate their own struggles, that we would want them to extend to us. We practice it every time we feel that surge of annoyance when someone does something we don't like, and then check ourselves and try to see the reason for their behavior from their perspective. We practice it every time we are gentle with others instead of being angry with them. And we practice it when we apply that same gentleness to ourselves: every time we accept that we are flawed and imperfect but are good despite that. We practice it in every recognition of each other's frailty and error.

As polyamorous people, we face particularly pressing needs to cultivate compassion for our partners, their partners and members of our community. But perhaps most important of all is compassion for ourselves. We are learning a new way of doing things. We're developing new skills that no one's taught us before and challenging ourselves in ways that many people never do. We're trying to learn how to treat not just one partner well, but an entire network of people whose well-being depends on what we do. And that's hard.

It's easy to beat yourself up for not being a perfect poly person, especially with the poly community putting its best face forward publicly in order to gain mainstream acceptance. Whether you're feeling jealous and insecure, or you're having trouble with anger management, or you can't figure out how to clearly communicate your needs...it's normal. You don't need to be a poly perfectionist. You're not the first person to have felt these things, not by a long shot. We've all been there. Try to treat yourself the same way you would treat someone you cared about who is having the same problem: with compassion and acceptance.

CHECK YOUR EXPECTATIONS

The dictionary defines *expectation* as "a belief centered on the future; a belief that something will or should happen in the future." That doesn't suggest the mischief our expectations can cause. Expectations lead to disappointment when they aren't met, and fear of that disappointment can cause us to hide our expectations—sometimes even from ourselves.

Expectations differ from related feelings like hopes, fantasies, wishes or desires. If you have the latter and they don't come true, you may feel disappointment or even grief, but we don't think that means it's bad to have them. *Expectations*, on the other hand, can fuck with you. The difference is that an expectation implies a responsibility on the part of another person (or at least an entity, like God or Fate or "the universe"). Perhaps even a sense of entitlement. So when it's not fulfilled, in addition to whatever disappointment you might otherwise feel, you also feel anger or blame.

We all have expectations. Most of the time, our expectations are reasonable and normal. We expect that when we turn on the tap, water will come out. On a more basic level, we expect that the laws that govern our interactions with the world are stable and immutable. We expect water to be wet, fire to be hot, gravity to make things fall. Our expectations form part of the basis for our perception of the world. They provide a sense of stability and predictability; if we had no expectations at all, living would become nearly impossible.

Things get more slippery when we talk about expectations regarding other people. People are self-determining, with their own motivations and priorities. We can expect some things of other people—we expect that our friends won't set fire to the house or steal the cat when they come to visit—but our expectations are always going to be hampered by the fact that we can't really tell what's happening inside another person's head. Sometimes people do set fire to houses or steal cats.

Let's talk about "reasonable" and "unreasonable" expectations. The difference is subjective, and there's a lot of fuzzy gray overlap. Some expectations are clearly reasonable. We expect our friends not to punch us in the nose without provocation. We expect our romantic partners not to drain our bank account and run off to Cancun with the grocer. Other expectations are just as clearly unreasonable. We would not expect a new date who's just shown up in a fancy formal dress to be enthusiastic if we say, "You need to go clean the cat box for me."

Between the two clear extremes lie the waters where reefs lurk, ready to shipwreck the unwary. Our expectations can run aground at just about any point in a relationship.

We do not, by and large, have the right to expect things of people without their consent. We cannot be angry at someone for failing to do something she did not agree to do in the first place. The skill of expectation management means more than trying to navigate between reasonable and unreasonable expectations. It means recognizing that a desire on my part does not constitute an obligation on your part. And we can never reasonably be upset at someone for failing to live up to our expectations if we haven't talked about our expectations in the first place.

QUESTIONS TO ASK YOURSELF

When you're thinking about what you want from your relationship life and how you'd like your relationships to be structured, here are some questions it might be useful to ask yourself (and talk over with your partner or partners, if you're in a relationship):

- *Why do I have relationships with other people?*

- *What needs do I have from my partners, in terms of time, emotional availability, commitment, communication and intimacy?*

- *What does "commitment" mean to me, and why?*

- *When I think about the future, what does it look like? Is there room for change and growth?*

- *How much do I value personal autonomy, transparency, cohabitation, having and raising children, shared finances, community, tradition, the opinions of my friends and family, adhering to social norms?*

- *What values are the most important to me in myself and in others?*

- *Are the choices I make in alignment with these values?*

- *Who are my mirrors? Whom do I rely on to call me on my mistakes?*

- *How do I respond to criticism from people close to me?*

- *How do I evaluate my choices when the effects of my actions are impossible to predict?*

- *What do I expect of others, and why?*

COMMUNICATION PITFALLS

*All words have not a single meaning
but a swarm of them, like bees around a hive.*

MAUREEN O'BRIEN

If you've heard anything about polyamory, you've likely heard this: "The first rule of polyamory is communicate, communicate, communicate." But what does that mean, exactly? Communication is trickier than it sounds. It covers a lot more than saying what's on your mind, and even saying what's on your mind can be surprisingly tough. Then there's the listening part. There are a thousand ways communication can fail and only a few ways for it to succeed. Yet good communication is a process, and it's essential to building trust, demonstrating respect and understanding the needs of the people you're close to.

When we talk about communication in polyamory, we're actually talking about a very specific *type* of communication: speaking the truth about ourselves, our needs and our boundaries with honesty and precision, and listening with grace when our partners speak of themselves, their needs and their boundaries. This kind of communication isn't really about words. It's about vulnerability, self-knowledge, integrity, empathy, compassion and a whole lot of other things.

Communication is such a complex subject that we've divided it into two chapters. This chapter addresses ways communication can run off a cliff, including being imprecise, dishonest, passive and coercive. The next chapter discusses strategies to help you succeed.

FUZZY LANGUAGE

In poly circles, people often complain that conversations about poly always seem to come back to semantics. This is actually a good thing. The poly community tends to focus on communication, and communication relies on words having shared meanings. Arriving at that mutual understanding is what semantics is all about.

On the one hand, language is a marvelously flexible and resilient tool. If you read a sentence containing non-English flutzpahs, even if you've never heard of flutzpahs before you can often glork their meaning from context. On the other hand, the simplest way for communication to go wrong is when one person uses a familiar word in a way that another person misinterprets. For example, Franklin once had a conversation with Celeste that went something like this:

CELESTE: Can you do me a favor and pass the sweeper?

FRANKLIN: What's a sweeper?

CELESTE: The thing that vacuums the rug. You know, the vacuum cleaner.

FRANKLIN: Oh! Right. Okay, here you go.

CELESTE: You never help me out around the house! You expect me to do everything! I ask you to do one thing and you won't do it!

FRANKLIN: Wait. You asked me to pass the sweeper, and I gave you the vacuum cleaner! It's what you wanted, right?

CELESTE: No, I asked you to vacuum for me. "Pass the sweeper" means "Pass it over the rug."

Small words can hide big misunderstandings. What is *sex?* What is a *relationship?* What do we mean by words such as *permission, consent* or *commitment?* A disagreement about the meaning of that last word popped up during a panel on polyamory Franklin once participated in at a convention:

AUDIENCE MEMBER: It's obvious that people with multiple romantic relationships can't be committed, because *commitment* means you're dedicated to only one person. Someone who is not committed can't be trusted, because they have no commitment to you.

FRANKLIN: But what if someone is committed to more than one person?

AUDIENCE MEMBER: Impossible. That's a logical contradiction. *Commitment* means "dedication to only one person." You can't be dedicated to two people any more than you can divide a circle into three halves. A person who has more than one partner has no commitment, and therefore can't be trusted.

What's obvious to one person may not be obvious to another. As we discuss in chapter 19, on sex, even defining the word *sex* can create a thorny tangle.

SLIPPERY WORDS

When the two of us communicate about relationships, we try to steer clear of certain words. Some words come preloaded with expectations and emotional baggage, which makes them prone to misuse. These words easily become tools of manipulation, because they sound reasonable on the surface but have meanings that are difficult to pin down.

Respect. Many people are fond of saying things like "New partners must respect my existing relationships." And it sounds reasonable: after all, who would go into a relationship saying, "I plan to disrespect all the other folks involved"?

But what does it mean to "respect" a relationship? Does it mean to yield to the people in that relationship all the time? Does it mean to always do what they say? Respect is reciprocal; what respect are the people in a relationship prepared to offer a new relationship?

Rather than use vague words like *respect*, you will benefit from spelling out what your expectations are. If you believe that older relationships have priority in terms of time and scheduling, for example, say so. Using vague words like *respect* creates an easy way to accuse others of breaking agreements any time they do something you don't like, without actually having to make explicit agreements.

Come first. Another agreeable-sounding but vague phrase we've heard often is "My existing obligations come first." Nobody enters a relationship with a clean slate; we all have previous commitments that require tending, perhaps to children, a sick relative, a demanding job or a business association. This is true in monogamous relationships as well as polyamorous ones.

So if we say, "Existing obligations come first," does it simply mean we have outstanding responsibilities we intend to discharge? That's reasonable in any sort of relationship. Or is it a way of saying "I will look after your needs only if they aren't inconvenient to the other people in my life," as all too often seems true? Does it mean that an existing partner may always usurp time allocated to a new partner?

Better to spell out what existing commitments you have, and what you need to do to discharge them, rather than simply say they "come first."

Fair and equal. These words can conjure up images of relationships where everyone is doled out the same-size slice of pumpkin pie, even if some folks are hungrier than others and some are allergic to pumpkins. Equality of opportunity is a very different thing than equality of circumstance; if people want different things, then it makes sense that their circumstances will be different. What's most fair is not necessarily an even division of resources, but rather a distribution that meets as many of the needs of all the people as possible.

Rights. In chapter 3, we talked about the high bar something must reach to be called a "right." Few things rise to that level, so "right" is a word that should be used very cautiously.

Some things you do *not* have a right to expect in any relationship: to never be challenged, to always be comfortable, to always have other people navigate around your triggers and discomforts. Things you do not have a right to do include to treat people as expendable, to extract promises that someone will never leave you, and to control other people's relationships. All these things require negotiation. Relationships are always voluntary; you have the right to end a relationship that does not meet your needs (and so does your partner), but you do not have the right to demand that your partner do what you want.

Success. When you think of successful relationships, what comes to mind? Relationships that last a certain amount of time? Relationships that have no disagreement? It can be tempting to call a relationship successful if it lasts, but what if the members of that relationship treat their other partners poorly?

"Success" should apply to everyone involved, not just some of them. If a poly couple stays together for a long time, but they treat their other partners poorly or hurt a lot of other people in the process, we would not necessarily consider their relationships a "success." When you use the word *success*, are you thinking only about a particular relationship or about all of them?

Reasonable. The word *reasonable* (and its evil twin, *unreasonable*) get tossed around very easily. Is it reasonable to want to tell a partner what positions she is allowed to have sex in? Is it reasonable for a partner to kiss someone else in front of you? The problem is, what's "reasonable" is largely cultural and subjective. Most people would probably say it's not reasonable to have multiple lovers in the first place!

Polyamory is still new enough that we have not yet established cultural norms of reasonableness. So instead of talking about what's "reasonable," talk about the specifics of how something makes you feel. How do you react when you see your partner kiss someone else in front of you? Why? How can you negotiate with your partner about ways to do things differently? Talk about what you need and how your partner can help you, and negotiate a solution that works for everyone.

Healthy. This is an especially dangerous word. Some relationships are genuinely healthy and others are unhealthy. But all too often, this word is used to judge behaviors we simply don't like. A relationship that violates your consent is indeed unhealthy. A relationship in which you are threatened with violence is unhealthy. A codependent or enabling relationship is unhealthy. But your partner doing something you don't like is not necessarily unhealthy. Sometimes healthy relationships are uncomfortable. Instead of using the word *healthy*, we recommend talking directly about behaviors that trouble you and why they do. If you sincerely believe your partner's behavior is unhealthy, it might be time to seek professional help (with your partner if possible, and for yourself if your partner won't participate; see page 53).

DISHONESTY

Honesty is one of the defining factors that separate polyamorous relationships from cheating. It's also, not surprisingly, one of the defining elements of good communication. However, it can be harder than it sounds. Even though we all probably agree that honesty is important in a relationship, it's surprising how often we still choose not to be honest. Otherwise well-intentioned people who generally act in good faith can end up making that choice, for any number of reasons.

The most common reason is emotional vulnerability: fear of rejection, fear of being ridiculed, fear of being wrong, of hearing no, of being found less desirable by our partners. And even as we claim to want honesty, we may subtly discourage our partners from being honest with us because we don't feel prepared to hear truths that might be painful.

People who are dishonest with their partners, especially when they are dishonest not by lying but by concealing things or not saying what's on their minds, often seek to control information as a way to control their partner's behavior. Another reason people can be dishonest is that they fear "upsetting" or "offending" their partners. Especially about sex. If you don't enjoy what your partner does, you may say nothing to avoid making him feel bad. This tends to backfire in long-term relationships, because someone who doesn't know that his partner is unsatisfied will never improve, and an unsatisfying relationship is always under stress.

Problem is, one of the most basic rules of life is that you cannot get what you want if you don't ask for what you want.

Franklin runs a website of educational resources about BDSM (activities related to dominance and submission or sadomasochism). Many years ago, a person read his site and wrote to say he'd always wanted to try exploring BDSM but never had. He'd been married for ten years but never talked to his wife about it, because he was afraid of how she might react. He asked Franklin, "What do you think I should do?"

Naturally Franklin said, "Talk to her. Tell her 'This is something I'm interested in. What do you think?' " About a week later Franklin received a reply. The guy finally worked up the courage to talk to his wife about exploring BDSM. He discovered that years before they met, she'd been involved in BDSM and enjoyed it quite a lot, but she had never talked to him about it... because she was afraid of how *he* would react!

Such failures to communicate happen when we lead with our fears instead of our hopes. If we spend too much time thinking about what can go wrong, we forget what can go right. Life is better when you lead with your hopes, not your fears.

Perhaps the most common justification for dishonesty in a relationship is the notion that the truth will hurt worse than a lie. A person who cheats on a partner may think, *If I tell the truth, I will hurt my partner, but if I don't, my partner won't need to experience that pain.* This reasoning says more about the person making the argument than it does about the person he is "protecting," because consent is not valid if it is not informed. By hiding the truth, we deny our partners the opportunity to consent to continuing a relationship with us. Controlling information to try to keep a partner (or to get a partner to do what we want) is one way we treat people as things.

And remember, honesty begins inside. A person who is dishonest with *himself* cannot be honest with anyone else. People are dishonest with themselves for many reasons, including having ideas about what they "should" be. If they think desiring multiple partners is dishonorable, they may convince themselves that they don't even if they do. Likewise, if someone wants only one partner, she may convince herself otherwise because she believes polyamory is more "enlightened." We can lie to ourselves for more subtle reasons as well. A woman whose husband is threatened by the idea of her having another male lover might tell herself, "Well, it's okay, I really don't *want* to be with another man," even if, in some corner of her mind, she would.

PASSIVE COMMUNICATION

Passive communication refers to communicating through subtext, avoiding direct statements, and looking for hidden meanings. Passive communicators may use techniques such as asking questions or making vague, indirect statements in place of stating needs, preferences or boundaries. Directly asking for what you want creates vulnerability, and passive communication often comes from a desire to avoid this vulnerability. Passive communication also offers plausible deniability; if we state a desire for something indirectly, and we don't get it, it's easy to claim we didn't really want it. Stating our needs means standing up for them and taking the risk that others may not agree to meet them.

One way this happens is by couching desires as questions: "Would you like to go out for Thai food tonight?" (Or worse, "Don't you think it's been a long time since we went out for dinner?") To a passive communicator, such a statement can be a coded way to say, "I would like to go out for Thai food tonight." The problem is, a direct communicator might naturally hear only what was said and give a direct answer: "No, I don't really feel like going out tonight." This can leave the passive communicator feeling disregarded; she might end up thinking, *He never pays attention to my needs!* when, to the direct communicator, no request was stated; he was asked how he felt. The direct communicator might end up thinking, "She never asks for what she wants. She expects me to read her mind! If she wanted to go out, she could have said so."

When we're talking about dinner, indirect communication might not matter too much. When we're talking about things that are more complicated, like emotional boundaries or relationship expectations, indirect communication can lead to crises of misunderstanding.

EVE'S STORY My relationship with Kira lasted only a few months, but the damage it left was lasting. By the time it ended, I felt profoundly unseen, unheard and unknown by someone I had only recently imagined I had a deep intimacy with. I felt not like a person, but like an actor who had been cast for a role. As though everything—the flirtation, the relationship, the breakup—was scripted in advance by

Kira's expectations and beliefs. And I felt that I had little influence over this trajectory because Kira and I could not communicate.

Kira was raised in a family that communicated passively, and she spent her adolescence in a culture where passive communication was the norm. The irony was that she valued, and often talked about, assertive communication—but her habits were too deeply ingrained for her to recognize them, let alone unlearn them. I learned quickly the disorienting, frustrating and often maddening consequences of being in love with someone for whom every statement had a double meaning.

To Kira, what mattered was not what I said, but what she *imagined* I had said, and that appeared to come from scripts deep in her psyche. Kira would imagine I wanted things I'd never asked for, give them to me as though they were her idea, and then blame me when she was unhappy about having given them. Her ideas that I wanted them came from cryptic readings of things I had said or done, and it did no good for me to deny I had wanted or asked for them. To her, I *had* asked. Passively. I was not permitted to deny the reality of the hidden meanings that Kira believed in but I had never meant.

Kira would forward me messages she had received from others, or ask me to view online conversations she was participating in, expecting me to be deeply offended or outraged by what I read. When I could not find the offensive statements, she would explain to me at length the hidden meaning of the conversation, what was "really" happening behind the words that were being said. She could create a detailed story from very few words.

Our relationship ended with her telling me such a story. I listened in disbelief and no small anguish as she told me what I had wanted, what I believed, what I expected—all of which had been read into my words or actions, and none of which was true. And the hardest part was that I couldn't counter any of it: passive communication was so second nature to Kira that it simply wasn't possible for her to believe that my words had meant exactly what I said they did—that not everything had a hidden meaning. To Kira, what she imagined lay behind my words was more important than my words—and that ended the possibility of communication between us.

Passive communication is the norm in many families, and indeed in many cultures. Every now and then some pop-psych article will surface that compares passive with direct communication and says that neither is inherently "better," and all you need to do is learn which style someone is using and adapt to it.

In polyamorous relationships, though, passive communication will fuck you right up—and your partners, and their partners. It's true that some cultures—the Middle Eastern culture that Kira grew up in, for example—do use very subtle, nuanced passive communication, and there's nothing wrong with that in its own cultural context. However, in cultures where passive communication is the norm, the paratext—the subtle verbal and nonverbal cues that tell you the hidden meaning—are shared and understood. We wrote this book for readers in the Western context, where it's almost certain that you, your partners and their partners will have grown up with different family and cultural backgrounds, and thus different assumptions about what subtle cues convey what unspoken meanings. Looking for hidden meanings in such a situation leads to a very high chance that you'll be quite simply wrong.

When passive communication includes implied threats or demands, it can tip over into manipulation. This can happen in many ways: concealing our real motivations by couching them in pleasant-sounding but leading language, for instance. "We wouldn't want anything unpleasant to happen now, would we?" Or by waiting for a partner to misinterpret our coded language and then springing something like "You never listen to me!"

EVE'S STORY I don't remember the exact circumstances under which I shared my Google calendar with Kira, or why. I remember asking her about it first, but she remembers it differently. I do remember that she had never shared a calendar before, and I wanted to show her how it worked. For me, sharing calendars was no big thing—at the time, many of my friends and people I worked with had access to both my personal and work calendars. If I wanted to keep information private, I would make a "private event."

We didn't discuss boundaries around the calendar or specific expectations about what sharing it meant. As it turned out, she had very different expectations than I did—but I didn't learn that until too late.

Because Kira was accustomed to passive communication, she understood my sharing my calendar with her to carry an implicit expectation that she would share hers, although this hadn't occurred to me—and I was quite surprised when she did. After sharing her calendar with me, she felt unacceptably exposed, as though I had full knowledge of her whereabouts at all times; in fact, I only viewed her calendar once during our relationship.

Ultimately the calendar was, to Kira, a symbol of the relationship escalator. Her fears about becoming bound by expectations or commitment became tied to it. The unfortunate part was, we never discussed any of this. She told me only when our relationship was at an end and any possibility of genuine communication had already been cut off.

A very common problem with passive communication is that people accustomed to it tend to see all communication as passive. They can't switch between passive and direct communication. No matter how direct you are, the passive communicator is certain there's a hidden message, an unstated request or a secret criticism buried somewhere deep in your words. Often a passive communicator will come up with interpretations that seem plain bizarre, even paranoid. But this just comes from their cultural expectations of how much meaning other people hide in their words.

The most effective way we've found for building good communication with a passive communicator is with patience, compassion and directness. Respond only to the surface words, without trying to divine or decode the hidden meaning. If the passive communicator becomes frustrated at your inability to see the actual message—and he will—reiterate that direct communication is the only way you know to make sure the message gets through.

Demonstrate clear, direct communication yourself. If your partner misinterprets something you've said, or extracts a meaning you didn't intend, be patient and forthright. State your intended meaning plainly. Reassure him that your words carry no hidden intent. Make it clear that you genuinely want to understand. Respond to vague statements with clear, direct questions. Ask for clarification when he says something ambiguous. And above all keep at it, and don't expect quick change. Passive communication takes a long time to learn, and just as long to unlearn.

STORYTELLING

Humans are storytelling animals. We tell stories to ourselves, dozens of times a day, without even being aware of it. We use these stories to make sense of the world and to understand the actions of the people around us. Many of these stories relate to other people's motives. We know that people's actions aren't random. We build models in our heads that help us understand others. And because we don't come from the factory equipped with magical mind-reading rubies in our foreheads, these models are flawed. They're made up of observation, guesswork, projection and empathy.

Unfortunately, it's natural to react as though our models are perfect. We don't usually say to ourselves, "I'm convinced to about 65 percent accuracy that he is trying to replace me in my lover's affections, but there's considerable room for error." Rather, we say, "That bastard is trying to get rid of me!" The motives we ascribe to other people's behavior are colored by our own fears and insecurities; if we're worried about being supplanted, we tend to read signs in everything.

Worse, we are predisposed to view all other people's motives less charitably than our own. Research has shown that we tend to explain our own behavior in terms of the situation we're in, while we believe the behavior of others goes directly to their character. When asked why we cut someone else off in traffic, we might say, "I was looking the other way and didn't see him," but when asked why someone else cut us off in traffic, we are more likely to say, "She's obviously a reckless driver who doesn't care about anyone else on the road." (Sociologists often refer to this as the "fundamental attribution error.")

In polyamorous relationships, as you might imagine, this behavior can get pretty ugly. When we tell ourselves stories about other people, we tend to run with those stories, rather than what the other people say about the matter. Of course so-and-so says he isn't trying to separate me from my partner; that's exactly what he wants me to believe!

We propose a radical strategy to deal with what people say: In the absence of concrete evidence to the contrary, believe them.

TRIANGULAR COMMUNICATION

If we were to set out axioms of good communication (as we try to do in the next chapter), one of them would be that communication about any issue ideally involves the people directly affected. This sounds simple, but it's surprisingly hard to implement. It starts from an early age. Most of us who grew up with siblings can remember at least one time when we said, "Mom, Danny's poking me!" or "Hey, Dad, Miranda won't stay on her side of the seat!" And thus the seed is sown for some of the most tenacious communication problems we will ever face.

Triangular communication happens when one person has a problem, concern or question for another person, but instead of bringing it up directly with that person, instead goes to someone else. It happens when a child has a problem with her brother's behavior and petitions a parent to settle it. It happens online when one person has a problem with somebody else and goes to the faceless masses of the Internet to seek validation. It happens when someone at a company has a problem with another person's performance and approaches a coworker about it. And it happens *all the time* in polyamorous relationships.

Triangular communication can also happen when one person wants to control the flow of information between the partners. Most of us don't like conflict, and controlling the flow of information can seem like a way to avoid or reduce conflict. It can sometimes be a means of minimizing tensions or disagreements; if your partners aren't getting along, you can be tempted to try to interpret one person's words for the other, in a way that shows the message in its most favorable light. It can also happen when you don't trust what your partners might say to each other.

In practice, triangular communication leads to diffusion of responsibility. It becomes easy to tell one partner, "I can't do what you want me to do because Suzie might not like it," rather than "I am choosing not to do what you want me to, because I think Suzie might not like it." (Veto is arguably an extreme example of this diffusion of responsibility. For more on this, see chapter 12.)

EVE'S STORY   Ray and his wife, Danielle, had a hierarchical relationship. Very early on, his wife stressed that I needed to remember she was primary. This was my first polyamorous relationship, I was head over heels for Ray, and Peter and I had assumed we would be using hierarchy as well, so at the time, it seemed entirely reasonable to agree to this. I was naively unaware of what it would actually mean—especially years in.

Danielle practiced what a friend of mine called "line-item veto." Ray and I were in a long-distance relationship, but if I came to visit him, I was expected to alternate nights with her, sometimes at a ratio of two nights hers and one night mine (in the case of a long weekend, for example). If we had plans together and she needed something from him, even if she'd just had a bad day, he had to cancel our plans so he could be with her—even if we weren't going to see each other again for weeks.

I tried negotiating directly with Danielle, which got even worse results—for example, I was going to be in town for a weekend, and she proposed that I share a meal with the two of them, as the only time I would see Ray. Over months, my frustration grew. I blamed Danielle: for being selfish, inconsiderate, demanding, needy. I was seeing a poly-specialist therapist at the time and was working with her through some of this frustration. She asked me why I was blaming Danielle for Ray's decisions. I didn't have a good answer.

I realized then that regardless of his reasons, it was Ray who was canceling dates. Ray who wasn't giving me the time or attention I wanted-ed. Ray who I needed to talk to about what I needed in the relationship, and Ray who could agree whether or not to provide it. This was an epiphany for me, and one that turned around my relationship with Ray. It simply hadn't occurred to me before to see Ray as the copilot of our relationship.

Eve's discovery was painful. It's much easier to blame a third party, casting you and your beloved as helpless victims, than to face the fact that your partner is choosing not to invest in your relationship. It can be hard to direct your anger and frustration at the person who is actually hurting you when he's someone you are intimately involved with. And for the pivot person in a vee relationship? It's a lot harder to do the gritty work of negotiating solutions among competing needs and deciding how to share your time and resources than it is to stand back and pretend that those solutions are something your partners need to work out between themselves.

Metamours are not children, and as a pivot partner you are not Halloween candy to divide up. Negotiating resource investments in relationships is not like deciding who gets how many Snickers bars and who is stuck with the malted milk balls. Three-way communication is useful to build trust and get a clear understanding of needs and capabilities, but ultimately the pivot partner is the master of her own decisions and resources. If someone isn't getting what he needs from her, that's something he needs to take up with her, *his partner*. And she needs to take responsibility.

The solution to triangular communication is simple in theory—don't do it—but difficult in practice, because it's easier to talk about things that bother us with anyone but the person whose behavior is at issue. And because when we feel wronged, it's natural to seek allies. In practical terms, you can't make other people communicate directly with each other. The best you can do is to limit your own participation in triangular communication. Just back out and tell the people they need to talk to each other. And *you* should address anything that bothers you directly with the person involved.

Try not to be drawn into the role of rescuer when someone comes to you complaining about that terrible thing so-and-so just did. Reserve judgment of other people in your relationship network, and encourage the parties at odds to talk directly to each other rather than through you, without allowing yourself to become a go-between.

If you do find yourself stuck in a pattern of triangular communication, it may be useful to pick up Harriet Lerner's *Dance of Intimacy*, listed in the resources. To see how triangular communication can go spectacularly wrong, we recommend reading *Othello*, by Shakespeare.

WHEN WE DON'T WANT TO COMMUNICATE

Everything we've talked about so far assumes that the people involved are trying to communicate with each other. We all grasp the value of communication intellectually, but turning that understanding into reality can be really hard, because often, we don't actually *want* to communicate.

Communication is scary. We fear open communication when we fear the vulnerability that comes with it. Open communication means exposing yourself to rejection or judgment or trouble. It may mean finding out that what you assumed your lover thinks and feels is wrong. It presents the possibility of hearing no to your deepest wishes, and it may mean having your needs or desires turned against you if the relationship is unhealthy. There is no communication—at least not meaningful communication—without vulnerability.

Communication can be hard when it leads to embarrassment or shame. If you were brought up to believe that there are certain things (like sex) that you just don't talk about, shame can interfere with communication...and you might end up wondering, "Why is my sex life so unsatisfying?" and being afraid to hear the answer.

Another barrier to communication is the notion that there are certain ways people in a relationship "should" be, so there's no need to talk about it. "If he really loves me, of course he will know to do thus-and-such. Why won't he do thus-and-such? Everyone knows this is part of a relationship! It must mean he doesn't love me!" Yet another of these emotional barriers is the common trap of thinking in generalities and allowing them to take precedence over the specific details of the people in the relationship. As one possible example: "Everyone knows that men love getting head. So that means I don't need to ask him how he feels about oral sex, because men love getting head. If he tells me he doesn't want me to go down on him, that must mean I'm doing it wrong and I'm bad at it."

If a relationship involves some element of consensual domination and submission, people can fail to communicate because they believe submissives should simply accept whatever the dominant partner wants. Or they may believe submissives shouldn't have a say in their relationship, because submissives like to do whatever they are told and never, ever voice their own needs. Some people take this to such an extreme that they even believe submissive partners in dominant/submissive relationships shouldn't *have* needs of their own.

Almost always, communication tends to be most difficult precisely when it's most important. As the relationship coach Marcia Baczynski has put it, "If you're afraid to say it, that means you need to say it." When we are feeling most raw, most vulnerable, most scared of opening up, those are the times we most need to open up. We can't expect others to respect our boundaries and limits if we don't talk about them or, worse, pretend they don't exist. It's a bit of a paradox that even as open communication makes us feel vulnerable and exposed, it's essential if we are to protect our boundaries from being violated. We can't expect others to respect our boundaries if we pretend they don't exist.

We've been asked whether talking about everything takes some of the mystery out of a relationship. We find that question surprising. We are all, every one of us, complicated and dynamic and always changing, and relationship dynamics are filled with mystery as it is. There's no need to invent more! There is easily enough mystery between two people to fill many lifetimes, even when they're both paying very close attention and are as honest and transparent with one another as it is possible to be.

Relationships based on honesty and transparency, in which the people really pay attention to each other and work to see and understand each other, are more subtle and profoundly complex than relationships that avoid this kind of honesty and knowledge. The more you get to know a person, the more you find that there is to know. And we are all moving targets; we change every day. There will always be new things to learn, no matter how much we communicate.

COERCIVE COMMUNICATION

Coercion doesn't always involve physical violence or direct threats. It's actually quite easy for relationships to become coercive when the stakes are high—and when we are deeply attached or committed to another person, they are high. Coercion happens any time you make the consequences of saying no so great that you've removed reasonable choice.

A subtle sort of coercion arises any time you believe that your partner owes you something. For example, if you think your partner owes you intimacy, and you are just "expressing your feelings" about what you're owed, there's a good chance you're being coercive. If your partner says no, and you start preparing for a fight instead of accepting their choice, you're probably being coercive.

If your partner sets a boundary or says no to a request, she probably has a good reason. That reason might not even be about you. It's important to respect a no even when you don't understand it. Show appreciation for your partner's self-advocacy and self-knowledge, be grateful for the intimacy she *has* shown you, and make it clear that you respect her autonomy and ability to make choices—even if you don't understand what's happening or why.

We're talking about boundaries your partner sets on herself, which as we discuss in chapters 9 and 10, are quite different from rules she places on you. It is always appropriate to negotiate things another person places on you, though it sometimes takes careful attention to recognize the difference.

It's also possible that in setting boundaries a partner is being manipulative, using boundary-setting as a way to coerce you. Withdrawal and silence, classic techniques of emotional blackmail, can initially be difficult to distinguish from healthy boundary-setting. A person could be withdrawing just to punish you. But that doesn't change what you should do. The solution is never to try to force someone to do something they don't want to do. Thank them, and respect their choice. If you can't respect their choice, it's time to examine your own boundaries.

If you're hurting because of a boundary your partner has set, knowing how to practice *active listening* can be especially useful. Active listening involves asking genuine, open-ended, non-leading questions, then listening quietly to the answer, and then repeating back what you heard so it's clear that you heard it correctly, as we discuss in the next chapter. It is especially critical in these moments to be careful not to twist your questions into accusations or statements of intent. "Why would you want to hurt me this way?" is a manipulative, coercive statement, not an attempt at genuine communication.

Even without disproportionate power, people manipulate one another in relationships in many subtle ways. People might seek agreement by shifting blame, appealing to a sense of fairness, or implying that the other person is negotiating in bad faith. Statements like "Why do you have to have sex with someone else when you know how much that hurts me?" are a common tactic that shifts responsibility for one person's emotional state onto another person.

Appealing to social norms is another way to try to coerce "agreement." This tends to be more common in mono/poly relationships or with couples who are opening up than in relationships that are poly from the beginning. It includes statements like "Why can't you just agree to normal relationships like other people?" (Eve's former partner Ray once said he could not accompany Eve and Peter on a vacation because he wouldn't be able to explain to their parents and social circle why he was going somewhere without his wife.)

Still another technique for manipulating agreement involves preying on fear of abandonment. Statements like "What would you do without me?" or "I don't know why I even stay here and let you do this to me" can be attempts to use emotional blackmail to compel agreement.

Now that we've covered the ways communication in poly relationships can go wrong, what strategies can you use to help it go *well*? That's the subject of the next chapter.

QUESTIONS TO ASK YOURSELF

Communication in relationships, and polyamorous relationships in particular, can be like a proverbial minefield. As you attempt to negotiate this potentially dangerous territory, here are some questions to guide you:

- *Do I use words the same way my partners do? Do I often find myself in discussions about the meanings of words?*

- *If I have a problem with someone's behavior, do I discuss the problem with that person?*

- *If my partners have a problem with someone else's behavior, do I encourage them to bring it up with that person?*

- *Do I communicate passively or directly?*

- *Do I look for hidden meanings in other people's words? Do I bury my real meaning?*

- *Do I communicate authentically in ways that make me vulnerable?*

- *In what ways do I actively listen to my partners?*

COMMUNICATION STRATEGIES

The best measure of the health of any relationship is the quality of the communication in it. Every single thing that we can't or won't talk about, openly and without fear or shame, is a crack in the relationship's foundation.

Therefore, strategies for successful communication are some of the most important tools in your relationship toolkit. Polyamory challenges us to communicate to a degree that other relationship models don't. In monogamous couples, for instance, if we're attracted to a third person, we're usually expected to pretend we're not. In poly relationships, communicating what we're feeling, even at the risk of making our partners uncomfortable, is the only way to build multiple sustainable relationships. Polyamory doesn't give us the luxury of avoiding tough, uncomfortable subjects.

A COMMUNICATION TOOLBOX

Before we look at some helpful communication strategies, there's something we have to say: You are, almost certainly, a lousy communicator. How can we say that when we don't know you? Because 99 percent of the population—ourselves included—are lousy communicators. Most of us are exceptionally good at misunderstanding each other, misreading each other's tone and intent, and failing to get our point across. But usually we don't realize it. Usually we think we've communicated just fine, and it's the other person who has a problem. Passive and passive-aggressive communicators tend to believe they are direct communicators. And all of us, being humans, are exceptionally good at storytelling: making up tales to explain things we don't understand without even realizing it.

Learning good communication skills is something we can't possibly cover thoroughly in this book. We'll cover only those communication issues most directly applicable to polyamory. We recommend, though, that you make a commitment to improving your communication skills on an ongoing basis if you're serious about success in polyamorous relationships, long after you finish this book.

Certain communication techniques should be in everyone's toolbox for any relationship. Each of the ones we'll discuss has many books dedicated to it, so we'll just briefly touch on them. You'll find great resources for developing these skills at the end of this book. Three of these essential communication tools are *active listening, direct communication* and *nonviolent communication.*

Active listening. When people think about communication, often their focus is on getting across what they want to say. But communication breaks down just as often—if not more often—in the listening as in the speaking. Active listening is a great technique not just for effective communication, but for connecting with your partner: making sure they *feel* heard. Active listening is often taught in conflict resolution courses and couples counseling.

As tough as it can be to practice, the mechanics of active listening are pretty simple. You listen intently to what the other person is saying, rather than using that time to think about the next thing *you* want to say. Then you repeat back to the other person what they have just said to you—in your own words, so that they know you understood. Then you trade roles. Because a need to be heard and understood is at the root of many interpersonal conflicts, active listening can go a long way toward defusing intense situations, even when a solution is not yet apparent.

Direct communication. This technique entails two things: being direct in what you say—without subtext, hidden meaning, coded language or tacit expectations—and assuming directness in what you hear, without looking for hidden meaning or buried messages.

Good communication is not a treasure hunt or a game of Where's Waldo's Meaning? Being direct in your speech means saying plainly what you think and asking plainly for what you need. It requires identifying what you want, then clearly and simply asking for it—not dropping hints or talking around the need. You assume that your partner will take your words at face value, without searching for hidden intent. You convey your meaning in the words you use, not in side channels such as posture, tone or body language. And you are willing to speak directly even when it might be uncomfortable.

In the previous chapter's story about passing the sweeper, communication started going wrong because Franklin and Celeste were using words differently, but that wasn't all that happened. When the first layer of communication failed, that created a situation where Celeste made assumptions about Franklin's motivations (that he didn't want to help with the housework). That made her upset, and communication ran further off the rails.

Direct listening starts from the premise that if your partner wants something, she will ask for it. You need to resist the impulse to infer a judgment, desire or need that's not explicitly stated. You assume that if your partner does not bring up an issue, she has no issue, and is not just being polite. Conversely, if she brings up an issue, she's not doing it to be confrontational or impolite, but to discuss it. You do not look for veiled intent, particularly veiled criticism, especially when talking about emotional or contentious matters.

Because direct communication is an indispensable skill in poly relationships, we return to it in more depth later in this chapter.

Nonviolent communication. Often called NVC, nonviolent communication involves separating observation from evaluation and judgment, and separating feelings and needs from strategies and actions. The speaker puts aside her assumptions about another's motivations and examines her own emotional responses. This is demanding cognitive work. It's surprisingly hard to do well, but when done right, it is an incredibly powerful tool for connection and conflict resolution. NVC is taught as a four-step process: observation, feeling, need, request.

The *observation* must be made without judgment or assumptions, stating only what a camera would capture. For instance, you say, "When I saw you come into the room and sit across from me at the table...," not "When you came into the room, you wouldn't sit next to me..."

The *feeling* must focus on what *you* felt, for example, "I felt lonely," or "I felt afraid," not on what you think the other felt or intended, such as "I felt that you were rejecting me."

The *need* also must focus on you, not the other person. You might say, "I need to feel supported when I'm in a group of people I don't know," not "I need you to sit next to me."

The *request* is usually a request for communication: "Will you talk to me about how you can help me feel supported when we go to events together?"

Nonviolent communication is, sadly, often abused. It can paradoxically become a weapon if your motivation is to change another person rather than connect with them. If you want to explore nonviolent communication, we strongly recommend that you take the time to learn it well. Start by picking up Marshall Rosenberg's book *Nonviolent Communication,* and consider enrolling in a workshop (available in many cities).

THE WORLD THROUGH OUR OWN LENSES

Communication extends beyond words. Even when everyone agrees on the meanings of words, things can go wrong when we have different conceptual frameworks—different ideas about the way the world works. After all, we see the world through the lens of our own experiences and ideologies. When we communicate, we filter the things another person says through these frameworks. If someone holds what to us seems an alien idea or a worldview we don't understand, or speaks from experiences very different from ours, communication can be lost. This happened to Franklin at a jealousy workshop:

FRANKLIN: Jealousy is an internal emotional state. A person who

says "I am jealous" is making a statement about an internal feeling.

You can't necessarily draw any conclusions about that person's

circumstance just from that statement.

AUDIENCE MEMBER: Hogwash! Jealousy is not always caused by internal feelings. A person might feel jealous because of something somebody did. You're just trying to dodge responsibility for your actions, that's all.

FRANKLIN: The idea that jealousy is an internal emotion doesn't say anything about the causes of the jealousy.

AUDIENCE MEMBER: Yes, it does! You're just repeating that tired old line that jealousy is all in someone's head and that person needs to just get over it already.

We can't help but see the world through our own lenses, and it's not always obvious where our perceptions of the world diverge from other people's. A big part of being able to communicate with someone who seems to hold a different worldview, or who has different experiences, is to listen and ask clarifying questions. It's tempting to impose our own understanding on other people—"You're just saying jealousy is all in my head!"—and if we don't pay attention, we can end up doing this without even being aware of it. Effective communication succeeds more often when we ask questions than when we tell other people what they're saying (or, God help us, tell them what they're thinking or feeling). In practice: "It sounds to me like you're saying I have to get over jealousy by myself, is that really what you're saying?"

TECHNIQUES FOR DIRECT COMMUNICATION

There's a way through the distortions of our own personal lens: direct communication. This skill does not come naturally to many, but it's one everyone can learn—and one that every polyamorous person *must* learn if they want to communicate effectively within their romantic networks.

Many excellent resources exist for learning direct communication. Many universities and continuing studies departments offer workshops in direct communication (sometimes called "assertiveness training"). The books by Harriet Lerner listed in the resources section offer good strategies for direct but compassionate communication. We urge you to explore this topic more if it is new to you, but we will touch briefly here on what direct communication is and why it's so important for poly relationships.

The single most effective way to start communicating directly is to use declarative statements rather than leading questions. For example, say "I would like to go out tonight" rather than "Would you like to go out tonight?" Statements that begin with "I want," "I feel" and "I need" are all markers of direct communication. They do not require a decoder ring to interpret correctly.

Plain language is another hallmark of direct communication. Make statements in active rather than passive voice ("I broke the vase," rather than "The vase got broken by my broom handle"). Use simple declarations rather than complex sentences ("I need you to take out the garbage," rather than "Taking care of this problem with the garbage was supposed to be your responsibility").

Use specific, concrete examples to illustrate what you're saying. Instead of saying, "You don't pay attention to my needs," list examples of times when you feel your needs weren't met. Take responsibility for your desires, thoughts and feelings. If you're asked to do something you'd rather not do, don't make excuses for not doing it. Rather, take ownership of it: "I don't want to do that." Try not to place responsibility for your feelings on your partner. Instead of saying, "You make me so angry," say "I feel angry." Give your partner the space to talk about her feelings as well.

Avoid hyperbole ("You always leave your socks on the coffee table," "You never close the garage door") and inferences of motivation ("You're only doing that because you want to get rid of me," "You clearly don't respect me").

Direct communication and active listening are complementary. Active listening means *paying attention* to what your partner is saying, rather than thinking of ways to refute what they're saying or interrupting. Direct communication is *saying clearly* what you want attention paid to.

There is one other element of direct communication: the ability to say yes and especially no without reservation. We've mentioned this before, but it's worth repeating: The ability to say no is vital to consent. Without the ability to say no, a relationship becomes coercive.

But there is another advantage to being able to say no. When you are accustomed to using passive communication, or unable to set boundaries, or when you feel you don't have the ability to say no to something, then it's very hard for your partners to have confidence in your yes. If you say yes to everything, then your yes might or might not be sincere, and your partner ends up trying to read tea leaves to figure out if you mean it or not. If you don't want to do something, you may become resentful when you do it, even if you said yes to it. Conversely, when you are able to say no and your partner knows it, he knows your yes is genuine.

ASK FOR WHAT YOU NEED

Asking for what we need is hard. And it's hard to learn to make requests in ways that are really requests, rather than demands, and are heard as such. But being able to ask for what you need, and in fact being *good* at asking, is pretty key to poly relationships—or any relationships.

For one thing, there's the obvious (yet somehow commonly overlooked) fact that if you ask for what you need, you are more likely to get it.

And then there's the fact that people who are getting their needs met will tend to be happier, and thus better (and less needy!) partners. We sometimes think we're being too needy when we ask for things...but when our needs are not being met, they tend to feel bottomless to us, and therefore to the people around us.

The simple act of formulating the request and deciding whom to ask, and how, forces you to get clear on what exactly you need—what's at the bottom of the emotions you're experiencing—and from whom, and why. But perhaps most importantly: Consistently asking for what you need means people can trust you to ask. They don't have to be second-guessing themselves, reading between the lines or worrying about you. They can simply enjoy being with you and discovering you and trust that they will know when you need something, because you will tell them. When you ask for what you need, you give a gift to the people you love.

Few of us are taught how to ask for what we need. Often we're socialized not to ask for things, because we're told that advocating for our needs is selfish. Sometimes we minimize them to conform to what we think is available. If we really want three cookies, we may think, *Well, three is a lot, and other people might want cookies too...I better ask for only one.* Then when someone else comes along and asks for three, we end up thinking, *Wait a minute! How come he's getting so many cookies and I'm not?*

Asking for what we need, rather than what we think might be available, is kind to our partners, because it communicates what we want authentically—as long as we are ready to hear a no. Asking for what we want isn't the same thing as "pressuring" someone, as long as the other person can say no and we can accept it. Some techniques that can help in asking for what you need:

- Ask for things in terms of "I need thus-and-such" rather than "I need more than any of your other partners get." When you state your needs as they stand, and not with respect to what you believe other people want or have, your partners will find it easier to meet them.
- Leave room for your partner to choose how to meet your needs. "I need to feel supported by you" is nicely open-ended; you can give examples of times when you have been supported, or things that help you feel that way, and then let your partner choose how to do that. "I need you to do things with me you will never do with anyone else" restricts your partner's options for responding.
- Remember that a need is not the same as a feeling. "I need to know you'll spend time to help me feel valued when I feel threatened" (direct communication of a need) is different from "I need to not feel threatened, so I need you to never date someone who makes me feel that way" (coercive communication).
- Be okay if the answer to your request is no. The difference between asking and demanding is what happens if the answer is no. If you're not okay with hearing a no, then you are demanding.
- Point out to your partners when your needs are being met, just as you tell them when they aren't. When your partners know they're doing right, this reinforces the right thing. It's better still when you can provide examples of how your partners are meeting your needs. This is also an important part of practicing gratitude, discussed in chapter 4.

If you've been socialized to not ask for your needs to be met, what tools can you use to learn how to ask?

- Practice communicating directly. When you ask for something, make sure you're actually asking! There is a difference between "I want to go to bed now," "Do you want to go to bed now?" "Are you coming to bed?" "I would like you to come to bed now" and "I would like your attention now." Be precise. Communicating directly may feel awkward at first, and you might not be good at it. That's okay. These are skills, and skills take practice.
- Talk about what you actually want, not what you think you *should* want or what you think might be available.
- Check your assumptions. If you think you hear implied criticism that was not stated directly, ask if that was what was intended. If not, you may be using passive communication. This is especially true when someone says something like "I don't want that" or "I don't need that." A person habituated to passive communication may hear "and therefore you shouldn't want or need that either," when the person was actually just talking about herself.
- Assume good intent. Your partners are with you because they love you and want to be with you. Even when problems arise, needs aren't being met or communication goes awry, this is still true. If you start with the assumption that your partners are acting out of malice, communication is never going to recover.
- When a partner has done the work of asking clearly for what she needs, take it seriously. Even small requests can be very hard to make, and they can lie at the tip of some very big emotions. If you can't meet the request, at least acknowledge it by saying no, and preferably explain why. If you can't do what your partner is asking, inquire about the underlying need; is there another way of meeting it? "No, I can't be with you next Thursday, but is there another time when I can help support you?" is better than just no.

TALK ABOUT THE REASONS

As scary as it can be to advocate for our needs, it can be even scarier to talk about *why* we want or need the things we want or need. Talking about the reasons leaves us naked; it opens us up to having our reasons, or even our motives, questioned. It also requires that we look inside ourselves and think about why we want what we want.

This can be difficult. "Because I just don't want that" is not good communication. If we ask for something, especially something that places limits on someone else's behavior—and most especially if it affects more people than just you and your partner—we need to talk about the "why" as well as the "what." This more effectively advocates for our needs, and it opens the door for a genuine dialogue in how to have them met.

Sometimes things that trigger us are hidden inside the statement "I just don't want that." For example, some people, usually heterosexual men, approach polyamory with the idea that it's okay if their partners have other female lovers, but feel threatened if their partners have other male lovers. It's certainly easier to say "I just don't want my partner to have sex with another man" than admit to feelings of vulnerability around sex, perhaps because you're afraid that if another man does what you do, you might be replaced. Talking about triggers* is necessary if we are to understand why we feel the way we do, and understanding our feelings is the only way to grow.

The purpose of talking about the things that trigger us is not to make our partners avoid them but to better understand them. When we can make sense of our emotional responses, we can more easily take responsibility for them, rather than making our partners (or, worse yet, our partners' partners) responsible for them. If, for example, you feel threatened by your lover having sex with another man, talking about why, and owning that feeling, can help you become more secure in your relationship. Discussing how you feel gives your partner an opportunity to explain what value she sees in you, and why another man doesn't have to be threatening to you.

"I just don't want that" tends to end rather than continue conversations. We encourage continuing discussion about what you want and, more importantly, why.

CUT THROUGH THE FOG

Being polyamorous doesn't confer immunity to negative feelings. Poly folks experience jealousy, insecurity, doubt and the full range of other human

---

* By triggers, we mean specific thoughts, actions, sights or events that set off an emotion that may not actually be related to the current situation, or may be much more powerful than the circumstances would seem to warrant. A trigger is usually tied to an earlier experience and may be connected to a traumatic event.

emotions. If we waited for immunity to uncomfortable emotions before traveling this road, we'd never budge. What's necessary is simply to understand that we don't have to put our emotions in the driver's seat. We feel what we feel; the secret is to understand that we still have power even in the face of our feelings. We can still choose to act with courage, compassion and grace, even when we're terrified, uncertain and insecure.

This notion that we can control our actions despite our emotions seems radical to many. The first part of making it happen is just realizing it's possible. Once you've turned that corner—and given all the social messages saying we're helpless in the face of our emotions, that's a tough thing to do—the rest is practice.

Some guidelines that help prevent you from turning over the wheel to your emotions:

- Understand that your emotions often lie to you. Feelings aren't fact. It's possible to feel threatened when there is no threat, for example, or feel powerless when you aren't.
- Avoid making decisions, especially irrevocable, life-altering decisions, when in the grip of strong emotions.
- Try not to validate, suppress, hang on to or deny your emotions. Just feel them, understand what they're trying to say...and then let them pass. Emotions are like weather; they come and go. Don't tell yourself you "shouldn't" feel them, but don't keep rehearsing things that keep them alive, either. Acknowledge them and let them go.
- Learn how you best process your emotions, and then advocate for doing that. Some people process their emotions by talking about them immediately; others need to withdraw for a while. Both approaches work, for different people. If you need to say "I don't want to go to bed angry. I would really like to talk about this now," say so. If you need to say "Look, I can't talk about this right now. Let's come back to it in the morning," do that.
- Take a deep breath from time to time and remind yourself that your lover is your partner, not the enemy. Enemies fight; partners work together toward a common good.

- Remember: This too shall pass. Our emotions tend to color our perceptions of the past and the future. When we're happy, we remember times in the past we've been happy and more easily see future happiness. When we're angry or frightened, we re-create our past and future accordingly. But emotions are transient. The things we feel today won't be what we feel tomorrow.

BE CURIOUS

Many conflicts arise because we've made judgments without full knowledge of the thoughts or feelings behind another person's actions. If the two (or more) sides in a conflict work from their own assumptions without checking whether these are true, no one feels understood, all become even more hurt and angry, and the conflict escalates.

Many conflict-resolution professionals stress the value of *curiosity*, accompanied by active listening. Many conflicts can be avoided or de-escalated if the parties involved are willing to set aside their prejudgments—and the intense feelings connected to them—and ask a question. And then be curious about the actual answer.

Not just any question, though. The question should be genuine and open-ended, a serious request for more information about another person's feelings, intentions or motivations. It should not be a choice between pre-defined alternatives, or an accusation followed by a demand for a response. It should be, as much as possible, unburdened from what you *think* will be the answer. That means being curious about what it really is.

Consider the following questions, arising from the same scenario:

"When we went to that dinner party, you didn't sit next to me. Obviously you're ashamed to be seen with me. Why are you even involved with me if you don't want people to know we're together?"

"Could you tell me why you chose that particular seat at the party?"

They both end with a question mark, but they are very different kinds of questions. One is a barely veiled accusation and expression of hurt; the other is a genuine request for information. The answer could turn out to be anything from "I wanted to talk to Bill over there about his project" to "Honestly, I'm worried that if the boss sees me with you, he'll think I'm cheating on my wife." Once the questioner understands where her partner is coming from, she will be able to respond to the situation using accurate information, not just her own stories. And she will stand a better chance of being able to express her own feelings about the situation to her partner without putting words in his mouth or putting him on the defensive, because he will know that she understands where he is coming from.

Moving away from defensiveness, assumptions and judgments and toward curiosity requires us to step outside ourselves. And that involves recognizing that the world may not be exactly as we think it is—we may have been wrong about our assessment of other people. It can be hard to restrain our emotional responses for long enough to express curiosity and try to understand the feelings of the very person we believe is responsible for our pain. But it can defuse a lot of conflicts before they start.

DON'T LET THE DISHES GET CRUSTY

Good communication is not just reactive, but proactive. That means regular checking in, just to see how things are going: and not just with your partners, but with yourself. Talk about things that bother you while they're still small. Express what you want early and often. Don't sit on things, hoping they'll go away. Don't wait until someone raises a specific problem before talking; develop the habit of letting your partners know where you're at emotionally, on an ongoing basis.

The purpose of checking in is simply to keep the lines of communication open, so problems can be spotted when they're still ripples rather than tsunamis. Noël Lynne Figart, author of the blog The Polyamorous Misanthrope, calls this "not letting the dishes get crusty." When everyone makes it a habit to wash the dishes as they use them rather than letting them pile up, no one has to confront the icky task of washing an entire sink full of crusty, three-day-old dishes.

HEALTHY SELF-EXPRESSION

Talking about our needs and feelings is tougher when we fear that we might come across as controlling: that is, dictating what another person should do. In a desire not to be seen as controlling, we may say nothing at all, which can let problems grow until we feel we have no choice but to blurt controllingly, "I want you to stop what you're doing right now!"

If you're used to passive communication, expressing a feeling can seem the same as being controlling. One of Franklin's partners grew up in a household where every statement of "I feel thus-and-such" contained an implicit "and it's your responsibility to do something about it!" If you don't want to be seen as manipulative and controlling (and you don't, right?), expressing yourself can feel dangerous, because it might be perceived that way.

The difference between expressing and controlling is in your expectations. What do you expect your partner to do? Is your goal to express your feelings or to change your partner's behavior? Just as the difference between asking and demanding lies in whether you can accept a no, the difference between expressing a feeling and being controlling is in whether it's okay for your partner to continue her present course of action. Are you *demanding*, or are you *informing* and *negotiating*?

While it may sound obvious, the simplest way to make your intention clear is to talk about it. You might say, for example, "I'm not telling you not to go on your date this Saturday, but I wanted to let you know I'm feeling some anxiety about it." From there, you can talk about the anxiety, and possibly even suggest ways that your partner can be supportive to you (for example, "I would like to connect with you after you get home," or "I would like to set aside some special time with you on Friday before you go"). Direct communication heads off passive assumptions about passive communication.

If you are negotiating, make that plain too. For example, you might say, "I'm feeling anxious about your date on Saturday. We're taking the dog to the vet that morning, and I might need your help taking care of him Saturday evening. Is it possible for you to reschedule for Friday instead?" Keep in mind, though, that sometimes the answer might be no, and that doesn't necessarily mean your partner doesn't care about you or your feelings. She may have schedule problems of her own.

MAKING COMMUNICATION SAFE

There's one more prerequisite for communication to succeed. It has to be safe for another person to communicate with you. We all want our partners to be honest with us. At the same time, nobody likes to hear bad news. From ancient empires to modern boardrooms, bearers of bad tidings have paid the price for delivering messages distasteful to the recipient's ears. Even in ordinary day-to-day conversations, there are all kinds of ways we can make it dangerous for others to say what we don't want to hear.

ADRIA'S STORY   Adria, a friend of Franklin's, had been dating her boyfriend for two years and wanted to get married. One day, her boyfriend came to her and said he had something to ask her. Adria was elated, because she was sure he was going to propose. She said, "You can ask me anything you want!"

Her heart sank when he didn't propose. Instead, he asked if they could try some new sexual things, like light bondage and spanking. Adria was hurt that he wasn't proposing, and also angry and hurt that he was asking to try these new things. She thought he was dissatisfied with her. She felt like he was saying she was a boring lover, because he couldn't enjoy "regular" sex with her. She yelled at him and told him he was a pervert, and said he was telling her she was bad in bed. He broke up with her shortly after that.

Adria's story contains a couple of lessons. The most immediate is that if you tell your partner "It's okay to ask for anything you want," *it better be true.* If you're not prepared to make it safe for your partner to open up to you, he won't. Because he'll feel he can't.

We don't always yell at people who say something we don't like to hear, but we often forget how many ways we can make it very expensive for people to be honest with us. When we love someone, it's hard even under the best of circumstances to say something that will make them unhappy. It requires a lot of vulnerability and courage to do that. We expose ourselves emotionally, because our partners' feelings affect ours. When that vulnerability is met with defensiveness, annoyance, passive-aggressiveness, silence, anger or resentment, honesty becomes damn near impossible.

If we want our lovers to be honest with us, we have to make it safe for them to be honest. We need to accept what we hear without anger, recriminations or blame, even when we're surprised or we hear something we really don't want to. We must be willing to take a deep breath, switch gears and say, "Thank you for sharing that with me."

HANDLING MISTAKES

Things will go wrong. You and your partners will make mistakes. People will get hurt. To paraphrase Voltaire, we are all born of frailty and error. What happens afterward depends on how capable we are to forgive one another for our errors, handle the consequences with grace and dignity, and learn from our mistakes.

Mistakes happen because someone is trying to solve a problem or meet a need. It's easy, in the emotional aftermath, to see the mistake as a consequence of selfishness or some other moral failing. But recovery from a mistake depends on being able to see our partners as human beings doing their best to solve a problem rather than as caricatures or monsters. Compassion, like communication, is one of those things that's most valuable when it's most difficult.

This kind of compassion is also needed when you're the one who makes a mistake. Sometimes it's easier to treat others with gentleness or compassion than it is to do the same for ourselves; we recognize the fallibility of those around us more readily than our own. You will make mistakes. It's the cost of being human. When you do, look to them as opportunities to learn, and remember that compassion begins at home.

QUESTIONS TO ASK YOURSELF

Strategies for better communication include, for starters, active listening, direct communication and nonviolent communication. As you practice these skills on a daily basis in your relationships, here are some questions to keep you on track:

- *How directly do I ask for what I want and need?*

- *What can I do to be more direct in my communication?*

- *If I hear a hidden meaning in a statement or question, do I ask for clarification before acting on my assumptions?*

- *Do I perceive criticism in my partner's statements even if they aren't directly critical?*

- *What do I do to check in with my partners?*

- *How well do I listen to my partners?*

- *What do I do to make sure it's safe for my partners to communicate with me, and to let them know it's safe?*

- *Does my communication show that I take responsibility for my actions and emotions?*

TAMING THE
GREEN-EYED MONSTER

*The worst thing about jealousy
is how low it makes you reach.*

ERICA JONG

So you're finally in a polyamorous relationship. You're involved with some-one who has another partner. There you are, cruising along, and *wham!* You see something, or hear something, or think about something, and now you're in the thick of it. Jealousy. It happens, sometimes when we least expect it. When it does, we can feel like we want to set fire to the world before running into a dark cave screaming "I will never let anyone get close to me ever again!" (Or maybe that's just us.)

We give such talismanic power to jealousy that the fear of it alone can shape our relationships. We've never heard anyone say "Polyamory? I wouldn't want to do that. What if I feel angry?" or "What if I feel sad?" But many people say "Polyamory? What if I feel jealous?" The fact is, at some point you will. Few people are born immune to jealousy. The good news is, jealousy is just an emotion like any other emotion. Sometimes you feel sad, sometimes you feel angry, but you don't let those feelings define you. They don't run your life. Jealousy doesn't need to either.

WHAT IS JEALOUSY?

Jealousy is the feeling we get when we drag tomorrow's rain cloud over today's sunshine. It's the feeling that we are about to lose something important to us, including maybe our self-worth, to someone else. It's the fear that we aren't good enough, that the people around us don't really love us, that everything is about to turn to ash. It comes like a thief in the night, stealing our joy. Jealousy is a sneaky thing. It sits behind us whispering that we are the victim, not the villain: that the people around us are wronging us, and we must act to protect ourselves. And perhaps most destructively, it tells us not to talk openly about the way we're feeling. It thrives on secrecy and silence. At its most toxic, it makes us angry at others and ashamed of ourselves at the same time.

Jealousy wears many faces because, unlike surprise or fear or anger, it is built of many emotions. Insecurity, fear of loss, territoriality, inadequacy, poor self-esteem, fear of abandonment...all these can pile onto one another to make what we think of as jealousy.

Is jealousy an intrinsic part of human nature? Some folks say yes, some no. We say it doesn't matter. We feel what we feel, but there is a difference between jealous feelings and jealous *actions*. Regardless of the origin of jealous feelings, the actions we take are within our control.

Jealous feelings come from a sense of loss, or a fear of it. Jealous actions are usually attempts to take back control over the things we're afraid of. For example, if you feel jealous when your partner has sex with her new partner in the Monkey with Lotus Blossom and Chainsaw position, you might be afraid that you're losing something special: "That's our position! What if this new person handles the chainsaw better than I do? What does she need me for, now that she's found someone else to do this with?"

The jealous *action* might be to say, "I don't want you to have sex with anyone but me in this position," which is an attempt to deal with the fear by taking back control. "If she stops doing this, I won't feel replaced anymore!" At least until the next threatening thing comes along.

These kinds of actions don't create safety or security. Rather, safety and security come from knowing that your partner loves, trusts and values you. Putting controls on your partner's behavior doesn't tell you how she loves, trusts and values you. It does exactly the opposite—restrictions undermine intimacy by telling your partner that you don't trust *her:* you don't believe her affection is genuine.

THE CHAMELEON EMOTION

Sometimes jealousy can be a relatively simple emotion, easy to detect and recognize. This is especially true when it happens in response to clear triggers, like watching a partner kiss another partner. The first time Eve saw Peter holding hands with Clio, the lurching feeling of the ground dropping out from beneath her feet was an unmistakable sign of jealousy. It was impossible to interpret as anything else, and the stimulus responsible for it was clear. That made the feeling, as scary as it was, relatively straightforward to confront.

But one of the things that can make jealousy such a challenge is that it's a shape-shifter: jealousy masquerades as other emotions. Before you can fight it, you need to see it for what it is. Some of the emotions that can have jealousy at their root are fear, loneliness, loss, sadness, anger, betrayal, envy and humiliation. If you are feeling these in connection to one of your partners or metamours and there's no obvious reason, or if the emotion is much stronger than the situation would seem to warrant, ask yourself if it might be jealousy.

On the other hand, those same emotions can arise in response to a genuinely hurtful external situation. In those cases it can be too easy to blame jealousy and duck the real issues. It's reasonable to ask yourself, "Am I really having these emotions just because I'm feeling jealous?" Take heed if someone frequently minimizes your emotions as "just jealousy." Do you feel you are being listened to? Are you being offered genuine insight about yourself by someone who knows and cares about you? Or are you being belittled and dismissed?

Jealousy can be a valuable signal that we have some soul-searching to do. Managing jealousy means having enough insight to tell it apart from its imposter emotions (and vice versa) as well as from external problems that may be developing. Distinguishing it from its look-alikes means knowing yourself (see chapter 4).

TRIGGERS FOR JEALOUSY

Sometimes jealousy is triggered by public behavior we often associate with "couplehood": holding hands in public, sending flowers to a partner's workplace, meeting a partner's parents. Peter felt jealous when Eve started wearing a gold necklace Ray had given her, and Eve felt jealous when Clio posted a picture on Facebook of a necklace Peter had made for her. As we discuss in chapter 18, on mono/poly relationships, Celeste felt jealous when Franklin's partner Bella wanted to have portraits taken with him, as did Mila when her metamour Nina posted family portraits to Facebook that included their partner Morgan.

These triggers usually happen when we fear losing the social status that comes from being part of a couple. In polyamorous relationships, such a loss is probably inevitable: poly relationships by definition include more than a couple. These triggers can often be avoided by using the strategies we talk about in the mono/poly chapter, such as including everyone in a family portrait. It also helps to demonstrate that you are not a victim or a pawn, but a full participant in the poly relationship. For example, if you're feeling jealous about your partner's new sweetie meeting his parents, scheduling the meeting when you can also be there will show his parents that it's not happening behind your back.

As mentioned, a common trigger for jealousy is seeing your partner being physically affectionate or flirty with someone else. This can bring up fears of being replaced or activate the "Why am I not enough?" script. It can also lead to destructive comparison with your partner's other partner: "Is she sexier than I am? Prettier? Smarter? Better?"

Physical evidence of intimacy between your partner and another lover, like a condom wrapper in the trash or extra slippers at the foot of the bed, can trigger jealous feelings. So can seeing your partner do something for the first time with a new lover—the "sushi effect" mentioned in chapter 5. Sometimes all it takes to deal with these triggers is to recognize the feelings for what they are and say, "I am feeling jealous because it seems like I'm learning to understand I'm not your only partner. Please bear with me while I work through this." Sometimes handling these triggers is more complicated, and we talk about more strategies in a bit.

LISTENING TO JEALOUSY

People often think of jealousy as evil. It can certainly make people do evil things, but by itself, jealousy is morally neutral. Like all emotions, it is the way the ancient, reptilian parts of our brains—parts that don't have language—try to communicate with us.

The problem is that as communicators go, jealousy is pretty inarticulate. It might be pointing to a significant problem in a relationship. Or it might just be our inner wordless three-year-old stomping its foot and saying "I'm not getting everything I want!" It might also be a symptom of a weak spot within us—some insecurity or self-doubt we're trying to protect. We have to decode the message if we are to decide what to do about it.

We can be tempted to approach jealousy by blaming whatever triggered it. "It's so simple! Just stop holding hands with your other partner!" We can also mistake it for other things, like territoriality or possessiveness or something else entirely. (And sometimes that's what it is; we'll get to that in a bit.)

FRANKLIN'S STORY   Ruby was smart, beautiful, strong, outgoing, opinionated—just the sort of person I find irresistible—and one of my first partners during my relationship with Celeste.

I was just out of school, and up to that point, I'd never experienced jealousy. I'd had partners who had other partners, and I'd never had even a twinge of bad feeling about it. I naively (and somewhat arrogantly) believed I was immune to jealousy—that it was something other people experienced, but not me.

I was utterly smitten with Ruby. Our relationship was emotional wildfire. Unfortunately, the terms of my agreement with Celeste didn't really permit a close, bonded relationship—which is exactly the kind of relationship Ruby and I were emotionally drawn into. We both chafed under the restrictions: no overnight stays, no public affection, a strict ceiling on how far the relationship would ever be allowed to grow. We both understood at some level that our relationship would never be permitted to become what we both needed it to be.

Before long, Ruby started another relationship with a close friend of mine, Newton. He was an excellent choice as a partner for her: quick-witted, laid-back, good-natured. His relationship with Ruby had no ceiling and no restrictions. Instinctively I knew that Newton could offer Ruby more than I could, and I was terrified that he would replace me in Ruby's heart.

The jealousy happened so fast and hit me so hard that I couldn't even recognize it for what it was. All I knew was that when I saw them together, I felt scared and angry. I assumed that because I felt this way, she must be doing something wrong, though it was difficult to figure out exactly what. I remember going to sleep replaying all my interactions with her in my head, looking for that thing she was doing to hurt me so much.

Because I was starting from the premise that she was doing something wrong—why else would I be feeling so bad?—I lashed out at her, accusing her of all kinds of wrongdoing, most of which existed only in my head. The tiniest, most trivial things she said or did that I didn't agree with were magnified to epic proportions. Before long, unsurprisingly, I had destroyed my relationship with Ruby, and not long after that, my friendship with her (and with Newton) as well. Not until more than a year later did I finally put together what had happened.

By the time I realized I was jealous, and that I had allowed my jealousy to poison our relationship, it was too late. I had done so much damage that neither Ruby nor Newton ever spoke to me again. I lost a partner and two friends.

Franklin destroyed his relationship with Ruby because he was unable to conceive that he might feel jealousy, and therefore he was unable to listen to it. In this case, the jealousy was saying, "You are encumbered by rules and constraints specifically intended to prevent you from having the kind of relationship both of you need. Newton is able to offer her a relationship without limits. If she wants that kind of relationship, you might be replaced."

Was Franklin actually in danger of being replaced? No. Ruby loved him very much. How might listening to the jealousy have changed the outcome? For one, Franklin might have seen how destructive the agreements he'd made with Celeste were, and this might have saved many other people—and Franklin and Celeste—a great deal of pain. More to the point, he might have been able to go to Ruby and say, "I'm feeling jealous. I realize that our relationship is constricted, and Newton does not have these limitations. Do you still value our relationship, even as circumscribed as it is? What do I offer you, and what do you value in me? How can we make sure we build a foundation that means you will continue to want to be with me?" And the outcome would probably have been very different.

It's so easy to pin responsibility for our emotions on other people. "You're making me feel this terrible thing. Stop doing that!" We forget that our emotions might be the result of our own insecurities rather than our partners' actions. When we transfer responsibility for our emotions to others, we yield control over our own lives.

CONFRONTING JEALOUSY

It's okay to feel jealous. That might sound strange, in a book about polyamory. But we, the authors of this book, have been there. Almost everyone you meet has been there. Being immune to jealousy is not a prerequisite for polyamory, and feeling jealous doesn't make you a bad poly person. So take a deep breath. Like all feelings, jealousy is not the sum of who you are. It won't kill you, even if it feels like it might. It doesn't necessarily mean something's wrong with you, or with your relationship.

Even when you're feeling jealous, you're still in control. Jealousy is like that creepy guy sitting behind the king whispering in his ear, "The ambassador has just insulted you most grievously, Your Grace! Attack his lands at once! Raze his villages!" But remember, you're still the king. You don't have to set the world on fire and run off to live in a cave, no matter how satisfying that sounds.

FRANKLIN'S STORY   About the time I was involved with Ruby, I had a friend who had a pet iguana, a huge green lizard more than four feet long. It was usually docile and friendly. But a pattern would play out every time she took it out of its cage. She would open the cage door and reach inside, and it would lash at her with its whip-like tail. She would jump back, then reach in the cage again. The second time, it would calmly climb up her arm to sit on her shoulder.

One day, when I watched her go through this ritual, she said, "I wish it would hit me with its tail, just once, so I wouldn't have to be afraid of it anymore."

In the aftermath of my relationship with Ruby, I was heartbroken. I spent long nights thinking about what had happened and wondering where our relationship, which had been such a source of joy to both of us, had gone so horribly wrong.

Eventually, I realized an inescapable truth: Our relationship had been destroyed because *I destroyed it.* It wasn't destroyed by her new relationship with Newton. It wasn't destroyed by anything she had done to me. I had destroyed it, because I had felt something I believed myself incapable of feeling and therefore couldn't handle when I did. She had been absolutely right to end the relationship with me. In the blindness of my own pain, I had been completely unaware of the pain I was causing her.

The things I felt during and after my relationship with Ruby were the worst I had ever felt in my life, and I didn't ever want to feel them again. And, gradually, I realized something else: *I didn't have to.* The secret of not ever feeling this way again was right in front of me. It had been all along.

First, after she broke up with me, I learned something valuable: I could lose someone, and I might want to curl up and die, but it wouldn't actually kill me. I knew what it felt like for the lizard to get me, and I didn't have to be afraid of it anymore. I would survive. I could even, eventually, be happy again.

Second, I realized she had the right to leave me. Everyone has the right to leave me. Whether they choose to leave me is something I have some control over, by the way I treat them. Ruby left because I did things that hurt her, and that drove her away. But it was within my power to do different things. It was not the hand of fate or the uncaring stars; it was the choices I made. If I had made different choices, if I had made decisions that drew my partners closer rather than pushing them away, I might have had a better outcome.

The implications of this idea took a long time to sink in. When they did, I felt empowered. Breakups weren't something that just happened to me; they happened because of the choices I and my partner both made. I might feel pain again, but I knew there was something on the other side. And I didn't have to be afraid anymore: I would have a hand in what happened to me.

As Franklin's painful breakup and subsequent epiphany demonstrate, jealousy can be confronted, dealt with, and banished back to the dark places where it slinks, powerless to damage your calm. Don't be discouraged. It might take work to get there, and some of that work might be uncomfortable.

Jealousy is a feeling, not an identity. You may feel jealous, but that doesn't make you a jealous person. It's an important distinction. If you say "I am a jealous person," you may find it hard to think about letting go of jealousy; it feels like letting go of something that makes you who you are. On the other hand, if you say "I am a person who sometimes feels jealous," that gives space to your other emotions. "I am a person who sometimes feels jealous, and sometimes feels happy, and sometimes feels sad, excited, afraid, angry or confused." Such a statement reinforces to yourself that jealousy is not who you are.

Remember, this too shall pass. When we are buried armpit-deep in an emotion, we can find it extraordinarily difficult to remember that emotions are transient. When we're sad, we can be hard put to remember what it's like to be happy, and when we're jealous, we can find it hard to remember what it's like not to feel that way. But there is another way to feel, even if we can't emotionally access it at the moment.

MILA'S STORY   When Mila fell in love with Morgan, a polyamorous man, she didn't really know what she was in for, but she knew it would be work. Morgan was already in a relationship with Nina when he started the relationship with Mila, and he started another new relationship not long after.

The first few months were hard for Mila. She didn't know where Morgan's relationships with her or his other partners would end up. Morgan's commitment to her was solid, but her clarity on the future was not. She had never been insecure or jealous before, and she had a hard time accepting herself for feeling this way.

She didn't know when the jealousy would hit her or what would trigger it. Sometimes it was Morgan and Nina's public displays of affection, sometimes it was when they attended events as a couple. But the feelings often overwhelmed her. She was motivated to make a poly relationship work, though: not just by her feelings for Morgan and his steady support of her, but by her own disillusionment with monogamy after an ex had cheated on her, and her belief that doing the work would lead them to a healthier relationship in the long run. So she hung on. And Morgan repeatedly created space for Mila to process her feelings and work on herself. He reassured her that it was okay to feel what she felt and did not try to fix her feelings for her.

Sometimes jealousy triggers come as a complete surprise, which is why trying to prevent your partners from doing things that trigger jealousy doesn't work. The triggers and the underlying causes are often quite different, so lasting relief from jealousy involves digging beneath the triggers to the roots. One strategy for dealing with jealousy looks like this:

Step 1. Accept the feelings. You can't deal with jealousy by wishing it away or by shaming yourself. Our emotions are what they are, and telling yourself "I shouldn't feel this!" won't work.

When you look around at the polyamorous community, it can be easy to convince yourself that everyone else has conquered their jealousy, and you're not a good poly person if you still feel it. That absolutely isn't true. Very few people say they've never felt it, and frankly, we suspect that just means they haven't felt it yet. Accept that there's nothing wrong with you for feeling this way.

Step 2. Separate triggers from causes. The next step is harder. It involves disassembling the jealousy to find those places where you are afraid and insecure.

Long-lasting jealousy management can come only from strengthening the places where your self-esteem is weak.

Examine your triggers, the specific thoughts, actions, sights or events that set off an emotion. It's easy to believe that these triggers "cause" the emotion, but the truth is a bit more complicated. We might feel that wild rush of jealousy when we see our partner kiss another person, but that doesn't mean the kiss itself is the root cause. Instead, it's more accurate to say that the kiss is the switch that turns on a complicated chain of emotions that brings us nose to claw with some internal beast—a fear of being replaced, maybe, or a sense of territoriality. The kiss might be the trigger, but the cause is something else—some inner insecurity, stirred from its slumber.

This chain reaction is why restrictions on specific actions or behaviors rarely do much to alleviate jealousy. The beast still lies there, waiting for some other poke or prod to awaken it. At some point, if we are to be free of jealousy, we have to confront the monster directly. That means digging deep to uncover and deal with the internal things—the wobbles in our sense of worthiness, the little fears that try to convince us we will be abandoned.

Step 3. Understand the feelings. Feelings need to be examined to be understood, and the first step in examining them is to accept them for what they are. But that doesn't necessarily mean we have to believe them. We're often told to trust our intuition or go with our gut. But your feelings often lie to you. For example, if you're afraid of snakes, you might feel panic at the sight of a harmless corn snake crossing your path. The fear is genuine, but the thing it's telling you—*This snake is a threat to me*—is not true.

Learning what our feelings are rooted in, without assuming that what they say is always true, is the place to start. Almost always, jealousy is rooted in some sort of fear: of abandonment, of being replaced, of losing the attention of someone you love, of being alone. Jealousy isn't really about the person you feel jealous of. It's about you: your feeling that you might lose something precious. What is it saying? What's the outcome you're afraid will happen?

Getting to the roots of your jealousy takes time. When you feel jealous, you often want to act on it immediately—usually in destructive ways. Instead, take the time to figure out what's actually going on, what your jealousy is trying to tell you.

Step 4: Talk about it. Jealousy management relies on calming fears directly, by talking about them and learning the way our partners feel about us. The first thing to do when jealousy arises is to talk about it, directly. And by "talk about it," we don't mean what Franklin did in his relationship with Ruby when he said, "You terrible person, how could you make me feel this way?" We mean acknowledge and own the fear, and ask for support to deal with it. "When you're on a date with him and you do that thing with your tongue, I feel jealous. That doesn't mean you shouldn't do it, but I sure could use some love and support."

This kind of communication is not always easy, especially when the jealousy arrives with a heaping side order of shame and doubt. Talking about it, though, can go a long way toward pulling out its fangs. One of the best ways to start addressing our fears in poly relationships is to ask our partners what they value in us...and trust that what they say is true. And if what they say doesn't stick, ask again. And listen. And keep at it until those things that make us magnificent in our partners' eyes start to sink in.

Step 5: Practice security. A particularly insidious thing about insecurity is that it tends to find—or invent—"evidence" to support itself. It sneaks up on you to whisper in your ear that you're not valued and not loved and your partner doesn't really want to be with you, even when those things aren't true. These things *feel* real. There is always the possibility that they are real, but regardless of whether they're real or not, it can be very difficult to tell whether you're actually in danger of being abandoned.

Again, we become good at what we practice. When we practice convincing ourselves that our partners don't want us, don't value us and don't really want to be involved with us, we become good at believing it. When we practice convincing ourselves that we have value and worth and our partners treasure us, we become good at believing that.

And often a relationship *becomes* what we believe about it. If you believe your partner does not love you and treasure you, then you may act in destructive ways. You might become withdrawn, sullen or defensive, which will cause your relationship to suffer. If you believe you are cherished and valued, then you start to act with confidence, trust and openness—and people like that are great to be around. Your relationships will blossom.

The Jealousy Workbook by Kathy Labriola, listed in the resources section, offers more exercises and advice for dealing with jealousy.

WHEN YOU FEEL LEFT OUT

"How do you deal with feeling lonely and left out when your partner is off on a date with someone else?" This is a question Franklin gets often in emails. The answer is, perhaps, not intuitive: it is not necessary to feel lonely and left out. This is more obvious when we aren't talking about polyamory. For example, what would we say to someone who says, "I feel lonely and left out for the eight hours a day my partner is at work"? We might think that was a little strange.

Our social values tell us it's okay for our partners to leave us for big chunks of time: for work, for errands, for military service, for all sorts of things. Yet we still tend to assume that if a partner is left behind for another romantic relationship, the natural response is to feel alienated and alone.

Of course, it's not only romantic relationships that trigger these feelings. Many people feel left out when their partners go to the bar with drinking buddies or join a roller derby league. It's as if we have two classes of activities: those where we don't expect to feel left behind, such as work or school, and those where we do, such as a date or a derby night. It's as though we expect to feel left out when our partner is engaged in a social activity, but not if a partner is engaged in a more mundane task. So really, the feeling isn't about a partner doing something without us. Only certain kinds of activities, usually involving social situations, make us feel this way.

Maybe this is because being in a romantic relationship carries social status. Maybe it's because we don't mind missing out on mundane activities but don't want to miss out on enjoyable ones. The solution might be to build your own hobbies and social circles, so you don't have to rely on your partner to provide for all your social needs. Or maybe the feelings come from a sense of exclusion—if a partner is building a relationship with his fishing buddies, we are being rejected. The solution to this might be to work on your sense of self-worth, as discussed in chapter 4.

Another fear closely related to the fear of being left out is the fear of playing "second fiddle." Perhaps your partner is starting a new relationship, and maybe you aren't really being left behind—but you aren't the number one focus anymore, either. This, too, isn't just a problem in polyamory. You can become second fiddle to a new child (or grandchild), to a new job, to a new hobby...hell, Franklin has seen someone whose partner became second fiddle to a pet. (It was a very cute cat, mind, but still...)

Again, the central issue is, how much do you trust your partner? If she wants to make you a priority, she will. If she doesn't, she won't. The type of relationship you're in doesn't matter. Every relationship has a natural ebb and flow. Sometimes we do get supplanted, at least for a time, in our partner's attentions. When Franklin's partner Amber started working on her master's thesis, Franklin lost some of her focus and attention. When a new baby comes along, we don't find it at all surprising when the baby becomes the center of everything. When these things happen, we trust that the time will come when we are a priority again. We understand that things happen that require more attention, and that's part of life. There is a balance; we merely need to have faith in our worth, in our partner's love for us, and in our ability to ask for the things we need to reassure ourselves that the pendulum will swing back and the balance will be restored.

KEEPING SCORE

Keeping score will drive you insane. Don't do it. If you start counting the nights (or dollars) spent together, the sexual acts engaged in, the hours on the phone or anything else of value, to compare it with what you're getting, believe us when we say that no good can come of this. You may be somewhat reassured if you come out ahead, but all keeping score will do is make you, your partners and their partners crazy and bitter without meeting the needs you're trying to get met.

AUDREY'S STORY After years of struggling with Jasmine's concerns over "losing" Joseph's time, Audrey and Joseph began using a spreadsheet. For two years, they used it to track the time they spent together: what scheduled time they missed, what unscheduled time they added. It tracked hours spent and lost, and whether Joseph spent time with Audrey and Jasmine individually or together as family time.

Time on the phone was logged in its own category. Their intention was to reassure Jasmine that their relationship wasn't growing outside of her comfort zone.

But all of this record-keeping didn't help anyone. Jasmine preferred to count only time that Joseph and Audrey added *over and above* their regularly scheduled time—a lunch, coffee date or vacation day now and then—in keeping with her fear that Joseph's relationship with Audrey was getting too big. Part of Joseph and Audrey's intent in using the spreadsheet was to also show the subtractions—dates that were missed. This was to help demonstrate that, despite Jasmine's fears that they were "growing," when you did both the addition *and* subtraction, they were actually staying "small."

However, the spreadsheet did not assuage Jasmine's fears. Joseph and Audrey are no longer keeping the spreadsheet, but Jasmine is still counting time.

If someone is keeping score, it's generally because they're afraid of something. The problem with using a scorecard to try to assuage that fear is that it does nothing to get to the root of it. Even an "even" scorecard is unlikely to diminish the fear, as Audrey's story illustrates.

Information, by itself, almost never changes feelings. If feeling secure in your relationship is contingent on seeing a certain balance on the scorecard, then you will always be comparing your relationship with another, rather than focusing on what is meaningful in your relationship: what your partner finds of value in *you*.

Taken to its conclusion, keeping score creates a relationship where people don't state their needs: they barter for what they want, using other people as the bartering chips. And this is a way of treating people as things.

PEOPLE ARE NOT INTERCHANGEABLE

Buried in the idea of building relationships by choice rather than by default is a powerful way to combat jealousy. All too often, our relationships *do* happen by default. We find the "best" person we can (whatever "best" means) and then stick that person into the "relationship slot." Sometimes, when we do this, we keep half an eye out for someone better to come along.

This approach to relationships is based on a tacit assumption that people are interchangeable. If you have a relationship with Zoe, and Bridget is hotter and richer, then you can replace Zoe with Bridget and you climb the ladder. This approach leads to insecurity; if Zoe knows that she can be replaced by Bridget, Zoe won't ever feel secure.

The idea that people are interchangeable is fundamentally flawed. When we value the things that make our partners who they are, no one person can ever replace another.

This is one place where that leap of faith to believe in our own worthiness really pays off. When we feel ourselves worthy of love in our own right, not for the things we do or how we look but because of who we are, we become more able to recognize our own unique irreplaceability—and the irreplaceability of our partners. When we believe ourselves to be worthy, we more easily see our partners as worthy too.

Many people in the polyamorous community say that comparisons are poisonous to poly relationships. "Don't compare one lover to another," they say. "If you do that, you'll breed insecurity." We'd like to suggest, perhaps counterintuitively, this is not necessarily so. Some comparisons are damaging. "Raj is better in bed than Franco is," for example, or perhaps "Bridget is hotter than Zoe." But there's a different kind of comparison, and that is noticing differences in a way that helps you remain aware of what makes everyone unique. That kind of comparison, which is more about treasuring the things that make people who they are than about ranking people, is awesome, because it reminds us that people are not interchangeable. Remembering that people are not interchangeable can go a long way toward calming the fear of being replaced.

SEPARATING REALITY FROM FALSEHOOD

Believing the best of your partner isn't always easy. And devils lurk in the details. Every now and then you may find yourself in a relationship that is genuinely unhealthy, or with a partner who really does have one foot out the door. It's hard to sort that out from your own insecurities and determine what is true if you don't have strong self-esteem to begin with.

There are no hard rules for distinguishing a situation where your insecurity is whispering falsehoods at you and a situation where your jealousy is a genuine signal of a painful truth. But there are external signs to look for.

One sign is a lack of empathy or compassion. A partner who brushes off your fears, or isn't willing to talk to you about your jealousy, may be telling you that she's looking to leave you for better options. If your partners want to support you, they will listen to your fears, even when they're irrational. What does your partner do when you say "Honey, I have this fear"? Does she listen with compassion? Does she empathize with your feelings, even if she thinks they're not grounded in fact? If she has done something that hurts you, does she genuinely feel sorry for it? Is she willing to take responsibility for it and make amends?

Another sign is an attitude of entitlement. This can be hard to call, because your partners are independent adults, carrying their own needs and feelings, and they really *are* entitled to make their own choices. But are they willing to work with you, to hear your complaints, and to make choices that support you in the long run even if you may not get everything you want in the short run? As we discuss in chapter 14, it may not be reasonable to restrict your partners to avoid dealing with your insecurities—but sometimes it is reasonable to ask your partners to help you, or even in extreme cases to agree to temporary and limited restrictions to give you the space you need.

What do your partners say when you ask for reassurance? If you ask for concrete reminders of how your partners love and value you, do you get them? And what does the relationship itself have to say? If we've been involved with someone for three months and already they seem restless and distracted, that might be cause for concern. But if we've been with someone for years and still wake every morning feeling that this is the day they will hopscotch out of our life, then maybe what we're feeling is more about our own insecurity than about our partner's desire to leave.

QUESTIONS TO ASK YOURSELF

When you've answered the questions below, you can start asking yourself why you feel the way you do. For example, let's say you answer yes to the question "Am I worried that if someone 'better' comes along, my partner will realize

I'm not good enough and want to replace me?" That might mean that your self-esteem is not high enough for you to recognize that your partner wants to be with you because he values and cherishes you; some part of you may be thinking, *Well, I'm not as good as he thinks I am, so I better keep him away from other people! Otherwise, he'll dump me in a heartbeat.* The antidote to those feelings is to build a sense of worthiness and understand what it is about yourself that your partner values.

Or say you answer yes to the question "Do I believe that if I am not my partner's only sexual partner, I am not special anymore?" The remedy there is to understand that value in a relationship comes from who you are, not from what you do, so if your partner has the same experience with another person that he has with you, the *feeling* of that experience is different, because nobody else is you.

- *Am I worried that if someone "better" comes along, my partner will realize I'm not good enough and want to replace me?*

- *Am I uncertain about the value my partner sees in me? Am I not sure why my partner wants to be with me?*

- *Does the idea of my partner having another lover mean that whatever my partner sees in me will no longer be valid, or that my partner will want to choose that other lover over me?*

- *Do I feel that most other people are sexier, more good-looking, more worthwhile, funnier, smarter or just generally better than I am, and I am not able to compete with them?*

- *Do I believe that if I am not jealous, I don't really love my partner?*

- *Do I think that if my partner falls in love with with another person, he will leave me for that person?*

- *Do I think that if my partner has sex with someone "better in bed" than I am, she won't want to have sex with me anymore or won't need me anymore?*

- *Is sex the glue that holds our relationship together? If my partner has sex with someone else, do I think the relationship will come unglued?*

- *Do I believe that other people are willing to do sexual things that I'm not willing to do, and therefore my partner will like having sex with them better?*

- *Am I afraid that if my partner has sex with someone else, she will start comparing me whenever we have sex?*

- *Am I afraid that anyone my partner has sex with will try to persuade her to leave me?*

PART 3

Poly Frameworks

BOUNDARIES

*Daring to set boundaries
is about having the courage to love ourselves,
even when we risk disappointing others.*

BRENÉ BROWN

When we create relationships, we invite other people deep into our hearts. We allow them intimate access to our minds, our bodies, our emotions. This intimacy is one of the most wonderful, most profoundly transformative things life has to offer. It changes who we are. It tells us that in all the vastness of the universe, we do not have to be alone. But it comes at a price. When we allow others into our heart, and they allow us into theirs, we become exquisitely vulnerable to each other. The people we choose to let in have the power to bring us incredible joy, and to hurt us deeply. If we are to respect the gifts of intimacy we are offered, we have an ethical obligation to treat one another with care.

In practice, this can be hard. Even when we allow only one person to affect us so deeply, there's a balance to be struck between allowing our partner to be who he is, and creating a framework where we feel safe. When more than one person has access to our heart, this balancing act becomes much more complicated—and scary.

Here in Part 3, we suggest frameworks we can use to create safety and security while still respecting the humanity and autonomy of the people we love. Just as Part 2 began with a chapter about our selves, so does Part 3, because secure poly frameworks begin with our selves and our boundaries. First, let's explain what we mean by that word, *boundaries*. Many people use the terms *rules, agreements* and *boundaries* interchangeably. But these terms have subtly different meanings, and being clear about those distinctions can cut through Gordian knots in relationships.

Any discussion of these three words has to start with boundaries, because boundaries are about you and your self. Understanding boundaries is essential to understanding what kinds of rules and agreements might maximize your happiness, empowerment and sense of well-being. (More on those in the next chapter.) Having poor personal boundaries can be damaging to the self. Strong boundaries are vital to building healthy relationships. Boundaries are also essential to consent, and relationships are healthy only when they are consensual.

DEFINING BOUNDARIES

Boundaries concern your self: what you alone own, and others may access only with your permission. Because boundaries are personal, we often don't realize where they are until they are crossed. But we can divide personal boundaries into two rough categories: physical (your body, your sexuality) and mental (your intimacy, your emotions, your affection).

Most people, unless they have suffered abuse, have a good sense of where their physical boundaries are. These begin where we feel physically affected by another person. For most of us they begin a little away from our physical edges, in what we call our "personal space." When we set physical boundaries, we are exercising our right to decide if, how and when we want to be crowded very closely or touched. Even in community spaces, where we can't necessarily control who enters our personal space, we have a choice; we have the right to not be there.

In romantic relationships, we often negotiate shared physical space, especially when we live with a lover. If "touch" for us begins beyond our skin, we may need to negotiate some space that we can control. For some people, this may be a room of our own. For some, it might be as simple as asking for quiet time on the couch. If you don't have the ability to negotiate for individual space when you need it, coercion has entered your relationship.

You may always set boundaries about your physical space and your body. If someone ever tells you it's not okay to assert a physical boundary—especially regarding who you will have sex with or who is allowed to touch you—look out! There's a problem.

Your mind is your mental and emotional experience of the world, your memories, your reality and your values. When you engage the world, you let people into this mental space. Finding the edges of your mind is trickier than finding your physical edges. We are social creatures, and even the most superficial interactions engage our mental and emotional boundaries. The boundaries of the mind are both the ones we most control and the ones easiest for others to cross.

When we engage in intimate relationships, we open up our mental boundaries. We let a chosen few affect us, deeply. This is beautiful and amazing, and one of the things that makes life worth living. But your mind always belongs to you, and you alone. Your intimate partners, your family, your boss and the woman at the grocery store only ever get your mind on loan, and if that intimacy is damaging you, you have the right to take it back. Always.

That means we all have a fundamental, inalienable right not to extend ourselves emotionally to anyone we don't choose to. Every one of us has the absolute right to chose whom we will or will not be intimate with, for any reason or no reason.

Setting mental boundaries is different from setting physical boundaries. When you set a physical boundary, you are exerting clear control over what you do with your body. "Don't touch me there," for example. "Don't move closer to me." "Leave my home." With emotional boundaries, we have to take care to not make others responsible for our mental state. When we tell another person, "Don't say or do things that upset me," we are not setting boundaries; we are trying to *manage* people whom we have already let too far over our boundaries. If we make others responsible for our own emotions, we introduce coercion into the relationship, and coercion erodes consent.

When we talk about setting boundaries, we're not talking about restrictions on another's behavior except as their behavior regards access to *you*. Of course, whether you choose to grant that access may in fact depend on how they are behaving. Examples of boundaries include:

- I will not be involved with someone who is not open and honest with all other partners about dating me.
- I will not have unbarriered sex with partners whose sexual behavior does not fall within my level of acceptable sexual health risk.
- I will not become involved with someone who is not already committed to polyamory.
- I will not remain in a relationship with a partner who threatens me or uses violence.
- I will choose the level of closeness I want with my partners' other partners, subject to their consent.

The difference between "boundaries we set for ourselves" and "rules we place on someone else" might just seem like one of semantics, but it is profound. *Rules* tend to come from the idea that it's acceptable, or even desirable, for you to control someone else's behavior, or for someone else to control yours. *Boundaries* derive from the idea that the only person you really control is yourself.

SACRIFICING YOUR SELF

One way to damage a relationship is to believe that your sense of self or self-worth comes from your partner or from being in a relationship. If you constantly seek reinforcement of your worth from your partner, your partner becomes your source of worth, rather than your equal. This kind of codependence is exhausting for your partner and destructive for you.

This is especially likely to happen if you have trouble setting boundaries. Fuzzy boundaries can lead to a loss of self-identity and an inability to tell where your self (and your responsibility to set your own boundaries) ends and your partner begins. Losing your self-identity opens you up to being manipulated or losing your ethical integrity. And you must be true to yourself if you are to be true to those you love. When you feel that you "need" a relationship, you may become afraid to raise your voice and assert the other things you need. It's hard to set boundaries in a relationship you feel you can't live without, because setting boundaries means admitting there are things that might end your relationship.

EVE'S STORY   I was probably eleven or twelve when I began believing that my worth was tied to a relationship. As a teenager, my favorite heroine was Éponine from *Les Misérables*. Her death from taking a bullet for the man she loved was one of the most romantic things I could imagine. I loved (and still love) Oscar Wilde's short story "The Nightingale and the Rose," in which a nightingale gives her life to help a boy woo the object of his adoration—who rejects him anyway.

So when I began to accept, ten years ago (give or take), that relationships were actually supposed to be fulfilling for *me*, that laying my own needs (and even my own personality) at the feet of a partner was not actually a noble or desirable thing, the idea was a game changer. It nearly ended my marriage—twice. And I still struggle with it.

Which is why I needed this poem, by Franklin's sweetie Maxine Green, which I coincidentally discovered online just a few months before I met and began dating Franklin:

I give, and you give, and we draw lines in ourselves where we stop.

I draw a line here, do you see it?

It's the place just before it hurts me to give,

because I know, if you love me, if you love the way I do, this is where you

would beg me to stop.

That poem, and some other things that happened to me around that time, helped me realize that loving someone—or giving to someone—is *not* supposed to hurt. And if it does, something is wrong. But drawing that line can be so, so hard. And on those occasions when I must do so, often the repercussions resonate at the same frequency as my own guilt and self-judgment until they shake the foundation of my convictions. For me, self-sacrifice is conditioning that goes very, very deep.

One form of sacrificing the self is embedded in many versions of the fairy tale. There are many toxic myths about love, but perhaps the worst is that "love conquers all." This myth hurts us in all kinds of ways—such as the untold zillions of hours and wasted tears spent by people trying to heal, reform or otherwise change a partner. Especially pernicious is the idea that we're supposed to "give until it hurts"—in fact, for some of us, that the measure of our worth is our ability to give, right down to the last drop of ourselves. That is wrong. Love isn't supposed to hurt, and we should not and do not need to sacrifice our selves for good relationships.

BOUNDARIES VS. RULES

For a person accustomed to passive communication (see chapter 6), the difference between a boundary and a rule may not be clear. A passive communicator may impose restrictions on a partner by stating the restriction as a boundary, using "I will" boundary language when she is actually applying "you will" restrictions. The difference is in what happens if the other person doesn't behave as desired.

For example, consider a reasonable boundary: "You are free to do what you like with your body with other people. I am free to decide my level of acceptable risk to my sexual health. If you engage in behavior that exceeds my level of risk, I reserve the right to use barriers with you, or perhaps not have sex with you at all." If this is a boundary, and the other person has sex that exceeds your level of risk, you assess the situation and take appropriate action. You might, for instance, say, "Since you are not choosing to use barriers with this other partner, I will use barriers with you," and then do so.

On the other hand, if this is actually a *rule* being stated in the *language* of boundaries, you may feel the other person did something he shouldn't have, or that you were *entitled* to make him always use safer-sex barriers with others. If there is recrimination, anger or punishment in response to your partner's choices, then you had instituted a *rule*, regardless of the wording.

Genuine boundaries recognize that others make their own choices, and we do not have the right (or ability) to control those choices. Rather, we have the right and ability to determine for ourselves what intimacy we choose to be involved in.

HEALTHY COMPROMISE

No two people have the same needs. Whenever we tie our lives to others, especially in romantic relationships, there will be times when we can't have everything we want. The ability to negotiate in good faith and to seek compromise when our needs and those of others conflict is a vital relationship skill. To understand where we can make compromises and where we can't, we must first know our own boundaries, which will limit what we can compromise on.

EVE'S STORY   In "Minding the gap" (pages 55–58), I told the story of Peter's first weekend together with Clio at our house. Before then, I had never taken the time to consider what boundaries I might need; I was so grateful for the freedom I'd had with Ray, I wanted to be able to reciprocate all at once. Unfortunately, boundaries are not transitive: the work Peter had done to become comfortable with me and Ray did not translate into my being equally comfortable with Peter and Clio.

I lay awake for most of their first night together. I spent the next day at a seminar, but could barely focus. As the day wore on, I felt more and more anxious, and more and more angry—but I knew Peter and Clio had done nothing wrong. I was upset because I hadn't taken care of *myself*.

I rushed home after the seminar and was barely through the door when I asked Peter to speak with me alone. I told him what I'd been feeling. I had five specific requests to make of him and Clio:

- I wanted them to clean up any signs of sex, including towels left on the floor, immediately afterward, before I woke up and saw them.
- I wanted Peter to wear a robe or other clothing when moving between my bedroom and the room he was staying in with Clio.
- I wanted Peter and Clio to shower after having sex and before coming to bed with me (we agreed after the first night to try co-sleeping).
- If Peter and Clio slept with me in our bed, I wanted them both to wear pajamas or other clothing.
- I wanted Peter to return to bed with me before he fell asleep.

We soon scuttled that last one, as I grew more comfortable and Peter and Clio's relationship deepened. I relaxed many of the others too, over time. (Now an empty condom wrapper on the floor elicits an eye-roll and smirk, at most.) They were crucial, though, in the early days of Peter and Clio's relationship, as my emotions struggled to catch up with my rational mind.

The best compromises are those that allow everyone to have their needs met in ethical, compassionate ways. For example, say you want to go on a date, but your partner wants you to spend more time with your kids. A compromise might be to schedule the date for late in the evening, after you've had time to help your children with their homework and they've gone to bed. Both objectives are met.

On the other hand, a compromise like agreeing not to have any other relationships until the kids have left home might be a boundary violation. If polyamory is essential to your happiness and part of your identity, this compromise requires giving up a part of who you are. With such a compromise, it's reasonable to question whether "spending time with the kids" has become a proxy for "I want a monogamous relationship, so I'm using concerns about the children as a pretext."

When we are asked to compromise in ways that require us to give up our agency or our ability to advocate for our needs, these compromises also threaten to violate our boundaries. Many parts of our lives are available for negotiation, but compromising away our agency or bodily integrity (for example, by agreeing to have sex with someone we might not want to, or agreeing to limits on what we are allowed to do with our bodies) means giving up control of our boundaries.

BOUNDARIES AND SINGLE/SOLO POLY PEOPLE

People who value autonomy highly and take a "solo poly" or "free agent" approach to polyamory face some special considerations around boundaries. Relationships that don't follow the traditional escalator (dating, moving in together, marrying, having kids) are often perceived as less important, serious or legitimate than traditional relationships. So, unsurprisingly, these relationships are sometimes not treated seriously, even in the poly community. Many polyamorous people still carry conventional social expectations about how relationships "should" look.

For these reasons, free agents must state their boundaries and advocate for their needs very early on. "I'm never likely to live with you, but I still consider this relationship significant, and I still want to feel free to express what I need and have you consider my needs" represents a reasonable boundary. As a single/solo poly person, you also need to be clear on the value your existing relationships have to you and what your commitment is to them, or they may be trivialized in the minds of potential partners who don't understand what commitment looks like to you.

A common complaint from solo poly folks is that many people assume they're only looking for casual sex. Because society so tightly conflates sex, relationships and life interconnection, this can be an easy mistake to make. But not wanting to move in does not necessarily mean only wanting casual sex. Negotiating boundaries around sex, particularly the expectations attached to it, is important to help solo poly people navigate the tangled thicket of assumptions that might pop up.

Because solo poly people place a high emphasis on personal autonomy, things such as veto, hierarchies and rules that constrain how the relationship is allowed to grow are especially problematic. Most solo polyamorists we have met will not enter such arrangements. Ironically, people who do seek prescriptive hierarchies and look for "secondary" partners will often gravitate toward solo poly people, erroneously believing that if solo poly people don't want the trappings of a conventional relationship, they don't become seriously invested in their relationships. This misperception often leads to pain.

The free-agent model can also have a dark side. Just as people who try to prescribe a specific relationship structure can misuse boundary language to control others, people who prefer a free-agent model can use boundaries around their personal decision-making as a way to avoid responsibility for the consequences of what they do. The choices we make belong to us, but so do their consequences. If you emphasize personal autonomy to the exclusion of listening to your partners' needs, you're not asserting boundaries, you're being a jerk.

SETTING NEW BOUNDARIES

Early in our relationships, when everything is going well, we're inclined to overlook faults and annoyances. Our hormones are telling us we want to become one with our partners: share everything with them, love them forever. This is when setting boundaries is most important in order to lay a good long-term foundation—and also when we're least likely to set them.

This is also when codependency can take root: patterns laid down now can entrench over the years, our personalities can polarize in over-functioning/underfunctioning dynamics (where one partner "takes care" of the other, removing their agency) or other unhealthy patterns, and the boundaries around our sense of self can blur. If we get stuck in a dysfunctional dynamic and want to reclaim our selves and re-establish a healthy relationship balance, we need to learn how to set new boundaries in old relationships.

Even in perfectly healthy relationships, people can change. What was okay last year may not be okay today. When relationships are good, they make us better, they make our lives bigger, and it's easy to forget about our boundaries, because there is no reason to enforce them. Yet when communication erodes, when trust comes into question, when we feel out of control or deeply unhappy and *then* we try to set a boundary, the experience can be terrifying.

Setting a new boundary is a change, and change is rarely comfortable. To your partner, the change can feel non-consensual. The key with boundaries is that you always set them around those things that are *yours*: your body, your mind, your emotions, your time, intimacy with you. You *always* have a right to regulate access to what is yours. But by the time the boundaries of your self have become blurred with those of your partner, setting boundaries and defining your self feels like taking something away from her that she had come to regard as hers.

Harriet Lerner's *Dance of Intimacy* (listed in the resources) is an excellent tool for anyone needing help with setting relationship boundaries. Lerner describes the "change back" responses that are common when a new boundary is set. When we establish a new way of doing things, our partners work to re-establish the old, comfortable pattern. Countermoves take numerous forms, from outright denial to criticism to threats to end the relationship. The trick with countermoves is to not try to stop them, but to allow them to happen while holding firm in the change we have made.

And if *your* partner is setting a new boundary, remember that he has a right to do so, even if it means he's revoking consent to things he agreed to before. The change may hurt, but the solution is not to violate the boundaries or try to talk your partner out of them. No one should ever be punished for setting personal boundaries, or for withholding or revoking consent.

PUSHING GENTLY BACK

People rarely cross our boundaries intentionally, unless we're in an actively abusive situation. However, people sometimes cross them accidentally. Because of this, healthy boundaries need flexibility. They can't be so brittle that the slightest touch threatens to end a relationship. There must be some allowance for the fact that we are all born of frailty and error. We need to be able to accept a certain amount of push, and reassert our boundaries by pushing gently back. We need to be able to say, "Hey, I would prefer you not do this thing," rather than "You monster! How dare you!"

This is a tricky balancing act, because predators and abusers are skilled at probing boundaries. One of the tools of a predator is to ignore a no in small ways, testing how we respond, finding weaknesses, and choosing people who won't reassert a no. (Gavin de Becker talks about the "tests" a predator gives to potential targets in his book *The Gift of Fear*.) Protecting ourselves from those who have genuinely evil intent means being willing to reassert our boundaries—or end a relationship—in the face of repeated infringement, even as we allow some flexibility for unintended boundary violations (such as the ones Eve experienced early in Peter's relationship with Clio, described earlier).

SUDDEN LEFT TURNS

Over the years, Franklin has received thousands of emails through his polyamory site. Some of these emails are heartbreaking: they might start off describing the ordinary sorts of difficulties that can happen in any poly relationship, but midway through, they suddenly veer off into wildly unhealthy, dysfunctional dynamics.

Franklin has started referring to these as "sudden left turn" emails. They start out normally, but then take a sudden left turn into the swamp. In one such email, a woman wrote to say that she and her fiancé had always had a monogamous relationship, with no mention of polyamory. Then, after the wedding, her husband told her he felt monogamy was unnatural and harmful (as she put it, "he said the idea of monogamy is even more perverted than homosexuality" and "monogamous relationships cause sexuality to atrophy"), and he demanded that he be free to have other lovers.

Another talked about a couple opening up to polyamory, in which the man told his wife, "If we do this, I only want you to have sex with other women. I don't want you to have sex with other men." As mentioned previously, it's common for men to feel threatened by other men and to seek to forbid their partners to have other male lovers. In this case, however, the woman identified as straight. Her partner demanded that she become bisexual.

A common problem Franklin has received many emails about concerns someone in a poly relationship—usually a partner of a person who's started dating someone new—who feels insecure. Insecurity can happen in any relationship, of course. In these cases, however, the insecure partner will try to deal with the insecurity by demanding to read every email and text with the new partner, hear everything they talk about (sometimes even listening in on phone conversations)—and become extremely angry at the suggestion that there might be some expectation of privacy.

Almost all of these emails end with "Is this normal? If I am polyamorous, does that mean I have to accept this?" No, it isn't. And no, you don't. Polyamory is a relatively new cultural phenomenon. Our society has a great deal of experience with monogamy, so the warning signs of coercion or abuse in a monogamous relationship are well-known. In polyamory, however, we are blazing a new trail. Few people have significant experience in polyamorous relationships, so the warning signs of trouble may not be so clear.

There are many signs of a harmful relationship dynamic, but the most unmistakable one is fear. *Why am I so afraid in this relationship when there's no imminent physical danger?* If you find you are asking yourself this question, check your boundaries. Do you know where they are? How much power have you given to others to affect your well-being, your self-esteem, even your desire to live? Remember, when you give someone the power to affect you and to come into your mind, you are only loaning what belongs to you. If you are afraid, you have given too much. When you look forward, do you see choices? Is leaving the relationship a viable option? Is changing the relationship a viable option? Is setting new boundaries an option? What happens if you say no?

It is unnerving when a relationship becomes permeated by fear, but this is often the trajectory of a relationship that lacks consent. It starts when you begin to bend yourself around your fears instead of embracing your dreams. We see plenty of relationships fall apart in sadness, anger, hurt and feelings of betrayal—but fear is worse.

If, on the other hand, your partner has started expressing new boundaries with you, ethics and decency demand a compassionate response. Remember that people express boundaries to protect themselves, and we all have the right to do this. Access to another person's body and mind is a privilege, not a right. Nobody should ever be punished for expressing a boundary or for revoking consent.

BOUNDARIES AND PSYCHOLOGICAL HEALTH

One place where boundaries in any romantic relationship can become especially difficult to navigate is around issues of mental health. Each of us has the right to set whatever boundaries we want, and these include boundaries concerning partners with mental health issues. We don't always like to acknowledge this, but it's true. A person who grew up with an alcoholic parent might be sensitive around dealing with substance abuse, for example, and might set a boundary that she will not start a relationship with someone who drinks or uses drugs.

That's a choice each of us is allowed to make. We can decline to enter into a relationship for any reason. This extends to mental health. We have a right to decide whether we will become—or remain—romantically involved with someone who suffers from depression, anxiety or any other psychological illness. While the stigma surrounding mental health issues needs to be confronted, and compassion and understanding for people coping with such issues are essential, we are not required to continue to engage in an intimate relationship with someone who suffers from a psychological health problem that may compromise our own well-being. This is each person's own choice to make.

When we have these boundaries, however, it is our responsibility to express them, preferably before we have put someone else's heart on the line. We cannot expect, with this or any other kind of boundary, another person to guess our boundaries.

And if we hear about a boundary that we know applies to us, it is also our responsibility to say so, even when it's difficult. Often mental health issues are surrounded by walls of shame and guilt; they are not easy to talk about. But again, people cannot consent to be in relationships with us if that consent is not informed. If a prospective partner has expressed a boundary and you don't feel safe sharing your history of mental health issues or substance abuse, that's okay, but it's still ethically necessary to tell that partner, "I don't think we're compatible."

We can't, though, guarantee to a partner that we'll never develop a mental health issue in the future. When this happens, it is certainly reasonable to ask your partner for help and support. But remember that your romantic partner is not your therapist. Expecting a partner to play that role is likely to place a heavy burden on your partner and the relationship, and unlikely to help you overcome serious issues. Talking to a qualified mental health professional is far more likely to succeed.

Having, and being able to assert, good personal boundaries is a vital prerequisite for the next part of creating frameworks for successful poly relationships, negotiating agreements and rules. Only by clearly understanding where your own boundaries lie can you hope to work out relationship agreements that meet your needs while still honoring the needs of everyone else involved.

QUESTIONS TO ASK YOURSELF

If you aren't sure whether a problem is just a normal bump or points instead to a boundary violation, ask yourself these questions. A yes for any of them is a sign of trouble.

- *Is my partner asking me to give up control of my autonomy, my body or my emotions?*

- *Am I being asked to consent to something in a way that I can't later withdraw my consent?*

- *Am I afraid to say I may need to leave this relationship?*

- *Am I afraid to say no or to disagree with my partner?*

- *Is someone threatening my well-being, safety or livelihood?*

- *Are decisions about my actions or access to my body being made without my involvement or consent?*

- *Am I being asked to participate in, or be complicit in, something I consider dishonest or unethical?*

- *Does my partner make me feel worse about myself?*

- *Am I being asked to give up relationships with friends or family?*

- *Do I feel I have no expectation of privacy in my other relationships?*

- *Do I feel that my partner considers me inferior to him or to his other partners?*

- *Am I asked to "respect" my partner or her other partners, but feel that this respect is not reciprocated?*

- *Am I afraid to express my boundaries? Do I feel they won't be respected?*

- *Am I treated as an adjunct to, or as an extension of, my partner's other relationships, rather than as a person in my own right?*

RULES AND AGREEMENTS

An intimate relationship is one in which neither party silences, sacrifices, or betrays the self and each party expresses strength and vulnerability, weakness and competence in a balanced way.

HARRIET LERNER

One of the first questions people new to poly often ask is "What kinds of rules should we have?" This is especially true when they are opening an existing relationship. The issue of rules is a complicated, charged topic. Many people have strong feelings about rules in poly relationships. Rules that work, rules that don't, alternatives to rules, distinctions between rules and agreements—these are issues we carefully take apart in the next few chapters.

For most people, monogamy comes with a set of expectations and rules bundled in. Some areas aren't necessarily clear—for example, some monogamous couples consider flirting to be a violation of the rules, while others don't—but for the most part, we know the expectations of monogamy. It's tempting, then, to look at the rules that come packaged with monogamy and say, "Okay, so what rules do we use for polyamory?"

This approach works for some people, but there are dangers in thinking about relationships in terms of rules. For instance, we both often hear people say, "Any rules are okay if you both agree to them." This saying underscores how stubbornly the assumptions of monogamy and couplehood can cling, even in communities that ostensibly practice non-monogamy. It assumes there are *only two* people, that those two will be negotiating with each other (but not with others), that their needs are of prime importance, that they will call the shots, and that they can make decisions for anyone else who becomes involved with either one of them about the best way to build relationships. What matters is what *they both* agree to, not what *everyone* agrees to.

We encourage an approach to relationships that gives a voice to all the stakeholders.

Many people starting polyamorous relationships also want to know: "How can I keep things from changing? And what guarantees do I have that things won't go wrong?" Rules are usually an attempt to answer these questions. The answers we offer are: you can't, and you don't have any. And that's okay.

Before we go into that, it's helpful to clarify the difference between a *rule* and an *agreement*. Rules, agreements and boundaries are all, at their core, mechanisms for changing behavior. The differences are in how these different things go about doing it, what assumptions they make, how they are created, and whom they apply to.

AGREEMENTS INVOLVE ALL PARTIES

As we use the word, *agreements* are negotiated codes of conduct established among people who are involved with each other. An agreement is a covenant negotiated by *all* the parties it affects. Something negotiated between one set of people—a couple, for example—and then presented as a take-it-or-leave-it proposition to others is not an agreement as we define it: we call that a *rule*. If Edouard says, "I never want you to spend the night with anyone else," and Maria says, "Okay," this is not an agreement—because it affects Maria's other partner Josef, who wasn't consulted. If his voice is absent from the negotiations, Edouard and Maria have instituted a rule.

Agreements also allow for renegotiation by any of the people they affect. An agreement that does not permit renegotiation is more like a rule. An agreement that is binding on people who did not negotiate it *is* a rule. Here are some examples of agreements:

- If one of us wants to spend the night with someone else, we will let the others know in advance so we can discuss it.

- If one of us wants to have sex with someone else without barriers, we will all first discuss sexual history, risk and testing before we reach a decision.
- We will immediately talk about a situation that make us feel threatened, rather than sitting on it.
- We will not start new relationships while there are problems in our existing relationships.
- We will negotiate safer-sex boundaries with each of our new partners.
- We will make our sexual health information available to new partners who want it.

Even when the negotiations include all parties, you must still take care to make the negotiations equitable for everyone. Power in a relationship is almost never distributed equally. When a new person starts a relationship with one or more people who are already together, the newcomer will probably have less power than they do. He is likely to bear the brunt of their disagreements or any resentments they have between each other. In an ethical negotiation, any person with a disproportionate amount of power must negotiate compassionately, rather than using that power to browbeat others to "consensus."

RULES PLACE RESTRICTIONS WITHOUT NEGOTIATION

As the term is used in this book, *rules* are binding limitations placed on someone's behavior that are not up for negotiation. Even when a rule is agreed to, it's a mandate that can only be obeyed or broken. Breaking a rule is assumed to have consequences, such as loss of the relationship.

Agreements sometimes become rules. The defining element of a rule is a restriction placed on someone without their input or negotiation. A trivial example of a rule is that Eve and Peter don't permit shoes to be worn in their home. Everyone visiting must follow it. The consequence of breaking it is that you will probably not be invited back. Some examples of poly rules we've seen people using or trying to use are:

- We will never spend the night at another lover's house; we will always come home at night.

- We will always use barriers when one of us has sex with another lover.
- We will not refer to any other partner by the same pet names we use with each other.
- We can have sex with other people, but we won't love another person as much as or more than we love each other.
- We will not bring any other lover to our favorite restaurant.
- If one of us wants the other to break up with another partner, we will do it. (This is called a "veto" and is discussed in chapter 12).
- We will not have sex with other partners in certain sexual positions, or if the other is not there.
- We will only start relationships with people who are willing to be in a relationship with both (or all) of us.
- We will only start relationships with people who are willing to be exclusive to both (or all) of us.

These rules may sound a lot like the agreements listed in the previous section. They all start with "We." The difference is that all of the rules listed here materially affect a third person who did not have a role in negotiating them, and that person must accept them or leave the relationship(s).

The absence or presence of empowerment is a litmus test for whether something is a rule or an agreement. Are all the people affected empowered to make their objections heard? Will the others consider the objections seriously, or will some people's objections always be overruled? What happens if someone wants a structure that doesn't work for someone else? Are negotiation and compromise possible, or is leaving the only alternative? Agreements empower people, whereas rules enforce power imbalances.

On a practical level, it is not always possible to make another person feel empowered. Indeed, we have noticed on many occasions that it's the person who feels disempowered who insists on rules, and then sees attempts to negotiate or modify the rules as further evidence of disempowerment. Feelings are not always congruent with reality.

Neither of us has met anyone who makes up rules by rolling dice or drawing words out of a hat. A rule is made to solve a problem or meet a need. However, making rules can quickly become complicated, because it's very easy to confuse *needs* with *feelings*. A person who says, "I don't ever want you to spend the night with another lover" might think the rule serves a need, such as "I need to wake up with you in the morning." But if we examine that need, it may come down to "I feel lonely if I wake up by myself." The rule is meant to prevent triggering a negative feeling, in this case a feeling of loneliness. The actual issue—"I feel lonely when I wake up alone"—is not being directly addressed.

Leading with the need ("How can we help make sure I understand how I am valued by you?"), rather than the action, opens the door to finding ways to solve the problem without imposing rules.

HOW AGREEMENTS BECOME RULES

When someone talks about why they need a *rule*, they tell you something about their fears. So it's not surprising that agreements become rules when they are grounded in fear. It often goes like this: people in a relationship—often a couple—sit down and negotiate a set of relationship agreements. At this point there aren't any new partners, so the people negotiating the agreements rarely consider the effect their agreements will have on others. Then a new person comes along. The partners present the new person with the agreement, with the expectation that the new person will sign on. She has little investment in the relationship at this point—and may be inexperienced with polyamory and unfamiliar with any other models of it—so she agrees.

After a time, one or more of the original people experience some sort of insecurity or feel threatened. The newer person is blamed for violating the agreement—sometimes a subtle, creative interpretation of it. The existing partners either end the relationship with the newer person over this infraction or use the infraction to justify imposing greater restrictions. Well, she agreed to it, right? What gives her the right to complain now?

When things go wrong—when an agreement is hurting someone or isn't having the intended effect and needs to be renegotiated—saying "But you agreed to this!" is just twisting the knife (and never helps solve the problem). At the beginning of a relationship, we are not yet emotionally invested in it, and we don't know how it will progress. So it can be easy to accept rules or agreements that later, as we become more vulnerable and more emotionally invested, become quite painful.

FRANKLIN'S STORY I had an agreement with my wife, Celeste, that no other partner would live with us. This agreement was presented to all of my new partners, including Bella and Amber. They both agreed to it—and why not? At the start of dating someone, living together often seems vague and remote.

So they agreed easily. There was no emotional investment yet, no pull toward a shared life. The prohibition on living together didn't become a source of pain until much later—in Bella's case, years later. Once we had built a deep, loving relationship, that pull toward a shared life began. And the agreement I had with Celeste left no room for that. The fact that Bella and Amber had signed on to this restriction up front did not change the fact that they were not allowed to express their needs when the nature of the relationship between us changed.

Bella was never allowed to renegotiate this agreement, and our relationship suffered because of it. Eventually it ended. After ten years of trying to remain within the constraints of my agreements with Celeste, Bella found it simply too painful to remain with me.

The truth, which we never acknowledged directly, was that my agreement with Celeste had less to do with sharing a roof than preventing certain types of relationships. My relationship with Bella was painful and crippled because the real, unspoken intent of the agreements, the reason these agreements were important to Celeste, was that she didn't want me in a relationship of such depth and significance that I *wanted* to live with another partner. The agreements achieved covertly what a direct statement could not do overtly: they created an environment so inflexible, so hostile to intimacy, that close, intimate relationships would suffer.

Rules that new partners are expected to sign on to, but which they have little or no say in, rarely provide space for new relationships to grow. Sometimes these rules are deliberately designed to keep new relationships away from sunlight and water, forcing them to remain stunted or to wither away altogether.

It's not possible to ever feel completely secure in a relationship whose structures are built on fear. Even if you follow all the rules, or the rules are easy for you, at some level you will always be aware that another person's potential fears are a driving force in the relationship. If the day comes when that person is afraid of you, look out.

In extreme cases, rules can become tools of emotional blackmail. They constitute a contract that specifies acts of betrayal, and a person who breaks a rule is cast in the role of the villain. Rules-based systems judge people's characters on the basis of adherence to the rules. When rules are used as a tool with which to attack someone's character—especially when the attacks are based on creative interpretations of the rules—they become a nearly invisible but extremely corrosive form of emotional abuse.

ALTERNATIVES TO RULES

Some of Franklin's most controversial (and popular) blog posts concern what he calls rules-based relationships. His skepticism about rules has led a lot of people to believe that he opposes them altogether. So we want to make clear that when we talk about relationships that are not rules-*based*, we're not talking about relationships with no rules whatever. Rather, we're talking about relationships that don't use rules as the first go-to problem-solving tactic, and which don't attempt to deal with emotional or security issues by creating frameworks of rules.

Many people say, "I need rules in my relationship," but when they are asked why, it quickly becomes obvious that what they need is actually something else. It is usually something like security or stability, a sense of empowerment, predictability, or safety. Those are all reasonable needs. What's not obvious is that it's possible to have those things without rules.

Conflating rules with needs is common, because we live in societies that teach us we need external structures and authority in order to act like civilized people. Many of us internalize the idea that the only way we can rely on people to behave with kindness, responsibility, respect and compassion is to create rigid codes compelling them to. We believe that if people make choices from personal autonomy, then responsibilities will be neglected and kindness will fade.

In reality, relationships without rules are (usually) far from a madhouse in which everyone does whatever they want without regard for anyone else. Instead, if you look at such relationships, they tend to show very high levels of communication, negotiation, compassion and understanding. Does this surprise you? We often think of "rules" and "commitment" as being almost interchangeable: we demonstrate commitment by agreeing to rules that limit our behavior. From that position, it can be hard to imagine what a relationship without rules would even look like, except perhaps a free-for-all.

Relationships, especially cohabiting relationships, often involve many commitments and responsibilities. One might think, *How can I be sure the kid will be picked up from school if I don't have a rule telling my partner to be home by 3:30 on weekdays? If there's no rule against late-night dates, how do I know my partner will be able to get up in the morning to go to work?* And the answer is: you don't. But if a partner is willing to skip out on commitments and responsibilities, she's probably *just as willing to break rules!*

To understand relationships that are not rules-based, we need to go back to two of the themes we emphasize in this book: trust and boundaries. You have to trust that your partners want to take care of you—that given the freedom to do whatever they choose, they will make choices that respect your needs and honor their commitments. Placing that level of trust in someone can be scary. Rules can feel safer. But they're not. And they hide the real concerns. Talking about the things I need can feel scary and vulnerable; it's easier to say, "I want you to be home every night before midnight" than to say "I feel lonely when I wake up in an empty bed without you. How can we work together to deal with that?"

Poly blogger Andrea Zanin has said: "Rules have an inverse relationship to trust. They are intended to bind someone to someone else's preferences. They are aimed at constraint. I will limit you, and you will limit me, and then we'll both be safe." The problem with rules, though, is we can never actually force our partners to abide by them. A partner who can't be trusted to meet your needs can't be trusted to follow your rules. What you need is a trustworthy partner. And you need to be trustworthy yourself.

Sometimes rules try to compensate for poor boundaries. We've talked to many people who say they use rules to "prevent drama" or to protect themselves from someone who might want to "split them up." We believe such rules aren't necessary if we know, have and assert good boundaries. Nobody can make you and your partner split up, or engage you in drama, if you don't agree to it. If you can simply say "No, I won't participate in this dynamic," or "I choose to remain with my partner. I'm not interested in dissolving this relationship," then you don't need to rely on structures or rules to attempt to do that for you.

In the end, whether you choose to rely on putting in place rules or agreements, or simply advocating for your needs and giving your partners the opportunity to address them, no relationship will succeed if your partners don't want to invest in it. If they cannot be trusted to make the relationship work, it won't, rules be damned.

RULES AS "TRAINING WHEELS"

Another common idea in the poly community is the notion of rules as "training wheels," a way to learn the skills to navigate poly relationships without feeling threatened. A person (or more often a couple) may start out with a list of highly restrictive rules, thinking they will learn trust by seeing other people obey the restrictions. Then, once that trust has been built, the rules can slowly be relaxed.

This idea may have become popular from the observation that lots of successful poly relationships seem to have grown this way. A couple or group will sometimes start out drawing up a long, detailed relationship agreement with many pages of rules and specifications, and then, as it's renegotiated over time, it becomes ever simpler and more general, until perhaps a ten-page document has been condensed to something like "Use good judgment. Be thoughtful. Take responsibility. Don't be a dick." The group's success makes this strategy look like a winner, and they proudly blog about it.

In fact, we believe the popularity of this idea confuses cause and effect. Because they were thoughtful people who take responsibility, they didn't need ten pages of rules in the first place. And if they hadn't been thoughtful people, the rules wouldn't have helped.

"Training wheels" rules are a seductive idea. They offer a justification for a tightly restricted model of poly, but also offer the promise that someday they won't be necessary. We have even been told that empowered poly relationships are only an option for people who already have lots of poly experience or a secure attachment style. Everyone else starting out is supposed to need the comfort of rules to learn the trust that leads to poly enlightenment.

The biggest problem with the "training wheels" metaphor is that it treats people as things. In the case of a couple, they're telling new partners, "We don't really trust you, and we don't have the skills to treat you well, so we're going to use you as practice to learn how to treat our future partners well." The idea is, if you don't trust your partner, the way to gain trust is to restrict her—and anyone else she is involved with.

But not everyone learns to ride a bike by using training wheels. Some people even believe that relying on training wheels teaches bad habits that must be unlearned when the training wheels come off. In polyamorous relationships, using rules to avoid dealing with thorny problems like jealousy and insecurity can cause us to learn some very bad relationship habits indeed. Even under the best of circumstances, talking about our fears and insecurities is hard. When we talk about our frailties, we become exposed and vulnerable, and that is uncomfortable. Relying on rules to deal with these feelings teaches us that we don't have to talk about them, which prevents us from learning the skills we need to find lasting solutions.

The entire purpose of many relationship rules is risk avoidance. If we already have a relationship when we start exploring polyamory, it's natural to say "I would like to protect the relationship I already have, so I want to explore polyamory without risk." If we come to poly when we're single, it's natural to say "I want to protect my heart, so when I have a partner, I will ask her not to do anything that makes me feel threatened."

Unfortunately, when you seek to reduce risk by imposing constraints on other people's behavior, you transfer that risk onto others. By doing this you say, "I want to explore polyamory but I don't want to take this risk, so I will transfer it onto any new partners, by asking them to be open and vulnerable while also limiting how much they are allowed to advocate for their own needs." We feel that doing this is a form of treating people as things.

We know we're expecting a great deal of courage by suggesting that you start exploring polyamory without relying on rules to feel safe. It does seem that the secret to healthy, dynamic relationships keeps coming back to courage. Forget training wheels. Forget trying to figure out the right rules that will keep you safe forever; there is no safe forever. Instead, go into the world seeking to treat others with compassion whenever you touch them. Try to leave people better than when you found them. Communicate your needs. Understand and advocate for your boundaries. And look for other people who will do the same. Trust them when they say they love you; where communication and compassion exist, you don't need rules to keep you safe. We don't learn how to be compassionate by disenfranchising other people; we learn how to be compassionate by practicing compassion.

LIMITED-DURATION RULES

Sometimes a rule can be useful, even necessary. When you're up to your ass in alligators, sometimes you just need the alligators off your ass for a while.

We recognize that the work it takes to become secure and confident is *hard*. In some situations, rules that are specific, narrow in scope and, most importantly, limited in duration can be valuable tools for problem-solving. If you've found that some thing your partners are doing just absolutely drives you crazy, asking them to temporarily stop doing it can give you the emotional space to process whatever's underneath.

EVE'S STORY   When I first started dating Ray, Peter and I had extremely strict boundaries around sexual health, which included barriers for giving and receiving oral sex. After a couple of months, and after Ray and I had exchanged STI test results, I wanted to stop using barriers for oral sex, but Peter didn't feel safe about it. I did my research and was able to give Peter what I believed were reliable sources showing how low the risk was that I would catch anything from Ray during those activities, but Peter was still uncomfortable.

He confessed that his discomfort was with the emotional implications of me and Ray having unprotected oral sex. I agreed to continue using barriers with Ray, as long as Peter agreed to work on his emotional blockage around the issue. We agreed to revisit the agreement in two weeks.

Two weeks later, we sat down again to talk about it. Peter said he had worked through his discomfort with me having that kind of sex with Ray, and our relationship proceeded.

Implementing time-limited rules can be helpful in specific situations, but there's also a risk in doing so: when we're comfortable, we tend to want to stay there. That's why we recommend a sunset clause in any rule: a way to say "After three weeks (or some other period of time), we will revisit this issue." And it goes on the calendar. How much time? That depends on the circumstances and the people, but broadly, for most people a week is too short and a year is too long.

A sunset clause doesn't mean you're under a deadline to fix the emotional issue. It's merely a promise to re-examine and renegotiate. You're asking your partners to trust that you are willing to work on whatever the underlying problem is. You're asking your partners to trust that you won't simply keep extending the rule every three weeks into infinity. Your partners are asking *you* to trust that they genuinely want to help support you in fixing the issue, that they are willing to give you space while you're working on it.

DO THE RULES SERVE THE PEOPLE?

It's incredibly easy to fall into prioritizing the rules of a relationship over the happiness of the people involved. We believe it's important to remember the ethical axiom: *The people in the relationship are more important than the relationship.* Sacrificing the happiness of human beings in the service of rules, rather than making rules that serve the needs of the people, takes us further away from joyful, fulfilling lives, not closer to them.

FRANKLIN'S STORY   Celeste and I negotiated rules that placed tight restrictions on me and my partners. Even when I became aware that these restrictions were not benefiting our relationships, I held on to the idea that I should honor my commitments above all else, even at the expense of my happiness. Only years later did I start to realize how much these restrictions were hurting not just me, but also my other partners.

It was easy to tell myself I was doing the right thing by saying "I will honor my commitments over my own needs." This gave me a sense of noble sacrifice: I loved Celeste so much, I was willing to give up my happiness for her! However, as years went by, doing this became harder when I saw that I was hurting other people too. Dismissing their pain by saying "It's okay, I'm honoring my commitments" started to feel unethical.

When my relationship with Celeste ended, we both became happier. We found relationships that were more aligned with what we wanted. In the end, my stubborn insistence on "honoring my commitment" without renegotiation deprived *her* of happiness, too.

Things ran off the rails when I started to believe I was subordinate to the needs of the commitments, rather than focusing on building commitments that served my needs and the needs of all the people I loved. When I made myself subordinate to the rules, it didn't make anyone happy—not me, not Celeste, and certainly not my other partners who ended up in harm's way because of it.

RE-EVALUATING AGREEMENTS

Anyone should be able to reopen discussions about an agreement at any time. It helps to think of agreements as mutable, organic things that will be revisited and modified as people grow and relationships change. When we see these structures as static, they can make relationships less rather than more stable, because they will fail to adapt to change...sometimes spectacularly.

A good relationship is not something you *have*, it's something you *do*. Over and over, the best, happiest relationships we have seen and been involved in are those whose members are constantly willing to renegotiate the groundwork beneath them. In fact, some people set periodic dates in their calendar when they will review their relationship agreements with each other to make sure they're still working and see if anything needs to change.

Both of us have experience with renegotiating our own long-term relationships. Eve tells three stories in this book (on pages 26–27, 62–63 and 296–98) about renegotiating her relationship with her husband, Peter. Franklin describes doing so with Amber on pages 29–30. These are lifelong partnerships that have endured because they were able to adapt to the changing circumstances around them and the changing people within them.

When looking at the structures of your relationship, ask yourself regularly: "Are they honest? Are they necessary? Are they kind? Are they respectful? Are they considerate of others?" If you've made agreements with an existing partner that you expect new partners to abide by, ask yourself, "Would I have become involved with my current partner if I were bound by these agreements at the start?"

CREEPING CONCESSIONS

Flexibility and willingness to renegotiate agreements are vital parts of a growing, thriving polyamorous relationship. There's a potential danger lurking in this flexibility, though, which we call "creeping concessions."

For example, neither one of us will ever enter a relationship with someone who has or wants a veto arrangement. That's a boundary. But sometimes people can end up in relationships that cross boundaries without their even noticing it. Perhaps you have a partner who's having difficulty and asks you to give up something while he works through his issue. You naturally want to support your partners, so you agree. Later that person may say, "Well, this still isn't working. Dreadfully sorry, but can you give up a little bit more? I'm really struggling with this."

Because our partner's happiness is important to you, you say yes. And perhaps time goes by and your partner says, "Look, um, I'm terribly sorry to bring this up, but I'm still having issues here. Can you perhaps find it in your heart to make this other small concession over here, just this one little thing that will really help me?" Bit by bit, inch by inch, you may find yourself negotiating away things that are important. If each individual step is small enough, you might give up a boundary without even seeing it.

At times we may be aware that we're conceding things we once thought inviolate, but we do it anyway because we've already invested so much. Economists have a name for this: the sunk cost fallacy. A "sunk cost" is an investment of time, energy, attention or something else that can't be recovered. If you spend a year in a relationship that isn't a good fit for you, you can't go back and get that year back again. The "fallacy" part involves making decisions for the future based on that past investment, rather than on whether the decisions are likely to benefit you in the future. Say, for example, you've bought tickets to a movie, and you realize early into the movie that you're not going to enjoy it. You've already bought the tickets; you can't get your money back. Do you stay and watch the movie and have a miserable time, or do you walk out and browse the bookstore, which is much more enjoyable? It's hard to walk away from the movie, although the cost of the tickets is gone either way.

When you're deciding whether to agree to a compromise or concession that gives you a sick feeling, knowing that the alternative might be to end the relationship, you might think, *I've invested a year of my life in this relationship. I can't let it go!* rather than *This relationship is not working, and if I make this concession, it's going to work even less. It is better to choose whether to agree based on my future happiness, not on the year I've already spent.*

AGREEMENTS ABOUT PRIVACY AND DISCLOSURE

We've talked a lot about how open, honest communication is, in our experience, absolutely essential to polyamory. However, we all have the right to set boundaries around access to our bodies and our emotions. One of those boundaries concerns privacy. The right to privacy is often considered a basic human right.

Balancing the need for disclosure with a reasonable expectation of privacy is not always easy. There is no bright line where one stops and the other starts. Rules that mandate either disclosure or secrecy can make sense. For example, communication about sexual boundaries and sexual health is necessary to give informed consent, and a rule that text messages will be kept private protects the intimacy and trust of partners. But it can be easy to go to extremes and create rules that violate someone's right to privacy or consent.

For example, as mentioned in the previous chapter, under "Sudden left turns," someone once emailed Franklin to say her husband wanted to see every single communication, such as texts and emails, between her and her boyfriend. Most of us would probably agree this is a serious violation of her boyfriend's privacy; it is difficult for intimacy to grow under the eye of an outside observer. We all need private spaces if we are to reveal to a lover the deepest parts of ourselves, the furthest corners of our hearts, and (especially!) the wounded and vulnerable places within ourselves.

Compulsory sharing is always a bit suspect. When others demand that we reveal ourselves, intimacy is undermined rather than strengthened, because something that is demanded cannot be shared freely as a gift. Intimacy is built by mutually consensual sharing, not by demands.

At the other extreme, some people insist on knowing absolutely nothing about a partner's other lovers. Not even how many, not even their names. These "Don't ask, don't tell" relationships raise troubling questions about boundaries, consent and denial. If we know nothing about a partner's other activities, we will find it difficult to make informed choices about our relationship—particularly the sexual aspects. "Don't ask, don't tell" relationships put outside lovers in an unenviable position too. Often such relationships include restrictions on calling a partner at home, and they almost always preclude visiting a partner at home, much less meeting the other partner to check on how this setup is sitting with him.

Demanding to know everything undermines intimacy, but so does demanding to know nothing. When we demand to know nothing, we cut ourselves off from a part of our partners' experience, and that must necessarily limit how intimate we can be.

The issue always seems to circle back to these questions: "How much do you trust your partners? How much do you trust your relationships? Do you trust your partners enough to allow intimacy, not limiting what you can hear? Do you trust your partners enough to leave them their private spaces, knowing that they will share things that are important and relevant to you so you can continue to make informed choices?"

DOUBLE STANDARDS

Rules that place different restrictions on different people are problematic in any situation, and polyamory is no exception. Double standards can be blatant and obvious: for example, Playboy founder Hugh Hefner is famous for having sexual relationships with multiple women simultaneously, all of whom are expected to have no lovers but him. But double standards can also be more subtle and sneaky. A common example is when a couple has a rule stating that they can interrupt each other's dates with other partners if a member of the couple needs attention, but their other partners are not allowed to interrupt the couple's dates with each other.

A double standard might not even be a hardship for the person agreeing to it. If someone genuinely does not want multiple partners, for instance, and is okay with his partner having other lovers, a rule that she can but he can't would not limit him. But it's still a double standard; the rules are still different for her than for him. (It also raises the question of why the rule exists. If she genuinely isn't interested in others, why was the rule imposed?)

Sometimes double standards are deliberately engineered to create different classes of people. If members of a couple claim the right to veto relationships with other people, but other partners are not given veto power over the couple's relationship, a deliberate double standard exists. The couple may see this double standard as a way to prevent new partners from "causing" them to break up.

Whenever rules apply unevenly to different people, there is potential for trouble, resentment and jealousy. (Ironically, double standards are often instituted as a way to prevent jealousy, at least within an established relationship, but far more often they end up creating it.) Rules that codify a double standard are disempowering. Be careful with rules that create double standards—both in setting them and, if you're starting a new relationship with someone who has them, in agreeing to them.

QUESTIONS TO ASK YOURSELF

When considering your needs for agreements or rules, or whether to sign on to someone else's, these questions can be useful.

- *What needs am I trying to address with this agreement?*

- *Does the agreement offer a path to success?*

- *Does everyone affected by the agreement have the opportunity to be involved in setting its terms?*

- *How is the agreement negotiated, and under what circumstances can it be renegotiated?*

- *What happens if the agreement doesn't work for my partners, or my partners' partners?*

- *Do I feel like I need rules to feel safe? If so, will the rules actually keep me safe?*

- *Are my rules equally binding on everyone they affect, or do they create a double standard?*

11
HIERARCHY AND PRIMARY/SECONDARY POLY

*You must love in such a way
that the person you love feels free.*

THÍCH NÁHT HẠNH

Whatever your position may be in a relationship network, polyamory brings risk. We have already talked about some of the ways people try to deal with these risks, not always wisely, and the strategies we recommend. Before we go further, we want to examine some of the underlying forces that shape any relationship. We're going to simplify—a lot—to construct a framework that lets us get our ideas across. The three main forces we will discuss here are *connection, commitment* and *power*.

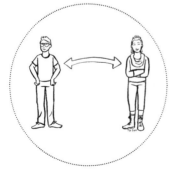

HOW HIERARCHIES EMERGE

Connection can mean a whole bunch of things, but here it represents what people see as the exciting bits of a relationship: intensity, passion, shared interests, sex, joy in each other's presence. It's the things that bring you together.

Commitment consists of what you build in a relationship over time. It includes expectations: perhaps of continuity, reliability, shared time and communication, activities that will be done together, or a certain public image. Commitment often supports life responsibilities, such as shared finances, a home, or children.

It's common for connection to start out very large and exciting and shrink as a relationship deepens and stabilizes, or sometimes to start out small, grow to a peak and then wane. Commitment tends to start small and grow. People in long-term, very committed relationships may still struggle to maintain connection.

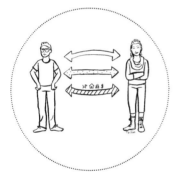

Each of these flows—connection, commitment—gives people *power* in a relationship. Power tends to be proportional to the size of the other flows. The more we've committed to a relationship, and the more connection we feel with someone, the greater the power that person has—to affect not only ourselves and our relationship with that person, but all our other relationships as well.

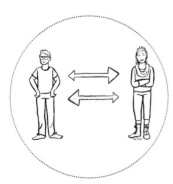

Ideally, the power flows within intimate relationships would always be equal. In practice, they often are not. Power imbalances tend to arise when the other flows are asymmetrical: when one person feels more connection or commitment than the other. That's normal. The person who feels less connection or commitment tends to hold more power. Other things influence power dynamics too, of course: things like economic or social status, physical dominance or persuasion skills.

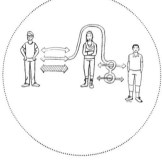

When someone is in a relationship with a large mutual commitment, especially when that commitment supports a lot of life responsibilities, it's common for a member of that relationship to feel threatened when a partner's new relationship has a really big connection—perhaps one that feels (and maybe really is) bigger than the existing connection.

Often, it's just the *idea* of a big connection that's scary, even when the flow is new and small. And the idea of a partner creating significant commitments to a new partner may feel (and sometimes is) threatening to the commitments that already exist.

One way people deal with this fear is by using the power from within their own relationship to restrict the connection, commitment, or both in other relationships.

Such restrictions have a couple of defining features:

- *Authority.* A person or people in one relationship, usually called the "primary" relationship, have the authority to restrict other relationships, often called "secondary."
- *Asymmetry.* The people within the secondary relationships do not have the same authority to limit the primary relationship.

When these two elements are present within a poly relationship, that relationship is hierarchical.

WHAT IS HIERARCHY?

Some people use the word *hierarchy* whenever one relationship has more commitments or responsibilities than another—for instance, members of a long-married couple with a house and kids becoming involved with a friend-with-benefits. This is *not* how we are using the word *hierarchy* in this book. When we talk here about a hierarchy, we mean a very specific *power dynamic:* where one relationship is subject to the control of someone outside that relationship. For instance, a hierarchy exists if a third party has the power to veto a relationship or limit the amount of time the people in it can spend together.

You can't throw a calendar in a group of poly people without hitting a hierarchical relationship. Hierarchical behavior might take the form of a rule that "No other partner may ever live with us," for example. Alternatively, it might manifest as restrictions on how strong another relationship is allowed to become, or on what a new person is allowed to do, where they are allowed to go, or what they are allowed to feel. Some common examples of prescriptions in hierarchical polyamory are:

- The primary couple always comes first with regard to time or other resources.
- Each member of the primary couple can veto any secondary partner of the other. (We discuss vetoes in detail in the next chapter.)
- Members of the primary couple are not permitted to spend the night with a secondary partner.
- Members of the primary couple pledge to love each other most.
- If the members of the primary relationship run into trouble or feel threatened, they can put secondary relationships "on hold" while they work things out between them.

People often assume these prescriptions are okay because secondary relationships are "casual"—but often they are not. Some secondary relationships are emotionally serious, long-lasting and deeply committed. (Franklin's hierarchical secondary relationship with Bella, described on pages 194–95, lasted a decade.) Nevertheless, secondary relationships are defined as relationships subordinate to a primary relationship—by rules, structures or agreements determined by the primary partners.

FRANKLIN'S STORY   When Celeste and I first started practicing polyamory in 1988, before we had the word *polyamory*, neither of us had any idea there were other people trying to do the same thing we were. Without the support of other polyamorous people, we had to make things up as we went along. We talked a great deal, trying to decide how we could do this non-monogamy thing. We tried to create rules for our relationship that we could both live with and that we thought would help us each feel secure and happy.

We were so busy thinking about protecting ourselves that we didn't think about the happiness of anyone else who might become involved with us. As a result, our rules focused on our own relationship. We thought that if we preserved the relationship between the two of us, the "core relationship," we were doing the right thing. We never considered that rules that worked for us might not work for the other people we would come to love, and we certainly never looked at our relationship from their perspective.

Prioritization of relationships does not necessarily imply hierarchy by our definition. For example, the two of us each have a partner (not each other) with whom we live and own property. Sharing a home means we have financial commitments that lead us to prioritize whom we spend money on. The mortgage must be paid before we spend a lot on dates! And if we start dating a new partner, that new person doesn't immediately get a vote on whether we sell the house.

Other examples: You probably don't give the keys to your car to someone on the first date. And most parents, mono or poly, are rightly cautious about whom they introduce their young children to, and when. Exercising your personal judgment in these kinds of decisions, and expecting your partners to make good judgments, is not displaying a hierarchy toward the person affected. Nor is requiring a partner to get your consent for things that concern both of you (such as property or children).

But if you control when and how your partner can make relationship decisions with *others*, and this prescription is intended to overrule the choices of your partner and his other partner, that is hierarchy.

Children are often used to justify hierarchy. If you are co-parenting, hopefully you are co-parenting with someone whose judgment you trust, and whom you trust to protect your children's interests. Deciding what parenting values you both share and will honor, and setting mutually agreed expectations for shared responsibilities and the structure you will provide for the children, is not imposing hierarchy per se, if the parents trust each other to make decisions within their other relationships that honor their commitments to one another and the kids.

The relationship structure becomes a hierarchy, though, when one partner expects to make decisions about how the other partner will conduct their other relationships, or what level those other relationships will be permitted to reach, to ensure that the commitments to the children are—in their opinion—met.

COUPLE FOCUS

Hierarchy almost always focuses on a couple. The couple may explicitly choose a hierarchical model as a way to add other relationships "on the side," or they may not realize how hierarchical they will become in a pinch, but to these people, the couple is always the relationship that matters. The emphasis on a "core couple" can permeate a relationship in ways that are both obvious and subtle. When it is taken to its extreme, a couple may see others as simply expendable, to be ditched without warning or explanation at any sign of trouble. A lot of single poly people who became involved with a couple who they thought loved and respected them have tales to tell about abrupt loss of all contact: phone calls and emails unanswered and no further communication.

FRANKLIN'S STORY   Celeste's family had a Christmas tradition: every year her entire family, no matter how far-flung, would get together at her parents' house for the holiday celebration. Because she and I were married we both attended, and because she was closeted about polyamory to her family, we never considered inviting any of my other partners—or even asking them what they might like to do for the holiday. I was simply unavailable to them, regardless of what they wanted. Far from being something that was negotiated, this situation was a given. Celeste and I didn't think to ask whether my other partners might want to spend time with me over the holidays, so I was blind to the idea that this might matter to them at all.

We had other, more far-reaching rules. At the beginning of our relationship, Celeste and I decided that no other partners would be allowed to live with us, that I would not love anyone else as much as I loved Celeste, that I would never say "I love you" to any other partner, and that I would never share finances with anyone else. We didn't consciously decide to ignore the needs or happiness of any secondary partners—we didn't think about them at all! We never considered, "What if someone wants to live with us?" or "What if being forbidden to tell someone I love her hurts her?"

People in hierarchical primary relationships may view a secondary partner's needs or expectations as a problem, or even imagine that future secondary partners should not have needs or expectations at all. If they even think that far: as with Franklin and Celeste, the happiness of the secondary partner may not even have occurred to them.

The members of a primary couple may have a belief—even a tacit, almost unconscious belief—that having more than one primary partner is not possible. Many new polyamorous people believe you can have only one primary partner, as in the monogamy ideal: they believe when push comes to shove, you can *really* only love one person. This model might be called "polyamory as modified monogamy," including the idea that you can only have one "soulmate" while still having multiple lovers.

REASONS FOR HIERARCHY

In many ways polyamory can be disruptive, and hierarchy can seem like a way to keep that disruption at bay. In our overwhelmingly monogamous culture, hierarchy can seem like a way to protect ourselves from risk by creating an agreement that our partner will always consider us more important than anyone else. For many people, hierarchy creates a powerful feeling of safety and control.

Hierarchy also seems to promise stability and continuity. It can seem like a way to explore a radical new relationship style without giving up the comfort and certainty promised by monogamy. It also seems to promise that we can have multiple relationships while still ensuring all our needs are met. If we need something, we'll get it; only after our needs are satisfied may secondary partners have our partner's time and attention.

Hierarchy may also feel like a way of buffering ourselves from our partner's other relationships. By packaging these up and keeping them at arm's length from the core couple, we may try to prevent them from affecting the life we have.

Outside of polyamory, the hierarchical model can sometimes work fine. The world of swinging is much larger than the poly world, and emotionally monogamous, hierarchical couples tend to dominate there. The focus is on sex for fun and adventure, with no emotional spillover allowed into the rest of life. If you have a partner and the two of you as a couple are strongly drawn to a hierarchical style, swinging may be an alternative to polyamory you might choose to investigate.

But the waters of poly are deeper, and for loving relationships, depth needs to be allowed—threatening as it may sometimes seem.

When we have been in an existing relationship for a long time, we might feel like some of the early intensity has faded. Watching a partner enter a wildly passionate, starry-eyed, intensely sexual new relationship can be quite uncomfortable. New relationship energy has quite a reputation in this regard. The existing partner may feel insecure enough to impose hierarchy to try to limit the intensity for his own comfort. You can see the smoldering fuses that this move sets.

The assumption lurking beneath a desire for hierarchy is that we can't really trust our partners to act well without a set of rules. That without a formal ranking to remind our partners that we come first, we will lose our status, lose the things we most value about our relationship, lose our sense of security, or even lose the relationship entirely. But as we've said before, if your partner can't be trusted to work with you on your needs when asked, she probably can't be trusted to follow rules.

THE POWER DYNAMICS OF HIERARCHY

In a hierarchical relationship by our definition, power is diverted from within one relationship to restrict another relationship, forming a sort of "gate" to limit commitment or connection. When the natural flow of connection or

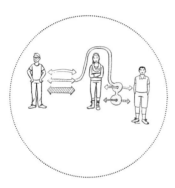

commitment is smaller than the width of that gate, everything is fine. This is usually what's going on where people point to hierarchical poly groups in which prescribed roles are working well for everyone involved. Of course, if the natural connection and commitment are small enough to fit within the "gate," hierarchy probably isn't necessary: that relationship would remain where it is on its own.

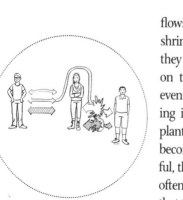

Problems arise when the natural flows are bigger than the gate. They won't shrink on their own, much as we might wish they would, so they continue to push back on the gate. The restriction might stifle or eventually kill the new relationship, stunting its growth in the way a sunshine-loving plant growing under the shade of a big tree becomes stunted. But if the flows are too powerful, they will eventually crash through the gate, often causing great damage to the relationship that the power originally emanated from.

Monogamous, one-true-soulmate conditioning goes very deep, and it's hard to root out all the ways it influences our thinking. It's hard work to consider the implications of our decisions on unknown future partners, and it's very tempting not to do that work. And it's particularly difficult to consider someone else's needs when we're scared. So it is often true that people in hierarchical relationships may behave in ways that are unnecessarily cruel to some partners—not out of malice, but merely out of thoughtlessness.

Returning to our garden analogy, you could think of a relationship about to be opened up as a big tree with deep roots—maybe one that's been bearing fruit for many years, seen a few rough seasons and spread its branches. Then you plant another seed in your garden: a new relationship. You don't know what the seed will grow into, but if you're like many primary partners, there's a good chance you have some hope, spoken or unspoken, that it will be an annual, or stay small, or at least thrive in the shade of that big tree. Certainly it won't ever get as big or demand as much space, right?

We tend to think of secondary relationships as "new" relationships, without giving thought to the fact that they might endure for years. It's common to hear variations on this theme: "But you can't expect a new partner to have the same rights as a spouse!" True, but relationships don't stay new forever. There was a time when your spouse of fifteen years was your new girlfriend or boyfriend, and a time could come when your relationship with your new partner will also be established. Sure, it's possible that you'll want the same kind of relationship in fifteen years that you wanted at six months, but it's unlikely.

Yet couples often seem to hope to keep secondary relationships frozen at that six-month size and shape forever. It doesn't work that way. If you plant an acorn in a flowerpot and the sapling manages to survive, you'll just end up with a broken flowerpot.

Often primary couples manage this structural flaw by simply jettisoning any relationship that threatens to grow bigger than the space they allotted to it. Many people often implicitly assume that a secondary relationship that becomes too well established may threaten the primary relationship—which is odd, considering the primary relationship has already had the time and energy to grow deep roots. Commonly, a secondary partner will sense that his happiness is not that big a concern to the primary couple, even if he can't put his finger on why. He may be sensing that even though the couple have never actually been callous or unethical, the structure of the relationship itself may not respect his rights and feelings, or give his relationship space to grow.

FRANKLIN'S STORY Over time, the agreements I had made with Celeste became painful to my other partners. A year or so after I started dating Amber, one of the things she wanted was to live with me. Celeste and I didn't know what to do; we didn't have a way to handle a situation where another relationship grew to the point where it threatened to overrun the limits we had placed on it. As a result, when Amber mentioned the idea of living with me, Celeste perceived this as an attempt to undermine her place in my life.

I thought it was most important to keep to my agreements, whatever the cost. This meant I hurt the people I loved, and who loved me, unfairly and unnecessarily. All this pain could have been avoided if I had simply thought about these agreements from someone else's point of view before I made them. Amber eventually did move in with us, after other events (discussed in the next chapter) led to an attempt at greater flexibility in my and Celeste's relationship.

Ironically, hierarchy can create precisely the situation the primary couple is trying to avoid. A person who feels relegated to a subordinate position may demand more decision-making power or more freedom to grow in the relationship. These demands may feel hostile to the primary couple. They respond by tightening the restrictions or by reminding the secondary partner, "Hey, you agreed to all these rules when you signed on," which only makes the secondary partner feel more disempowered. And the next thing you know, what could have been a positive and healthy relationship ends up eating itself in a big ball of suck.

Another danger unique to hierarchical relationships is that a secondary partner might start a new relationship with someone else, someone who does not subscribe to hierarchy, and that new relationship can feel threatening to the partner in the primary relationship...not because it's a threat to the couple, but because the new relationship offers things the hierarchical relationship forbids. Franklin's relationship with Ruby, described in chapter 8 (pages 128-29), is a perfect example of how this can happen, and we've both seen it many times. People in hierarchical relationships typically find that letting a *secondary* partner have other partners is scarier than letting their *primary* partner have others!

NOT EVERYONE USES "PRIMARY" AND "SECONDARY"

The words *primary* and *secondary* to refer to partners first became popular among early-generation poly people (some people even had "tertiary" partners). Often these adjectives got pressed into service as nouns themselves, so people had "primaries" and "secondaries." In many places, these words remain popular, and it's still fairly common to hear people talk about primary relationships, but the word secondary is falling out of favor (although some people simply use "non-primary" instead).

This language can get confusing, because not everyone who uses the words primary and secondary is talking about a hierarchical relationship. The confusion arises because these words may be used in two different ways: *prescriptively* (as when a primary couple decides in advance what limitations any other relationship will be subject to) or *descriptively* (to describe whether a relationship has naturally grown to be more or less entangled than another). For example, some people use "primary" to refer to all live-in relationships and "secondary" for all relationships that aren't financially or domestically entwined. As well, hierarchical polyamorists often (though not always) expect that there can be only one primary relationship, whereas with descriptive "primary/secondary" relationships, someone may have several primary partners. We've even heard people who practice non-hierarchical poly say, "My primary is whichever partner I'm with at the time" (even if it's more than one partner).

Neither one of us describes any of our relationships as "primary" or "secondary," and neither do our partners, their partners or most of our close associates. Many poly people have made the choice not to do this, and they tend to find that words such as *partner, lover, girlfriend, boyfriend, fiancé* and *spouse* convey more meaning than the words *primary* and *secondary*. The two of us call the people we live with "nesting partners"; some people also refer to "domestic partners." *Co-parent* and *life partner* are also commonly used; we've also heard "life mate." *Um friend* is sometimes used for casual lovers (as in, "He's my, um, friend"). Many poly people, including us, refer to all their partners as "sweeties" or "loves," and the term *paramour* (from which *metamour* is derived) is popular in the United Kingdom. There are plenty of made-up terms and phrases too—you may have noticed that poly people are good at making up words!

Despite the fact that some people still use the words *primary* and *secondary* descriptively, we discourage this use—particularly *secondary*—because it is confusing, and because many people find the word *secondary* hurtful outside of (and sometimes within!) hierarchies. In this book, we only use these terms when speaking of explicitly hierarchical relationships.

SERVICE SECONDARIES

One common feature of hierarchical relationships is the notion that the secondary partner must provide the primary couple with some form of service as compensation for being in a relationship with one of them. For instance, the secondary partner may have to babysit. (We even know of a case where the secondary partner was expected to present in public as the couple's nanny.) Or the service could be other domestic duties. Sex is another service that secondary partners are often asked to provide, in cases where they are expected to be sexually involved with both members of a couple.

We refer to such arrangements as "service secondaries," and you would be well advised to avoid them—no matter which role you would play in the structure. What's wrong with these arrangements? Isn't it fair to look for partners who will want to support you, help around the house and participate in your family life, if that's what matters to you? Well, sure. But starting out with the view that a new partner is *taking something away*, and therefore *needs to compensate* by doing work for the couple, is not a healthy foundation for a relationship.

Let's take a deeper look at this. First, we're not talking about mutually supportive relationships where everyone pitches in and helps each other. These arrangements are nonreciprocal. If you don't see the primary couple showing up at the secondary partner's house on a Friday night to do her dishes and laundry, the service arrangement is probably one-way.

Second, some help-out arrangements may be perfectly reasonable at the start—particularly if the secondary partner actually likes the chore—but they can become coercive as the partners bond and as the job becomes habitual. Once the relationship has become established, the secondary partner may feel he has to continue doing the work in order to "pay" for continued access to intimacy.

Finally, in prescribing in advance what service they expect a secondary partner to perform, the couple is objectifying any potential new partners.

Service secondary arrangements enshrine the idea that the secondary partner must compensate the couple for being there. There's something inherently demeaning about telling someone they have to perform a service for you in exchange for enriching your life. If a partner doesn't add to your life, then why are you bringing her into it? If she does add to your life, then why make her work for you in order to be there?

Many people do like to express their love (or have love expressed for them) through acts of service, and there's absolutely nothing wrong with that. And many people like to go out of their way to extend themselves to a new metamour, to make them feel welcome and cared for. But if you want to know whether you're looking at a mutually supportive relationship that may include acts of service as expressions of love, or you're slipping into a hierarchical "service secondary" arrangement, here are some things to think about:

- Is what I am looking for reciprocal—am I ready to offer as much care and service as I'm expecting in return?
- Is my partner free to choose the acts of service that he uses to express his love for me?
- Am I making access to a relationship contingent upon continued acts of service?
- Am I choosing partners on the basis of the service they are willing to provide?

FIND A PRIMARY OF YOUR OWN?

We've discussed before that people are not need-fulfillment machines, and that (except in certain limited instances) the "My needs aren't being met, let's find someone else" approach to poly problem-solving is fraught with peril. Nowhere is this more true than in the idea that if a secondary partner wants more time and attention, the solution is for him to go find a primary of his own.

FRANKLIN'S STORY Bella wanted a committed, closely bonded relationship with me, but the terms of my agreement with Celeste relegated my other partners to a prescribed secondary status. Bella and I thought, seemingly reasonably, that if she had another "primary" partner, her needs for that kind of relationship would be met, and she would no longer need those things from me.

That idea turned out to be disastrously wrong. The thing she wanted wasn't "a primary," it was a closer relationship *with me*. Being close to other people didn't meet that need. When she did find another partner, she discovered this didn't change what she wanted from me.

Our relationship ended because not being able to have her needs met damaged it beyond our ability to repair. When she ended the relationship, she was clear that she did not believe it was possible for someone to be close to me under the terms that Celeste and I wanted, regardless of whether that person had an existing "primary" relationship or not. I struggled to understand why. Because I was still trapped in the mindset that polyamory was something Celeste allowed me to do, and protecting that "main" relationship with her had to be my first priority, I could not see how I was treating Bella as an accessory to my relationship rather than as a real person. I did not realize that thinking Bella just needed a primary of her own was actually a way of saying her feelings for me were not okay, and that she needed to transfer those feelings to someone else.

Bella and I had been together for ten years when she called it off. I was devastated, but for a long time, I held on to the belief that what went wrong was somehow her fault: that if she had just stayed in the space Celeste and I had set aside for her, everything would have been okay. Only much later did I understand why making that space for her and telling her to stay put inside it was not a kind or loving thing for me to do—and when I did figure that out, the pain was much worse.

If your car needs an alternator, you can go to an auto parts store and pick one off the shelf. But people are not car parts. Each of us is unique, and it's the things that make us unique that matter. Swapping one person for another in the hopes that the new person will meet the needs unfilled by the old really doesn't work.

HIERARCHY AND ETHICS

Is it possible to practice hierarchical polyamory in a caring and ethical way? Yes, but it takes special attention to avoid hurting people. A secondary partner is in a uniquely vulnerable position and may feel she has limited recourse when problems arise. It is particularly vital to consider this whenever you make decisions that affect a secondary partner directly. This doesn't mean that consideration for the secondary partner should override any and all needs within the primary relationship. Avoid either-or thinking: that if someone's needs don't come first, that must mean another's needs do. Instead, work together to give everyone space to voice their needs. There might be many ways to have certain needs met, and needs do not always have to be in conflict even when they seem to be.

Primary partners should be especially conscious of how their decisions will impact their secondary partners, and take care to treat the secondary partner's needs and feelings gently and with compassion. In particular, when things get stormy in a primary relationship, it's easy to become so concerned with our own issues that we forget to pay attention to the secondary being hurt. Franklin has been guilty of this himself, and he knows how easy it can be.

In chapter 3 we introduced our Relationship Bill of Rights. It contains, we believe, standards by which to judge whether a hierarchical relationship is ethical and healthy. These rights apply to all relationships, but hierarchical relationships in particular risk abridging many of them. The following are examples of specific relationship rights that are at risk in hierarchical relationships and ways in which these rights are commonly overridden:

- *to choose the level of involvement and intimacy you want, and to revoke consent to any form of intimacy at any time.* Both the pivot partner (the person in the middle) and the secondary partner in a hierarchical vee structure can have this right violated if the primary partner restricts the intimacy they can choose with each other, or if the primary partner requires that the secondary partner be intimate with her too.

- *to revoke consent to any form of intimacy at any time.* This right can be violated when the primary couple keeps relevant information from the secondary partner.

- *to hold and express differing points of view.* It's common for primary couples to shut down complaints or concerns from the secondary partner if they contradict the primary couple's rules, or to forbid a secondary partner from attempting to renegotiate the rules.

- *to feel all your emotions.* Both the pivot and secondary partners may be subject to rules restricting what they are allowed to feel.

- *to feel and communicate your emotions and needs.* Generally speaking, rules against specific emotions are really rules against communicating feelings, since people cannot control what they feel, but only what they express. When a secondary partner does express "forbidden" emotions, they are often dismissed as unreal or less important than those of the primary couple.

- *to set boundaries concerning your privacy needs.* Some primary couples do not recognize the right to privacy of the members of a secondary relationship. There may, for example, be expectations that the primary partner will tell the other primary intimate details that the secondary partner considers private.
- *to seek balance between what you give to the relationship and what is given back to you.* It is common to see secondary partners expected to give things to the primary couple that are not reciprocated.
- *to know that your partner will work with you to resolve issues that arise.* Often secondary relationships are subject to rules that were put in place before the secondary partner came on the scene. If a rule is not working for the secondary relationship, will the original members of the relationship renegotiate?
- *to make mistakes.* There may be an expectation that a secondary relationship will be ended the first time the secondary partner makes a mistake.
- *to decide how many partners you want and to choose your own partners.* Hierarchy often includes a "screening veto," discussed in the next chapter, that restricts people from selecting their own partners.
- *to have an equal say with each of your partners in deciding the form your relationship with that partner will take.* In many hierarchies, the primary couple has more say than the secondary partner in deciding this.
- *to choose the level of time and investment you will offer to each partner.* The pivot partner's ability to choose the level of investment she wants to give to each of her relationships may be limited by pre-existing rules set by the primary relationship.
- *to understand clearly any rules that will apply to your relationship before entering into it.* Many secondary partners feel that they did not fully understand what they were getting into.
- *to discuss with your partners decisions that affect you.* Many primary couples make decisions about the secondary relationship, then present them as a fait accompli.
- *to have time alone with each of your partners.* Some primary couples have rules prohibiting this.

- *to enjoy passion and special moments with each of your partners.*
  Hierarchical relationships often have rules restricting the amount
  of intimacy or "specialness" the secondary relationship can have.
- *to choose the level of involvement and intimacy you want with your
  partners' other partners.* Hierarchical relationships often seek to
  prescribe the relationships with more than one person, sometimes
  even requiring the secondary partner to be sexually or romantically
  involved with both members of the primary couple.
- *to seek compromise.* Often the primary couple expects to dictate
  terms.
- *to have relationships with people, not with relationships.* The primary
  couple may expect the secondary partner to interact with them as a
  unit, limiting the individual relationships that may develop.
- *to have plans made with your partner be respected; for instance, not
  changed at the last minute for trivial reasons.* Primary couples often
  assume they are free to change plans whenever they "have to."
- *to be treated as a peer of every other person, not as a subordinate, even
  when differing levels of commitment or responsibility exist.* Hierarchical
  relationships tend to be disempowering to at least the secondary
  partner, and often to the pivot partner in the core couple as well.

So, are hierarchical relationships inherently disempowering? Or can
they be practiced fairly and ethically, in a way that benefits everyone and does
not violate the Relationship Bill of Rights? We are hesitant to give a categori-
cal yes or no. Because of the popularity of hierarchical poly relationships, we
would like to be able to say, "Yes, it is possible to conduct hierarchical relationships ethically and responsibly, for the benefit of everyone involved."
But the truth is, in all our years of practicing polyamory, in the thousands of
emails Franklin has received and the hundreds of stories people have shared
online, we have never seen a hierarchical relationship that worked well for
everyone over the long term.

It's common to hear people say that a hierarchical relationship "works
for us," and by "us" they mean the primary couple. But if you look at their
relationship histories, you'll often find a string of past secondary partners
who were either vetoed for trying to renegotiate the rules once they became

too constricting or who left the relationship because of poor treatment. (This, sadly, describes Franklin's history of secondary relationships during his eighteen years with Celeste.)

Many people who have been a secondary partner in a hierarchy have sworn never to do it again. It's difficult to say that hierarchy is "working" when we include these people in our assessment. On the other hand, couples often complain that they just can't seem to find secondary partners who are "really poly"—that is, who won't want a say in the rules that govern them. When couples consistently can't find partners willing to participate in their flavor of hierarchy, it's difficult to say that hierarchy is working for *them*, either.

You *do* see relationship networks where people have carefully worked to maximize well-being and respect the relationship rights of everyone involved, while upholding their commitments to their partners. But in our experience, by the time someone has managed to avoid the pitfalls above and remains focused on, say, a long-standing lifetime partnership while treating newer or less-entwined partners with integrity and compassion, the structure that is left tends to no longer resemble a hierarchy. Such relationships instead begin to look like empowered relationships, the subject of chapter 13. But first we need to talk about a particular kind of agreement that's a keystone of many hierarchical poly relationships: the veto.

QUESTIONS TO ASK YOURSELF

You may encounter relationship hierarchy in one of two ways: by instituting it in one or more of your relationships, or by entering a relationship with someone who is already part of a hierarchical structure. The questions to ask yourself will differ depending on which situation you're in.

If you are considering implementing a relationship hierarchy:

* *How do I view potential new partners, both for myself and for my existing partners? Do I see them as potential problems to be managed? Or do I see them as potential sources of joy to enrich my partner's life? How does my approach to hierarchy reflect that view?*

- *Are there specific assets, commitments or people (such as children) I am seeking to protect with a hierarchy? Can I imagine other avenues for achieving that protection?*

- *Am I open to secondary relationships someday becoming primary relationships, given enough time and investment?*

- *What will I do if a secondary partner becomes dissatisfied with the rules that apply to them? Am I willing or able to involve that partner in renegotiations of those rules?*

If you are considering entering a hierarchy as a secondary partner:

- *Do I clearly understand both the letter and the intent of the rules that will apply to my relationship? Am I comfortable maintaining a relationship within those rules? Am I comfortable with the reasons for the rules?*

- *Do I know whether the rules that apply to my relationship are subject to change? If so, who may change them, and how? What input will I have into those changes?*

- *Will the term secondary be applied to my relationship, and if so, do I understand how the primary couple is defining the word? Am I comfortable with the definition?*

- *Will it be possible for the secondary nature of my relationship to evolve into primary, if my partner and I desire that? If not, how will I feel about my relationship remaining secondary long into the future—say, ten or fifteen years?*

VETO
ARRANGEMENTS

May your choices reflect your hopes,
not your fears.

NELSON MANDELA

The word *veto* is Latin for "I forbid." It refers to one person's power to prevent something from happening. In law—where the English use of the word comes from—a veto is something that happens at the *end* of a deliberative process. When we talk about "veto" in polyamorous relationships, we're talking about something very specific: the agreed-upon ability for one person to tell another "I want you to break up with your lover," and have the breakup happen.

Identifying a real veto situation can at times be tricky, because some people use the word *veto* to describe things that aren't veto by this definition. For instance, we often run into people who say, "We have the right to talk to our partner if one of her other relationships becomes a problem, discuss the problems we see and ask for resolutions, which might include changes up to and including ending the relationship." We prefer to call this sort of arrangement "good communication," not "veto." If you have something you call "veto" that looks like this, we are not talking about you.

A veto, for the purpose of this discussion, is a one-sided decision to halt a relationship between two other people. It is not a negotiation or a request.

The key elements of a veto are that it is *unilateral* (that is, only one person needs to think there's a problem) and it is *binding* (that is, the person exercising a veto has reason to believe the other will obey it). A veto moves the locus of control away from the people in a particular relationship and gives it to a third party.

Veto arrangements are one of the most common, and most zealously guarded, of all the rules in hierarchical relationships. In our experience, most hierarchies include a veto arrangement, even when they include few of the other rules we've talked about. Vetoes promise the ultimate fallback: if a partner's relationship becomes too difficult, or their other lover is too unlikeable, or jealousy becomes too unbearable, veto can make the problem just go away.

Over the years, Franklin has received scores of emails from people who had their relationship ended by a veto. These stories varied in detail, but all had one common thread: the person who was vetoed felt that the veto was unfair.

The subject of veto is likely to generate controversy in any discussion about polyamory. Some people feel passionate about the value of veto. The word itself is powerful: it conjures up feelings of empowerment and control. Even people who don't have a veto according to our definition will often insist on using the word *veto* because the word itself creates such a compelling feeling of safety.

VETO OF AN EXISTING RELATIONSHIP

For people who are subject to a veto but do not hold one—for example, the new partner of a person whose pre-existing partner has a veto—the word *veto* is just as powerful, but often it is powerfully negative. It creates an environment where no matter what you do or what kind of investment you make, your relationship can be ripped away at a moment's notice, without discussion or appeal. It summons an image of the sword of Damocles, always dangling over the relationship by a thread, ready to fall at any misstep. This creates an environment where it's nearly impossible to feel safe in that relationship.

We have both been affected by vetoes. Eve had a relationship vetoed by another person. Franklin has been vetoed and has also had someone veto a partner of his. Vetoes are like nuclear weapons: they may keep others in line, but their use tends to forever alter the landscape.

FRANKLIN'S STORY For Celeste, veto was a security blanket, a way to stop relationships that threatened her position as the number-one person in my life.

She used that veto to end my relationship with Elaine. At the time, I had known Elaine for about five years and been in a relationship with her for about three. Our relationship was incredibly powerful and passionate. We were very well matched as partners, and our sexual connection was extraordinary. This was hard for Celeste to see; watching a long-term partner have an intense, passionate connection with someone else can be scary.

The day Celeste exercised her veto, I was driving to work with my partner Amber, who worked from the same office. Celeste called me to demand that I end my relationship with Elaine immediately and never contact her again.

As Celeste instructed, I called Elaine and broke up with her immediately. I was devastated. I remember pulling into the parking lot of a fast-food restaurant with Amber, unable to stop crying. I was so hurt and upset that I never made it to the office that afternoon. Amber wrote about that day: "I have never seen him break down like that, before or since. His body broke down into convulsions of crying. I don't think I've ever seen him in so much pain."

To this day, I still do not completely understand why Celeste made the choice she did. When she used the veto, I felt violated. I was angry, not just that she could veto a partner I'd been with so long, but that she could do it in a way that allowed no argument for or defense of my relationship with Elaine. My control over my own romantic life had been ripped away from me. Even though I had agreed to give Celeste this veto power, that didn't change the loss of control I felt when she used it.

That sense of violation and my feelings of anger seeped into my relationship with Celeste. None of the theoretical, abstract discussions we'd had about veto prepared me for the raw emotional impact of being told to end a relationship with someone I loved. I saw, for the first time, how damaging veto was, and I resolved not to allow this to happen again, to me or to any of my partners. I told Celeste that I would not accept another veto.

My relationship with Celeste never fully recovered from the veto. We divorced less than two years later. Many other factors were in play, as always in the disintegration of a decades-long relationship. But that veto was like an earthquake at sea, which initiated a tidal wave that would eventually consume everything Celeste and I had built together.

Many hierarchical relationships have a veto provision that can be exercised at any time, even after another relationship has been well established. This kind of veto is popular because it seems to provide a safety switch to shut down a relationship that becomes too intense or threatening. But that sense of safety can carry a very high price. We have both seen many couples who have executed a veto only to break up shortly thereafter. Any time we choose to break our partner's heart, the damage to our own relationship may be permanent.

When a partner of yours vetoes another partner, you actually do have a choice. You can either end the relationship that's being vetoed, or you can say "No, I refuse to accept this veto." But neither option is likely to lead anywhere constructive. If you say "No, I refuse to accept this," your partner who used the veto now has a choice to make: Stay in the relationship and sulk? Leave? Whatever choices each person makes, bitterness is pretty much guaranteed.

EVE'S STORY   My relationship with Ray ended when his wife vetoed me, but it wasn't the veto that ended it. Ray and I had a long-distance relationship, and his wife and I had little contact. Ray and I had been involved for close to two years when he told me that I had been vetoed—several months earlier! He had continued to visit me, have sex with me and have almost daily contact with me, without his wife's knowledge. When I learned of this I told him I couldn't see him anymore. I am ashamed to say it took me nearly 24 hours to come to that decision.

It was painful enough that after two years with me, Ray wouldn't stand up to his wife to defend our relationship. But it was especially bad that *I* was put in the position of implementing the veto that Ray did not have the courage to either accept or refuse. Rather than take responsibility for the situation and stand up to either one of us, he chose to lie to us both.

Even if your partner uses a veto, responsibility for the breakup is still yours. If your relationship has been vetoed, it's easy to say "I am ending this relationship because my partner made me do it." Franklin did this when Celeste used her veto. In reality, the ethical responsibility belonged only to him.

SCREENING VETO

Not all vetoes work to cancel an existing relationship. Some people use what might be called a "screening veto." This means a potential new relationship may be vetoed before it becomes established, but not after. In a newspaper column in 2007, kink and polyamory writer Mistress Matisse described this as "starting the feedback before emotions and slippery bits get involved." A screening veto is safer than a post-relationship veto in that it is less likely to create a sense of violation. However, even this variety of veto can have damaging consequences.

FRANKLIN'S STORY   Meadow and I met a few years ago, under strange and complicated circumstances. We hit it off at once. We both felt drawn to each other, and soon after we met, we went on a date. It was one of the best first dates I've ever had. There wasn't anything unusual about the date itself—we sat in a restaurant and talked—but we both had an absolutely fantastic time, chatting about everything from movies to neurobiology. The chemistry between us was delightful.

After the date, I took her home and met her husband. We spoke briefly, and then I went home.

I emailed her the next day to let her know I'd had a delightful time and was looking forward to seeing her again. No response. I texted her a couple of days later, and again, no reply. *Huh*, I thought. *I guess she didn't have as good a time as I thought.*

Months later, I found out through mutual friends that Meadow had been so thrilled and excited by our date, and so giddy at the thought of dating me, that her husband vetoed me on the spot. What's more, he forbade her to ever speak to me again—even to tell me I'd been vetoed! I would never have found out if we hadn't had overlapping circles of friends.

This veto experienced by Franklin seems to have come entirely from a place of fear and threat. It can be intimidating to see a partner excited about a new relationship, especially when we feel insecure ourselves. All the demons start whispering in our ears: "What if I'm not good enough? What if this person is more exciting than I am?"

A screening veto has problems because, like all vetoes, it tends to end conversations rather than start them. Had Meadow's husband chosen to talk about his feelings rather than using a veto, their relationship might have improved. But it can be hard to say "Wow, seeing you excited like this makes me feel insecure. Let's talk about what that means, and how we can work together to strengthen and support our relationship until what we have brings you this much joy." It's much easier to say "I don't want you to see him again."

While it's not as damaging to veto a person before a relationship begins, depriving a partner of a source of joy is still a dangerous thing to do. When we see a partner clearly excited about something and take that thing away, we risk undermining our partner's happiness, and that, too, is likely to damage our relationship.

It might be tempting to look at the examples above and call them abuses of veto, rather than situations where veto is useful and appropriate. We disagree. The problem is that nobody with veto power believes he uses it capriciously. We all tend to be the heroes of our own stories, acting on motives wise and pure. The problem with veto is not that some use it inappropriately; the problem is that it tends to cause damage no matter how it is used. And sometimes veto becomes a way to defend our own dysfunctions and entrench them.

You may hear the following idea in poly circles: that you should only add relationships that enhance your existing ones. Or that you should screen new partners to make sure their communication and relationship styles mesh with your existing relationship. That does seem like a good way to avoid drama and promote stability. But just as often, it can lead to enabling behaviors. You can easily end up constructing an echo chamber in your existing relationship where dysfunctional relationship patterns go unchallenged.

But what if we have reason to be concerned that the new person is disruptive, manipulative, a bad influence, emotionally unstable or dangerous to our partner? We've heard all these and more as reasons why someone "had to" use veto. After all, our beloved is all caught up in twitterpation, aglow with hormones, and can't think clearly. It's true, we all gloss over flaws in the flush of a new crush. Isn't it our partner's job to see with eyes unclouded when we are blinded? To see warning signs and tell us?

Well, yes, but there's no reason to imagine that the veto-wielding partner is any more objective than the twitterpated partner. After all, it's scary to watch your partner get distracted by the new shiny. And when you're scared, you don't make wise decisions either. Which isn't to say that the veto-wielding partner is always wrong and the infatuated partner is always right. There's just no particular reason to assume one is necessarily more "right" than the other. The only way through the swamp is to communicate openly about whatever concerns or misgivings you have, and then to let the person *in* the relationship be the one to make the decision. Because even if his choice of partner is a mistake, it is his mistake to make.

"Screening veto" agreements deprive us of our ability to make our own mistakes, and learn and grow from them. Early in Eve's relationship with Peter, they talked about using a veto as part of their transition from monogamy to polyamory. But after they discussed it for a while, they both agreed that a veto might reduce their opportunities to learn.

EVE'S STORY   Peter has been in a relationship with Gwen for over five years. He started seeing her just a couple of months after he began his relationship with Clio, and while he was still traveling frequently to look after his mom. I was still adjusting to all the change and was completely unprepared for him to begin another new relationship. Moreover, I didn't like Gwen. When I met her, I had difficulty understanding her. I just had a gut feeling I didn't really like her, and I didn't feel like I was going to enjoy having her around. I told Peter so, but he continued to see Gwen.

If Peter and I had had a screening veto, I might have vetoed Gwen. And that would have been a huge mistake. Because in this case, Peter has proven to be a much better judge than I was of what will make him happy and what sort of person Gwen is. She has been an overwhelmingly positive addition to both our lives, and a stable, secure and supportive partner for Peter. I am immensely grateful not only for her presence in Peter's life, but for the agreement Peter and I made early on that we would not have the right to choose whom the other could become involved with.

ETHICAL PROBLEMS WITH VETO

There's nothing wrong with trying to manage risk—we do it every time we put on a seatbelt. Managing risk through veto, though, raises serious ethical concerns. It violates both of our core ethical principles: *The people in the relationship are more important than the relationship,* and *Don't treat people as things.*

How does a veto treat people as things? A veto of an existing relationship makes a person expendable. It does not give her input into whether or not her own relationship is ended. While it's true that even in monogamous relationships the person being broken up with often doesn't get a say in the matter, the poly veto situation is unique. Here a third party *who is not actually in the relationship* is ending something that both of the people in it still want.

A veto arrangement also makes the relationship more important than the people in it, because it requires that a relationship be ended without consideration for whether it is healthy or beneficial to the people in it. Nor does it consider the harm that may be done to them by the veto.

It's true that when we have several relationships, some may cause pain in others. Despite raising the issues, despite ongoing negotiation, the pivot partner may choose to remain in a relationship that one of her partners thinks is harmful. If you are the partner who might want to issue a veto, consider *stating boundaries for yourself instead.* You could say, "This situation is degrading my happiness to the point where I can no longer imagine being happy if it continues. If you keep going down this course, I won't be able to remain in this relationship." Indeed, it's an important part of consent: you always have the right to withdraw consent, for any reason. You *never* have to remain in a situation that hurts you.

Issues of power and risk come up. If you have veto power and you say "I cannot stay with you if you remain in this relationship," you know ahead of time that you will "win" this particular play. Your partner has promised you in advance—probably when his other partner was still hypothetical and not yet a real person—that if this scenario ever arose, he would "choose" you.

Because you're pretty sure what the outcome will be, the risk for you in enacting a veto is lowered. You can deliver an ultimatum and still *not lose the relationship.* You do not have to shoulder the risk and vulnerability of saying you are prepared to leave and *really mean it.* In other words, the consequences of your actions—and thus the bar you need to reach before you issue an ultimatum—are lowered for you, giving you more power and less incentive to act in good faith.

At the same time, *all* of that risk is unloaded onto the other partner. This shifting of risk—telling another person to bear both the normal risk that comes with any relationship plus extra risk shifted from the other relationship—is one of the things that makes vetoes unethical.

If, on the other hand, you do *not* have veto power, the outcome is not predetermined. There is a chance that your partner will not break up with his other partner. So you have to accept the vulnerability of telling your partner, "I can't take this anymore. I will have to leave if you continue that relationship." You have to be *sure.* It seems to us that if you're ready to take a step as serious as ending another person's intimate relationship, it's fair to ask that you put as much on the line as they have.

And then, without a veto, your partner has the opportunity to do what he believes will be best for him in the long run, what will bring him the most happiness—rather than having to make a choice he may not want to make because it was agreed to long before a third real human being was involved. *The people in the relationship remain more important than the relationship.* Including that third person. When the outcome is predetermined through a veto arrangement, she has no room to negotiate or to defend herself or her relationship. Maybe she even has a case for why she is a better partner for him than you are—and she should have the right to make that case.

Even if you have a strictly hierarchical, primary/secondary relationship, the ethical considerations of veto deserve some attention. Any relationship can end, for any number of reasons. Not all relationships last; that's a fact of life (see chapter 22). But even when the primary partner in a hierarchical relationship decides he needs his partner's secondary relationship to end, the ethical thing to do is to involve the secondary partner in the discussion and allow her to respond to concerns.

PRACTICAL PROBLEMS WITH VETO

Aside from ethical concerns, and aside from the pain and bitterness a veto may cause, veto arrangements present other practical problems you may not have thought of. For example, a veto arrangement that's justified by a bad past experience holds a bad actor's actions against a new person who never even knew him. Say your partner became involved with Bob last year, and Bob rained drama and chaos all over. If that makes you ask for veto, then when Charles comes along, you're making him pay for the sins of Bob. You are perpetuating Bob's drama.

Another problem is escalation. We can't, short of use of force, actually make a partner break up with someone else. When we use a veto, even a mutually agreed-upon veto, we are giving our partner a choice: break up with your other partner, or else. The "or else" part is often left unspecified; few veto negotiations include provisions for what might happen if the veto is ignored. But a veto can, in fact, be ignored. Then what?

Veto creates a trust imbalance. The new person is often told, "Trust us. We won't use this veto inappropriately." But what does this say to the new person? "I want you to trust that I won't veto you inappropriately, but we have a veto arrangement because *we* don't trust *you*." Is it reasonable to ask someone we don't trust to trust us?

On an even more pragmatic note, we observe that people who make the best partners in poly relationships—people who have experience with polyamory, have demonstrated good communication skills, are compassionate problem-solvers with good conflict-resolution skills, and have a high reputation in the community for these abilities—usually avoid anyone who has veto. So by having a veto in place, you stack the deck *toward* relationship problems, because so many experienced poly people with good skills will avoid you. Both of us use "Do you have a veto agreement?" as a screening question with potential partners. If the answer is yes, it's a deal-breaker.

ALTERNATIVES TO VETO

People can become confused when talking about relationships without veto because they may have a mistaken notion that "no veto" means "no input." Some new partners can indeed be damaging or even dangerous, and it's important to be able to speak up when you see problems. Think about "right of consultation" as an alternative to "right of veto." You want conversation to open up, whereas a veto ends conversation. You need to be able to say, "I got a bad feeling from the way he treated you there at the bus stop," or "I went online and found he has a restraining order against him"—and have that not be perceived as a threat, but as useful information. Your partner needs to know you will go on to say, "So please be extra careful, and I'd like it if you could phone home often."

The most common justification we hear for veto power is that it's necessary to prevent a new partner from trying to break up the existing relationship. There certainly are people who will try to do this. They're common enough that the poly community has a name for them: "cowboys" (or "cowgirls"), because they ride up hoping to rope one out of the poly herd.

Unfortunately, veto treats all new partners as bad actors simply because some might be. And your partner isn't a delicate Grecian urn, an object to be stolen away by an enterprising burglar. Your partner is a person, and people can't be stolen. If some new shiny tries to "steal" him, he has to consent to being stolen. Veto or no veto, if he wants to stay with you, he will.

So the real question is not "How can I protect myself from cowboys?" The real question is, do you trust your partner to want to be with you, even if some cute young thing asks her to leave you? If someone says "run away with me," what do you think your partner will say?

Trust isn't something most of us are taught when growing up. The conventional fairy tale tells us to find true love and we'll be happy ever after. It doesn't mention trusting our partners even when we're afraid. It doesn't tell us how to assert good boundaries when faced with potentially disrupting relationships. Committing yourself to trusting that your partner wants to be with you, and will choose to be with you even if someone else tries to tug him away, takes courage. Asserting good boundaries around your partner's other partners takes work. But in the end, your partner is going to make the choices he makes whatever rules you put in place, so what other options do you really have?

Solid boundary-setting is another important tool in managing veto-free relationships (see chapter 9). Your partner may choose a partner you don't particularly like to be around. She may choose a partner who encourages her to make choices that hurt you. At these times, you need to be able to set clear guidelines about what you will and won't accept *within your own relationship.* You do not need to spend time with someone you don't like. If you feel uncomfortable or unsafe with a certain person in your home or your bed (or around your children), you have a right to (and should) set limits about who you will permit in your space.

Of course, your partner also has the right to choose a different living arrangement if your boundaries become unworkable for her.

If you expect certain standards of behavior—to be told the truth, for example, or to have plans reliably kept—that the other relationship is interfering with, you can express these expectations to your partner without managing the other relationship. And of course, if you are in a relationship without veto, it is especially important to respect the boundaries your partner sets around her body, her mind, her choices and her space with regard to your other partners, even when they inconvenience you.

Chapter 4 talked about the idea of self-efficacy—your belief in your own ability to make yourself heard and to positively affect your own situation. Veto can seem like a form of self-efficacy, but we believe self-efficacy lies in believing that if your partner's new relationship starts to go horribly wrong, you can talk about it and make yourself heard. Veto is an indicator of low self-efficacy; it is a way of saying "I don't believe I can get my partner to listen to my concerns unless I have a kill switch."

The higher a person's self-efficacy, though, the less likely that person will enter a relationship with a veto provision in the first place. If you value the ability to have a say in your own relationships, you're unlikely to agree to give someone else ultimate authority over whether your relationship lives or dies.

We talk more about setting boundaries with your partners' other partners in chapter 23, on metamours, and about negotiating directly with your own partners in chapters 6 and 7.

LINE-ITEM VETOES AND FORCE OF DRAMA

Many people who don't have a formally negotiated veto arrangement come up with ways to veto their partners' relationships anyway. If you see patterns like this, it's time for you and your partner to talk. Like most ways of getting our way when direct negotiation has failed, these can be emotional blackmail.

First, there's the line-item veto. That's when, on a case-by-case basis, you restrict what your partner can do with her other partners and when. Eventually enough dates get canceled or interrupted, enough activities curtailed, that the relationship withers and dies. You don't have to demand that your partner end a relationship in order to make it end; you just have to starve it of the resources it needs to thrive.

Another form of veto-by-another-name is what Eve likes to call "force of drama." This is a weapon you can use when you don't want your partner to do something—like go on a date, continue a relationship or engage in a certain activity—but you have not been able to negotiate up front what you want. Your partner, after considering your input, has decided to make another choice: go on the date, continue the relationship, do that thing. But instead of accepting your partner's choice, you make sure that it carries a price. You have an emotional meltdown an hour before that date, and he has to stay home with you. You send him anxious text messages every five minutes whenever he's with the partner you don't like. You keep making nonspecific threats of disaster—emotional or physical—when he does what you don't want.

As damaging as this behavior is, we often unintentionally reinforce it when it happens. We want to be there for our partners, we don't want to hurt them, and most of us don't really like conflict. If her objection to that thing I wanted to do is so important to her, I don't *really* need to do it, right? That one date really isn't so important; I can schedule another one... The trouble is, people use this behavior because it works: it gets them what they want.

Some people object to the use of the word *drama*, on the grounds that it is used to minimize and dismiss. In the sense we are using it, however, "force of drama" has another name: emotional blackmail. If you recognize what we're describing, either in your own behavior or your partner's, you owe it to yourself and your partners to read the book *Emotional Blackmail*, listed in the resources.

Of course, we think we have really good reasons—every time we do it. None of us wants to believe that we're manipulating our partner, and we're very good at justifying our actions, even to ourselves. To the person conducting the line-item veto or wielding force of drama, every instance seems necessary and justified. And everyone is allowed the occasional freak-out, outburst or temper tantrum. But if this is happening on a regular basis—and if your partners are giving in to your demands simply to avoid dealing with your behavior—you may want to consider getting professional help to cope with your emotions.

If your partner exhibits this kind of behavior often, if most of your decisions she doesn't like involve you paying an emotional price, or if her drama continues more than a couple of months into a new relationship, then you have a problem—a potentially serious one, with no easy solution. The two of you will need to learn more appropriate negotiation techniques that do not involve emotional threats. Point out the behavior to her and explain the effect it is having on your relationships. Consider reading *Emotional Blackmail* together, and consider getting professional help from a poly-friendly counselor. If the behavior does not stop, you may need to consider ending the relationship.

POCKET VETOES

A "pocket veto" is when you stop your partner from doing something you don't want her to do, simply by doing nothing. In polyamory, this usually comes in the form of "I am afraid of X. Please don't do X until I stop being afraid."

SARA'S STORY   An example of this involves Franklin's friend Sara. Sara was in a relationship with Owen, who was married to Kate. Sara started a new relationship with Mark. Kate told Sara that she didn't feel comfortable with Sara having sex with Mark until Kate knew him better, and requested a three-month waiting period for everyone to get to know each other before Sara and Mark had sex. Sara agreed, and three months passed—three very busy months, in which Kate never had time to get together with Mark. So at the end of the three months, Kate asked Sara to wait another three months, since Kate hadn't had time to "feel safe" with Mark. Sara and Kate were not even lovers; they simply shared a partner.

We've known a few people who have been in relationships with monogamously inclined partners who agreed to a polyamorous relationship, but only after they "felt secure in the relationship." That turned out to be...never. Of course, if your reward for feeling secure is something you don't want, you don't have much incentive to ever feel secure. These relationships can last for years before ending. We know of at least one that has been going on for six years, the polyamorous partner still wistfully hopeful that someday his monogamous partner will "get there."

We have talked of being judicious about when you start new relationships: that perhaps it's better not to bring in new partners when an existing relationship is in crisis, just after a major life upheaval, or when serious mental health issues are erupting, to name a few. The trouble is that this idea of "poly readiness" can become a pocket veto if it does not include a clear statute of limitations. If you need time to work through an issue, get used to a new partner or adjust to the idea, then agree to a time limit on it. If the time limit expires and you still want to say no, or if you want to renew the time limit, understand that you have crossed into pocket veto territory. That is not, in and of itself, a bad thing—provided you're okay with using a veto. But recognize that this is what you are doing.

QUESTIONS TO ASK YOURSELF

The questions around veto fall into three categories: those for people who want to have veto over their partners' relationships, those for people who are considering giving veto power to another, and those for people who are considering becoming involved with someone whose partner has a veto.

If you want your partner to give you veto power over his or her other relationships:

- *Under what circumstances do I feel it's appropriate for me to use it?*

- *Who do I think should have the final say in deciding whether a relationship ends? Why?*

- *What do I believe will happen if I ask a partner to end another relationship, and he or she says no? Why will that thing happen?*

- *Do I trust my partner to consider my needs and well-being in his decisions about whether to stay in a relationship that is hurting me? Why or why not? If not, what can I do to improve that trust?*

- *Do I trust my partner to make good decisions about whom she starts relationships with? Why or why not? What might the consequences be if she makes a poor decision, and how might I deal with those consequences?*

- *Do I use the word veto to describe something other than an ability to unilaterally end a partner's relationship—for example, when I give input to my partners about how I feel about their other relationships? If so, why? Is there something about the word that reassures me in a way that words like negotiation and input do not?*

If you are considering giving your partner(s) veto:

- *Am I prepared to bring someone I care about (or will come to care about) into a situation where I must dump them at someone else's will?*

- *Can I think of a way to make a new partner feel safe in a relationship with me under these conditions?*

- *Do I understand the needs my partner is seeking to meet by requesting veto, and have I considered alternative ways of meeting those needs?*

If you are considering starting a relationship with someone whose partner has a veto:

- *If I start a relationship with someone who is already partnered, what kind of input do I feel it's reasonable for their other partners to have in our relationship?*

- *Do I feel safe opening my heart to someone who has given the power to end our relationship to someone else?*

EMPOWERED RELATIONSHIPS

I've worked really hard to eliminate the words
"have to" from my vocabulary. Because the reality is,
I'm choosing to. I'm choosing to show up and meet
my commitments.

People who are empowered in their romantic relationships can express needs and ask for them to be met. They can talk about problems. They can say what works for them and expect that their partners will try to accommodate their needs as much as they can.

It's not possible to *make* a person feel empowered, just as it's not possible to make a person feel secure. The best we can hope to do is to create an environment that welcomes participation and encourages empowerment. We can, however, *dis*empower people, and that can be very dangerous, as we hope the previous chapters impressed upon you. People who are disempowered have little to lose by breaking the rules. The worst possible outcome—losing the relationship—is something they're already risking by chafing under restrictions; by this point losing the relationship might not seem like such a bad idea.

Some key defining elements of empowerment in a romantic relationship are:

- engaging and participating in the decision-making process for decisions that affect you
- having a full range of options available when decisions are made, not a simple yes or no option (or, in extreme cases, the "Accept it or leave" option)
- having agency over one's own body, relationships and life
- being able to express needs, opinions, desires and boundaries
- having access to the information that materially affects your relationship, person, safety or security
- being able to propose alternatives
- having the ability to object to, and open negotiations about, rules, agreements or structures of the relationship
- having the ability to give, withhold or withdraw consent

It's no coincidence that many of these characteristics resemble some of the relationship rights.

When we use these criteria to define empowerment, it can become clear that an empowered relationship is not necessarily one in which everyone has equal power. Rather, it is one in which no one is *dis*empowered, intentionally or unintentionally, by a hierarchical structure.

EMPOWERMENT IS NOT EQUALITY

When you bring up the notion of poly relationships without hierarchy, people often imagine you're talking about "equal" relationships, where "equal" means "Everyone has the same things." That might mean, for example, trying to create a relationship structure in which everyone has the same amount of time, the same status or the same resources. Perhaps it means everyone is having sex with everyone else, everyone lives under the same roof or everyone loves everyone else "equally."

You will hear people argue for hierarchical polyamory on just these grounds. It's not reasonable, they'll say, to give the long-distance boyfriend you've been dating for a year the same influence over major life decisions as you give your wife. And that's usually true. But as we've said, we find it more useful, when thinking of alternatives to hierarchy, to speak of *empowerment*. This means full opportunity to voice needs, negotiate agreements and advocate for building the kind of relationship you want. Because different people want different things, empowerment is more useful than sameness as a relationship principle.

To continue our garden metaphor: Attempting to build relationships where everyone is equal is a bit like lopping the top half off pine trees and placing rose bushes in pots on tall pedestals to make everything the same height. What if one person naturally wants more time with a shared partner, and another less? Is it reasonable to tell them both they're only allowed to have the same amount of time? What if one relationship has existed for six years, another for six months? Expecting the same level of commitment and entwinement from each would be high-order foolishness.

VESNA'S STORY   Vesna lives with her partner Ahmad and has been in a relationship with Erin for more than a decade. She has also become close friends (and occasionally lovers) with Erin's wife Georgina. Vesna and Erin clicked powerfully the first day they met, and their connection has endured not just across the years, but across the several hundred miles that now separate them. But their relationship isn't suited to an entwined, live-in situation—they're too much alike, Vesna says, and it's just a kind of relationship she's never craved with Erin. So despite their close bond, they live apart, each with nesting relationships of their own.

None of them planned their relationships to be this way. For example, Erin and Georgina never had an agreement that Erin couldn't form a life-entwined partnership with someone else. And Vesna is open to the possibility of having more than one such relationship at a time. The current arrangement is just the way things developed: a way that expresses the differently compatible personalities of everyone involved.

Vesna describes every one of these relationships as remarkably low stress. She says it helps that her relationships—and most of her social circle—are queer, poly and feminist. They talk a lot, and they have a shared language for doing so. She feels their involvement with kink helps them with its focus on negotiation. Vesna says, "I love the synergy with which all of this comes together in how my life and relationships are constructed."

Eve and Franklin each have one partner we live with, and other partners who are highly independent and choose not to share a home with us (or with anyone else); they prefer living alone. A literal take on "equality" might be that everyone should have the same obligations to share a home and same vote in how to handle the mortgage. A more rational take on equality might mean that everyone has equal power to choose how they run their lives.

A partner who doesn't live with us might, for example, someday ask, "I would like to consider sharing a home with you. How do you feel about that?" but would not have an equal say in whether we decide to sell the house we currently live in.

People who have long been together often have a vested "sweat equity" in the relationship. They've made sacrifices and incurred obligations together. Those obligations look like the big commitment arrows on the illustrations in chapter 11. In an empowered relationship, a person is not told, "You have the same standing and the same voice in these existing obligations and responsibilities." Rather, that person is told, "As you invest in the relationship, you, too, will build sweat equity. You will not be denied the opportunity to do this."

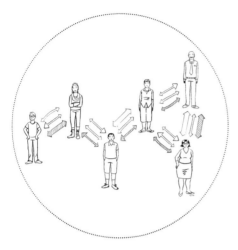

In the context of polyamory, an empowered relationship means that no one outside a relationship has the authority to place restrictions on that relationship. The flows of connection, commitment and power within a relationship can be of any size, and can even be unequal within relationships. But the defining element of hierarchy—*power from within one relationship that controls or restricts another relationship*—is absent.

Franklin's partner Amy likes to say that empowered poly relationships are not ones where every person is "equal" to every other, but rather relationships in which you are negotiating from an equal footing with *your* partner. That is, third parties, such as your partner's other partners, do not have more power in *your* relationship than you do.

We've seen cases where "equality" meant an equality of bad behavior. Franklin knows a married couple who had opened their marriage to polyamory. The wife had a girlfriend for many years before the husband finally found another partner. When the husband started dating, the wife became increasingly jealous. Finally, after several months, she told her husband, "I can't do this anymore. I want you to break up with your girlfriend. But it's okay, I will break up with my girlfriend too, so it's fair." This might be an extreme example, but the impulse often exists, when we're faced with unpleasant emotions, to treat people as expendable.

OWNING YOUR POWER

Non-monogamous relationships clearly highlight the gap between our *perception* of our power and the *reality* of our power. It is often easier to see someone else's power than to see our own. If our partner begins a new relationship, we might see how he invests in the new relationship, and we feel powerless—without recognizing how the established structures, history, commitments and shared life experiences in our own relationship give us a tremendous amount of power that the newer partner doesn't have. The new partner, however, is often *keenly* aware of the power the existing partner has.

A key to practicing empowered relationships is to recognize and understand the power we hold. For this, we need to return to the ideas about security and worthiness in chapter 4. Without a strong *internal* sense of security and worthiness, we will find it nearly impossible to be aware of our power in our romantic relationships. When we feel unworthy, we feel disconnected—even when our loved ones are craving connection with us. We feel isolated and alienated, even when we're surrounded by love and support.

While we're working on the project of our own worthiness, though, we can also seek to understand our own power—even if we don't yet feel it in our hearts. Here, to go back to our mushroom-hunting metaphor: we look for evidence. If you are terrified of losing a ten-year relationship, step back and think about the fact that your partner has chosen to be in a relationship with you *for ten years*. This didn't happen by accident! It happened because for ten years, you have added value to your partner's life.

If you feel you need hierarchy to protect a co-parenting relationship, think about what it means that your partner has chosen to make the enormous commitment of having children with you, and look at evidence she gives you daily in the form of care and investment in your children. Practice gratitude for all of the ways, large and small, your partner invests in your relationship. It will help you understand the value of the relationship to them.

STARTING NEW RELATIONSHIPS IN THE FACE OF EXISTING COMMITMENTS

When starting a new relationship, it's important to be forthright and clear with the new person about your existing commitments. In fact, demonstrating that you keep your commitments to others is a good way to show a new partner that you are worthy of his trust and investment as well. But remember, there's more than one way to shave a walrus. Most poly commitments should offer multiple paths to meeting those commitments while still making room for new partners.

Agreements to support existing commitments succeed best when they offer flexibility about *how* the commitments are met. First and foremost, flexibility honors the agency of the people involved. An agreement to meet your obligation to pay the mortgage offers more flexibility than a rule that you may never spend more than $30 on a date—even if the purpose of the rule is to make sure the mortgage gets paid. A flexible agreement spells out the nature of the obligation and empowers adults to make decisions as they see fit, so long as the obligation is met.

Flexibility also allows for renegotiation of agreements, including the ways in which commitments are met when new relationships alter the playing field. We aren't suggesting, of course, that someone who begins dating a partner already in a long-term relationship be given the keys or invited to sign the mortgage on the first date. Instead, relationships usually work best when the newcomer is not forbidden in advance from doing such things *ever*, but rather knows that the situation has room to evolve. As with everything in polyamory, flexibility is key.

EMPOWERED RELATIONSHIPS AND CHILDREN

Children are the most important commitment many people will ever make. If you're a parent now, they are probably the most important things in your life. Children are dependent: they need people to take care of them, and their parents need to prioritize meeting those needs. Only slowly do they develop good judgment and free agency, and decision-making power on their way to adulthood, so they need special consideration and protection for many years. These overriding needs can get in the way of adult partnerships, which is tough. If you have or want children, you likely (and hopefully) choose partners who understand this fact.

So surely, given the unique vulnerability of children, hierarchy must be necessary for poly families with kids—right? Surely, as someone we know put it, "Coupled-with-kids, especially young kids, is intrinsically a hierarchical situation. No way around it. And without some guidelines or structure, the hierarchy can descend into chaos and the kids would suffer." Are empowered poly relationships even possible with children?

CLARA'S STORY   When Clara and Elijah decided to open their marriage, their two children were very young, one a toddler. They did not enact a hierarchy before opening their relationship, but adopted open communication as their main strategy. Instead of rules, restrictions or veto power, they agreed that if one of them was having trouble with another relationship, they would negotiate a solution case by case.

Their children meant that time management was a central concern. As part of their agreement to open up, Elijah agreed to take on more of the household responsibilities to fill in when Clara was away with another partner.

Clara became involved with Ramon, who had three children with his wife, Caitlin. With Elijah and Caitlin's help, Ramon and Clara worked out a schedule for seeing each other that involved minimal time away from their children. Caitlin often took her children away from home on short trips and to visit family, allowing Clara to spend the night with Ramon alone in a quiet house. Because Elijah worked early in the morning, Clara needed to be at the house before he left. She left her own house after her children were asleep and returned in the morning before they woke up. Ramon would also occasionally spend the night at Clara and Elijah's home.

Just as many monogamous people would, Clara waited to introduce Ramon to her children until she was certain their relationship had staying power. Rather than asking her non-co-parenting partners to babysit (or requiring it, as discussed in "Service secondaries," pages 192–93), she prefers to rely on friends. She also makes sure to schedule time alone with her children, so they understand how much she values her relationship with them and they never feel like Ramon is "taking her away."

As far as we know, no magic pixie dust gets sprinkled on parents at the moment of their child's birth to make them incapable of honoring commitments and responsibilities on their own. If you were a responsible adult before your kids were born, you will remain a responsible (if highly sleep deprived) adult after.

Responsible adults do not secretly want to ignore their children's well-being so badly that, if not for hierarchy, that's what they'd do. If people can be trusted to make good decisions in other realms of life, such as friendships, employment or hobbies, they can be trusted in their romantic relationships. We have the optimistic view that if you are given the ability to make your own choices, you will honor your agreements, uphold your responsibilities and care for the people you love—partners and children.

Perhaps the best way for parents to work toward stable and loving homes is to seek partners who are other mature grown-ups and share their values and priorities, then work to build a strong foundation to all their relationships, demonstrate over time that they are reliable and trustworthy, and then trust each other to make decisions that will benefit their relationships and their families.

In empowered relationships, when a co-parent is about to make a choice that another parent doesn't feel is best for the family, she can raise her concerns. The adults can talk about the concerns and make their choices with those concerns in mind. If one person in the partnership begins consistently making choices that aren't best for the family, then it may be time to re-evaluate that partnership—just as happens in monogamous relationships. And just as happens in monogamous relationships, sometimes the best thing for everyone may be for the parental dyad to share parenting some other way—such as living apart, or in a live-in, platonic co-parenting relationship (an arrangement we've seen often among poly people).

If you don't like how someone is (or isn't) honoring their commitments to you, or you don't feel they can be trusted to honor their commitments and you can't talk it through with them, then they may not be a good choice as a co-parent. If an adult is willing to abandon her commitments, then hierarchy isn't going to force her to keep them!

So what happens if the original parental dyad does dissolve? Surely this scenario must be prevented at all costs if there are kids involved—right?

Relationships end. In a family with children, the end of a relationship will be sad and stressful for everyone. But the same thing happens in monogamous families, and there are ways to minimize the stress on the children. Often, in fact, a new relationship created with a more recent partner is more beneficial for a child than its parents' relationship was, if the parents' relationship was dysfunctional. We've seen this with monogamous blended families as well as poly families. Game changers, discussed in the next chapter, happen to everyone, not just to poly people. Sometimes children are affected.

CLARA'S STORY   Clara and Ramon's relationship was a game changer for both of them. Ramon raised the bar for her in terms of what she wanted out of relationships, and in the end, her relationship with Elijah did not survive—nor did Ramon's with Caitlin. Clara and Ramon are now separated from their spouses and living with each other.

It's always hard for kids when parents separate, but all four parents have worked hard to minimize the effects of the separation on their children. Clara and her children still live in the same home as before, and their schedules have remained the same. Elijah comes to visit them two nights a week, and they spend the night with him every Saturday. This is less than he used to see them, and the elder child has experienced some grief at seeing her father less often.

Ramon and Caitlin's children live with Caitlin and visit Ramon several times a week, including overnights. They have had a rougher time with their parents' separation than have Clara and Elijah's children, because they are somewhat older, with a better grasp of the situation, and have overheard conversations that have exposed them to some of

Caitlin's emotional distress. Both Clara and Ramon have experienced serious parental shaming from friends and family.

Despite the struggles, Clara feels clear that she made the right decision. She believes that had she stayed with Elijah, her unhappiness would have undoubtedly affected her children.

Many of us still carry an idea, preserved from the soulmate fairy tale, that a parental dyad is critical, often above all other concerns, for a child's well-being—even more important than family happiness or functionality. Many imagine that keeping someone in an unhappy relationship "for the sake of the children" is better than allowing two parents to live apart. We learned that from monogamous culture, after all. Among some poly people, this extends to a belief that is it dangerous to allow each adult to make her own choices in a way she needs while also allowing her to honor her relationships and commitments as best she can.

For a child, having happy, fulfilled parents who are committed to that child (in whatever configuration those parents come, and even if that configuration changes), and who are living lives that fulfill them, is far superior to having two parents who are "together" dysfunctionally only because rules and a hierarchy keep them in line. And this situation is certainly better than having people in the household who are treated as secondary to other people. If children observe such behavior in their families, they will take those ideas out into the world and treat other people the same way.

An empowered approach to polyamorous parenting might include agreements that look like this:

I have chosen to parent with you because you share my values and hopes, and I trust you to honor your commitments to me and to make decisions in your relationships that are in the best interest of our family. If your decisions do not support us, I will tell you how and why, and I trust you to work with me— and your other partners, if necessary—to make it right. If you begin behaving in a way that is harmful to me, our relationship or our child, and you don't

rectify it, we will need to renegotiate the terms of our relationship and our co-

parenting arrangement.

It is absolutely true that guidelines and structure benefit children. They are naturally conservative creatures, thriving on order, predictability and outside direction, and falling apart when given freedom they can't yet handle. Parents can create structure and prioritize their children without making one adult partner subject to restrictions created by another partner. Guidelines and structure can be achieved without hierarchy, because adults can be trusted to build a family out of goodwill, free choice, and their love for their partner and their child.

TRUST AND COURAGE

In chapter 8 you met Mila, whose story we return to in chapter 18. Mila, new to poly and planning to have a child with her partner, found the idea of hierarchy seductive, but deliberately turned away from it because of her own values and her concerns for her partner and metamours. She worked through her fears and built a strong relationship with her partner, Morgan, based on trust—in Morgan's love and integrity, and in her own ability to handle what came her way.

Empowered relationships rely on trust. Trust your partner to want to cherish and support you. Trust that if you make your needs known, your partner will want to meet your needs. This requires courage. Building relationships on a shared understanding of needs means having the courage to stand in the face of a negative emotion and ask, "What is this feeling telling me? Is there a need that is not being met? Is there something I can do to enlist my partner as my ally in dealing with this?"

If you're the person whose partner is experiencing emotional hardship, it can be tempting to read this chapter as a way of saying "You have the responsibility to deal with your own emotions, so I don't want you putting restrictions on me." That is partly true, in the sense that you can't solve someone else's problem for them, and if your partner places restrictions on your behavior, those restrictions rarely resolve the underlying issue.

But it's a mistake to put what Douglas Adams calls a Somebody Else's Problem field around a partner's distress. If you care, you will help. Behaving with compassion means working *together* to overcome relationship issues. That's how relationships become strong and healthy.

Another valuable technique in the toolkit of strategies for happy, trusting relationships is to let go of attachment to the *form* that a partner's behavior must take. For example, suppose you feel you aren't getting enough time with your partner. One way to address this is to insist, for example, that he be home by nine o'clock. This may or may not succeed. In one instance Franklin has seen, it did not work even though the person did start coming home by nine, because he would then spend the rest of the evening talking or texting with the person he had just left. The partner who made the request had assumed that being home at nine meant paying attention to her needs, but that wasn't what she actually asked for. What did work was junking the nine o'clock rule in favor of a direct statement: "I need some of your undivided attention every day."

When Franklin has a need, he tells his partners: "These are the things I need in order to feel loved and cherished. These are the things that make me feel special in your eyes." He says these things without expectation or compulsion. He says them without attachment to the way they have to happen. For example, he might say something like "I feel loved and cherished when you spend time with me and reassure me whenever I feel threatened." And then he lets his partners do those things.

Life is occasionally chaotic and unpredictable, from flat tires to late-night emergency-room visits. Sometimes, even when we make a good-faith effort to meet our partners' needs, life gets in the way. Flexibility is important. Resiliency in the face of adversity is a powerful tool for building happy relationships.

QUESTIONS TO ASK YOURSELF

Empowerment in poly relationships and structures can be difficult to define, but its presence or absence is usually clearly felt. The following are some questions that can help you and your partners think about the level of empowerment in your relationships:

- *How do I encourage decision-making participation by all my partners? In what ways do I show my partners they are empowered?*

- *If I feel a desire to restrict relationships between my partners and their partners, what underlying need am I trying to meet?*

- *What are my existing commitments? How can I meet them while still making room for new relationships?*

- *What evidence do I have that my partners love and care for me?*

- *Are there specific things I can ask my partners to do for me to help me feel loved and cared for?*

- *In what ways am I empowered in my relationships? What things help me to feel empowered?*

- *Can I renegotiate the agreements in my relationships? Can my partners?*

PRACTICAL POLY AGREEMENTS

*You cannot shake hands
with a clenched fist.*

INDIRA GANDHI

Most relationships require some bare minimum of structure. Without it, it's difficult to navigate commitments and responsibilities. In the last few chapters, we talked about the distinctions between rules, boundaries and agreements, and we made a case for why we think rules-based structures can create problems in poly relationships. Preparing the ground for relationships to flourish means thinking carefully about not just how to meet your needs, but how to meet the needs of all the people involved. In this chapter, we discuss practical strategies for approaching relationship agreements with this careful analysis as your foundation. It starts with thinking about why people do what they do.

FRANKLIN'S STORY Many years ago I ran a small consulting business. I had an office in downtown Tampa, Florida. Every day on the way to the office, I drove past a building where people applied for passports. The application office was very small, with room for perhaps five people to sit inside. On most days I would see at least twenty people outside, waiting in line to get in.

Just outside the building was a wall about three feet high. The people in line often sat on the wall. It's easy to understand why. They might have more than an hour's wait in the hot Florida sun.

Whoever managed the passport office was offended by people sitting on the wall. I would see sheets of paper that read "Do Not Sit On Wall" taped to the wall. The signs were routinely ignored. The workers in the passport office didn't want people sitting on the wall, but they didn't think about *why* people sat on the wall. When you're waiting in a hot concrete courtyard for an hour, you're going to get tired and want to sit down. The rule was guaranteed to fail.

A more effective way to prevent people from sitting on the wall, if that was really a problem, would have been to address the need rather than the action—say, by installing benches.

The memory of that office and its courtyard has stuck with me. In my own relationships, when I see people doing things I'd rather they didn't do, I try to find out why they're doing it and what might help take care of the need. I try to put benches in the courtyard, rather than putting up signs telling them not to sit on the wall.

Effective relationship strategies take work. They are things that meet people's needs. And meeting these needs involves asking why people are doing whatever you wish they wouldn't do. What need does their behavior meet? What function does it serve? Is there something else, something that might be less threatening, that could meet the same need? How invested is the person in doing that particular thing, and why?

Creating such strategies also involves looking at some scary things inside yourself. Why is it not okay with you if that person does that thing? Are the problems you see really problems? Is passing a rule actually an attempt to shift responsibility for your own emotions onto someone else? Does the person doing the thing reasonably have a right to do it? How much does it really affect others, and in what way? Are you just trying to avoid discomfort? If so, is your discomfort more important than someone else's choices?

From there, you can work on finding the park bench. What might help everyone get their needs met? If something makes you uncomfortable, how can the person do it and still support you?

WHY BE SKEPTICAL OF RULES?

Monogamous society teaches us that to keep our partners faithful and ourselves secure, we should limit their opportunity, keeping them away from desirable people. If that mindset carries over into poly, it leads to trying to keep ourselves secure by limiting who our partners are allowed to have relationships with, or how much time they can be together, or what they do. If we're setting these rules because we are afraid, deep inside, that we aren't good enough and our partners might replace us, a self-reinforcing cycle can develop. We feel low self-esteem, so we make rules to feel safe, and then we don't want to develop self-esteem because if we do that, we won't need rules anymore, and if we don't have rules, we won't feel safe!

Sometimes we can try to use rules to address things we are shy about discussing. It feels scary to talk about our vulnerabilities and insecurities. Often talking about rules becomes a way to try to do that by proxy. It doesn't work, because if we can't talk about the reason for the rule, our partners won't understand the rule's intent, and that leads to trouble, mischief and rules-lawyering: insisting on the letter of the rule without being clear on the intent.

Not all rules are intrinsically bad (see, for instance, "Limited-duration rules," pages 172–73). However, rules always have the potential to become straitjackets, constraining relationships and not allowing them to grow. Sometimes this is intentional—and such rules can be very damaging indeed. If your partner tells you, "I don't want you ever to grow any new relationship beyond this point," and eventually a relationship comes along that you want to see flourish, your original relationship may fail—not in spite of the rule, but *because* of it.

Rules that seek to dictate the structure of a relationship that is yet to exist (for example, "We will only be in a quad") are attempts to map a country you have not yet seen. These types of rules, we have seen, are most often created by people with little experience in polyamorous relationships. Often they attempt to impose order on something that seems mysterious and dangerous. Psychologists have discovered that we are remarkably poor at predicting how we will respond to novel situations. We want certainty; we don't want to get too far from familiar land. But we cannot explore the ocean if we're unwilling to lose sight of the shore. Trying to retain the certainty and order of monogamy against the apparent scary disorder of polyamory usually ends up creating failures in both.

Some rules indicate fears or discomforts that someone doesn't want to face. Someone might say, "We want to have other partners, but the thought of my partner prioritizing anyone else when I want attention brings up my fears of abandonment. So we will pass a rule saying I can always interrupt my partner's other dates, or I must approve my partner's scheduled time with other people."* When two (or more) people have discomforts they're trying to avoid, they may play the mutual-assured-destruction game: I will let you control me to avoid your discomforts, if you let me control you to avoid my discomforts. Or, as the poly blogger Andrea Zanin has written, "I will limit you, and you will limit me, and then we'll both be safe." Avoiding discomfort isn't really the same thing as creating happiness; real happiness is often on the other side of our comfort zone. If our relationships aren't creating happiness, what's the point?

CREATING EFFECTIVE RELATIONSHIP AGREEMENTS

Agreements and boundaries will be part of any polyamorous relationship. Some expectations are reasonable, though "reasonable" and "unreasonable" carry a great deal of wibbly-wobbly subjectivity. Here is one crude tell-tale sign of unreasonable rules that we use: When people have agreements that are *reasonable*, such as around safer sex, they generally can talk about them calmly and dispassionately. When someone states a rule and then refuses to

---

* Note, however, that restrictions on sex in a shared bed are a very common limited-duration rule, discussed in chapter 10.

discuss it, answers questions about it with "That's just how I feel," or becomes offended or upset about it, look out. Something else is going on—something that isn't being addressed directly.

Healthy agreements are those *that encourage moving in the direction of greatest courage.* "I feel threatened by the idea of my woman having sex with other men. She can't do that" is based on fear and insecurity, not courage. "I feel threatened by this idea, so when you do this, I will ask for your support and I will want some time with you afterward to help ground and settle me" is a request that moves in the direction of greatest courage. It recognizes that the other person has the right to choose her partners, while at the same time asking for the support to help deal with unpleasant emotional responses.

The agreements that work most consistently are those that are rooted in compassion, encourage mutual respect and empowerment, leave it to our partners' judgment how to implement them, and have input from—and apply equally to—everyone affected by them. These include principles like the following: Treat all others with kindness. Don't try to force relationships to be something they are not. Don't try to impose yourself on other people. Understand when things are Not About You. Understand that just because you feel bad, it doesn't necessarily mean someone else did something wrong. Know that your feelings sometimes lie to you. Own your own mess. Favor trust over rules.

Here are some other common characteristics of successful relationship agreements:

- *They are not games of Mao.* Named for the Chinese ruler Mao Zedong, Mao is a card game where at the start of the game none of the players except the dealer know the rules...and the players are penalized for breaking the rules. The players who figure out the rules the slowest lose. If you are to have relationship agreements, they must be clear and comprehensible. Everyone involved should know and understand them—and equally important, understand the intent behind them: the spirit as well as the letter.
- *They seek to place controls on one's self, not one's partners.* You can't really control anyone but yourself. "You must," "You cannot...": Those kinds of statements work only if other people choose to let them.

- *They offer a clear path to success.* Rules that try to protect anyone ever from feeling uncomfortable, for instance, don't have a clear path to success—discomfort often accompanies change, and sometimes attempting to prevent one person from being uncomfortable will make someone else uncomfortable.
- *They are clear, specific and limited in scope.* "You must care for me more than you care for her" is not clear or specific. It doesn't define what "care for me" means or what steps can be taken to get there. "We will not have unbarriered exchange of bodily fluids before discussing it with each other" is clear, specific and limited in scope.
- *They have a defined practical purpose.* "Don't do this because it makes me feel threatened" is vague and impractical. It places responsibility for the feeling on the partner of the person having the feeling. It's not always clear what need a particular feeling may be trying to communicate, and it can take some effort to work down from a feeling to discover the underlying need. Successful agreements address needs directly, rather than trying to address feelings about them.
- *They do not seek to sweep problems under the rug.* "I get jealous when I see you kiss someone, so don't kiss anyone in front of me" does not deal with the jealousy, it only addresses the trigger. The jealousy is still there, just waiting to emerge in some other way.
- *They have a sunset clause if they are meant to provide space for dealing with a problem.* A sunset clause (see also page 173) means a restriction expires on a certain date. If there is no sunset clause, once the emotional trigger has been removed, it can be all too easy to say "I'll work on the problem tomorrow." And tomorrow becomes next week, then next month.
- *They aren't aimed at unspoken expectations.* For example, "Don't spend the night at a lover's house" may actually be a way of saying "Make sure I am never lonely." The overnight rule might sound reasonable, but the underlying expectation is not. We are human beings; we feel many things, including, from time to time, things we don't like, such as loneliness.
- *They are renegotiable.* Any agreement should be open to discussion at any time by anyone it affects. This includes anyone who enters a

relationship after an agreement is made. Life is change; deal with it. Even if life never changed, we rarely build something exactly right the first time.

- *They do not disempower people.* It's common for a couple, or people in a romantic network, to pass rules governing in advance the behavior of a future new arrival, without giving that person a say. In ethical relationships, every adult has a voice.
- *They do not try to legislate feelings.* People cannot provide feelings on demand. Attempting to legislate feelings (for example, by saying "You must love both of us equally" or "You are not allowed to feel jealous") usually works about as well as trying to legislate the weather.

NEGOTIATING IN GOOD FAITH

When you are negotiating agreements in your relationship, it can be hard to hear that your partners have different needs or sensitivities than you do. Truly understanding that other people are as real as you are is hard. If you want to negotiate in good faith, here are some things to keep in mind:

- *Focus on mutual benefit.* To succeed, an agreement must benefit everyone. Even when people have what seem to be contradictory goals, it may be possible to find a solution by looking for the need underneath a proposed rule.
- *Pay attention to the needs.* If a partner tells you, "I don't want you to take any dates to Bob's Crab Shack" because that's a special place for the two of you, their statement may spring from a desire to feel unique in your eyes. Finding ways to show your partner that you consider him unique and irreplaceable may solve the need better than avoiding Bob's Crab Shack.
- *Treat the other people in the negotiation as partners, not problems.* It's easy to think, *If only you would do what I say, everything would be okay! Why aren't you doing what I want?* Remember that these people are not your adversaries; you *all* want happy relationships. Treat people with compassion.
- *Don't compromise on behalf of other people without their input and consent.* When you agree to limitations on your actions with other people, you are limiting them as well. They deserve a place at the negotiating table.

WHEN YOU DIDN'T WRITE THE RULES

In polyamory, you will likely find yourself starting relationships with people who already have partners. And that may mean going into relationships that have rules already in place. Accepting someone else's rules at the beginning of a relationship sets a dangerous precedent: it says that you're on board with relationships that are built around other people's needs.

Anyone who goes into a rules-based relationship, knowing the rules up front, is agreeing voluntarily to be bound by them, right? Well, maybe. All kinds of things might cause someone to enter a relationship that isn't a good fit—a scarcity model of relationships, for example.

It's absolutely true that if you enter a rules-based relationship you are, implicitly and explicitly, agreeing to those rules. And yet "You knew the rules when you signed on!" is so often the parting shot amidst a relationship's wreckage. Consider why. Most of the time, when we start a relationship, we expect our partners to meet us in the middle, to negotiate with us, to consider our needs. Those seem like reasonable expectations, right? So it can be quite a shock when your partner suddenly slams the door on something and says it's non-negotiable. ("What *is* this about Bob's Crab Shack, anyway? Why can't I go there with you? I just want to get some seafood!")

Rules might seem reasonable at first but end up leading to absurd outcomes. In one relationship we know of, a married couple had rules concerning what sexual positions could and couldn't be used with "new" partners. When the wife started a relationship with someone else, those rules remained in force a decade into the "new" relationship. I think most of us would probably agree that a ten-year relationship is not a "new" relationship. We probably expect, reasonably, that if a rule takes us to an absurd destination, it should be revisited—and we can be shocked to be met with "No, sorry, you knew the rule when you signed on."

It is okay to assume that flexibility and agency in our relationships are part of the social contract. It probably wouldn't occur to us even to *have* to say "By the way, if I've been with you for ten years, I expect you to be willing to consider my needs." So in that sense, "You knew the rules when you signed on" is not actually true. *We did not grasp* that flexibility and negotiation were forbidden.

At the beginning of a relationship, we can't predict what feelings we will have, or how deeply we will attach to someone, because *we aren't there yet.*

Therefore, it's easy to say yes to rules that treat us as disposable, or don't give us a voice in advocating for our needs, because we don't have the needs yet. The true test of compassion is what we do when compassion is hard. Any well-implemented set of agreements needs to allow for the vulnerability of human hearts and the unpredictability of life.

RULES THAT CAUSE PROBLEMS

We have seen certain relationship rules among poly people fail again and again. The following agreements have proven to be fraught with problems and require great care if you attempt them.

"Don't ask, don't tell" agreements. In these arrangements, a person says, "You can have other lovers, but I don't want to know about them." This often indicates that someone wishes the relationship weren't poly at all and hopes to pretend it's not happening. This charade makes it impossible to communicate about important things, or for new partners to verify that the relationship is in fact open. "We're in a 'Don't ask, don't tell!'" is a favorite lie that monogamous cheaters use to explain why you can't just call their spouse to check out whether the relationship is really open.

Rules that require a person to be sexually involved with another, or that require some other form of service. When you make sex or intimacy with one person the price of sex or intimacy with another, you plant the seeds of coercion, as discussed in the section titled "Service secondaries" on pages 192–93.

Rules that fetishize or objectify people. We have known people who treat a partner's other lovers as fetish objects, demanding detailed, blow-by-blow accounts of every sexual encounter for their own gratification. Your partner's significant others are not your sex aids. Unless they consent to having the details of their sexual encounters shared with a third person for the purpose of arousal, they have a reasonable expectation of privacy.

Rules that restrict certain things, places, activities or sex acts to one partner. These rules are often seen as ways to protect the "specialness" of one relationship. A person who does not already feel unique in her partner's eyes, however, is unlikely to gain greater self-worth by restricting others from "special" things.

And over time, the *symbols* of specialness, like Bob's Crab Shack, can start to be more important than the actual *fact* of specialness. They begin to feel hollow, because they are. The feeling of specialness actually arises from all of the daily ways in which we invest in a relationship and express love. Such rules also court disaster when the lists of limited activities become—as they may over the years—long and complicated.

LEILA'S STORY Molly and Jeff are a married couple with a notebook filled with rules, including a detailed list of which sexual activities are permitted with which partners. When Leila became involved with Jeff, the rules in the book were applied to her too. One of the rules was that Leila could not touch another partner on an area of the body covered by underwear without Jeff's permission. Leila assumed "underwear" meant briefs; Jeff assumed boxers. While on a date, she touched a new partner on the inner thigh. This led to recriminations and accusations, with Jeff claiming Leila had violated an agreement.

After the relationship ended, Leila described to us the feeling of trying to navigate these labyrinthine rules. She said, "A rule is not just an agreed-upon avoidance of consequences. Rules-based systems judge your moral character based on your adherence to the rules. It's a contract that frames things as acts of betrayal and leaves the 'betrayer' buried under moral judgment. The guilt or potential guilt in that situation is like breathing acid."

"LOVE ME, LOVE MY PARTNER" RULES

Human beings don't fall in love at the same time in the same way at the same rate with two people at once. It just doesn't happen. And when rules make assumptions about sexual access to someone's body ("If you have sex with me, you must have sex with my partner too"), they can quickly overrun personal boundaries, or even become coercive: Sex with one person becomes the grit-your-teeth price that must be paid to have a relationship with the other. Such rules discourage honesty. If your new partner loves you but not your partner, will she tell you that, knowing that telling you means being kicked out?

Rules that specify what happens if one relationship runs into trouble. For example, there could be a rule that other relationships must be ended or scaled back. When a couple agrees "If we run into trouble, we'll drop any other relationships to work on the problem," they treat their other partners as disposable things. If a couple had three kids and decided to send two of them into foster homes to focus on a problem the third one was having, we might call them monsters. This kind of behavior is also a questionable way to treat romantic partners.

Rules that are disguised as personal preferences. Sometimes a person might present a rule as just a statement of personal preference. An example from Franklin's experience is a married couple who had a rule that the wife was not permitted to have any male partners. When Franklin asked why this rule existed, she said it was just her personal preference; she didn't want any male partners.

So then why was the rule made at all? This was a big warning flag of underlying issues in the marriage. It took about two years for the wife to admit that, yes, she really *did* want male partners; she'd said she didn't to reassure her husband, who felt threatened by the idea and obtained the rule at what seemed like no cost to anyone. It took another five years for the dust to settle. In the end, she was able to have another boyfriend, but it took a lot of unnecessary turmoil and drama to get there. As uncomfortable as it was for her husband to come to terms with her hidden need, two years of him naively believing that she didn't want other male lovers only made him feel worse about the reality when he found out. Honesty from the beginning would have saved everyone considerable grief.

PAGING DR. MÜNCHAUSEN

There's one rule, quite common in hierarchical relationships, which we believe is particularly dangerous and deserves special attention: a rule that a person who is sick, injured or in crisis will only be supported by the primary partner. Other partners are not permitted to care for that person. This rule was part of Franklin's relationship with Celeste.

You will often see caring for someone in need billed as a way for a primary partner to preserve a sense of intimacy and specialness. Caring for a partner is one of the most loving things we can do, but the idea that only one person should be able to do it is very troubling.

When someone is sick or injured or in crisis, the focus should be on that person. Rules that say "Only the primary can provide support" divert the focus from the person in need, shifting it to the issue of who can do what. Worse, if a person's sense of specialness or intimacy *depends* on caring for someone in need, that's codependency. In its most extreme form, it becomes Münchausen by proxy syndrome, a recognized psychiatric disorder. When someone is in the hospital or laid up, this is not the time for displays of territoriality or ego.

WRITING IT DOWN

"Good fences make good neighbors"—or so they say. Many people who give poly advice will urge you to write down and even sign your agreements. The "relationship contract" is quite common in polyamory (and is growing in popularity even among monogamous people, or so we hear: Mark Zuckerberg's wife famously negotiated a contract with him guaranteeing 100 minutes of his undivided time for her each week). These written agreements can range from a few sentences on a Post-It note to, in one case we've seen, approximately 48 pages of single-spaced type.

Certainly there are many situations in which explicit, written agreements are just common sense. Eve won't do business with a new client without a contract (and usually a deposit). It's too easy even for honest people to remember a verbal agreement very differently from each other, or for one to genuinely forget they even made it.

But while written relationship contracts might seem like good communication, they contain a hidden trap. Communication is a dialogue. A contract—especially one that's presented to new people as a done deal—very often isn't. Communication and discussion are essential for the health of any relationship. This is why, as we have said before, we see agreements as far better than rules. The difference is that agreements are mutually agreed to among equals, but turning an agreement into paperwork too soon can become an expression of power.

We've seen two different types of written relationship contracts: those that are written when all the people affected come together to work out a solution to a problem everyone is facing, and pre-emptive contracts that one set of people (often a couple) writes down, expecting any new partners they meet to sign on.

Some written relationship agreements are intended to address only a particularly narrow subject, such as safer sex boundaries, or whom the partners can be out to, or whether a veto exists and how it may be used. (Some people have found it just as helpful to record that veto does not exist as to record that it does—such a reminder can be helpful when times get rough.) Other agreements include some of the provisions mentioned above, concerning permitted or forbidden sex acts or restaurants, ranging all the way to pet names that new partners are not allowed to use. We even know of one contract that limits playing certain kinds of strategy war games to only certain partners.

In general, written agreements are more successful when they

- are short enough to remember without needing to reference them often—generally less than one or two pages long
- have a narrow focus
- are intended to solve a specific problem among a specific group of people
- concern only those people present in negotiating them: in other words, "I will do this for you," not "Others will or will not do this" or "I will or won't do this with others."
- include statements of goals or intentions: the purpose of the agreement (such as Eve's wedding vows, on page 272).
- are flexible and open to review and renegotiation

Written agreements tend to work poorly when they

- are lengthy and highly detailed
- attempt to define or regulate every aspect of a situation
- affect people who are not present in negotiating the agreement

- prescribe specific actions to implement a stated intention (that is, allowing only one way to get there)
- attempt to control things beyond the control of the negotiating partners, such as future intimacy (see pages 263–64) or the behavior of others
- allow no room for renegotiation or change

Successful written agreements are documents that you hold *yourself* to, not something others hold you to. They are reminders to yourself of commitments you have made and tools for communicating those commitments to other partners. They should not be used as devices to shame, manipulate or punish. And remember our ethical axiom: *The people in the relationship are more important than the relationship.* If you find yourselves haggling over clauses in an agreement and whether they have been violated, rather than discussing the hurt feelings, the needs behind a partner's actions and ways to make amends, you've probably reached a place where the people are serving the rules, and not the other way around.

Perhaps the most serious danger in written contracts is when they are inflexible. The longer and more complex they are, the more they are likely to be trying to script a relationship or treat people (at best) as a threat to be managed and (at worst) as a commodity. If one partner is finding herself unable to hold to a provision of the agreement, there's a good chance the agreement needs to be renegotiated to work for all partners—and not that she is dishonest or doesn't care about the agreement.

People who keep long, complex written agreements often build relationships that are unable to change when their needs change. They often spend a lot of time rules-lawyering (consider the story of Leila and Jeff).

Imagine that you were looking for a conventional monogamous relationship, and on a date, somewhere between the Caesar salad and the barbecued shrimp, your date pulled out a 48-page document and said, "This contract spells out how our relationship will go from here. Sign here, here and here, and initial here, please." You would quite likely find it off-putting—especially if the contract specified that you couldn't play Scrabble, couldn't go to Bob's Crab Shack, and were expected not to engage in oral sex, all so that your date's best friend from college wouldn't feel threatened by you.

Good written agreements are instead reminders of our own bound-aries or commitments. One very short contract we've seen contains elements such as "My partner is important," "Do your chores before going on a date," "Don't spend joint money on your own dates," and "Don't fuck it up." An agreement that's about what you will each do to care for each other is a very different thing from an agreement that tells new partners how *they* are expected to behave.

We urge those of you considering written agreements to draw up short, specific lists of boundaries or intentions, rather than than long, complex documents that tell others what they are and aren't allowed to do. Ultimately, remember that your relationship belongs to the living, feeling people in-volved in it, not a list of rules. Make sure that *people*, not pieces of paper, are always at the center of your relationships.

DROP THE PERMISSION MODEL

A factor that often portends failure of a rule is whether it's linked to a "permission model" of relationships. This is the idea that when we enter a relationship, we give up control over our actions to our partner. If we wish to do things like enter into another relationship, visit another partner or take a new lover, we must seek the permission of our existing partner. As soon as we start a relationship with someone, that person becomes the gatekeeper to all our future relationships.

In our experience, relationships that provide everyone in them the most happiness follow a different model. The people who seem happiest in rela-tionships start with the premise "I can have the kind of relationship I want. I can make choices I want to. My best course of action is to learn to choose people who want something similar, to take responsibility for the conse-quences of my choices, and to pay attention to the effects my choices have on the people around me."

When evaluating agreements or structures, look also to the language built into them. Watch for the slippery words we talked about in the com-munication chapters. *Respect* is one of those words. You can hardly argue with it; when faced with a provision that says, "You must treat me and my other partners with respect," few would say, "Well, you know, I think I'd rather be disrespectful." Most people will agree to such a provision without a second thought. But what, exactly, does *respect* mean? If respect means "be subordinate to," it creates a very different relationship dynamic than if *respect* means "take seriously and treat with compassion."

The best agreements are not ones that steer people away from bad things, but rather ones that point us toward good things. We both subscribe to the radical idea that the best way to create security in a relationship is to create happiness: the people in the relationship are more important than the relationship. To that end, when you make agreements, look for the ones that move in the direction of greatest happiness. Franklin's partner Sylvia likes to say her primary relationship rule is "If I am not a positive aspect of your life, I don't want to be in your life, and vice versa." While it sounds simple, that approach to relationship requires courage—especially the courage to know that you can lose a relationship that does not make you happy, and that's okay.

GAME CHANGERS

When we open our hearts to multiple relationships, every now and then someone comes along who changes everything. This is one of the truths of polyamory rarely talked about: the game changer.

A game changer is a relationship that causes us to rethink all our relationships, and maybe even our lives, entirely. It may be a relationship with someone who fits with us so naturally that the person raises the bar on what we want and need from other relationships. It may be a connection so profound that it causes us to look at our lives in a new way. It's a relationship that alters the landscape of life. A game changer doesn't even have to be a good relationship. It can be one that's dysfunctional on such a deep level that it changes what we look for thereafter.

A game-changing relationship is invariably disruptive. It makes us see things in a new light. It opens us to new ways of thinking, or perhaps answers needs we didn't know we had (or didn't think could be met). Because of that, game-changing relationships are scary. Indeed, they are arguably one of the scariest things that can happen in poly relationships.

Many rules in poly relationships can be seen as ways to control the fear of a game changer. Franklin has experienced not one but two game-changing relationships, both of which substantially rearranged his life. Given how scary and disruptive game changers are, many people try to set up barriers to prevent them, erecting fortifications to protect their lives and hearts from disruption. In practice, this is often about as effective as building a tornado shelter from straw. Love is a powerful thing. Sometimes it transforms us.

Not only are structures designed to prevent game-changing relationships unlikely to work, it wouldn't necessarily be a good thing if they did. Change is scary, but that doesn't make it bad. There is nothing noble in trying to preserve the status quo from things that can make our lives better.

Unfortunately, when a game changer happens to someone who's already in a relationship, it tends to concentrate the wonderfulness in one place but spread the disruption around. So when your partner starts new relationships, you may feel compelled to seek reassurances that things won't change for you, at least in ways you don't like. It can feel very reassuring to extract a pledge from your partner that you will always have some measure of control. Good luck with that.

Game changers change things. It's in the name. They upset existing arrangements. People confronted with a game-changing relationship will not be likely to remain happy with old rules and agreements for long; the definition of a game-changing relationship is that it reshuffles priorities. Expecting an agreement to protect you from a game changer is a bit like expecting a river to obey a law against flooding.

Being a parent is not a protection against game changers. In chapter 13 we told the story of Clara and Elijah, a married couple with children who separated after Clara's game-changing relationship with Ramon. Of game changers, Clara says, "You realize what's really important to you in a relationship and re-evaluate what you have." She doesn't regret the decisions she's made, despite the changes they've caused to her co-parenting relationship.

Game changers are not just a poly thing: they happen in monogamous relationships all the time. Nearly half of marriages end in divorce, and game-changing affairs are one major reason. Sometimes, game-changing events have nothing to do with romantic relationships. A promotion, a baby, a car accident, a job loss, a death in the family—all these can permanently and irrevocably alter our lives, and our relationships, in ways we can't predict. We accept the reality of game changers all the time when they don't come in the form of romantic relationships, as happened in Eve's life.

EVE'S STORY   Arguably the biggest game changer in my marriage was my mother-in-law. In 2008 she had a massive stroke that paralyzed her on one side. In just a few minutes, this active, healthy, youthful sixty-seven-year-old woman became completely dependent on round-the-clock care. That stroke represented a seismic shift in my marriage, dictating our priorities, budget and travel schedules for years. Peter made the ten-hour round trip over the mountains to visit her and his father every two to four weeks for years. In 2012 he went to live with his parents for over eight months, to assist his father, who was facing burnout.

Few would fault him. Elder care is accepted as something that often is a game changer. And yet it resulted in significant strain on our lives and our relationship.

We understand that no promise of "forever" can stand up to the #39 bus with bad brakes that puts someone in a coma. These are the risks we take when we open our hearts to someone else. Sometimes things really change. Relationships take courage.

Still, polyamory complicates the emotional calculus in new ways. Relationship game changers feel more frightening than other kinds. Whether it's insecurities that whisper that others are prettier, smarter and more deserving; or the social fable that romantic love connects us to only one person at a time; or the idea that every new connection our partner makes takes away our specialness (as though specialness were a currency sitting in a bank account somewhere, available in limited quantities, with substantial penalties for early withdrawal)—relationships seem uniquely able to push our buttons.

The desire not to lose what you have because your partner meets someone new is rational and reasonable. What is neither rational nor reasonable, though, is attempting to build structures that allow your partner to have other relationships while guaranteeing that nothing will change for you. Relationships don't work that way. We live in a world with no guarantees.

FRANKLIN'S STORY   I spent my first five or six years of non-monogamous relationships trying very hard to create a system of rules that would guarantee I always felt safe and in control. When I didn't feel safe, it seemed like I hadn't found quite the right rules. So I returned to the rules, tinkering with them, adding exceptions and new clauses, searching for just the right combination that would protect me from changes I did not want to face.

In the end, this strategy didn't work. When the first game-changing relationship came along, neither I nor Celeste were prepared for it. I met Amber, who is still my partner as I write this. She tried very hard to fit herself into the space we'd carved out for her with our rules, and something profound happened. For the first time, I was able to see how contorting herself to fit into the space left by our fears and our desire for safety hurt her. As soon as I saw that, the relationship became a game changer.

Had we been more flexible, or had Celeste and I been more open to the possibility that parts of our relationship could change *and we'd still be okay,* I might have been able to accommodate the new relationship in a way that allowed me to strengthen my bond with Celeste, and my life would look very different now.

That's the funny thing about fear of change. Sometimes the more rigid we are when we insist that we do not want our lives to change, the more catastrophically things break when change comes along. I handled my own game-changing relationship poorly. Rather than facing down my fears, having the courage to accept change and the flexibility to adapt to it gracefully, I had become so invested in the idea that polyamory would not mean changing my existing relationship that on the day this became impossible, I had no tools for handling change.

The starting point to a happy poly life is the ability to say "Our relationships can change, and that is okay. My partner and I can still build things that will make us both happy even if they don't look quite the way they do now." As we've said, this takes courage. And it means having trust in your partner and yourself.

From there, the next step is to say "Even if things change, I have worth. I believe my partners will make choices that honor and cherish our connection, whatever may come, because I add value to their lives. I will build relationships that are resilient enough to handle change, flexible enough to accommodate change, and supportive enough to create a foundation that welcomes change. Change is the one eternal of life. What I have now I will cherish, and what we build tomorrow I will cherish, without fear."

Life rewards courage. The game changer that turns everything upside down might just leave you in a better place. The only real control you have in your relationships comes from working together to express the things you need even while change is happening all around you.

QUESTIONS TO ASK YOURSELF

Relationship agreements work best when they do not impose limits on what form new relationships are allowed to take; when they serve the needs of all the people involved, including the people yet to show up; and when they are flexible and adaptable as you change and grow. These questions can help guide you toward ethical agreements that work.

When considering an agreement:

- *What is the purpose of this agreement?*

- *Does the agreement serve the purpose it is intended to serve?*

- *Is this agreement the only way to serve this purpose?*

- *What will happen if someone breaks the agreement? Do we have a path for re-establishing trust?*

- *Is everyone affected by the agreement at the table in negotiating it?*

- *Can the agreement be renegotiated?*

When renegotiating an agreement:

- *Are the needs now the same as the needs when we agreed to this?*

- *Has this agreement been successful in meeting the needs it was intended to meet?*

- *Has anyone been harmed by this agreement?*

- *Is this agreement serving the people involved, or are the people serving it?*

PART 4

The Poly Reality

HOW POLY RELATIONSHIPS ARE DIFFERENT

It will be a little messy, but embrace the mess.
It will be complicated, but rejoice in the complications.
It will not be anything like what you think it will be like,
but surprises are good for you.

NORA EPHRON

Despite what you may think after the past 256 pages, most of the time poly relationships are pretty much like monogamous relationships. There's coffee and movies and cuddling and sex and talking, meals and arguments and chores and balancing the house accounts. (Okay, maybe there's more talking.) Plenty of situations are unique to poly, though, and many things that crop up in monogamous relationships involve special considerations when more than two people are involved. And there are a few poly bogeys—scary situations and problems with no easy solutions, which no one really likes to talk about but which exist all the same.

In Part 4 we go deep into the nuts and bolts of poly relationships: things like time management, sex and, yes, those scary, no-easy-solution problems. We've already talked about the idea of the "relationship escalator": the script deeply ingrained in monogamous culture that defines the default path for "successful" relationships, from dating to sex to living together to marriage and kids. You may jump off the escalator and start again from the bottom with someone else, but the assumed goal is to find the right one for the trip all the way to the top, at which point you're done. As we've said, polyamory can free you from the relationship escalator, allowing you to grow relationships that nourish everyone in the ways they most need.

The variety of poly relationships is, as we've mentioned, huge. We can't make assumptions about the shape or path of your relationships. However, most poly relationships do pass through certain stages: things like new relationship energy, and the start of a new relationship while in an established one. These stages present uniquely poly challenges. Here are some places where poly relationships diverge from monogamous relationships and the old templates no longer apply.

THE TIMING OF NEW RELATIONSHIPS

There's no perfect time for a new relationship to start, nor a set schedule for how quickly or slowly it should develop. Sometimes opportunity knocks at the most inopportune times. New relationships are wonderful, joyous and stressful. Attempting to script how and when they develop amid your existing ones is like trying to corral elephants; these things have a certain inertia of their own, and sometimes all you can do is learn to be nimble on your feet.

Some people prefer to start new relationships infrequently, and to impose a moratorium after a new one begins to allow it to grow roots. Others choose not to start a new relationship if there are problems in any existing relationship, or during times of turbulence or stress. Still others prefer to remain open to new relationships whenever connections might occur. None of these strategies is always effective. Allowing relationships time to solidify before taking on new partners is not a guarantee that new partners won't be disruptive, and being open to new relationships all the time doesn't necessarily mean a lot of romantic churn.

To some extent, the approach you'll take depends on your personal poly styles. People who favor a closely connected network of intimate relationships tend to decline opportunities for new relationships shortly after taking a new partner, whereas people with a more solo or independent poly style are more likely to be open to relationships whenever and however they form. New partnerings can often feel threatening or, at the very least, destabilizing. This is where many people adopt another strategy: moving at the pace of the slowest person. "Move at the speed of the slowest person" is such common advice in poly discussion groups that it's become a trope.

Making sure everyone has time to process changes in a relationship, especially big changes, certainly has its advantages. The gotcha is that "Move at the pace of the slowest person" can turn into a pocket veto. "Not now, not yet" can, if unchecked, quietly become "Not ever." If one person is urging others to slow down, there must be a recognition that she needs to show she is making some progress toward being comfortable with things. Otherwise, "Move at the speed of the slowest person" turns into "Don't move at all." If "no movement" is a person's intent, they should say so up front.

Rushing into a new relationship can lead to instability. But moving more slowly than what's natural for the relationship can also damage it. Relationships, like living things, have a natural pacing and rhythm. Artificially limiting a relationship's growth can leave people feeling hurt and frustrated. Counterintuitively, it can cause the relationship to be *more* disruptive. Imagine how much more desperate Romeo and Juliet felt because their parents tried to keep them apart, and how much less turbulent the story would have been if their parents had said, "Eh, you two work it out."

In any relationship, it pays to check in often with yourself and your partner about the state of the union. Is it growing in ways that serve your needs? Is the pace of the relationship appropriate for your mutual desires? Does it cause unnecessary difficulties for your other partners?

NEW RELATIONSHIP ENERGY

Few things raise trepidation in the hearts of poly people faster than new relationship energy. NRE, as it's (un)affectionately known, is that crazy, giddy, I-can't-stop-thinking-of-you, everything-about-you-is-marvelous feeling you get at the start of a new relationship.

The biochemistry of NRE is becoming fairly well understood. During the early stages of a romantic relationship, our brains go a little haywire. Several neurotransmitters, most notably dopamine, serotonin and norepinephrine,[*] are produced in greater quantities, generally producing emotional effects that are part attraction and devotion, part obsessive-compulsive disorder, part mystical experience and part physical lust. We become infatuated and twitterpated whenever the person is near. In this state, we're biochemically predisposed to overlook their flaws and faults, see the best in everything they do, convince ourselves that we are meant to be with them, and crave their attention. When people make distinctions between "love" and "being in love,"

---

[*] *Some people also implicate another neurotransmitter, phenylethylamine (PEA), in attraction and pair-bonding, though this assertion is still controversial. Some studies have suggested it plays a role, but other studies have not supported this conclusion.*

what they describe as "being in love" is generally something like new relationship energy.

Psychologist Dorothy Tennov coined the term *limerence* in 1979 to describe a state of romantic attraction characterized by intrusive thoughts of a person, overwhelming fear of rejection by that person, and powerful, obsessive need for reciprocation. Limerence, in other words, is what we feel when we fall in love with someone regardless of whether they like us in return; new relationship energy is limerence in an actual new relationship.

For the partner of a person starting a new relationship, NRE is scary stuff. The overwhelming feelings can make existing relationships feel drab by comparison. Worse, the tendency to idolize new partners can easily trick us into making too many commitments too quickly, which can create chaos in the existing relationships.

We're not saying NRE is a bad thing. On the contrary, it's transcendent. NRE lets us start a relationship bathed in delight. There's a reason this biochemical response exists: the excitement and giddiness can help lay the emotional foundation for a rewarding, loving partnership. But to make it through NRE while preserving our other relationships, we need to recognize it for what it is, nurture our other partners when we feel it, and not mistake it for love.

We've seen a lot of policies in poly relationships designed to mitigate the effects of new relationship energy, but none that seem terribly successful. When it comes to people's brain chemistry, rules and agreements have a way of falling by the wayside.

A more effective way to deal with with a partner's NRE involves both communication and patience. The good news is that this biochemical madness doesn't last forever; the bad news is that it can last as long as two or three years. Patience is important, because a person experiencing NRE literally isn't quite in their right mind. Communication is important too; when you observe your partner behaving in ways that make you feel insecure, neglected, threatened or taken for granted, you need to say so. Patience *in* communication is also key, because a partner in the throes of NRE may not hear you the first time.

When you're the one experiencing NRE, mindfulness is the only consistently successful strategy we've seen. Be aware that you're not in your right mind, that your perceptions are distorted, and that your judgment is impaired. Don't make life-altering decisions while intoxicated. Don't pledge your life to this marvelous person you met last week. Be aware that you will be predisposed to neglect your existing relationships, and try not to do that. Be willing to do a reality check.

A particularly insidious pattern can set in when the hormonal cocktail begins to wear off. A person who doesn't understand what's happening may become convinced that the relationship is no longer interesting and was probably a mistake from the start, and she starts casting around for a new relationship, which she pursues with zeal until that NRE too wears off. In monogamous culture this takes the form of short-term serial relationships. In polyamory, this pattern can present as a series of ongoing relationships that begin explosively and then wither from neglect. In either case, the chemical high of NRE is mistaken for love, and the sufferer seeks the next new hit like an addict.

LIVING TOGETHER

Being involved with multiple partners complicates the logistics of cohabitation. When many people first hear about polyamory, they envision a bunch of people living together in a commune. While that does sometimes happen, it's really not that common. More often, we see households of two or three people, some or all of whom may have non-live-in relationships with other people. Some of those other people might have live-in relationships with their other partners.

As we've said, there's no standard model. Whether the people in a poly relationship live together depends only on their own needs and choices. After all, just because you love Eunice and you love Taj, and you can see yourself living with either or both of them, that doesn't necessarily mean Eunice and Taj can live with each other! Not everyone wants to live with even one lover. Some folks prefer having their own space. In fact, for people who practice a solo model of poly relationships, living alone may be vastly preferable to sharing a home, regardless of how committed the relationship is or how long it continues.

An entire class of problems can appear when we do live with multiple partners. Living with anyone in itself can be a source of stress and discomfort. A friend of ours likes to say these stresses aren't poly problems; they're roommate problems. We don't tend to consider live-in romantic partners the same way we think about roommates, but a lot of unnecessary suffering can be avoided when we employ the same strategies as for non-romantic roommates—strategies like negotiation and clear expectations around dishes in the sink, household chores, basic courtesy, respect for other people's sleeping schedules, and willingness to clean up after ourselves.

Take laundry, for instance. Who does the laundry in polyamorous relationships? In the monogamous world, that job tends to get assigned by default, more often than not along gender lines. In poly relationships we negotiate everything, including the division of domestic labor. Talk about who does the laundry. (In Eve's household, as in many poly households, there's an agreement that whoever has a lover over to the house changes and washes the sheets afterward.)

COMMITMENTS IN POLY RELATIONSHIPS

The huge variation in poly relationships means there won't be a clear road map for what commitment looks like. Some folks argue this means polyamorous relationships can't be committed. Naturally we disagree, though we will say commitment in poly relationships is often quite different from the monogamous template. In monogamous culture, many commitments look like the relationship escalator. People who start dating each other and continue a while often expect a commitment to stop dating other people. Most monogamous dating couples who don't break up will eventually live together. Most people living together who don't break up will eventually feel they need to commit to getting married, owning property and maybe having kids together.

There are less tangible commitments as well. Most monogamous couples would probably agree that they have a commitment to seeing the relationship continue as long as it can. Most monogamous couples have a commitment to one another's well-being, which might mean anything from bringing chicken soup to a partner who's sick to driving a partner to work if her car breaks down.

Part of the beauty of poly relationships is they can look like almost anything the people involved want them to. But that means poly people are responsible for consciously designing our relationships. It's essential to be crystal clear when making commitments, and to *never* assume a commitment unless it's been explicitly stated. Simply being in a relationship with someone is not a commitment to the traditional relationship escalator. A pattern is not a commitment—and an assumption that it is can lead to a feeling of entitlement on one side and confusion on the other. Polyamory means creating relationships deliberately, not making assumptions about what they "should" look like. If you want your partner to make a certain commitment to you, *don't assume*...ask. If you are uncertain what commitments your partner thinks he or she has made, ask.

And be realistic about what commitments you can make. This means not just being realistic about your other commitments now, but about the flexibility you may require in the future when a new person enters your life. One challenge with polyamorous relationships is they require a willingness to leave space for other people who have their own needs and desires. This means that some types of commitments are especially problematic in poly relationships, and the need for flexibility on everybody's part is much greater.

For example, longer-term commitments are trickier than short-term ones. I can easily commit to a date with you next week, but to commit to a date with you the same night every week forever? That overlooks the fact that I may someday have someone new in my life, and that's the only night she can see me. Or maybe I'll someday want to go to Mexico for a week with her, which will mean canceling our date night. Commitments to always put one person "first" in certain things, or to always restrict certain activities to one person, can become problematic if someone enters the picture for whom one of the restricted activities is important. And everyone needs to be put first sometimes.

And then there are commitments that specify *how* other commitments are to be met. "I commit to sharing equally in our parenting responsibilities" is very different from "I commit to never spending the night away so that I will always be there for the kids' breakfast." Similarly, "I commit to living with you, remaining your ally throughout your life, and looking after you in your old age" is different from "I commit to never living with anyone else, never being a lifelong ally to someone else, and never taking time away from our relationship to care for another partner who needs help."

Another type of commitment that can trip you up is commitment to future intimacy. Many of the commitments we make in relationships—things like legal and financial responsibilities, a shared home or children—are actually commitments to life-building, not to feelings. And not to never changing your boundaries. When we're head over heels in love (or feeling NRE), we may want to promise to love our partner forever. We may even want to promise to desire them forever—as much as we do now. But as much as you may want to build a life with someone, consent to intimacy exists only right now, right here, in this moment. Consent means that you will be able to choose at all times the intimacy you participate in.

Being in a consensual romantic relationship means you are never obligated to any future intimacy, meaning anything that enters your personal boundaries. It can be sleeping together, having sex, hugging and kissing, sharing emotions, living together, having certain shared experiences or making shared choices. You can state future *intentions*, but you cannot pre-consent, and both people must recognize and respect personal boundaries in the present time, regardless of intentions stated in the past. This is important to understand, or else the relationship can easily become coercive.

Many people build structures against free exercise of consent in the future to protect themselves from their fears: "Never leave me." "Love me forever." Such statements are you or your partner asking for future control of the other's feelings and choices. But even if you have already made such promises, you can always withdraw consent, always draw new boundaries, or it's not consent at all. The moment you begin *expecting* any form of intimacy from a partner because of a commitment he has made to you, or ignore boundaries because you feel your partner has no right to set them because of prior commitments, your relationship has become coercive.

Financial commitments in polyamory need special attention. It's common for people in a relationship to combine their finances. In poly, we believe it's important to have access to some money that's just yours, even if you have joint finances with another person. This helps avoid one source of resentment and conflict. We have seen many people get upset when they feel that a partner is spending joint money on dates with someone else. This opens an avenue for control; a person who doesn't want his partner to have other relationships can simply forbid using "their" money to do so. When each person has some amount of money that is theirs to use as they wish, this helps eliminate the feeling that one person is subsidizing another's romantic life.

COMMITMENTS AND SOLO POLY

Advocating for needs and navigating commitments can be a special challenge for solo poly folks, whose relationships don't follow the usual script. We're accustomed to judging a relationship's significance by how far it's gone up the escalator. So when we don't see the conventional markers of a "serious" relationship, we may underestimate its depth and how much investment has gone into it. People who take a free-agent approach often look for partners who value them and their needs even when the relationship doesn't follow a traditional trajectory. So it's often not their partners who misunderstand the importance of their relationships, but their metamours. A partner's other partner can easily trivialize a relationship that doesn't appear "committed" because it doesn't have the normal markers (such as moving in together) that society associates with commitment.

FRANKLIN'S STORY   Amy and I started dating in 2004. Amy is solo poly, and our relationship has never been on course for the two of us to share finances or live together. During the time we've been partners, she has always maintained a high degree of autonomy, living by herself and making her own decisions. We didn't have a plan for our relationship; we let it take its own path.

In the years since, we have always been there for each other, through good times and bad. We have celebrated joy together, held each other through heartbreak, supported each other through the occasional bumps that any partnership faces. Despite that, we've never felt a need to develop a more traditional relationship.

It has sometimes been difficult for other people to recognize how committed Amy and I are to one another. This has been true with partners of mine who don't understand how we can "really" be committed to one another if we aren't planning an entwined future, and to partners of hers who don't consider ours a "real" relationship because, despite all the years we've been with each other, we haven't made any move toward living together. At times I've felt it necessary to stand up for our relationship against assumptions that it can't really be serious, and she has had to set boundaries when new or potential partners consider her entirely single because our relationship is almost invisible to them.

Many solo poly people, when considering a relationship with a person who is already partnered, find it essential to talk about their expectations and ideas about commitment early on.

LONG-DISTANCE RELATIONSHIPS

When you look around at poly people, you'll see a disproportionate number of long-distance relationships. Often you'll see deeply committed, long-term LDRs—something that's fairly rare among monogamous people.

Monogamy makes assumptions that are poorly suited to distance, and it's difficult to maintain sexual exclusivity for long periods when your partner is far away. But because polyamory doesn't necessarily include expectations that partners will live together, and because it doesn't restrict sex and intimacy to one person, long-distance poly relationships are more feasible. Another reason you see so many is that many poly folks meet online, and because poly people represent a relatively small portion of the population, the selection of local poly partners can be limited. Our relationship with each other is long-distance, and Eve has one other LDR and Franklin, three.

Long-distance relationships exist in a constrained space. Time with a long-distance partner is scarce, meaning it's at a premium whenever the opportunity comes up. But there are many ways to nourish an LDR when the partners are apart; the two of us, for example, spend a lot of time on Skype, and we're both avid texters.

The time when long-distance partners are physically together, surprisingly, can create the most stress. When you have both local and long-distance partners (as both of us do, and all our long-distance partners do), it can be easy to get so caught up in the normal, day-to-day relationship with a local partner that you forget to make space for the distant one. Sometimes literally. A long-distance partner can be a sort of "invisible" person: someone whose needs aren't necessarily obvious. For example, do you leave a place in your home for your long-distance partner to stay on visits? If you have a regular schedule with local partners—every Friday is date night, say—are you flexible enough for a long-distance visitor to interrupt that routine?

Local partners may resent visits that disrupt regular schedules. When your long-distance partner is in town, naturally you want to maximize the time you spend with him. From the perspective of a local partner, the visits can look like all grapes and no cucumbers (a distinction we explain in the next chapter). You may go out to eat more often, take trips, spend more time playing tourist, and do other "fun" things to make the most of the limited time. Your local partner might end up saying, "Hey! When do I get to have that fun?" If your long-distance partner visits for a week and you want to spend every night with him, your local partner might say, "That's not fair! When do I get to spend the night with you?" (The answer, of course, might be "During all the other fifty-one weeks in the year.")

Long-distance relationships concentrate the fun, flashy parts of a relationship, but at the cost of all the small things that build intimacy every day. We know few local partners who would be willing to trade places with a long-distance partner! LDRs also create special concerns around relations *between* metamours, because visits may not allow much time to build metamour friendships. The partners in the long-distance relationship may need to sacrifice some dyad time to allow for metamours to get to know each other. Metamours, for their part, need to be able to recognize the scarcity of time the long-distance partners have with each other, and realize that it's probably not personal if they don't get as much time as they'd like to get to know the long-distance partner. Because distance makes time such a valuable commodity, flexibility from everyone is vital.

POLYAMORY WITH CHILDREN

Polyamory can be a tremendously positive thing for children. We have both seen or been involved in polyamorous relationships with people who have thriving, happy children. Polyamory potentially means there are more loving adults in the family. It allows children to see more examples of healthy, positive, loving relationships. It exposes children to the idea that love is abundant and can take many forms.

Evidence-based research on long-term outcomes for kids raised in poly families is still scarce. But a fifteen-year longitudinal study by the sociologist Elisabeth Sheff, summarized in her 2013 book, *The Polyamorists Next Door* (highly recommended reading if you are poly with children), found that the kids from poly homes are often strikingly robust and emotionally healthy—though she admits that her sample has a self-selection bias. Her generally positive conclusions about kids in poly families match observations that are common throughout the self-identified poly community.

Children of poly parents grow up with adults in all kinds of configurations. Many poly parents end up living with a non-parental partner, some of whom have kids of their own. It's quite common to see live-in vees consisting of a couple with children plus another adult partner who often participates in child care and may have a close, stepparent-like relationship with the children. Quads and quints, bigger networks living in a great big house with six or seven kids—it's all been done. Some non-parental partners are more like aunts or uncles, some more like friends of the family who don't have much involvement with their partners' kids. Some (but not many) poly people hide their poly relationships from their children, seeing partners outside the home or treating them as "friends" (we talk more about coming out to children—and coming out *with* children—in chapter 25).

There is no magic formula for poly parenting, no configuration that will work best for every family. The strongest, healthiest homes for children are those with happy, emotionally healthy adults who model integrity and good communication. The child's needs must be cared for, and the parents absolutely need to be *present* for and *committed* to their children, but that does not mean sacrificing their own needs, happiness or interests to every want of the child. Most people seem ready to accept parents' complexities and trade-offs for other things, such as careers—not just when both parents work, but when a parent needs to uproot the family to move cross-country for a career or educational opportunity. It's really not so different for relationships.

If you have children or plan to have them, and you want to open up to polyamory, it's worth taking some time to unpack your ideas about what it means to be a good parent. Our society has long idealized nuclear families, but there are all kinds of families, including plenty of children who grow up without "traditional" nuclear families. A lifelong, live-in romantic dyad is *not* the only healthy or acceptable way to raise children, and in fact the isolated nuclear family is a historically recent aberration. As a polyamorous person, you might end up creating a beautiful live-in quad or triad with dedicated co-parents, not unlike the way your great-grandparents grew up, surrounded by aunts and uncles. Or you might lose your romantic relationship with your co-parent. You might end up as a single parent or in a platonic co-parenting arrangement with your former partner, or in something that resembles a monogamous blended family (separated parents living with stepparents).

Few things are more controversial among poly people than how polyamorous families with children should behave. Parental shaming is rampant in the wider culture. We are immersed in so many messages about what "good parenting" looks like that by the time we get around to having kids, it can be tough to shake off the guilt *no matter what we do.* Mom working outside the home? How can you be so selfish? Not working? You'll never afford a safe town with good schools! Don't want to (or can't) breastfeed? You're ruining your child's chance at a future! *Oh, my God,* is that *non-organic* baby food? Didn't play her music in the womb? Didn't read to her for an hour a day from birth? There are a million ways for parents to "fail," and parents are measuring themselves and others against every one of them. If we don't get it right, our kids will grow up to be drug addicts, incapable of intimacy, unemployed and homeless, or maybe they'll just miss their chance at that Nobel Prize—and it's *all our fault.*

Well, polyamorous parents get shamed from all sides, mono and poly. Parent-shaming is the next cultural narrative you have to confront after slut-shaming. Under these circumstances, creating healthy, ethical, egalitarian relationships when you have children can be especially tricky.

Our monogamous friends tell us that when we have kids, we'll settle down—grow out of this whole "poly" thing. Our poly friends tell us that egalitarian poly relationships are impossible with children, because without a hierarchical structure, no one would look after the children's needs. Everyone tells us that good parents always put their kids first. But what that means is very culturally specific. Everyone thinks they know what's best for kids, and damn near everyone is ready with judgment and blame when the parents they know (truthfully: usually the mothers) fail to meet their expectations. Add the fact that poly people are in a PR war in which we're putting our happiest, most stable and photogenic poly families out in front, and that gives poly parents just one more thing to measure up against.

In her 2013 book *Lean In*, Facebook CEO Sheryl Sandberg discusses parental shaming, unrealistic expectations of mothers, and research concerning child care responsibilities and child well-being. The research she cites shows that stay-at-home parenting is not the only healthy way, or even the best way, to raise children. Some data even suggest that kids do better *without* parents who are dedicated to filling their every need 24/7. Very young children, of course, may need 24/7 *caregivers*, but these do not have to be parents. In fact, children benefit from being able to attach to adults other than their parents (often grandparents, aunts, uncles or a close friend of the family), and they often benefit from group settings such as day care. As Sandberg says, "Guilt management can be just as important as time management for mothers."

Are you okay with the idea of raising your kids in a family that doesn't meet the societal script of a romantic dyad? Do you believe you can still do right by your kids if you end up raising them in a home with one or three or more parents—something that looks different from what you expected? Or will you feel you have "failed" your children? If you are going to live in fear every time your partner is away with another partner because you believe that if you can't maintain a "primary" romantic dyad you'll somehow be harming your children, then you might want to reconsider whether this is the best time for you to make the leap into polyamory.

Children certainly do complicate time management. Young children especially require huge time commitments from parents. It's essential to be realistic about how much time you have available to invest in romantic relationships, including with your co-parent, and whether that time is enough to allow you to treat another partner well—especially if a relationship becomes serious. (And making a rule that a relationship can't become serious will likely lead to problems, as we discuss in chapters 10 and 11, on rules and hierarchies.) If you or your co-parent are extremely fearful of the loss of time for your children that another relationship might represent, again it is worth considering whether polyamory is a good choice for you at this stage in life.

One final thing to consider is the situation of new parents. Many thoughtful people try to space out new relationships, allowing time for each to become secure and established and aiming to understand the impact it will have on their lives, before being open to another one. A new baby is also a new relationship. And given the emotional upheaval, life changes and sleep deprivation that come with having a new baby, this is an especially good time to be cautious when deciding whether you are available for new connections. In fact, many established relationships, both mono and poly, end due to the stress brought on by the birth of a child. Remember: Whatever your reasons, if the circumstances of your life do not allow you to treat multiple partners ethically, then it is not ethical to seek them. Many people say that a new baby makes it hard or impossible for them to treat new partners with compassion. If that's the case for you, it's not a good time to start new relationships.

WHAT ABOUT MARRIAGE?

Poly relationships may be live-in or separate, local or long-distance, sexual or nonsexual, entwined for life or autonomous, open or closed, shared or networked or entirely independent. Given that, some people ask, "Why would a polyamorous person even bother to get married?" But many people are polyamorous and married, for all sorts of reasons.

Eve and Peter have been married for four years, together for more than fourteen. On their wedding day, they had been living polyamorously for two years. His two other partners—and their partners—attended the wedding. On the whole, it's not Eve's monogamous friends who are puzzled by her marriage; it's her poly friends. "Why get married if you're not going to spend your life with one person? Isn't marriage a remnant of couple privilege or an archaic approach to relationships? Isn't it about ownership?"

EVE'S STORY   When we decided to get married, Peter and I had been together for about nine years. My relationship with Ray had forced a major re-evaluation of my life with Peter, and in the course of that, we came to the realization that the future we were building together was lifelong, and we wanted it to stay that way. And watching Peter's father take care of my mother-in-law, severely disabled from a recent stroke, drove home the importance of having people in your life who are deeply committed to you, people you know you can always rely on no matter what.

We were married a year later. These were the vows we spoke:

In the presence of the Light and in the love of family and friends I take thee to be my beloved, promising to be a loving and faithful partner. I ask you to be none other than yourself. I promise to cherish and delight in your spirit and individuality, to face life's challenges with patience and humor, to celebrate our differences, and to nurture our growth. I make this commitment in love, keep it in faith, live it in hope, and make it eternally new.

So if we aren't monogamous, and we aren't sexual, what does it mean for me to be married to Peter? It means I've tied my life to his. It's not just financial, though that's a big part of it: we are creating one financial future together, built on pooled resources that we share equally. We also know that we'll always be there for each other, and that our lives are tied in parallel if not identical trajectories. Whatever happens to one of us, the other is in it with them. Each of us will take care of the other if they can't take care of themselves. In making our choices, we have to take the other person into account—even if we don't always put their needs first. And each of us has a responsibility to the other to help them reach their full potential, realize their dreams, through support and even a little pushing when needed. We don't share one life, but the path of my life proceeds in cycles that are tied to the cycles of Peter's, and his to mine. And whatever we might have to face in our lives, we have someone to face it with.

Plenty of polyamorous people choose to marry, though their marriages lack the pledge of sexual exclusivity that is a hallmark of traditional marriages. They do so for the same reasons monogamous people get married: for someone to build a life with, to build wealth with, to raise children with, to grow old with. Polyamory does offer a great deal more flexibility in how you structure a marriage, what elements you make a part of it. For example, it need not include sex or children, shared finances, or even living together. A marriage is a commitment between two—or in the case of poly sometimes more than two—people. What that commitment includes is up to them.

FRANKLIN'S STORY   A few years after I moved to Portland, Vera and I had a commitment ceremony attended by fifty or sixty of our friends and family. Vera is already legally married to her husband, Charles, who attended the ceremony. During our ceremony, I exchanged rings with Vera, to symbolize the shared life we were building together.

I exchanged rings with Amber when she moved away to attend grad school. The rings were symbols of the fact that we have committed to being one another's family, however far apart we may be and whatever our relationship may look like. So I now wear two wedding rings.

Vera and I wanted a formal commitment ceremony because we had been living together for some time and wanted to recognize the life we were building together. We called our ceremony a "complicity," because it was a pledge from each of us to be complicit in one another's lives—to adventure together, plan together, jointly aid one another and encourage each other in our endeavors. (The name "complicity" was chosen as a playful suggestion that we work together to achieve dubious deeds.)

The recognition of our community is an important part of why we chose to have a commitment ceremony. Just as in traditional relationships, we in poly relationships value recognition of our partnerships, and for many of the same reasons.

When I had been married previously, Celeste identified as monogamous; for eighteen years we were in a mono/poly relationship—a relationship between a polyamorous person and a monogamous person. An important distinction between my relationships with Amber and Vera and my marriage with Celeste is that the solemnizing of my relationships with Amber and Vera in no way serves to place these relationships ahead of any other. Celeste had wanted a partnership in which her needs always superseded those of others, something that ultimately contributed to its end. I am open to commitment ceremonies, possibly including legal marriage, with other partners, without having these commitments impose obstacles or limits on any other relationships I have or may start.

A marriage is also, often, a public celebration of the commitment. People who have been in a relationship for a long time and are making a serious commitment to each other often want to share their joy in that commitment and declare it to the world, which is another great reason why many poly people do choose to marry.

QUESTIONS TO ASK YOURSELF

Building poly relationships means carefully assessing how we define our commitments and expectations, how we think about partnership, and how we think about the paths our relationships should take. These kinds of relationships also require us to build our commitments with an eye toward making space available for future partners. Here are some questions that can help:

- *What are my existing commitments? How much time do they leave for new partners?*

- *When am I open to taking new partners?*

- *What assumptions do I make about commitments in my relationships?*

- *What do I need from my relationships? How often do I re-evaluate my needs?*

- *How do I define "commitment"? Do my definitions leave room for nontraditional commitments and nontraditional relationship trajectories?*

- *How do I leave space for new people to come into my life?*

If you have children, or are thinking of having them, here are some additional questions worth considering:

- *When I think about family structures that are healthy for children, what features do they all have in common?*

- *How can I and the other adults in my life contribute to an environment that is safe and nurturing for children?*

- *Do I trust my partners and their partners to be supportive of my responsibilities to my children, and do I have confidence in my ability to select supportive partners?*

IN THE MIDDLE

When I dwell less on the conflicts and compromises,
and more on being fully engaged
with the task at hand, the center holds and I feel content.

SHERYL SANDBERG

When you have more than one partner, at some point you may face the unique challenges that come with being the pivot: the person in the middle, between two partners. The waters here can be turbulent. Your partners may have contradictory needs, or want the same thing from you at the same time, or end up in conflict with each other. You may find it difficult, when this happens, not to feel pulled in two directions.

Even when your partners are romantically involved with each other in an intimate relationship of their own, there will be times when you're in the middle. Maybe they'll both want your attention, but in different ways or for different reasons. Maybe each has different plans for the day and wants you to participate. This will happen, sure as night follows day. It's not necessarily a bad thing, but it helps to be prepared.

Of course, this situation isn't unique to polyamory, as anyone with more than one child can tell you. When you're asked to care for, support and cherish two (or more) people who have different ideas and needs, life can be a balancing act. The difference in polyamory is that you're not the boss. You're dealing with self-determining adults, which means "Because I said so!" is not a workable fallback argument. You'll be asked to make decisions that are ethical and responsible while still respecting the autonomy of each of your partners.

BOUNDARIES FOR THE PIVOT

Successfully navigating your role as the pivot starts with good boundaries. When your partners have competing needs or desires, if you don't have good boundaries you can become a prize to be fought over, rather than an autonomous person with decision-making capability and needs of your own. This can happen even when everyone is acting in good faith.

When faced with tension between your partners, the first thing to do is to ask yourself, "Does it involve me directly?" If not, you're well advised to leave the conflict to them to work out themselves. If it does, the next question is, what do *I* want? When people you love have different ideas or opinions, the question of what *you* want can easily get lost in the struggle to please others. Moreover, if you're focused on trying to please your partners rather than taking responsibility for your choices, it becomes easy for your partners to focus on *each other* as the reason you're not doing what each of them wants. Advocating for what *you* want when you're being pulled in different directions is a powerful tool to help resolve conflict, contrary to what you might imagine.

Boundaries around communication are another important part of balancing your role as a pivot. We discussed triangular communication in chapter 6 (pages 99–102). Short version: It's a trap to stay out of. As a pivot, triangular communication can be tempting in two ways:

- If your partners are unhappy with *your* choices, or feel their needs aren't being met, it is very easy for you to shift the blame onto another partner. "I can't see you tonight because Sophie won't let me." "I want to go to that event with you, but Owen is insisting I go out with him." Don't blame others for your choices; it's your choice to accept Sophie's demand or to go with Owen. We will talk about this more under "Who owns your choices?"
- If your partners are in conflict, it's also easy to slip into the role of trying to play the mediator, or of "translating" them to each other. This is dangerous ground, because if they don't resolve the conflict

themselves, it's not resolved at all. Attempting to mediate can end up estranging them from each other and eroding their trust in you.

Part of setting good boundaries as the pivot is to speak only for yourself, not your partners. If a partner asks you what another is thinking or feeling, what he wants or why he did something, *resist the urge to answer.* The best response is, "I think you should ask him yourself."

WHO OWNS YOUR CHOICES?

We talk so much about communication and negotiation in poly that it can be easy to forget that the pivot actually holds a great deal of responsibility for *making decisions.* And make them you must. Negotiation is important, but it's also important not to lose sight of the *purpose* of a negotiation, which is ultimately to make a choice. A choice, hopefully, that upholds your commitments and honors the needs of everyone affected, but a choice nonetheless. Gather data, certainly. Discuss, negotiate, listen and empathize. But then make a decision.

EVE'S STORY   In the early months of Peter's relationship with Clio, she and I did a lot of planning for him, to make sure they were able to visit each other. In fact, he would sometimes joke about how we could just figure things out for him. But that changed about six months in, and that change altered not just our relationship with Peter, but my approach to poly relationships since then.

Peter and I had each been to visit Clio separately, but this was our first visit together to her house. The first night, we were trying to decide who was going to sleep where. Peter wanted Clio and me to make the decision, but neither of us wanted to make it for him. Peter asked each of us—we were in separate rooms—what we wanted to do about sleeping arrangements, and ended up running back and forth relaying messages between the two of us. He also wouldn't tell us what *he* wanted. He became frustrated—and finally slept on the couch, while Clio and I slept in Clio's bed.

It hadn't occurred to us that there was a flaw in our decision-making process; we were all pretty happy with the results up to then. But we realized that weekend that Peter wasn't taking an active role. He was letting Clio and me figure things out for him. The couch incident was the first time the three of us had been confronted with a situation where we had to make a spur-of-the-moment decision all together.

The next morning, we each talked with each other in our three separate dyads, and then the three of us all talked together. The outcome of all this talking was that Peter needed to take a more proactive role in making our group decisions. Peter initially resisted, though today, neither he nor I remembers why. Clio explained the role we wanted him to take as being like a central data processor: collecting information from both of us, interpreting it in the context of his own needs and wants, and making his decisions in line with his priorities of nurturing our relationships.

Our process changed after that. Peter became much more independent in making plans with Clio. Rather than asking me to make decisions concerning visits or sleeping arrangements, he would ask me about my feelings or plans, then make proposals for me to respond to. Quite quickly, he became fully independent in managing his relationships.

Writer Ferret Steinmetz has called this "ping-pong poly": a pattern of running back and forth between your partners, trying to please everyone but rarely making a choice (or worse, making decisions that only last until you see your other partner). Nearly everyone who's been a pivot has probably committed ping-pong poly at least once; it's an easy pattern to fall into. But if it becomes chronic, it will wear you and your partners down and damage trust among all of you.

Shifting responsibility for your choices onto your other partners ("Sophie made me do it!") is cowardly. If your partners buy into this—and many will—you will be able to deflect their unhappiness onto each other instead of you. However, this ploy serves you poorly, for a couple of reasons. One, taking responsibility for your choices is a sign of integrity, which helps build trust. Shifting that responsibility will, over time, undermine not just your partners' trust in each other, but their trust in you. Two, even if your partners never become close, it's in your interest for them to trust each other and feel safe communicating with one another. Deflecting tensions from their relationship with you onto whatever friction they may have with each other can easily create confusion and conflict.

Your choices are always yours, regardless of whether they make you or your partners happy or unhappy. Own up to them. If you use phrases such as "Jill won't let me," or "Karen made me," or even "The rules say I have to," you are shifting responsibility.

TIME MANAGEMENT

Discussed a lot in poly support groups, time management is one of the toughest parts of having multiple relationships—for some folks, it's harder than issues like jealousy. It also doesn't come naturally to many people.

As with many other poly skills, effective time management really comes down to communication. Good communication about time includes being clear about what time commitments you are available for, how much time you need in each relationship (including how much needs to be dyad time as opposed to group time), how much you need for yourself (especially important if you're introverted), and what time commitments you already have. It also includes being very clear about what you are committing to and with whom—which can be harder than it sounds.

For example, on two occasions Eve scheduled vacation days off work for plans she'd made with a partner. In both cases, at the beginning (and once in the middle!) of her time with them, the partner informed her they had made plans with others for part of the time scheduled. In both cases, the partner was self-employed or in school and didn't understand that "I'm scheduling vacation time" represents a serious commitment for someone in a salaried job. Her partners had considered the plans to be tentative. For his part, Franklin has more than once invited partners to participate in his plans with other partners without asking the latter, only to find out, too late, that the partners he had made plans with expected to be alone with him.

Many poly people set up regular "date nights" with specific partners. For people who are into scheduling, this is a good tool to help let everyone know what to expect—though, as with everything else, you need to be somewhat flexible. Life isn't always tidy, and should a conflict come up, or a partner become ill or injured, it's reasonable to be able to rearrange the schedule without causing undue grief. As with anything, use judgment: if a long-distance partner comes into town for a week every six months, it's reasonable to expect date night to get rescheduled. Be aware, too, that schedules may need to change permanently to accommodate a new relationship.

Regular date nights are a great way to help nurture any relationship. They create a setting where the people involved can get back in touch with the romantic part of the relationship, free of distractions like chores, housework and kids. Sometimes polyamory makes this easier; when you have more than two people involved, it becomes easier to trade off one person taking care of the little things that always need taking care of while the two others spend time alone together. As long as the same opportunities are available to everyone, and everyone treats one another compassionately and without resentment, scheduled, focused time with each partner helps all the relationships thrive. (It's important that this not become a "service secondary" issue, as discussed in chapter 11.)

Google Calendar has become tremendously popular among poly people for time management. There's a standing joke that poly couldn't take off until Google Calendar was invented. It's so popular because, unlike a paper day planner or similar tools, it's also a *communication* tool: calendars can be shared among multiple people, with different levels of access, and several people's calendars can be viewed simultaneously. You can pull up six or seven calendars at once to look for opportunities for dates, shared time, and so on.

Google Calendar is so powerful that it requires careful negotiation before you start to use it. Failure to set explicit expectations about the purpose and use of the calendar can lead to serious misunderstandings and hurt feelings. In chapter 6 (pages 97–98), Eve told one story about how a lack of communication around calendar expectations helped sink a relationship.

What are your boundaries about what you are willing to share, and how you want your partners to interact with your calendar? Do you want them to see only free or busy times, have read-only access or have write access? You can schedule private events, which can only be viewed by those with owner-level permissions on your calendar—so even if someone has read or write access, you can keep some of your life private. When scheduling shared events, do you prefer to have the event added directly to your calendar or sent to you as an invitation that you can accept or decline?

Shared calendars can also pose a couple of special problems in poly. If a person doesn't feel her needs are being met, but sees on her partner's calendar the time he is spending with other partners (or doing other things), this can trigger jealousy. Some people find it easy to slip into feeling that unscheduled time should be theirs—it can be easy to forget that time for one's self is just as (or more) important, and is not a snub. Also, if Joe has write access to Jane's calendar, and Jane trusts him to schedule events without asking, Joe needs to remember that the time he is scheduling does not belong to him.

Different people have very different boundaries around sharing calendars and assumptions about what sharing means. For some it's a deeply intimate exchange, while for others it's just a logistical convenience. Discussing these meanings can help avoid misunderstandings and heartache.

ZERO-SUM AND INCLUSIVE RELATIONSHIPS

People new to polyamory often fear that embarking on this road means giving up time; every minute that your partner's other partner gets is a minute that you don't, right? That need not be true—if you and your partner's other partner get along well. When you can spend time with your partner together with his or her other lover, a minute given to that person does not necessarily mean a minute taken away from you.

Time-management issues can be eased or worsened by how comfortable you all are spending time together as a group, and whether you can get some of the same things from group time as from dyad time. That is, how much time needs to be one-on-one, and how much can be shared activities? Is your time a zero-sum affair, to be carved up among your different partners and other commitments, or are you able to take a more inclusive approach, where parts of your relationships and time are shared?

There is no right answer, though you often hear people forcefully arguing for one approach or another. Each approach has benefits and trade-offs, and some people are simply better suited for one approach than another. Watch out if you end up in relationships with people who are suited to different approaches—the styles often don't mix well. Both of us, happily, like spending time with all our partners together. We also don't feel cheated if another comes along with the two of us, if it's someone we both get along with. When this works, it's a tremendous benefit: We've met some awesome people through our partners, people who have become friends independent of our connection by dating the same person.

But if you assume that your relationships *have* to be inclusive, one of your partners may find himself spending a lot of time in the presence of someone he doesn't much care for. Each person needs to be able to set boundaries without blame. As much as we may crave inclusive relationships, it's not okay to force them. It's not okay to try to shame or threaten our partners into liking each other, even when, as we've seen happen, you're angry at them for not getting along. If an important relationship is contingent on any other relationship, this can introduce a strain that is not just about getting along, but about feeling like something deep in you is being violated—a loss of consent. If your partners are to be free from coercion, then separate time, or even complete separation, needs to remain an option.

Of course, there are consequences of such zero-sum relationships. Intimacy will be affected. And you may have to grieve for what is lost when those boundaries are set. Those losses may include one or more of your relationships. But don't blame. It needs to be okay, in every moment, for your partners to set boundaries—with you, and with each other.

TYRANNY OF THE CALENDAR

With a few exceptions, poly people are good at time management—or learn to be good at it out of necessity. So good at it, in fact, that many of us treat our calendars like games of Tetris, seeing how much we can pack into a day, week or month. We're scheduled to the hilt. Among poly people, you'll often hear complaints like these:

> *"I feel like I have to make an appointment to be with my husband."*
>
> *"I wish I could be more spontaneous."*
>
> *"Sometimes I just really feel like I need to be with Greg, but I have to keep my date with Alice."*
>
> *"I'm exhausted. I don't have any time for myself."*

We tend to have lots of commitments—not just relationships, but work, projects, social lives. Many of us sometimes end up feeling like all our time is allocated to other people—even like we've lost control over our lives.

When Eve (briefly, for a couple of months) had four partners, three of whom were local, she often found herself committed to each of them one night a week, with business engagements at least two nights, and social engagements on the seventh. She began to feel like an automaton, numbly moving from one commitment to the next, with little room—it felt—for personal choice and zero room for spontaneity or self-care. And she felt helpless in the face of this: she loved her partners, and each one of them needed and deserved her time. She came to call this state "the tyranny of the calendar."

Less extreme examples also prevail. In the flush of a new relationship, it's normal to crave the presence of a new partner almost constantly. Or when you're going through a breakup and are heartbroken, maybe all you want to do is hide in your room watching *Doctor Who* and eating pints of Ben & Jerry's. It can be difficult to balance your desire to be with someone when your calendar says you need to be elsewhere. But part of personal integrity is showing up and meeting your commitments. Blowing off dates with your long-standing partners—or your kids—to go running through a sunbeam-filled meadow with your new shiny isn't going to win you points in the integrity department.

So it's important to keep your commitments, to show up—not just physically, but with your whole heart. When you're with someone, work on being present with her. She will feel it if you're not, and if it happens enough, it will damage your relationship with her. Maybe someone else is on your mind, but the person you've committed your time to is in front of you *right now*. This is essentially a practice of *mindfulness*—being fully present with each of our loves, and open to the person we're with in the moment—and it's an advanced but essential poly skill that isn't often discussed. It takes years to become good at. But it makes us better partners.

And in all this, don't forget that you need to make time for yourself. Avoid the mistake Eve made in scheduling herself 24/7. Now she blocks off time on her calendar as "Eve time," and everyone who shares her calendar sees this. We know quite a few poly people who forget this. Taking time for yourself can be crucial in maintaining the emotional balance required for the other challenging aspects of being poly.

WHO OWNS YOUR TIME?

One of the default assumptions that many of us carry from monogamous culture is that in a long-term relationship, especially when we live with a partner, our partner's time becomes "ours" by default. So when he chooses to do something social that's independent of us, it's outside the norm—and thus can feel like he's taking away something that rightfully belongs to us.

AUDREY'S STORY   From the beginning, Audrey and Joseph have planned their time together around their many pre-existing commitments. Joseph and his wife, Jasmine, have a standing three evenings and one weekend day together. Joseph and Audrey have two evenings a week together. What little remains of Joseph's time isn't specifically allocated, and he considers it his—but in practice, with home and family commitments, it's usually spent at home. Even though that time does not "belong" to Jasmine, Jasmine sees it as an *opportunity* to spend time with Joseph; thus, when Joseph spends some of his free time with Audrey, Jasmine feels it as a loss.

Jasmine has always been concerned about how "big" the relationship with Audrey will become. Will they let their time "creep" and eventually take over the marriage? This has not happened in the decade-long relationship, but Jasmine still wants Joseph to agree to a limit—which he is unwilling to do. Joseph is willing to say what time he *will* spend with Jasmine, and the amount of time above that that he expects to be home to meet his responsibilities, but has been unwilling to agree to a specific limit on his relationship with Audrey.

Joseph and Audrey are working from an intent to honor pre-existing commitments, allocating time to those first, with the *result* being that their own relationship is limited in time. Jasmine wants to *start* from a time limit and define that first. Although the end result may be the same—Joseph and Audrey's time is constrained—Jasmine hasn't gained the reassurance she needs, because of the lack of a cap. Audrey characterizes the underlying issue as one of different ideas about who Joseph's time belongs to.

Understand and accept that each person owns his own time. A relationship, even one designated "primary," does not confer ownership of another person's time. When someone gives time to his partners, it is just that—a gift. While promises can certainly be made, and should be honored, gifts of time in the absence of promises do not constitute entitlements for similar gifts in the future. People can (and should) express their needs and wants, and a skilled pivot will take these into account when choosing how to allocate time.

Such an approach can benefit you and your partners in a few ways. First, if you start from the premise that you are an autonomous adult responsible for your own allocation of time, your partners will be less likely to see you as a commodity to be fought over. Second, if you start from the assumption that your time is yours until it's given to someone, this reduces (but doesn't eliminate) the possibility that a partner will see time given to another as a personal loss. But, perhaps most importantly, when you understand that time spent with a partner is a *gift* and not an *entitlement*, this will help you cultivate a sense of gratitude for it, and gratitude is a powerful shield against jealousy and fear.

FAIRNESS BEGINS WITH COMPASSION

"That's not fair!" Below a certain age, we hear people say this all the time. Past that age our vision gets longer, and we learn that fairness operates best on a global, not a local, scale. If you did the dishes last night and it's your sister's turn tonight, but she isn't doing the dishes because she just got back from dental surgery, it may seem unfair to you from a purely selfish perspective... but really, would you want to trade places with her? And if you were the one who'd just been through the root canal, wouldn't you appreciate a pass on the dishes tonight? Sometimes compassion dictates that a rigid schedule should change.

By the time we're adults, we've pretty much figured this out. That, or we've just given in to exhaustion and stopped worrying so much about what's "fair" on such a granular level. Yet in relationships, and *especially* in polyamorous relationships, the little whisperings of our five-year-old selves poke through and say, "That's not fair!" when things don't go the way we expect. Even when we don't talk about our expectations. Even when we know our expectations are silly. Hell, sometimes even when what's happening is not only fair, but most excellent as well. When you're balancing more than one partner, you will surely hear this sentiment. The words may change, but the meaning is predictably constant: "That's not fair!"

In dealing with human beings, issues of "fairness" sometimes need to go right out the window. People change and needs change, but often our notions about what is "fair" remain static, so deeply buried that we're not even aware of them. The fairness that is important in relationships isn't the tit-for-tat "I did the dishes last night, so it isn't fair that I have to do them tonight too!" variety. In fact, sometimes a tit-for-tat approach to fairness creates a situation that's decidedly *unfair*. In chapter 13, you read about Franklin's acquaintance who demanded that her husband break up with his girlfriend and told him "I'll break up with my girlfriend too, so it will be fair." Three broken hearts for the price of one is a peculiar definition of the word *fair*, and it illustrates an important point: *Symmetry is not the same thing as fairness.*

The kind of fairness that really counts is the kind that begins with compassion. Doing the dishes two days in a row because your sister has just had a root canal is compassionate (we've both had root canals, and believe us, the last thing you want to be doing when the anesthetic wears off is standing upright). On the other hand, saying "I'll dump my partner of many years just to get you to dump yours" is hardly compassionate. Fairness means saying things like "I realize that my insecurity belongs to me, so I will not use it as a blunt instrument on you, nor expect you to plot your life around it. I may, however, ask you to talk to me while I'm dealing with it."

This isn't the kind of fairness our inner five-year-old understands; he's far more likely to be worried about someone else getting something that he doesn't have, or getting something for a lower "price" than he paid for it. At the end of the day, though, our mental five-year-old isn't likely to make our lives better, no matter how much of a fuss he puts up.

OF MONKEYS AND CUCUMBERS

You may have seen this on YouTube or TED by now: primatologist Frans de Waal has experimented with primate reactions to inequality by placing two monkeys within sight of each other and rewarding them for doing a small task, such as handing a rock to a human lab aide. The reward is either a tasty piece of cucumber or an even tastier grape. When both monkeys get a cucumber, everything's fine—they'll happily complete the task dozens of times. But give one of them a cucumber and one of them a grape, and watch out! The "lower paid" monkey completely loses it: it throws the cucumber back at the aide, pounds the floor, rattles the cage. Like any good scientist, De Waal has repeated this experiment many times, with different species and variations. Same result.

We prefer to avoid the quagmire of evolutionary psychology; our intent with this example isn't to talk about how our feelings about fairness may be rooted deep in our brains. Instead, we want to talk about how we decide what are "cucumbers" and what are "grapes" in our relationships. By way of example, think of Ali, Tatiana and Alexis, three people whom we've fictionalized a bit only because theirs is *such* a common pattern in polyamory that it's more of an archetype. (In fact, both of us are in positions similar to Ali's.) Ali lives with Tatiana and is also in a relationship with Alexis. Ali and Tatiana have two young children. Their relationship involves a lot of housework, diaper changes and arguing over the budget. Their downtime together consists of a lot of cuddling in front of *Doctor Who* but not much sex and only the occasional night out.

Ali and Alexis only see each other a couple of times a month, so their time together is intense. They usually spend half of it having sex, the other half in deep conversation or doing exciting things—all focused on one another. Maybe once or twice a year they'll get away together for a long weekend at a bed-and-breakfast.

Most people in Tatiana's position would feel like she's getting all the cucumbers and Alexis is getting all the grapes. The things Ali and Alexis do are *fun*, right? They're *dates*—something long-established couples can have a tendency to forget about, or not have time for. And it *is* very important for live-in couples to take time to care for their relationship, so they don't take each other for granted. But it's also worth considering why we might think Tatiana is getting the cucumbers—and how, to Alexis, they might actually look a lot like grapes.

Ali and Alexis might have a vacation relationship—they may have more fun together, and Ali and Tatiana more work. But Ali and Tatiana share some things that are arguably far more precious, and which Alexis may never have access to. Things like

- being able to wake up nearly every morning together
- having each other close enough to touch, almost all the time
- curling up on a rainy afternoon with each other, snuggling beneath warm covers

- building a private language from a shared history of experience
- standing by each other through the shared struggles of building a life
- being able to plan a future with each other
- working together to bring two small humans into the world

After all, Ali and Tatiana *chose* the life they have together. If they had wanted, they could have had a relationship that looked instead like Ali and Alexis's. They did not have to move in together, mingle finances or have children. They *chose* to. They valued the things on this list. When people talk about taking a relationship—or a partner—for granted, these sorts of things are often discounted. And these things, in a relationship, can be very sweet indeed.

If one of your partners feels like he's getting all the cucumbers and someone else is getting all the grapes, remember that you and your partner chose to have the kind of relationship you have. Take time to notice and express gratitude for the benefits that come from it. If you have a live-in partner, those benefits might be the small touches, the opportunities to care for each other (even if it's grumbling as you pick up someone's dirty socks), the chance to sleep close to each other, the cuddles and shared meals, your small daily interactions, the future you're building together. If you live apart and see each other less frequently, the benefit may be the fact that your partner is carving out time from her busy and full life to focus exclusively on *you*.

This is another reason why fairness is not the same thing as symmetry. Tatiana and Alexis may envy each other for the things each has with Ali. They may need to work with Ali to reshape their relationships, so that each gets more of what they need. But it's possible that we primates all have a hard time seeing the value of what we have when we are busy looking at what someone else is getting. The monkeys in the experiment threw their cucumbers away—cucumbers that a few minutes before, they were eager to have. And it's also important to remember, if you're in the middle, that very few relationships can survive on only cucumbers or only grapes. Most relationships need a mix of work and play to grow strong over the long term.

INTRODUCING YOUR PARTNERS

If you're involved with two or more partners who don't already know each other, sooner or later it will be a good idea for them to meet. *When* is largely a matter of personal preference—yours and theirs—and is something we discuss at length in chapter 23. However, a couple of things are worth mentioning specifically to the pivot.

Some people like their existing partners to meet potential new partners right away, before any relationship begins to grow—and many people, likewise, want to meet the existing partners of someone they're considering becoming involved with. Others—often people who place a higher value on autonomy—prefer to wait until a relationship is taking root, when they're fairly certain that a new person is going to be important in their life, before expending the time and energy to meet "the family"—particularly if the family is large or far-flung.

Of course, as the pivot, you can't (and shouldn't) *stop* your partners from meeting, even if you don't feel ready. Trying to dissuade your partners from having contact raises an instant red flag among poly people that something dishonest may be going on, even if it isn't, and lays the groundwork for mistrust. If your partners want to meet, let them. But there's another important point of etiquette to bear in mind.

When two monogamous folks are dating, and their relationship grows serious, at some point it gets to be meet-the-family time. Bringing someone home to meet the parents (or whoever else is in your family unit) is typically taken as a statement: "This person is important to me. I am considering making this person part of my family."

Don't underestimate the importance of a little ritual like this in introducing new partners to the rest of your network. Sure, your partners are grown-ups who are capable of calling up another grown-up for a coffee date. But it can feel a little awkward, a little intrusive—and often, a little humiliating—for Glen to call up Juan and say, "Hey, I know Petra hasn't introduced us yet, but I've been seeing her for awhile now, and I think it's time for you and me to meet." That puts Glen in the position of saying to one of the most important people in Petra's life that Petra is important to Glen...but maybe Glen is not quite as important to Petra, or she would have set this up herself. To meet someone who may have an important influence on your future happiness under this awkward circumstance can be profoundly disempowering.

So it's good etiquette for the pivot to take the initiative and ask the others if they would like to meet. If one of your partners expresses an interest first in meeting the other, be the one to make it happen, and make it clear that the meeting matters to *you*, too. How you introduce a new partner to your network can make all the difference in how welcome she feels.

JEALOUSY IN THE MIDDLE

Dealing with your own jealousy is hard. Dealing with your partner's jealousy about another partner when you're stuck between them is no picnic either. When you have two lovers and one or both is feeling jealous of your time and attention, you can easily feel pulled apart. When one feels threatened by the other, a cooperative situation can quickly turn competitive, and a jealous partner may blame you for his jealousy. He might ask for things that hurt your other partner. Your other partner might have limits on what accommodations she is willing to make for him, and those limits might be perfectly reasonable. And there you are, poor sod, caught between.

This is a miserable place to be. Your power in this situation is limited; no matter what you do, you cannot solve someone else's jealousy. You may be able to make it easier for him to deal with it, but that's all. The good news is that it will pass. As long as everyone is committed to working through the issues, jealousy—as painful and intractable as it may seem in the moment—is a conquerable emotion. Millions of polyamorous people, though they may still grapple with the occasional wibbles (a poly term for minor jealous twinges), have learned coping skills and are able to have relationships that are relatively unburdened by jealousy.

Although your partner has to do the heavy lifting himself, there are things you can do to help make his work easier. The first is to listen. Nobody *wants* to be jealous. Nobody enjoys it. Your partner isn't doing this to hurt you, or out of spite. So listen, compassionately, without judging or shaming. Allow space for him to feel what he's feeling. Remember that saying "You shouldn't feel that" probably won't change anything. Creating a safe space for your partner to talk openly about his feelings goes a long way toward making a solution possible.

Reassure your partner. A lot. Talk about the things you value in him and the ways you love him. (And, really, do this even when your partners aren't in crisis. There's never a bad time to remind them how much you cherish them.) When you're done, reassure him some more. Accept that he is feeling what he's feeling, even though it's inconvenient.

Sometimes you may be able to change things about your relationship to help accommodate the jealous partner. For example, you might slow down the progress of a new relationship to give your old partner time to adjust. An analogy Franklin likes to use for dealing with relationship problems is fixing a broken refrigerator. If the refrigerator isn't working, it might be a good idea to stop putting things into it until you get it fixed.

There's danger lurking here, though. You can all too easily get so caught up in a jealous partner's pain that you agree to accommodations that hurt your other partner. Damaging one relationship to try to fix another usually ends up creating two broken relationships. Another danger: If the accommodations by you and your others make the jealous partner too comfortable, while discomfiting everyone else, he may have little motivation to work through his jealousy. Accommodations rarely solve jealousy; its solution comes almost always from within. Remember, you are your partners' advocates. This doesn't go just one way. You have a right, and a responsibility, to advocate for all your relationships. It's not okay to damage one relationship or hurt one person to try to help another.

The only strategies we've ever found that work long term are identifying and resolving the insecurities and fears that *underlie* jealousy. Ironically, trying to make compromises to accommodate a jealous partner can actually make the jealousy worse. For example, if your partner is afraid of abandonment, and demands that you never spend the night at another partner's house, maybe what he needs to get past the fear is to see that you can spend a night away from home and you'll still come back to him. If you give in to the demand and never spend the night with another lover, he may never let go of that fear. Not only will he never have the opportunity to see that you'll come back, you've shown him that he can control your behavior as long as he holds onto that fear.

Even the most insightful, self-aware person can't make deeply rooted insecurities vanish overnight. In our experience, working through jealousy normally takes weeks or months, especially if it's a partner's first experience sharing. If the process is taking years, though, something's stuck. Either your partner has become invested in the status quo and is dragging his heels, or he needs professional assistance to do the work (or both).

In the analogy of the refrigerator: once you've stopped putting more things into it, you can't just shove it in a corner and forget about it. You have to fix it, so that you can use it again. You and your partner should be able to see and feel progress.

You also must be willing to set boundaries, not only with your partner who isn't experiencing the jealousy, but with the one who is. If you don't, you may find yourself playing ping-pong poly again (see page 280): bouncing back and forth without making a decision. If, in your estimation, some accommodation your jealous partner is asking for seems reasonable, then say so. If it doesn't seem reasonable, then say so too. If he asks for something that would damage your other relationships, decline. You may have to make a decision someone doesn't like, but that's better than being tossed around on the rocks indefinitely.

For most people, the bottom line in dealing with a partner's jealousy is listening and loving. Reassure your partners, be diligent in honoring your commitments, and let them feel all their feelings. And remember that, as long as everyone is committed to working through the issues, it won't stay this hard forever.

QUESTIONS TO ASK YOURSELF

If you're the pivot person between two or more others, being able to set good boundaries for yourself and advocate for your needs, while also being considerate of your partners, can feel hard. As you build the skills to do this, here are some questions to ask yourself:

- *When my partners have competing desires, how well do I express what I need? Do I make sure my own desires aren't lost in the shuffle?*

- *Do I take responsibility for my choices, or do I expect my partners to make them for me?*

- *What does "fairness" mean to me? How does this affect the way I make choices and interact with my partners?*

- *What do I value most in each of my relationships?*

- *Do I prefer to spend time with my partners separately or together? How do they feel about that? Do I respect their other time commitments?*

- *What boundaries do I set for myself in relation to each of my partners?*

- *What accommodations do I make if one of my partners experiences jealousy?*

- *Do my accommodations improve my relationships or create other problems?*

- *Do I support my partners' relationships with one another in ways that respect their agency and right to choose their level of intimacy?*

- *How can I help support a partner who is feeling jealous or passed over?*

- *How do I handle my own feelings of jealousy?*

OPENING FROM A COUPLE

If you love someone, set them free. If they fly away, they were never yours to begin with. If they come back, be grateful and sweet and happy they are near you, and recognize that they can fly away any time, so just don't be an asshole, okay?

EDWARD MARTIN III

Many people come to polyamory from an established monogamous couple. Monogamy is the default for most relationships, and even people for whom polyamory is the best fit often discover it only after starting monogamous relationships. But the journey from monogamy to polyamory has many potential pitfalls. We aren't taught how to navigate multiple relationships, and if we try too hard to protect an existing relationship from monogamy, we can end up doing damage to others close to us. This is a journey Eve and her husband Peter made, and many couples will likely find similarities in their travels.

EVE'S STORY   After Peter and I had been together monogamously for four years, we separated. We were both unhappy in the relationship, but we also cared deeply for each other. After sleeping apart for several months, we began to reconcile. The separation gave us a chance to start fresh in many ways, and to renegotiate the terms of our relationship into something that worked better for both of us.

One of the things we agreed on almost right away was that we did not want monogamy. I can't even remember which of us mentioned it first. I do remember that I read him the swinging chapter from Dan Savage's book *Skipping Towards Gomorrah* (which, ironically, we had borrowed from my mother), and that served as a jumping-off point for the discussion. Initially, swinging seemed appealing: a safe, controlled, relatively uncomplicated way to have sexual variety without threatening our own relationship. We checked out some swinging groups nearby, went to a swinging party (and watched but didn't play), and set up profiles on sites such as AdultFriendFinder.com. But that world left us feeling a little flat.

About a year later, I had a late-night, drunken flirtation with a very old and dear friend, which led to lots of processing between me and Peter about the possibility of permitting scary things like emotion and intimacy with people other than each other. I realized that I have a hard time forming sexual connections with people I have no emotional connection with, so an open relationship that allowed only casual sex was not, for me, particularly open. Peter—eventually—agreed we could be open to more intimate connections. It was, shall we say, a slippery slope from there to out-and-out polyamory.

For years we read everything we could (including Franklin's web-site). I started following and interacting with people on various poly blogs. We each went on a few dates. We left the small town we were living in and moved to a large city, where we began attending the local poly group. Finally, fully four years after reading that Dan Savage book, one of us (me) finally started up a new relationship with someone else, my now ex-boyfriend Ray.

Four years went by between our agreeing to open up and actually doing it, but during those four years we weren't static: we were connecting with poly people and reading and preparing. Even then, though, I can't say we were really ready. The reality reminded me a bit of going to study in India when I was twenty: no amount of planning could have truly prepared me for setting foot on the ground in that country. I started a relationship with Ray, and the months that followed were filled with rapid change and many hours of conversation. My relationship with Peter almost didn't survive the transition. All the preparation helped, though. Those early dates had provided opportunities to handle small pangs of jealousy. We had at least a theoretical basis for structuring our relationships and dealing with issues. And perhaps most importantly, we had a poly support system we could turn to with our struggles, whose first response wouldn't be to blame our problems on the fact that we were poly.

People who want to transition their relationship from monogamous to polyamorous tend to ask a lot of questions like: How can I protect the relationship I've already built? How can I ensure that my existing obligations will continue to be met? What do I do if someone gets jealous? What happens if a new relationship threatens the existing one? What if my partner meets someone she loves more? How can I still feel special? How can I control what other people do? (The answer to that one is easy: you can't.) How do I find poly people to date? How do I tell my partner I want this?

The last question needs to be dealt with first, so that's where we'll start. (The other questions are what much of the rest of this book is about.)

BRINGING IT UP

There is no "right" time or "right" way to bring up the idea of polyamory with your partner. You're talking about negotiating a change in the most basic structures of your relationship. This is not likely to be a conversation that happens in five minutes while you're chopping vegetables. "Hi there, I want to totally change the foundation of our relationship, whaddya think? Can you pass the salt?" is probably not how this conversation will go. The idea will probably take a while to sink in. It may be weeks or months—or longer!—before you're finished talking about it. Likely both of you will need some time to come to terms with this degree of change.

Start simply. Ask your partner, "I've been hearing about polyamory. What do you think of it?" And then, *listen to the answer.* This is a dialogue, and dialogues are two-way; half of communication is *listening.* If you go into the conversation with the goal of persuading your partner to do what you want, he may end up feeling pressured or browbeaten. Read about it. Do some research. If there's an organized poly group in your area, consider talking to the people in it; many of them will have come from the same place you're coming from. You don't have to be polyamorous to go to a poly discussion group! Read books about polyamory, together if you can.

Talk to your partner about how you came to this idea. More importantly, talk about *why.* Talk about what interests you and what you find appealing about it. Be direct and honest, but also compassionate. If your partner has fears, listen to them. Talk about your own fears. And then listen some more. If a poly relationship is to be healthy and successful, it has to work for everyone.

That means your partner can't just do it for your sake; it has to work for her too. Going into polyamory when it isn't a good fit for *you*, just because your partner wants it, means there's tension baked in from the start, and in our experience that inevitably causes problems down the road.

Unfortunately, usually the innocent new partners bear the brunt of these problems. One member of a couple can very easily sabotage new relationships in incredibly subtle ways (even unconsciously) if he or she is only reluctantly poly. This problem is amplified if you're going along with a partner's desire to be poly because you feel you couldn't stand to be alone or lose your partner. That creates a circumstance where you feel you have no choice but to agree, and people who don't have a choice cannot give meaningful consent.

When you start discussing the idea of polyamory, remember there's a very real chance your partner may *never* be on board with a non-monogamous relationship. Some people are happiest in monogamy, and that's okay. If your partner is monogamous, that isn't a rejection of you, and it doesn't mean your partner is unevolved or unenlightened. It may, however, mean you have to make a choice: how important is polyamory to you? Can you be happy if your partner wants you to remain monogamous for life? If not, you may be faced with ending the relationship.

Also, while it might not necessarily be obvious, once you've had this conversation, *your relationship has changed.* Even if you ultimately decide not to pursue polyamory, just the fact that you've expressed interest means a part of your relationship is now different. Simply having the question raised is, for some people, a difficult thing to accept.

If your partner accepts the idea of polyamory, it's normal to sit down and try to negotiate agreements about how you will approach it. Be careful! Think about what effects any agreements you make will have on future people who get involved with you. Think about what assumptions your agreements are based on. It can be easy to forget that each of us has the right to build a life suited to our needs. Polyamory isn't a privilege your partner extends to you. If you start from the premise that you don't actually have any right to be polyamorous, that your partner is doing you a favor by permitting you to "get away with" having other lovers, you can end up believing that you should accept whatever conditions your partner may impose, even if they mean anyone you start a relationship with will be treated badly.

GIVING IT A TRY

Moving from monogamy to polyamory demands new skills and new ways of thinking about relationships. So many couples try to ease into it gradually, often making many rules that tightly constrain new relationships or try to limit their speed. We talk a great deal in the next few chapters about using structures and limits to try to manage fear and insecurity. But before we do, we'd like to address a common trap.

If you're in a monogamous relationship and your partner suggests polyamory, or if you're single and considering dating someone who's poly, it's tempting to think, *Okay, sure, I can give this a go. If it doesn't work, we can go back to being exclusive.* That makes sense at first blush, but consider what would happen if you had no children and your partner said, "Honey, I'd like to have kids." Would you say, "Sure, we can try it, but if I don't like how it works out, let's go back to being childless"?

What venturing into polyamory and having a child have in common is this: they involve other people. People who weren't part of your discussion. When we have a child, we know the decision can't be undone; the needs of the child will always matter, and we must take them into account. With polyamory, as soon as another person is involved in the relationship, that person's heart is on the line too. That person's feelings matter. Polyamory isn't something you can try on like a new set of clothes. If you expect to be able to dump everyone else and go back to monogamy, you're saying you have the right to break someone else's heart, or to demand that your partner break someone's heart. You are treating people as things.

You'll often hear poly people talking about how scary it is to open an existing relationship. You don't hear as much from people who are starting a relationship with a member of an established couple, even though it's just as scary. Couples are able to make all kinds of rules and structures to transfer their risk onto new partners, without recognizing that a person starting a relationship with one or both of them is already assuming a lot of risk. When we fall in love, we are all vulnerable; we all put our hearts in other people's hands, knowing they might be broken. Too often, the vulnerability and fear within an existing couple is given the highest priority, with little or no recognition of the vulnerability and fear of a new person starting a relationship with them. Everyone in the foxhole is at risk, but that doesn't make it okay to use someone there as your human shield.

Polyamory, like child-rearing, isn't for everyone. And, like child-rearing, you can't predict what effect it will have on your life. We're not saying you can never close a relationship after opening it—but when other people are involved, it's dangerous to assume your desires should always supersede theirs. And if you try to go back to your old mono relationship, you will find that it has changed.

We know of couples who have agreements that any decision to renegotiate the relationship will happen only when neither of them has any other partners. As long as one of them is in a relationship with someone else, the option of returning to monogamy is off the table.

SEEKING A CLOSED TRIAD

A very, very common chain of reasoning among male-female couples, usually where the woman is bisexual and the man isn't, goes something like this: "We want to open our relationship to new people. But if it's completely open, what will be left? If we don't set limits on how open it gets, what's to prevent us from just running around having a bunch of hookups? Can you really have commitment like that? It feels less scary to keep things more limited. And what happens if one of us finds a partner and the other doesn't? How can we keep from feeling jealous and left out?

"Aha! Maybe we can date together! If we present ourselves as a package deal, nobody will be able to come between us. We need a bisexual woman, of course, so she can have sex with both of us—and the thought of another man in the mix is uncomfortable anyway. That woman can be with both of us, so she won't come between us or make one of us feel left out. And we'll make it an exclusive triad. She'll be just with us, so we won't feel threatened by her other partners. That way, we will both feel safe and comfortable."

Couples looking for this setup are so common that they're a cliché among poly people. Very, very few such couples ever find such an imagined third person. (Franklin knows one couple who have been searching for that bisexual woman for more than forty years, without success.) These couples often join organized poly groups, but become frustrated and upset that their requirements are rebuffed. Many poly women do identify as bisexual, and more than a few are open to a man and a woman as partners, but experienced people almost always say no whenever a hopeful couple approaches. The couple usually offers an unequal balance of power, even when they believe they're offering equality; after all, they're the ones setting the terms of the relationship. (A term for this is couple privilege.)

So if you're the couple and those are your thoughts, know that you've chosen a difficult row to hoe and you will most likely never find such a person. Indeed, women willing to sign on to such a relationship are often called "unicorns," because they're about as thin on the ground as mythical horned horses. As reasonable as this idea sounds from your perspective, it is very unreasonable from her perspective. If you were her, think what the offer would look like. First, the couple says they want you to date both of them. Almost always, you will be expected to have sex with both of them, and you may also be told you can't have sex with one without the other there (because that might breed jealousy or resentment). And you will be expected to love both of them "equally."

From the start, you're put in a position where you have little voice. Your relationships have already been scripted. Alas, the human heart rarely follows scripts. It is rare for someone to be attracted to two other people in the same way at the same rate at the same time—in fact, we've never seen it happen. So you're likely to be more attracted to and more connected with one member of the couple than the other, and that's likely to create tension. For many couples, if you express more attraction for one person than the other, you'll be kicked out immediately.

Not everyone who's poly is an exhibitionist or likes group sex. Asking someone to have sex only in a group and only with two people is likely to come across as controlling, even to someone who *does* like group sex. All healthy relationships need some one-on-one time.

But let's say you agree and start dating them both—and, somewhere down the road, some sort of problem or incompatibility arises with one of them. What happens then? The relationship becomes coercive. You'll probably be told, "You *knew* we were a package deal. If you stop having sex with one of us or stop wanting a relationship with one of us, we will both break up with you." That puts you in the unenviable position of being told your only choices are 1) to continue having sex with or being romantically vulnerable to someone you don't feel close to; or 2) to have your heart broken.

As for the polyfidelity requirement, most of us come to polyamory because we reject the idea that being in a relationship means being forbidden to be with anyone else. Yet that's what's being offered in this arrangement. People who identify as polyamorous generally won't be excited about entering a restrictive relationship. Franklin has known several people who have dated both members of a couple under these circumstances. Without exception, they were badly hurt and say they would never do it again.

We're not saying polyfidelitous triads don't exist. All the ones we've seen, however, have formed when a member of a couple starts dating a new partner and then, some time later, that new partner develops an attraction for the other member of the couple. They formed organically, rather than being scripted.

The truth is, structure can never solve the problem of jealousy (as we talk about in chapter 8). Going to a polyfidelitous relationship can seem like a way to "ease in" to polyamory, but it's a bit like trying to ease into skydiving by saying, "I don't want to just jump out of the plane. That's too scary. So I'll climb out carefully, maybe sit on the wing for a while—to get a feel for what it's like, and get comfortable trusting my parachute." Not only will this not work, it will put you and your fellow skydivers in jeopardy.

If you don't trust your parachute, skydiving probably isn't for you. By "trust your parachute," we mean building the tools of communication and jealousy management, trusting your partner, and believing that she wants to take care of you even if other partners are involved in the mix...*before* you open up.

COUPLEHOOD AND IDENTITY

One of the problems that can arise in opening from a couple to polyamory is the competing expectations of monogamous culture and poly culture. Marriages are often portrayed as combining two lives into one. Society expects that couples do almost everything together. A spouse is often called "my other half." In extreme cases, this tips into codependence: each person becomes so dependent on the other that they're unable to express their needs as individuals or make decisions alone.

Yet when you're looking for a partner, very often it's who you are as an individual that makes you attractive. Couples who think of themselves as a unit aren't likely to be seen as attractive prospects, because it can seem as if there's no room for anyone else. If the two people think of themselves as one, where's the room to have and express individual, distinct relationships with each of them? Is a new relationship going to involve each member of the couple as an individual, or will it be required to address the couple as one entity? If the latter, what happens if a conflict arises within the couple, or between you and one member?

Yet attempts to assert individuality can feel very threatening, especially to couples who have been together a long time. As scary as it may be, asserting individuality doesn't mean damaging your existing relationship. You were individuals when you met, and that worked out, didn't it? You can still be individuals while you maintain close, intimate bonds with your partner. Presenting yourself as a whole person who is closely connected with another and can become closely connected with new people too, rather than as half of a unit, makes finding new partners and developing new relationships much easier. And it helps prevent codependence.

WHEN NOT TO OPEN UP

There's never a perfect time to start a new relationship. Life is messy and complicated. It's rare that the merry-go-round of our day-to-day lives stops long enough to let someone aboard without a fuss. That said, some times are less opportune than others. Those times might include when your current relationship is unhealthy or when you have young children.

There's a snarky saying among poly folks, often delivered with an eye-roll: "Relationship broken? Add more people!" This expression is used to refer to people—often but not always in monogamous couplehood—who seek new partners to try to fix issues in their own relationship. Perhaps they're feeling bored or stifled. Maybe the sexual spark is gone. Perhaps they're having difficulty talking about their needs. Regardless, the solution (or so it seems) is to open up to new, exciting relationships, in hopes of turbocharging what's already there or fixing the broken bits.

Polyamory won't fix a broken relationship. We're not saying a relationship needs to be perfect before you open it to polyamory, but polyamory will put pressure on any weakness that exists. It is not a solution to relationship problems. Polyamory may make it easy for one person to escape an issue temporarily by retreating into the new shiny, but the issue will always come back—often worse than before. And once you have more partners, there are more people to be hurt.

There may be certain narrow exceptions. For example, we've known people with specific sexual kinks not shared by their partner who have started relationships with others who share those kinks. And if, as with Eve and Peter, monogamy itself is the problem with your relationship—if you are compatible partners but are chafing at trying to squeeze yourself into a monogamous mold—then polyamory might help. Generally speaking, though, polyamory will work best when any and all of your existing relationships are in good shape. People are not duct tape, something you wrap around the leaky pipes of your current relationship until you can get a plumber in to fix the problem for real.

FROM SWINGING TO POLY

Some folks who hear about polyamory confuse it with swinging, though it isn't really the same thing—at least not the lurid, Hollywood stereotype of swinging, where people throw lavish parties, drink champagne and have sex with all and sundry. Mind you, that's not the way most people who practice swinging go about it either; much swinging is a private affair, where a small group of people, often close friends, will get together and have sex. Long-term personal friendships can and do develop out of this kind of swinging.

An overlap does exist between swingers and polyamorous people, and many people come to poly from the (much larger) world of swinging. After all, sex and intimacy are closely linked, and many's the time a person in a swinging relationship has found himself getting attached to his partners. Sometimes things go the other way too: a person may be polyamorous and also enjoy casual sex. The difference between swinging and polyamory is largely a matter of whether sex or relationships are the prime focus, but some of the difference is simply in the different cultures that have developed around each.

Franklin has been peripherally involved in several swingers' groups in several cities. Many, though not all, swingers he's spoken to self-identify as monogamous. Often swingers are married couples who consider themselves emotionally fidelitous but sexually non-fidelitous. Quite a few swingers operate under the premise that they are free to explore sex outside their relationship, at least in controlled settings such as parties, but love and emotional intimacy are not permitted. This doesn't describe all swingers, of course. But it is a common theme among many swingers. We've met swingers who have operated under these conditions for years, and then...*wham!* They wake up one day to discover someone has fallen in love, and they have no idea what happens next.

If you arrive at polyamory from swinging, you'll likely find the transition a lot easier if your swinging didn't include the assumption of emotional fidelity. If it did start from that assumption, welcome! You'll probably find a lot in common with people in mono/poly relationships (relationships where one person is polyamorous and the other monogamous). Some of the challenges will likely be easier. You've likely already resolved at least some of the sexual jealousy that people in a mono/poly relationship may face, though many swingers deal with this jealousy by only having sex with others while they're together, and this may not be sustainable in a polyamorous relationship. Other challenges, like mourning and letting go of the desire for emotional monogamy, will probably be similar, and the same strategies apply to dealing with them. And, again, we highly recommend finding a poly discussion group where you can talk to other people who have already walked your path.

POLYAMORY AFTER CHEATING

Franklin has received dozens of emails from people looking for a path to polyamory after an episode of cheating. Often a person will cheat, and then after confessing or being caught will want to start a polyamorous relationship with the person he was cheating with. Some poly folks have a history of cheating in monogamous relationships, often because monogamy felt stifling, but they didn't know that non-monogamy was possible. When they find out about poly, they set out to build poly relationships.

Other people cheat on a partner, then try to transition that relationship to poly. We've talked to people who have made this journey from cheating to polyamory. It is possible, but it's a long and rough road and the success rate is not high. Moving from failed monogamous relationships into starting new relationships openly on a polyamorous footing is much easier than trying to rebuild a relationship damaged by cheating.

That's because cheating represents a profound betrayal of trust. It's the trust, more than the sex, that creates a hard path to polyamory. The cornerstones of ethical polyamory, as we've discussed, are consent and communication. Cheating undermines both, and it's nearly impossible to rebuild a relationship until trust and communication are restored.

There are many reasons why a person might cheat. Some people like the thrill of the forbidden, or the rush that comes with doing something they might be caught at. Some people cheat because they want to experience something new but don't know how to ask for it, or they believe it is not available to them. Some people want to experience multiple sex partners but don't want their partner to do the same thing—which, as you can imagine, is especially problematic from a polyamorous perspective. Others just fall in love but don't want to lose their partners or families, and they don't know that any other option exists.

The reasons a person chooses to cheat are important when looking for a path from cheating to honest non-monogamy. And yes, it is a choice. Many folks who are caught cheating say, "It was an accident!" as though they slipped on an icy sidewalk and fell into someone's bed. Cheating might not be planned, but "unplanned" is not the same thing as "accidental." Calling cheating an accident is a way of avoiding responsibility for making the decision.

Finding the path to polyamory starts with acknowledging the affair—and, just as importantly, acknowledging that it was a choice, not an accident. It also requires assuming responsibility for the cheating. All too often, cheaters shift the blame. "If my partner were thus-and-such, then I wouldn't have needed to cheat." The "thus and such" might be "more sexually available" or "more adventurous" or "less reluctant to do what I want." In reality, the affair is a choice made by the cheating partner, and that's where the responsibility lies.

Rebuilding trust is hard. In fact, it's so hard after cheating that we advise talking to an experienced, poly-friendly counselor or therapist (we talk in chapter 25 about finding one). Professional help will almost certainly be an important part of building the trust necessary for an ethical polyamorous relationship.

That trust will never be rebuilt unless you are willing to tell the truth, about everything. Come 100 percent clean. No evasions, no holding back. The path from cheating to poly isn't easy, and an absolute commitment to honesty is the only thing that makes it possible. Honest, open transparency is a learned skill, and mastering it takes time and effort. A relationship might have all sorts of patterns that make honesty hard. Again, this is something a qualified counselor or therapist can help with.

In this case, it's also important to think about whether polyamory is really what you want. Many of the people Franklin has spoken to who try to move from cheating to polyamory originally started their affairs because having an affair seemed less scary than talking openly with their partners. As often as not, the scary part about open non-monogamy was the idea that their partner might also want another lover. In other words, they cheated because they wanted to have additional lovers but didn't want their partner to.

Sometimes, when caught in this situation, people are tempted to say, "We can start a polyfidelitous relationship with the person I was cheating with!" This can feel like a solution that lets the cheater go on having the affair, sometimes with a "side helping" of watching his spouse and his illicit partner getting it on with each other, but without the fear of having his spouse explore other relationships. As you can guess, we view this fantasy very skeptically. For starters, a person who has already shown a willingness to cheat in a monogamous relationship may well cheat in a polyfidelitous relationship. The same factors that led to the affair may still be present. Moreover, it's difficult to sympathize with the notion that "we'll be polyfidelitous so I can keep my illicit partner but you can't have one."

Finding the path from cheating to polyamory requires the active buy-in of everyone, and building fairness means *not* starting from the assumption that the cheated-upon person will never have other partners in the future, even if they can't imagine wanting them now. If you're trying to move from cheating to polyamory, be prepared to question *everything* about your relationship. It's also reasonable for the cheated-upon person to need time. Expecting someone who's just been cheated on to embrace polyamory immediately after learning of the infidelity is excessively optimistic. For a functional poly relationship to arise overnight from the ashes of an affair is highly unlikely.

Even when a relationship does move from cheating to polyamory, you don't always get to keep your illicit lover. Often the illicit lover won't be okay with this. Even if he is, the cheated-upon person may never be okay with someone who's already shown a reckless disregard for his needs and boundaries. And when we say finding the path requires the active participation of everyone involved, that includes the third person. For the relationship to transition to polyamory with the same cast of characters, that person is going to need to feel included, empowered and welcomed. Yes, welcomed. Like we said, this isn't easy.

In most situations, couples counselors recommend that a person caught in an affair cut off all contact with the third person. Obviously, if the goal is to create a working polyamorous relationship, that's not going to be good advice. But you can't have it both ways. Relationships tend to work when everyone feels empowered. A polyamorous relationship isn't likely to succeed if the third person is simultaneously treated like a partner and a resented outsider. As uncomfortable as it may be, including that person in counseling might be a good idea.

During this transition it might help for each person to consider what they want the new relationship to look like, and then negotiate for that. After infidelity, you're essentially creating an entirely new relationship. Being willing to start from first principles, and build something that reflects the needs of everyone involved, is going to be necessary.

Of course, not all cheating is the same. Different people have different ideas of where the "cheating" line is. To some, cybersex chat with strangers is cheating; to others it's their spouse's harmless fun. The point is, there are levels of cheating and differences of opinion about it. Generally speaking, if you're doing something you can't tell your partner about, you're probably cheating.

Because there are gradations of cheating, some violations are easier to recover from than others. If your relationship prohibits kissing someone else, it will probably be easier to recover from a kiss than from someone getting pregnant. In any case, talking to your partner and coming clean will almost certainly be easier if you do it sooner rather than later. Put another way, if you steal first base, talk to your partner before you hit a home run.

QUESTIONS TO ASK YOURSELF

If you're thinking about transitioning from a monogamous relationship into polyamory, you're not alone, but you're in for some pretty big changes. The things you probably think are important likely won't be, and things you haven't thought about might matter most. Here are some questions that may be helpful:

- *What assumptions do I have about what my relationships "should" look like? How are these assumptions influenced by the cultural narratives about monogamy, and how much are they truly mine?*

- *What parts of my relationships are most important? How can I preserve those elements while knowing that my relationships will change over time?*

- *What guarantees do I want from my relationships? Are they realistic?*

- *How much space do I have to devote to new relationships right now?*

- *As I seek new relationships, what guarantees can I offer my new partners that I will make space for them, listen to their needs, and be able to change to accommodate these new relationships?*

- *Where does my sense of security come from in my relationships? What am I willing to do to help my partners feel secure, and will those things come at a cost to any new relationships I may start?*

MONO/POLY
RELATIONSHIPS

Surely the most ubiquitous misunderstanding of love is "love hurts."
Loving never hurts—it's wanting others to be different from how
they are, and not getting what you want, that we find so painful.

CHRISTOPHER WALLIS

A fish and a bird can fall in love, so the saying goes...and so can a monogamist and a polyamorist. It happens a lot, actually. This isn't surprising, given how outnumbered poly people are by mono people. But it sure puts the fairy-tale idea that "true love conquers all" to the test (spoiler alert: it doesn't). What can you do? Is your relationship doomed? Can such a pairing ever work? The good news is that the mono/poly relationship is common enough that it's become something of a poly archetype, so there are plenty of people willing to share their experiences.

A good mono/poly relationship is possible. We have both seen examples of successful, happy relationships between a monogamous and a polyamorous person. But getting there is hard. In fact, it is among the most difficult poly structures to navigate in a way that promotes and respects the happiness of everyone involved. These relationships require patience, persistence and compassion. They require careful communication and a willingness to do some deep soul-searching. The people must be willing to work together, and the poly person's other partners also need to be willing to show sensitivity and kindness to the needs of the monogamous person.

DEFINING MONOGAMY

The concept of monogamy is more complicated than it seems. When someone calls herself "monogamous," talk about what expectations she has. Some people consider themselves monogamous because *they* want only one partner, but it's okay if the partner has other lovers. Others identify as monogamous because they want a relationship in which their one partner is also exclusively faithful to them. The concept gets more complicated, because different people have different ideas about what constitutes fidelity. Some swingers self-identify as monogamous; for them, sex without emotional attachment doesn't count. Other people consider even a platonic relationship, perhaps online where the people never meet, to be a profound betrayal.

As you might imagine, a poly relationship with a monogamous partner who says, "I only want her, but it's okay if she has other relationships" is a lot easier than a poly relationship with someone who says, "I want it to be only you and me." Mono/poly relationships also follow a different course when the monogamous person falls in love with a poly person who already has other partners than when a couple start a relationship together and the door to polyamory opens later.

The two of us have extensive experience with mono/poly relationships of both varieties. For eighteen years Franklin was in a mono/poly relationship with his ex-wife Celeste, who strongly preferred a relationship involving only two people, and for three of those years, he had a second partner who was this variety of monogamous as well. Today he has a partner whose husband self-identifies as monogamous but is okay with his wife having multiple relationships. Eve's ex-partner Ray was married to a monogamous woman. Both of us have close friends in mono/poly pairings. We have learned a lot of lessons from these experiences.

YOU WON'T CHANGE EACH OTHER

Poly folks have heard this story a million times: George and Iris have been together a couple of years. He's poly, she's mono. In fact, Iris says the very thought of polyamory exhausts her. But George believes she will someday "wake up" to its advantages. Iris believes that George will eventually "settle down" to monogamy. George has even said he would marry Iris if it didn't mean pledging a lifetime of exclusivity to her. They're in love, and each is prepared to patiently wait for the other to change.

We have a word in the poly world for monogamous people like Iris who knowingly pair up with a poly person, hoping to change them: cowgirls (or cowboys). They ride up alongside a poly crowd to "rope one out of the herd." There's no special nickname for the poly person who hopes to change his mono partner, but there should be. Both are setting themselves up for long-term pain and thwarted dreams.

The cowgirl/cowboy story usually goes like this: the monogamous person has internalized the narrative of monogamous culture—that polyamory is just a phase, that when he meets The One (who is, of course, herself), he'll settle down. The poly person, meanwhile, believes the mono person will come around once she feels secure, or starts to want variety, or sees other poly relationships working, or just sees the light.

Each *says* they accept the other's nature. The monogamous person may even agree to an open relationship in theory—just not yet, not until the relationship is stable and feels secure. And the poly person gives her that time. And more time. And whenever they talk about opening the relationship, there's some reason not to. Maybe there's some external stressor, or there's something wrong with the person the poly partner wants to date. And after a lot of time has passed, and the two are deeply bonded, and the poly person seriously falls for someone new...well, of course that person is seen as a threat, because the poly person wants to change the now-long-established default.

The problem is that both parties entered, and continued, the relationship on the assumption that they would eventually change the other. Yet for many people, polyamory and monogamy aren't things they can simply change; they are fundamental. Mistress Matisse put it well when, in her column on cowboys and cowgirls, she said, "Dismissing people's stated definitions of their sexuality as something you can make them change is not love." Mono/poly relationships only work when each person wholeheartedly embraces who the other is, allowing them to live the way that's most authentic for them, without judgment. Solid intimate relationships do not come from a place of wishing our loved ones would be someone else. Intimacy comes from accepting and loving others for who they are.

THE COST OF MONO/POLY RELATIONSHIPS

That's all well and good when both start the relationship understanding who the other is. It's harder when they both planned on a monogamous relationship and then one of them realizes his or her true poly nature or beliefs. In this case, giving up monogamy is a scarier step. The monogamous person may feel deep loss: the relationship doesn't look the way he wants or the way other relationships look. It can feel like the polyamorous person is always getting what she wants—other lovers, other intimate companions. The monogamous person can feel like he's losing time, attention and focus—and sometimes this may be absolutely true.

From the poly person's point of view, a mono/poly relationship can feel constricting. The poly person may feel that she is not permitted to follow her heart. She may feel controlled. She may feel that her partner doesn't really understand or accept her, and that she is being forced to live out a dream deferred.

We don't want to paint a picture that's entirely doom and gloom. As we said, we both know people in happy, successful mono/poly relationships. At the same time, we don't want to whitewash the challenges you may face if you choose this kind of relationship.

CHALLENGES FOR THE MONOGAMOUS PARTNER

A monogamous person embarking on a poly relationship will probably spend some time mourning the loss of the relationship she expected, and coming to terms with polyamory. This is a process. The polyamorous partner needs to treat the process with respect and compassion. A monogamous partner may see polyamory as a problem to be managed, rather than a source of joy for a loved one. She may find it difficult to recognize that polyamory isn't a flaw or a failing; it's a different way of seeing relationships, and a positive one at that.

Many monogamous people we've met try to establish security by limiting what their poly partners do. That's a dangerous road, as we've said, in part because the people who usually suffer the most are the polyamorous person's *other partners*. Monogamous social structures don't equip us to treat a lover's other lovers compassionately. Yet learning to extend compassion to a partner's other lovers is a vital skill in mono/poly relationships.

When a poly person is allowed to invite people into her heart—but not too far—it often creates a situation where everyone is unhappy, and the people who suffer the most also have the least power to ask for things to help end their suffering. This is especially true if those other partners are also poly and want a relationship that includes being part of the family.

FRANKLIN'S STORY   When I started my relationship with Bella, it wasn't the sex that Celeste felt most threatened by. It was the things that normally signify family, like love, cohabitation and planning for the future.

Bella wanted the freedom to love and be loved by me, to participate in my day-to-day life, and even, if the time came, to be able to live with me. Celeste wanted above everything else to be the sole person to fill that role in my life. In my desire to make Celeste feel comfortable and secure, I made it clear to Bella those options were permanently off the table, which caused great pain for both of us and undermined our relationship. Bella felt, rightly, that I had invited her in without *allowing* her in, or giving her a way to ask for what she needed.

CHALLENGES FOR THE POLYAMOROUS PARTNER

In a mono/poly relationship, the poly person may see her monogamous partner's needs as obstacles to be worked around, or as unreasonable expectations to be dealt with. She may feel that if the monogamous person would just *get with the program,* these needs would fall by the wayside. The poly person must recognize that monogamy is not an imposition—it's a valid, healthy and reasonable way to conduct romantic relationships. The monogamous partner isn't unevolved, unenlightened or selfish. There is nothing wrong with wanting one exclusive partner. Compassion for the feelings and expectations of the monogamous partner is essential.

If you are the poly partner of a monogamous person, you have some work to do. What compromises can you make, while still conducting your other relationships with integrity? How can you set boundaries that create a safe space for your monogamous partner, but not at the expense of your other partners? This balancing act requires flexibility, adaptability, self-knowledge and compassion.

ASSUMPTIONS AND SOCIAL EXPECTATIONS

We all carry a pile of social assumptions, which may or may not be true, into our relationships. In poly relationships, some of our standard expectations certainly won't be true.

Expectations are often invisible unless we specifically look for them. In mono/poly relationships, these expectations can be land mines, ready to blow up at any step. Communication is especially vital in mono/poly relationships, because when we don't talk openly about something, the default social norms tend to dominate.

Some of the assumptions Franklin has experienced firsthand from his monogamous partners include ideas like "If you truly love me, I should be enough for you" and "If I am not enough for you, something is wrong with me." This would come up most often in the earliest stages of a new connection. Often Celeste would respond to a new flirtation by asking, "Why aren't the partners you have enough?" or "What's missing from your life that you need to go out and look for something more?"

These are difficult questions to answer, because to a poly person they come from assumptions that don't make sense. Answers such as "It isn't about being 'enough.' Even if I were with partners who were perfect in every way, I'd still be open to new connections," or "Nothing is missing from my life. Relationships aren't about filling in missing spaces"—these were never very satisfying to Celeste.

One of the most difficult hurdles to overcome can be the assumption that a person is polyamorous because something is missing. Sometimes polyamory does offer an opportunity to satisfy an unmet need; we've both met poly people who are interested in BDSM but have a partner who isn't, or who have an asexual partner. But even in those situations, polyamory isn't a reflection on the deficiencies of the monogamous person; it's just a recognition of a difference.

Polyamory can even be a benefit to the monogamous partner. We've both met people who feel guilty over not being able to provide their partners with something. A friend of Franklin's, for instance, is not interested in bondage but has a female partner who absolutely loves it. When she started dating a new partner who was also enthusiastic about bondage, he felt intimidated at first. Would she leave him? After time went by and that didn't happen, he no longer felt guilty about not being able to provide her with what she wanted.

This idea seems easier to grasp for old relationships than for new ones. When Franklin was married to Celeste, he started a relationship with Elaine, who also self-identified as monogamous.* She did not feel threatened by Franklin's two existing partners. Because they predated his relationship with her, it seemed obvious that their existence wasn't a reflection on her worth. However, a year later, when someone else expressed an interest in Franklin, Elaine became very upset and asked, "Why am I not enough? What am I lacking that makes you need to start dating someone else?"

When a monogamous person begins dating a polyamorous person, existing relationships are part of the landscape. Simply being comfortable with existing relationships is not necessarily a good indicator of how much success a monogamous person will have in a mono/poly relationship. Be ready to talk about that.

From the perspective of a monogamous person, polyamory may look like a license to behave indiscriminately. It can be difficult to shake the notion that commitment and exclusivity are the same thing. This can lead to thoughts that a polyamorous person can't or won't commit, and therefore must be unreliable or wildly promiscuous.

Nor is polyamory (necessarily) about a need for sexual variety. Franklin once had a discussion with a monogamous person who asked, "If my partner is polyamorous, can't he be satisfied if we role-play different characters in bed?" Polyamory might look like a need for sexual variety, but a better way to think about it is in terms of openness to deep personal connection, not too different from the way most people are open to making new friends.

Social recognition is also a big issue in the mono/poly relationships we've seen and been part of. A monogamous person in a poly relationship often wants the social recognition that comes with being conventionally partnered, and often feels uncomfortable with public signs of partnership that involve others. Celeste was not comfortable with Franklin holding hands with anyone

---

* You might question Franklin's wisdom in starting two simultaneous mono/poly relationships. You'd probably be right.

else in public, and she did not want her social circle to know that Franklin had other partners. She also felt threatened when Franklin's partner Bella wanted to have portraits taken with him. The social recognition as Franklin's partner was important to her and wasn't something she wanted to share.

MILA'S STORY   In Mila's perfect world, she would have a monogamous relationship with her partner, Morgan. When she fell in love with him, she knew he was poly and that he was already in a relationship with Nina. Intellectually, polyamory made sense to her, but the emotional reality was different. Coming to terms with and even finding joy in her mono/poly relationship with Morgan was not an easy road.

One of the things Mila consistently found triggering were public expressions of Morgan and Nina's relationship. She was deeply hurt when Nina had family photos taken with Morgan and posted them on Facebook. She struggled with the swinging relationship they had with another couple—it wasn't the sex that bothered her, but the fact that Morgan and Nina participated as a couple. And she panicked when Morgan made arrangements for Nina to meet his parents (over the same holiday week, coincidentally, when Mila was to meet them).

Mila was tempted to restrict Morgan's relationship with Nina, particularly displays of public "coupledom." But she chose instead to work through the roots of the feelings. In some cases, she negotiated temporary boundaries with Morgan and Nina, such as restraining public displays of affection when the three of them were at dinner with friends, while she worked through her feelings.

Her biggest fear, she discovered, was of being perceived as a victim or having people feel sorry for her. In the case of meeting Morgan's parents, she found it helped her to be present at the meeting, and to plan with Morgan and Nina beforehand how they would all present a united front. In doing so, she demonstrated to Morgan's parents that she was fully consenting to the situation and had agency in her relationship with Morgan.

Placing restrictions on public affection with other partners usually doesn't work. In our experience, it creates resentment; there can be a sense of being forced into fakery. Sometimes this is just an issue that people need time and space to work through. Sometimes it can be dealt with by inclusion. Franklin and Celeste dealt with Celeste's discomfort around having portraits taken by going together as a group and having portraits taken that showed Franklin and Celeste, that showed Franklin and Bella, and that showed all three. (The portrait photographer handled this with grace.)

MILA'S STORY   During the early months of Mila's relationship with Morgan, sharing him was hard. She had never felt insecure or jealous before. There were lots of tears and emotional outbursts. Mila struggled to set boundaries, to find her bottom line in her relationship with Morgan.

Morgan worked hard with Mila to establish trust. Without his integrity and patience, she's not sure she would have made it through. He said the hard things to her when they needed to be said and never wavered in them—even when it would have been easier to not say them, to let her pretend their relationship was something other than what it was. He created a safe space for her and gave her time to process her feelings. He didn't try to get involved when she was upset or put words in her mouth. He let her be "an emotional wreck" and reassured her that her feelings were okay. She says, "I was allowed to have a hard time, to be insecure. I didn't feel rushed to figure it all out." Ultimately, Morgan's integrity and communication skills were an important part of her motivation to see the relationship through.

CULTIVATING TRUST

By now, you've probably noticed that a theme in this book is trust. We believe that trust between partners is an essential part of happy, stable relationships. A surprisingly large number of poly problems are actually about trust. Trusting in your partner's enthusiastic willingness to take care of you, and your partner demonstrating that this trust is well placed, solves many problems in poly relationships. But this can be tricky in mono/poly relationships, because it's hard to trust someone whose motivations you don't fully understand. When someone's motivations don't make sense to you, you will find it difficult to predict what choices they might make.

FRANKLIN'S STORY   During the time I was with both Celeste and Elaine, I attended a week-long computer convention out of town. While I was there, Celeste and Elaine spent a great deal of time talking to each other, and somehow convinced each other that I was engaging in all sorts of random, no-strings sex with the beautiful women they imagined I was meeting at the convention. The reality was far more mundane: I spent all day at workshops on computer programming and network administration, and most nights in the hotel room watching reruns of *Law & Order*. I did not have even a single sexual encounter, much less the dozens they imagined to be filling my nights. There was no reason to believe I would be looking for flings; I've never had a taste for casual sex. But because they both struggled to understand why I wasn't satisfied with conventional romantic relationships, they believed they couldn't predict how I might behave, so they ended up imagining far-fetched fantasies.

When two people don't see eye to eye, it's easy for a tiny seed of doubt to blossom into a full-blown breakdown of trust. Mono/poly relationships require special commitment to trust and communication. Being willing to take a leap of faith that your partner is dedicated to your relationship, even if you don't understand your partner's motivations, becomes especially important. On the other side, as the poly person, when opportunities to build trust arise, you really have to behave with integrity. If you've made promises to your monogamous partner, keep them. Even if you don't understand why he wants them. If they create real problems, don't break them, renegotiate them. Cultivate trust by demonstrating that you are worthy of trust.

Finally, for the monogamous person, trust in yourself—in your self-efficacy—is as important as trust in your partner. Mila found that sticking with it and getting through those early struggles gave her confidence that she could get through future struggles. She was terrified at the beginning of her relationship with Morgan when polyamory was a complete unknown. Now, she trusts that if hard times come back, she can get through them and be okay.

STRATEGIES FOR THE MONOGAMOUS PARTNER

Being happy in a mono/poly relationship means finding a way to make the relationship work for you. For example, if you know there's something you can't offer a partner, it might take stress off you when your partner finds someone else who can. If you're introverted and your partner is extroverted, polyamory might let you spend time doing things you want while your partner is socializing with another lover. If you see polyamory as a problem to be worked around, you're less likely to be happy than if you find a way to make it benefit you too. That doesn't necessarily mean you have to have multiple relationships yourself; it might mean polyamory gives you the opportunity to explore other interests or hobbies. (We talk more about this in the strategies section, later in this chapter.)

Your partner is poly because he is poly. *There is nothing wrong with you.* No matter who you are, no matter what you could be or do, he would still be poly. If you have a child and you decide to add another, it probably isn't because there's something wrong with the first child. It's about bringing more love and intimacy into your life. Polyamory is the same.

You don't have to make peace with this all at once. It's okay to need time. Polyamory is a radical change, and sometimes it takes a while to process change. There *will* be times when you'll feel jealous or insecure. That's okay. It doesn't mean you're doing something wrong. It's also okay to ask your partner for help when this happens. Not help as in "I don't want you ever to have other partners," but help as in "I need your reassurance and support here." There's nothing wrong with asking your partner to take time to show you why you're valued.

There's nothing wrong with being monogamous. If you don't want other lovers, don't try to force yourself to have other lovers. If you want to explore what it's like, that's one thing, but you don't have to in order to be with a polyamorous person! There's nothing wrong with being who you are. And there's nothing wrong with your partner for being poly. It isn't a moral failing. It isn't because poly people can't commit. That's important to keep in mind. Suggesting that polyamory is a problem or that there's something wrong with your partner is unlikely to make your relationship better.

Your partner's other partners are human beings. It can be hard at times not to resent them. It can be tempting to tell yourself they have no right to be there. That's not true. Polyamory is a valid relationship model, and the people involved in a poly relationship have a right to be there, just as you do. Your partner's other partners are not your enemy. They don't necessarily have to be your family, or even your friends, but respecting them and treating them kindly as people your partner loves, and who add value to your partner's life, will definitely help the relationship run smoothly.

As we like to emphasize, people are not interchangeable. It may seem that if your partner has another lover who is similar to you, or likes the same things you do, then she doesn't need you anymore. But remember, she's non-monogamous and doesn't think that way. She loves you for who you are.

Doing something with you is an entirely different experience from doing the same thing with someone else. And if your partner has a lover who's very different from you, it's not a covert way of saying that the different things about you aren't good, wonderful or valuable, or that she wants you to be like someone else.

Accept the reality that your partner *has* other partners! Attempting to hang on to the trappings of monogamy, for example by maintaining a "Don't ask, don't tell" relationship, is likely to create a lot more trouble than it solves. When we don't know what's happening, our fears run wild. We can start to think that all our partner's other partners are far smarter, more dazzling and more sophisticated while we sit at home with the cat. This creates a potent environment for resentment to spread.

Franklin calls denial the "Miami approach" to mono/poly relationships. Imagine that you really want to live in Miami. Sun-drenched beaches and swaying palm trees call out to you. But you find yourself living in New York instead. You're unlikely to succeed in adapting to New York life if you stubbornly insist you're in Miami. If you wear shorts in December and refuse to recognize snow, you'll probably find your unhappiness increasing. You'll be happier if you acknowledge that snow is going to be part of your life, and that New York actually has a lot going for it.

Another strategy that some people try is to create a privileged relationship tier that places the needs of the monogamous person over the needs of anyone else. As we discuss in chapter 11, this is apt to create problems as well.

If you're accustomed to monogamy, every time your partner touches someone else affectionately, that can feel like a rejection of you. This can cause you to pull away from your partner, which makes the feeling even worse. These feelings are hard to address directly, because when you're feeling rejected, the last thing you want to do is make yourself vulnerable by opening up to your partner about what you're feeling. The only way we've found to avoid a self-reinforcing cycle of rejection and defensiveness is to confront the feeling head-on. When your partner is affectionate with someone else, understand that it's not about you. Speak up and ask for support.

STRATEGIES FOR THE POLYAMOROUS PARTNER

You're asking your partner to believe, in the face of overwhelming social messages to the contrary, that you're not looking to replace him; that the reason you're open to other partners is not because there's something wrong with him; that you're not asking for permission to cheat; and that you don't have one foot out the door. That's a lot to deal with. You're asking your partner to accept that having other lovers isn't just a way for you to move from one relationship to the next. Make sure that's true. Make sure you are worthy of that trust.

We can't turn a lifetime of expectations around on a dime. Give your partner space and time. Allow your partner room to experience her emotions, to have freakouts, and to get through to the other side. Be compassionate. As we described above in the section on trust, a huge factor in Mila's relationship was Morgan's ability to give her time and space to process, without blaming her or expecting too much too soon.

Being polyamorous is not a license to do whatever you want. There will be times when your partner struggles and needs your support. Be there. Be supportive. Be willing to hold his hand when things are tough. Be willing to go the extra mile to talk about what you value in him, why you love your relationship with him, and why you want to be with him.

Time management is important in any poly relationship, but especially in a mono/poly relationship. Your partner may not be accustomed to spending time alone. Be transparent about your plans and intentions. Communicate openly about your schedule. Work with your partner to apportion time in a way that works for both of you.

Your partner may never want to explore other relationships, and that's okay. Avoid starting from the idea that your being poly is fair if your partner is "allowed" to have multiple relationships just like you. If your partner doesn't want them, the opportunity to have them isn't a benefit. Don't assume that your partner will suddenly become polyamorous as soon as he discovers how wonderful it is.

STRATEGIES FOR MONO/POLY RELATIONSHIPS

Many strategies for successful mono/poly relationships are the same as for any poly relationships: communication, flexibility, willingness to face discomfort, and all the other things we talk about in this book. In any poly partnership, some people might be off with a different lover while another person is home alone. This happens often. In a mono/poly relationship, it's likely to happen much more often. Because of this, the monogamous partner will benefit from developing a rich life separate from her partner. Hobbies, social activities and other interests can be really helpful.

MILA'S STORY In her early attempts to adjust to her mono/poly relationship with Morgan, Mila turned to her monogamous friends for support. The advice they gave was unhelpful. They blamed Morgan, told Mila to disregard Morgan and Nina's feelings, told her to put her foot down and say no to the situation. She found herself in the awful position of having to defend Morgan while seeking support.

A turning point for Mila came when she reached out to her local poly community. She found a small monthly discussion group that met her needs for empathy and shared wisdom. She was able to get support and advice for her struggles from people who had experience in poly relationships, and who did not immediately blame all her problems with Morgan on polyamory. They helped her counter some of the internal scripts from monogamous culture that she still struggles with. They helped support her sense that Morgan and his other partners had good intentions toward her and were trustworthy, despite everything she was being told by societal norms and well-meaning mono friends.

The monogamous person needs to have people—preferably outside the relationship—with whom she can talk and process her emotions. But finding such support can be difficult. Ideally such a confidant(e) won't just point to polyamory and say "See, here's the problem!" Yet a person whose relationship background is entirely monogamous might not have poly-friendly friends to confide in. We strongly recommend finding a poly discussion group in your area, if you can. An online search for polyamory in your area can help turn up many of these. Most discussion groups will have several members in mono/poly relationships, and having other such people to turn to can be an invaluable source of support.

Recognize that there are times, especially early on, when your relationship is going to be uncomfortable. Happiness is not merely the absence of discomfort; it requires doing the work, facing down fears and insecurities, and being willing to talk about and confront unpleasant things. There's nothing wrong with discomfort; challenging our comfort zone is how we grow, and succeeding in a mono/poly relationship requires growth.

Transparency is important. The polyamorous partner may hesitate to tell the monogamous person about new interests for fear of hurting him. The monogamous person might not want to talk about fears or insecurities for fear of upsetting the polyamorous partner. Wrong and wrong. Relationships live or die on the quality of the communication in them. It's vital that both people talk openly, even when talking openly is difficult.

As discussed in chapter 17, it might be tempting to think, *Okay, I can give this poly stuff a try, but if it doesn't work out, we can go back to monogamy.* Approaching polyamory this way is dangerous. It's one thing to talk about reverting back to monogamy when no one else is involved yet; it's quite another to discard other loves to do it. Treating other partners as disposable is not ethical. It will also damage your relationship. Telling a partner "Okay, I've changed my mind, get rid of this other person you love" will probably hurt both of you.

A tempting idea, particularly for monogamous people in a poly relationship, is to seek a feeling of safety and comfort by being able to reject the polyamorous person's other partners if they seem too threatening. As we discussed in chapter 12, that idea often backfires.

FINDING YOUR BOTTOM LINE

Mono/poly relationships require flexibility, negotiation and willingness to compromise. They also require a good understanding of our personal boundaries, and the things we can't compromise on. We talked about creeping concessions in chapter 10 (pages 175–76). Mono/poly relationships are especially prone to these. When people have radically different ideas about what their ideal relationship should look like, they will be especially tempted to make compromises that, over time, bargain away more than they intended. When negotiating a mono/poly relationship, ask yourself, "What are the essential things I must have? At what point will my needs no longer be met? What are my values? What must I have in order to act with integrity?" Don't compromise on those. If you negotiate away your integrity, ethics or agency, you are no longer a full and equal participant in the relationship.

You must also be aware of your partner's boundaries, and not ask (or expect) her to compromise past those points. Talk about what she needs to have a happy, functioning relationship, and where these needs overlap with yours. Be careful not to compromise on behalf of other people. Sometimes when we're trying to find a way out of an impasse, we may be tempted to make compromises that affect others—especially when those others are still hypothetical. It can be tempting to try to ease stress by bargaining away their agency in advance, such as by agreeing to limitations on their behavior. When we do this, we are using the agency of other people as bargaining chips.

Instead, focus on practical things your partner does have control over. If you need more time with her, say "I need more time with you," not "I don't want you spending so much time with other people." Be concrete about the things that are bothering you—schedules, chores, responsibilities, time with the kids, fun time together—and negotiate for those things specifically.

YOUR RELATIONSHIP IS A CHOICE

Overwhelmingly, the social message we're given about relationships is that falling in love means moving in together, getting married, settling down, starting a family. The "relationship escalator" narrative doesn't dwell much on the notion of choice; it can seem that once we fall in love, we're on that ride whether we want to be or not. It can be surprisingly easy to lose track of the fact that we do in reality have choices, even if they're difficult.

FRANKLIN'S STORY   When I met Celeste, she knew I'd never been in a monogamous relationship. We didn't expect to become romantic partners, much less married. The relationship that developed between us took us both by surprise. Throughout our relationship, we both had the idea that falling in love meant there was a path we were supposed to follow, and we were committed to that path. Celeste would say things like "I'm in love with you, which means I can never leave."

Because of this, we both ended up feeling that neither one of us had ever fully agreed to the relationship. Celeste felt like she hadn't quite consented to polyamory, even though she was aware I was not monogamous, because as soon as we were in love we would have to follow the path.

I felt the same way. At this point the word *polyamory* wasn't in circulation yet, and I had never met anyone who wanted the same things I did. I felt I was alone in wanting non-monogamy, so any relationship I was in would have this built-in difference in goals and desires, and so I had to make it work with Celeste. If I didn't, I would just have to start the same thing over with someone else, have the same arguments, make the same compromises.

Because neither of us believed we had a choice, we were both held hostage to our feelings. We didn't think leaving the relationship was possible, and we didn't have good tools to deal with the differences in what we wanted. As a result, Celeste felt that polyamory was being inflicted on her without her consent, and I felt that she couldn't really understand me.

In a mono/poly relationship, it is especially important that the people involved feel they are agreeing to the relationship on purpose, because they each see value in the other that makes the relationship a positive choice for both of them. When we believe, in contrast, that we must keep the relationship at all costs, it becomes difficult to give consent. As Franklin's partner Amber says, "When we enter into a romantic relationship, we make a choice.

Over time, we build a life. This may involve legal and financial commitments and responsibilities. But there is a difference between life-building and intimacy. Consent is about intimacy, and in every moment of every day, we should feel that we have a choice in the intimacy we participate in."

And remember that no matter how much you love each other, you are not obligated to be in a relationship with each other. You have a choice. If it doesn't work, if one of you is hurting too much, it's okay to let it go. The fairy tale is wrong: True love really doesn't conquer all, all the time.

QUESTIONS TO ASK YOURSELF

Mono/poly relationships offer some unique challenges and require careful negotiation if they are to succeed. Before embarking on a mono/poly relationship, here are a few things to consider:

If you are the monogamous partner:

- *Why do I identify as monogamous? Is it because I only want one partner for myself, or because I want my partner to be only with me, or both?*

- *Do I enjoy time to myself or without my partner? Do I have hobbies I enjoy alone or with others, and a social life that does not rely on my partner?*

- *Am I prepared to face uncomfortable feelings such as jealousy, insecurity and fear about my partner's loyalty, and to put in the work required to overcome them?*

If you are the poly partner:

- *Am I prepared to give my monogamous partner time and space to process his feelings about my polyamory?*

- *Am I prepared to make concessions in my relationship to help the monogamous person work through his feelings?*

- *Are there limits on the concessions I will make, either in terms of what I will agree to or the time span of the agreement?*

For both partners:

- *Do I fully understand my partner's choice to be monogamous or polyamorous, and am I able to accept my partner for who she is?*

- *Can I build a relationship that respects the agency not only of each of us, but of others who are involved as well?*

SEX AND LAUNDRY

> *Love's mysteries in souls do grow,*
> *But yet the body is his book.*
>
> JOHN DONNE

In the introduction, we said the first question most people ask when they hear about polyamory is "Who does the laundry?" That was naughty of us. The first question people usually ask is "Who sleeps with whom?" The question about laundry usually comes much later.

People in poly relationships are probably not having as much sex as you think. Polyamory, with its emphasis on intimate romantic relationships, isn't really about sex. Poly people don't necessarily have high sex drives, aren't necessarily kinky, aren't necessarily into group sex, and may not be interested in casual sex. Many poly people hold traditional views about sex. Indeed, as we've mentioned, polyamory is often attractive to asexual people, since it allows close, intimate relationships without the pressure (or guilt) of being a partner's only sexual outlet.

Having said that, sex is part of most romantic relationships, and poly relationships involve special considerations about sex. So it's a good idea to be fully up to speed about the physical and emotional risks (and special joys) that come with it. In this chapter, we address considerations other than sexual health and the risks of sexually transmitted infections (STIs), which are discussed in the next chapter.

DEFINING SEX

Before we talk about polyamory and sex, we have to clear up a minor detail: What is sex? Traditional heterosexual relationships give us a narrow definition: Sex is a penis entering a vagina (short form: PIV sex). Other sexual activities tend to be minimized or dismissed, as happened when a certain U.S. president sparked a national discussion over whether oral sex "counts." In gay and lesbian relationships the definition might get a little more complicated, but still tends to revolve around who does what with which genitals. A surprisingly large percentage of people will call themselves "virgins" even after they engage in oral or anal sex, which raises interesting and unfortunate implications for emotional and sexual health.

In polyamory, just as there's no single model for a romantic relationship, there's no single model for a sexual relationship. Partners in poly relationships may never engage in conventional penis-in-vagina sex (if they have bodies that permit that; not all poly people are heterosexual or cisgender!).* They may or may not expect that unbarriered sex (for instance, without a condom) will ever become part of the relationship. Poly relationships may involve a wide range of sexual activities, without including conventional sexual intercourse (or even genital contact) at all.

Defining sex is more than a word game. It matters for the agreements that people negotiate with each other. It affects sexual health boundaries. It influences what people may wish to be notified about, and what parts of a person's sexual past might need to be disclosed. In negotiations about sexual boundaries, therefore, everyone needs to be on the same page about what constitutes "sex."

---

* *Cisgender refers to a person whose experience of gender identity matches the gender that was assigned to them at birth.*

FRANKLIN'S STORY While I was visiting an out-of-town sweetie, I met a lovely young woman, Amelia. She and I quickly became friends. At one point during my visit, the partner I was visiting wanted to spend some time with one of her other boyfriends, so the two of them spent the night together. Amelia and I shared a bed that night, as there was only one other bedroom in the house where we were staying.

Amelia and I were not lovers, but during the course of the evening, she asked (in charming fashion) if I would object to her masturbating. I didn't mind at all, though I didn't participate in any way.

It would not have occurred to me (or my partners) to think of that night I spent with Amelia as sex, or of her as anything other than a non-sexual partner. But many people would consider the night we spent together to be a sexual activity, and one that would need to be disclosed to other partners. Certainly many monogamous people would consider this to be a violation of their relationship agreements.

This isn't an everyday sort of occurrence, but it does show how the definition of "sex" can be slippery, and how activities one person doesn't consider sexual, another might.

There is tremendous potential for hurt or resentment when our definitions of "sex" are misaligned. Sexual boundaries are among the most personal and intimate ones, with the potential to cause grave damage if crossed. Different kinds of sexual activity also involve different levels of physical risk. Mismatched definitions of "sex" create fuzziness around risk boundaries. We're better off overanalyzing how we define sex than not to be analyzing it enough. So we need to be able to discuss sex and sexual acts openly with our partners, without fear or shame. Unfortunately, most of us have not grown up accustomed to doing that, so it can be hard. The anxiety of talking openly about sex, though, pales beside the anxiety of having sexual boundaries stepped on, even inadvertently.

Two keys to having low-stress conversations about sex are being direct and asking questions. Listen and ask questions about how your partners define sex. Coded language and euphemisms only muddy things and create embarrassment. Here are some questions to open the discussion. Do you consider kissing sex? How about making out? Erotic massage? Clothed or unclothed fondling? Oral sex? Anal sex? Mutual masturbation? Same-room masturbation? Text or cybersex? Sharing sexual fantasies? Phone sex? What kinds of activities do you want to know about? At what point do you consider someone a sexual partner? If you ask about a prospective partner's sexual past, do you and she have similar ideas about what makes someone a lover?

SEX AND VULNERABILITY

Sexual risk is not always physical. We usually become emotionally attached and vulnerable to our lovers. As people who have explored cybersex can attest, physical touch is not necessarily a prerequisite for emotional vulnerability.

FRANKLIN'S STORY   Sex has always been strongly linked to emotional intimacy for me. I tend to get attached to my lovers, even if that's not my intention. Many years ago, I was traveling abroad to visit one of my partners. She and her other partners and their other partners and I all traveled to a remote castle in France, where we stayed for about a week.

While we were there, I met a lovely woman—a member of the extended poly network, linked to my partner through one of her partners. She and I connected quickly. I am normally cautious about extending physical intimacy to people, because I know I tend to get attached to my lovers whether I plan to or not. In this case, I extended more intimacy more quickly than I normally do.

Later we had a disagreement about something that should have been inconsequential. She said some things that should not have been able to hurt me, but did—because I had already let her in. I had permitted her too far inside my own boundaries, because we had been physically intimate, and that made the things she said far more wounding than they needed to be.

Some people can engage their bodies without engaging their hearts. Whether you can do this can be hard to predict, though. Whenever we let someone physically close, we've let them through a layer of our boundaries; Franklin has met several people, mostly former swingers, who once believed they could have sex entirely detached from intimacy, then found themselves getting unexpectedly attached to a casual lover. Nobody is immune to emotional vulnerability through physical vulnerability.

SEX AND EMOTIONAL BOUNDARIES

The boundaries that come up most often around sex involve STI risk, and we'll talk about those in a bit. But people have emotional boundaries around sex that need attention too. If you have a partner who has, or is considering, another lover, do you want to know what sexual activities might happen, or is that something you don't care about? When do you want to know that someone may become a new sexual partner? Some people like to be informed well in advance. For other people, if they're told sex might be a possibility during an upcoming date, that's enough.

How do you want to be informed? Do you want an in-person discussion with your partner before she takes a new lover, or would a text message do saying "Hey, having a wonderful time, think we might end up in bed"? Is it enough just to be told the next day? You will need to communicate these preferences clearly. Because people have different ideas about what is "sex," miscommunication can happen with surprising ease.

AMY'S STORY   Franklin's partner Amy was in a poly relationship that included an agreement about informing her current partner, Stephan, before she had sex with a new partner. She and Stephan did not agree on what this meant—though at first they did not know this.

Amy went on a third date with an old, close friend. A decade previously, the two of them had danced around the idea of a relationship, and now, they were discovering that their chemistry was stronger than ever. Back at her place they engaged in some heavy petting, but did not have intercourse.

Stephan believed Amy had violated their agreement, even though no intercourse had happened. To him, Amy had broken their agreement by failing to notify him that sex *might have been possible*, even though Amy believed that no sex had *taken place*. Because of this incident, Stephan decided Amy couldn't be trusted to honor agreements, so he wanted her to agree to restrictions on when and how she would see other people. Their relationship ended as a result of this conflict.

Good boundaries around sex must also be made knowing that everyone has a right to privacy about the details of their intimacy. There's no hard and fast line that clearly separates one person's right to be informed from another's right to privacy; setting these boundaries requires compassion and negotiation. Certainly, you have the right to know about your partner's sexual activities with other people in general terms, but at the same time, the details of intimate acts are things that your partner and his partner can reasonably expect to keep to themselves if they don't want to share them.

APPROACHES TO UNBARRIERED SEX

In poly relationships, often people have a select few partners, or perhaps one partner, with whom they will have unbarriered sex, and they use various forms of protection with others. For some folks, unbarriered sex is an intimate form of bonding.

Some people assume that certain kinds of relationships, such as marriage, come with an unspoken understanding that the partners will dispense with condoms and other barriers. But unspoken assumptions should never substitute for explicit negotiation. Polyamory means examining all of our assumptions about sex. If a married couple wants unbarriered sex, that may be awesome, but it's not necessarily right for everyone or every circumstance.

Another tacit assumption is that partners who have chosen unprotected sex will have unprotected sex forever. Poly people have even (of course) made up a term to describe the decision to have unprotected sex: *fluid bonding.* The word *bond* implies, to many, a promise that this will be ongoing.

Not all poly people use the term *fluid bonding;* many prefer to simply talk about using barriers or not, specifically to divest the idea of unbarriered sex from the emotional overtones that the term *fluid bonding* carries. They prefer to view unbarriered sex as a risk-management decision and, like all agreements, as something that can be renegotiated if necessary. Other people are deeply invested in fluid bonding and consider it an important part of intimacy.

EVE'S STORY   When I started seeing Ray, I was fluid-bonded with Peter. Ray and I were tested for STIs at the beginning of our relationship, and again six months in. I had recently had the HPV vaccine, and Ray was using condoms as a birth control method with his wife. So after the second set of tests, Ray, Peter and I sat down and agreed that Ray and I would have unbarriered sex. We agreed that we would inform each other when we had a new sexual partner, and that none of us would have unbarriered sex with anyone outside our trio without first discussing it with the others.

About six months later, Ray had unbarriered sex with a friend at a party. He called me the next day and told me. I said we would have to begin using barriers for another three months, until he could be tested again, and then we would need to discuss whether we wanted to fluid-bond again. I was hurt, because I valued the ability to have unbarriered sex with Ray, and I felt he had casually tossed that away. But I saw the issue as a risk-management problem that we could work through.

Peter, on the other hand—whom I told a week later (before I'd had an opportunity to have sex with either him or Ray)—considered Ray's decision a serious betrayal, especially because Ray had not taken the effort to tell Peter personally. Peter had a much more serious view of the "bond" element of a fluid bond than Ray or I had understood. But more than that, the broken agreement became a flashpoint for anger that had long been simmering for many other, unrelated reasons.

Eve, Ray and Peter ran into difficulty because unbarriered sex meant different things to each of them, with differing levels of emotional significance, and because they weren't all in agreement about protocols for disclosure regarding what might lead to resuming use of barriers.

When you're considering unbarriered sex with a partner, you want to be clear about your approach and expectations: whether you are making a risk-management decision that's open to future negotiation, whether the step you are taking has emotional significance for you, and whether you expect the agreement to be temporary or permanent. Perhaps most important is to agree in advance on what protocols you will follow when someone makes a mistake—because they will—or breaks an agreement.

WHEN UNBARRIERED SEX HAS EMOTIONAL SIGNIFICANCE

A common poly arrangement is for partners who have chosen to have unprotected sex with each other to pass rules prohibiting unprotected sex with others. Sometimes this is actually an attempt to control emotional intimacy. We aren't suggesting this is always true, but it's something to be aware of when discussing sexual boundaries. A conversation about safer sex shouldn't become a covert way to try to control your partner's emotional connection with others.

An agreement within a group to keep a barrier wall to the outside world, but not among one another, is called a "condom compact." This agreement has a poor reputation among poly people—because of the guilt, sense of betrayal and drama all around if one person breaks it. Having so much emotional weight hanging over the situation creates a big incentive for the violator not to tell the others, poisoning honesty and potentially exposing the whole group to STIs when they thought they were safe.

Instead, the approach both of us take is that any of our partners are free to have whatever kind of sex they want with whomever they want, provided they are honest about it. We then take charge of our own precautions. We communicate our sexual health boundaries, and our partners who value being able to have unprotected sex with us respect those boundaries. Should a partner choose not to, then we may choose to use barriers with that partner. This arrangement protects the right of all the people involved to make choices about their own bodies and level of risk, and to take responsibility for their own protection.

That sounds perfectly rational, but sex is rarely entirely rational. It's okay for unbarriered sex to be connected with feelings of intimacy. Being open to fluid bonding is sometimes a sign that a relationship has grown to the point where the intimacy is worth whatever risks might be associated with forgoing barriers.

Because fluid bonding is emotionally significant, it's useful to talk about an "exit strategy" with someone you're thinking about having unbarriered sex with. Under what circumstances will you continue having unbarriered sex, and under what circumstances will you go back to using barriers? What does having unbarriered sex mean to each of you—not just in practical terms like risk levels, but emotionally? If you choose to stop having unbarriered sex, what will that mean for your intimacy? What measures are you willing to take to protect being fluid-bonded? Often it can feel like a punishment if a partner decides to resume barrier use. Knowing the answers to these questions in advance can help avoid hurt feelings if the exit strategy is invoked.

Not everyone wants or values unprotected sex. Many people, especially people who identify as solo poly, prefer to maintain safer-sex practices with all their partners. This way, they can protect themselves without relying on their partners to inform them of changes to their sexual status, and they feel more free to make their own choices about sexual activity and sexual health.

PREGNANCY, THE OTHER RISK

Conversations about safer sex usually revolve around mitigating the risk of sexually transmitted infections (STIs), and it's surprising how many polyamorous people don't talk about pregnancy. It is a fact of nature often unacknowledged that when fertile heterosexual people have PIV sex, pregnancy sometimes results. Even, occasionally, when using contraception. It pays to talk about pregnancy risks and contingencies. What happens if someone accidentally becomes pregnant? By whom? Consider each possible combination. What are your expectations and contingencies concerning pregnancy and child-rearing?

In monogamous relationships, when one person says to another, "Honey, I think I might be pregnant," that usually starts a discussion. In poly relationships, "I think I might be pregnant" sometimes leads to incredulity, as if basic biology doesn't apply to polyamory. Especially, it seems, in hierarchical relationships with a secondary partner. Rather than being a statistically malleable consequence of a penis entering a vagina, pregnancy is sometimes treated as a betrayal, or a violation of the rules, or occasionally even an act of malice. Don't do this.

Talk beforehand about what you'll do about an unplanned pregnancy. There are a lot of divergent options. Will you abort? We've seen people in primary/secondary hierarchies start with the premise that if one of the primary partners gets pregnant, the other primary partner will be assumed to be the father, and they will raise the child accordingly. We've seen live-in relationships whose members have decided that in the event of pregnancy, all the men will have parenting duties. In other relationships, the woman will get a paternity test to determine the biological father.

Some poly partners who don't live together discuss raising the child in separate households with joint custody. Others say in the event of pregnancy, they will move in together. Be careful, though; in prescriptive primary/secondary relationships, this agreement can collide with rules that prohibit cohabitating with secondary partners! Any prescriptive hierarchy needs to have groundwork in place in the event of an unplanned pregnancy.

The contingency plans had better be more robust than "I won't let this happen." For if slippery bits are touching, it's always a possibility. If you use *two* birth control methods together, such as an IUD (one of the most effective methods) and condoms, the risk becomes very tiny. But very tiny is not zero. A friend of Franklin's once got pregnant—with triplets!—even though she was using an IUD *and* her boyfriend was using condoms. It happens. "I promise it won't" is about as realistic as promising it won't rain on your birthday.

Something not to try to legislate in advance is that any future partner will be required to have an abortion or won't be permitted to have an abortion. We don't believe a woman can be forced to carry to term or terminate a pregnancy. We also realize that this is an emotionally charged topic that many people have strong feelings about. If you don't agree with us, talk to any new partner about your expectations *before* tab A enters slot B.

No matter what discussions you have, you're probably going to feel some pretty strong emotions if pregnancy occurs. That's normal. Pregnancy is a big deal and likely to be disruptive for everyone. Talk about it before it happens. Give yourselves time to process your feelings, then talk some more. Please don't postpone the discussion until too late. For more about these issues, how to have these conversations, and how to prepare to start a poly family with kids, see Jessica Burde's book *The Polyamory on Purpose Guide to Poly and Pregnancy*, listed in the resources.

NONSEXUAL ROMANTIC RELATIONSHIPS

We tend to assume that sex is part of any romantic relationship, but some *asexual* people want intimate relationships without sex. *Demisexuals* want little. It's also very common for sexual desire to decline (or disappear) in long-term relationships. As with every element of polyamory, sex should not be assumed: it requires negotiation. Emotional closeness, support, love, touch and cuddling can all exist independent of sex. For many asexual people, polyamory offers an opportunity for romantic relationships without feeling obligated to provide for a partner's sexual needs.

Not desiring sex does not mean being frigid, cold or distant. Nonsexual relationships can be physically affectionate and warm. Romantic relationships without sex are not "merely" friendships. They can and do include passionate emotional intimacy, living together, shared goals and dreams, and lifelong plans.

Every comedian's repertoire has jokes about sexless married couples. They're not terribly funny, but they're sure to get a laugh. The loss of excitement in the familiar scares poly newbies and veterans alike. "What if my partner finds someone who she's hotter for than boring old me? How can I compete with all the frantic sex of a new relationship?" The answer is, you probably can't. This is normal, and it's not about you. So stop worrying. The newness of the new person will wear off too.

According to the U.S. National Health and Social Life Survey, about 15 percent of all married men and women reported having sex never or just a few times in the past year. We would all benefit from letting go of the idea that a relationship "has to" involve sex, or that there's a right amount of sex that romantic partners "should" have, and instead allowing relationships to be what they are, without pressure or expectation.

SHARING SEX

Not everyone is into group sex, and not all poly relationships include it. In fact, popular perceptions (and the Showtime *Polyamory* series) aside, group sex is more the exception than the norm among poly people. For those to whom it appeals, though, it can be great fun and great bonding, and the possibility of group sex with multiple people you love can be one of the big perks of polyamory.

If you've never had group sex before, it can trigger unexpected responses. You might imagine that you can avoid jealousy by controlling what your partner does with the other people, but sex tends to be a dynamic, messy, complicated business, and you won't be able to script the entire encounter. You can, however, establish general guidelines and boundaries in advance. For example, you might want to require barriers (and define what that means) all around, or take certain activities off the table. These kinds of boundaries usually work best when they're kept general (common ones are things like "No penetration" or "No male-male genital contact"), with an expectation of talk and negotiation throughout the encounter. With that in mind, make sure that in your first experience with group sex—or anyone's first experience together—judgment and communication are not overly impaired by alcohol or other substances.

This should go without saying, but everyone should have input about what goes on. Going into group sex thinking that it's all about you, or perhaps all about one couple, rather than a shared experience for everyone, is likely to lead to trouble. Don't do it if you feel bullied or pressured, and don't bully or pressure others into it. This, too, should go without saying.

It is normal for unexpected feelings to happen. When they do, step back, take a deep breath, and remember that your emotions don't have to be in the driver's seat. If you feel an unexpected negative emotion, say so calmly and clearly. Be willing to set boundaries, without having a temper tantrum. If something isn't working for someone else, change what you're doing—even if it's something you were really into. Remember, it's only by playing nicely that you get to play again!

It's better to end feeling that there is more you wanted to do than that you went too far. You might discover that group sex isn't for you. That's okay. Being poly doesn't mean you *have* to like threesomes or orgies. If you do, though, polyamory can offer the chance for all sorts of fun. For those who like it, group sex is a rewarding, amazing, intimate bonding experience. It isn't the exclusive domain of people who are bisexual or pansexual. A shared sexual experience does not have to involve every combination of people, unless all want it to. (For example, Franklin is straight; when he has group sex involving other men, he does not have sexual contact with them.) It can be two (or more) people focusing on one (or more) person in rotation...and boy, is it fun to be the one in the middle!

It can involve trading off attention, where one person alternates back and forth between two or more lovers. It's nice, and very connecting, when the person who's doing the alternating maintains contact with all of her lovers, even if it's just a hand resting on one person's shoulder while her attention is focused on another. As one poly fan of group sex says, "Group lovemaking can turn into an amazing thing, awash with amplifying feedback waves of different feelings going in complex directions that aren't really predictable. Getting good at surfing those waves, and sculpting them into something grand among your dearest lovers—there's just nothing like it."

EXPECTATIONS OF GROUP SEX

Some people try to mandate group sex, creating rules that if one member of an established couple takes a new partner, she is not allowed to have sex with the new person unless the other member of the couple is there—watching, if not involved. This is often meant to prevent sexual jealousy by keeping sexual access available to everyone. This looks good on paper but doesn't work well in practice, because usually jealousy isn't about allocation of resources; it's about insecurity, self-doubt, and feelings of unworthiness or fear. It's possible to be in the middle of a threesome and still feel sexual jealousy. Simply having sexual access to your partner's lover doesn't make jealousy go away. And to assume that if someone likes one person she should be sexually available to that person's partner comes across as very, very creepy. Which is part of why couples who take this approach find it so difficult to find partners.

BRUCE'S STORY   Many years ago, Bruce and his wife, Megan, decided to try polyamory. Since they didn't have experience with it, they thought dating together would be a good way to avoid jealousy. After years of searching, they finally hit the jackpot: an attractive, sexually alluring bisexual woman, Alicia, who agreed to date both of them.

The celebration didn't last long. Even though Bruce and Megan were both having sex with Alicia at the same time, jealousy still flared up whenever she seemed to be enjoying attention from one of them more than the other, or if she seemed to be paying more attention to one than the other. Even the normal ebb and flow of attention was enough to create jealousy.

At first they tried making rules that restricted her even more. The jealousy problems got worse. Before long, it became almost impossible for any two of them to pay attention to each other without the third person feeling jealous, even when all three were together. Needless to say, the relationship didn't survive.

Some people are happy to date and/or have sex with a couple. Such folks are thin on the ground, though, and even if a couple finds one, they may be surprised to discover feelings of jealousy and threat. As we have said many times, attempting to regulate the form a relationship may take is no substitute for dealing with things like insecurity and low self-confidence, and dealing with these things benefits any relationship, regardless of its form.

QUESTIONS TO ASK YOURSELF

When you have multiple sex partners, everyone needs to be clear with regard to sexual boundaries and expectations. Here are some questions to help get you there:

* *How do I define "sex"? What activities are sex? What aren't?*

* *Is sex a mandatory part of an intimate relationship for me? Would I consider a relationship with someone uninterested in sex or stay in a relationship with someone who loses interest in sex with me?*

* *Does unbarriered sex carry emotional significance to me?*

* *How do I feel about having unbarriered sex with someone who is having unbarriered sex with someone else?*

* *How do I feel about group sex and sexual exhibitionism?*

* *How do I feel about sex outside a romantic relationship?*

* *What happens if I or a partner of mine has an unexpected pregnancy?*

SEXUAL HEALTH

> *Fears are educated into us and can,*
> *if we wish, be educated out.*

KARL A. MENNINGER

The two of us grew up in the 1980s, when it was impossible to avoid public service announcements about the dangers of sex and potentially deadly infections like AIDS. This campaign unquestionably saved a great many lives, but it has also caused us as a society to be distrustful of sex—to see it as a dangerous business. Handling a lover can feel a bit like handling an unexploded munition of dubious provenance. Being polyamorous means navigating the risk involved in having multiple sexual partners. That risk isn't as great as many people fear, but it needs to be acknowledged, and risk-mitigation strategies are an important part of polyamory.

STI RISK IN POLYAMORY

People in monogamous relationships often pay little attention to sexual health and safety, partly because they associate sexual risk with promiscuity. By conflating promiscuity and risk, monogamous people create a false sense of reassurance for themselves: if I want monogamy, I don't need to talk about sexual health, right? It's only those non-monogamous folks who have to worry about that, right?

The reality is dramatically, surprisingly different. Few people in contemporary Western societies are monogamous by the strict technical definition (that is, having only one sexual partner for life). Even fewer of these, wittingly or not, mate with another person who is just as strictly monogamous. Far more common is serial monogamy, being monogamous with whoever you're with right now—and given the high prevalence of cheating in nominally monogamous relationships, even serial monogamy is often not what it appears.

Several studies suggest that a common course for nominally monogamous relationships includes having sex before committing to monogamy, getting tested for sexually transmitted infections (STIs) after having sex if at all, and discontinuing barrier use before being tested. This strongly suggests that monogamous relationships offer less protection for sexual health than many people believe.

When we consider how often sexual infidelity occurs within supposedly monogamous relationships, the picture becomes even murkier. An article in the *Journal of Sexual Medicine* reveals that the overall risk of STI infection is higher in monogamous relationships involving cheating than in openly non-monogamous relationships. The report also found that openly non-monogamous people are more likely to talk about sexual boundaries and sexual health, more likely to use barriers with partners, and more likely to have frequent STI screening than the population as a whole. As a result, the STI risk in communities of openly non-monogamous people is significantly lower than intuition might suggest (and the risk in monogamous relationships is likely higher).

The information in this book is as accurate as we can make it. However, this is an area where new research is being done all the time. The information you'll find here is current as of spring 2014, but we encourage you to do your own research and keep up with new findings. Our numerous sources are listed in the notes for this chapter.

SAFER SEX

Sexual health protection begins with you. You are the person most responsible for your health, which means it's always acceptable for you to make choices to protect yourself. While monogamy is not a guarantee of safety, risk does increase with more partners. This is true for any form of non-monogamy, including cheating, swinging and, yes, polyamory. When we get into a car, we minimize risk by doing things like wearing a seat belt; when we have sex, it is wise to minimize risk as well.

When most of us think about protection during sex, we tend to think "condoms." Male condoms are an excellent way to protect ourselves from many STIs, including the worst ones. They're effective contraception as well when they're used correctly. New materials such as polyisoprene and poly-urethane make condoms available for people with latex sensitivities. Many poly people use condoms with some or all of their partners for some or all types of sexual contact. We often tend to associate STI risk with vaginal or anal intercourse, but other types of activity, including oral sex, can be a risk factor too. Female condoms are less well known. They're more expensive and often harder to find than male condoms, but they provide a high degree of protection during vaginal and anal intercourse.

Some people also use dental dams for cunnilingus. These are square sheets of latex or silicone that are placed over the labia during oral sex; they're effective at preventing STIs by preventing direct contact between one person's mouth and the other person's sexual fluids. Impermeable plastic kitchen wrap also works and is much cheaper and handier. "Breathable" wrap has many microscopic holes and is not suitable for this use.

Some people go even further, preferring to use barriers such as gloves even for manual stimulation during sex. The odds of transmitting dangerous STIs such as HIV during manual sex are very low (though gloves are wise if you have unhealed cuts or cracked cuticles that tend to bleed), but there is a small risk of spreading HPV (human papillomavirus) or HSV (herpes simplex virus) through manual contact. Using latex gloves and being careful not to touch yourself after touching your partner can reduce this risk considerably.

Some poly people engage in sadomasochistic sexual activities. Even though these activities don't necessarily meet the conventional definition of "sex," some forms of BDSM play can transmit STIs. Any contact with blood or other bodily fluids can spread infection. Activities such as cutting and needle play represent a risk of exposure to blood-borne pathogens. People involved in BDSM usually make sure they use sterile, disposable implements for this kind of play, and wear gloves with partners they're not willing to exchange bodily fluids with.

Vaccinations are another important tool for STI risk management. Vaccinations against hepatitis A and B and the most serious strains of HPV are widely available, and a vaccine against herpes is entering clinical trials. We believe that sexually active people should, where medically appropriate, make use of these vaccinations. Talking about your vaccination status, along with testing, sexual history and test results, is an important part of discussing STI safety. (And while we're at it, seasonal flu shots are immensely helpful in preventing a nasty flu from sweeping through a romantic network.)

A relatively new approach to HIV prevention among people at high risk (including gay men and heterosexual couples with one partner positive for HIV) is the use of antiretroviral drugs by uninfected people. Studies have shown that use of antiretroviral drugs as a preventive measure significantly reduces the incidence of HIV transmission, by as much as 75 percent or more. This use of antiretrovirals is still relatively new. As we write this, a quarterly antiretroviral injection is being studied for HIV prevention. Although it's not a vaccination, it holds promise for significantly slowing the spread of HIV.

People carrying herpes, both types 1 and 2, can use a common antiviral such as acyclovir to reduce outbreaks and minimize their risk of transmitting the virus.

But the best protections aren't mechanical or medical, they're behavioral. They start with having a proactive attitude about sexual health. Transparency about sexual behavior and risk management, and the ability to talk about sex without fear or shame, are the foundation for a good STI risk-management strategy. Your attitude toward sexual health determines not only the risk-management strategies you use, but also how you communicate with your partners.

DISCLOSURE

Ethical polyamorous relationships require disclosure of your current partners, because without full disclosure, people can't give informed consent to be involved with you. Different people require different levels of disclosure, which means part of responsible disclosure is proactively asking questions about a person's boundaries, definitions and need for information.

The purpose of this disclosure is not merely to provide information for sexual health and STI risk assessment, but to give a complete impression of the romantic obligations and commitments you have made and other factors that might limit the time and emotional energy you can offer. When Franklin talks to a prospective new partner, he talks about all of his romantic relationships, even his nonsexual relationship with Amber.

A complete STI risk profile also requires disclosing all past sexual partners. Many people in the poly community feel that merely exchanging STI test results is not sufficient. Test results are a snapshot, recording STI status at a particular point in time; past sexual history gives a more complete picture, showing patterns of conduct and level of risk tolerance. The most important risk factor for HPV (discussed later in this chapter), for instance, is the number of sexual partners someone has had in the past year. Many poly people will want information about a prospective partner's sexual history before making dating and/or sexual decisions.

Some people feel this level of disclosure is unnecessary, especially for people who won't be engaging in unprotected sex. However, relying on barriers alone is not sufficient for everyone, as barriers are not 100 percent effective. And some viruses, such as herpes and HPV, can be transmitted by skin-to-skin contact, so barriers are less effective at preventing these than they are for other STIs. Because different people have different thresholds of acceptable risk, you must be willing to talk openly about sexual history and boundaries (or, at the very least, be willing to say "I don't think we are compatible partners" to someone who wants this level of disclosure).

People from monogamous backgrounds, or who have come to polyamory from swinging, may not be accustomed to this level of discourse about sexual history and behavior. Within the poly community, it is often (though not universally) considered a routine part of negotiating sexual boundaries.

RISK ASSESSMENT

Fact: You are terrible at objectively assessing risk. So are we, and so is everyone you're likely to meet. Our brains are poor at evaluating real risk vs. perceived risk. We fear riding in airplanes but get into a car, which is a more dangerous way to travel, without a second thought. Our emotional assessment of risk is strongly skewed toward spectacular but unlikely scenarios, and biased away from situations where we feel a sense of control. Our brains are also terrible at understanding probability, which leads us to irrational decisions. For example, if you drive ten miles to buy a lottery ticket, you are far more likely to be killed in a car crash getting there than to win the lottery. Furthermore, research has demonstrated that our perception of risk is collective; it relies more on the particular social group we are part of than on the actual level of risk.

This inability to assess risk applies just as strongly to sexual health as to anything else in our lives. We fear AIDS but not hepatitis, even though hepatitis is more common and kills more people in the United States every year. Add to that the stigma associated with sexual health, and it's no surprise that realistic assessment of STI risk is difficult. We tend to treat someone who has had gonorrhea very differently than someone who has had strep throat, even though both are bacterial infections that are sometimes antibiotic-resistant, sometimes dangerous, but generally treatable.

Our emotional perception of risk makes us likely to rate risk higher when we have no direct benefit from it than when we do. This means that we're likely to feel more afraid when a partner has other lovers than when we have other lovers ourselves, even if the risk profile is the same, and even though we have an extra degree of separation from our lover's lovers.

The first thing to understand about STIs is that, like driving a car or climbing a ladder, there is no way to guarantee sex will be absolutely safe. Even if previously celibate people start a totally monogamous relationship, that is not a guarantee. Many nominally sexually transmitted infections, including herpes and HPV, are often transmitted nonsexually as well. In the U.S., more people contract herpes 1 (often expressed as cold sores) by nonsexual means than by sexual means, usually during childhood.

Given that sex carries some degree of risk, the real question isn't "How can we be totally safe?" but rather "What level of risk is acceptable?" Different people have very different answers. Barrier use, regular testing and open discussion about sexual history are an effective combination for STI prevention. They don't guarantee absolute safety, but the combination of these things will probably bring the risk below that of many things we do every day, like driving to the grocery store or using a stepladder.

The management strategy that the two of us use is that we are screened for STIs regularly, usually annually and whenever we are considering starting a new sexual relationship. We exchange test results with a potential new partner before any activity that might involve fluid exchange. Eve, like many others, keeps a spreadsheet with her testing and immunization history, plus a one-year sexual history, in a Google Drive folder, along with PDFs of test results and immunization records. Since she can access these documents on her phone, she can show them to anyone who might need to see them, whenever she is asked. She also shares the folder with long-term partners.

STI TESTING

Another fact: Verifying negative test results is highly effective protection against the most common STIs. That's one of the reasons why testing is the go-to method for STI prevention among poly people. Most poly people get tested at regular intervals, typically ranging from every six months to every year, depending on the stability of their immediate network. Asking to see copies of test results doesn't typically raise eyebrows among poly people: "Trust but verify" is a phrase you'll often hear. Making verification a standard procedure protects everyone against the possibility of dishonesty or NRE-addled poor judgment while not pointing any fingers.

Different STI tests have different windows of effectiveness. The chart on pages 358-59 provides information on testing windows as of 2014, but STI testing is something to discuss with a medical professional, who can provide you with up-to-date details about the types of tests and their effectiveness. Don't be afraid to ask questions about the details of the tests you'll be receiving! Our chart includes types of tests and testing windows for various STIs. We created the chart by compiling research on the prevalence of various STIs and the risk of transmission from various types of sexual activities. The information here represents a survey of the current literature in North America. Of course, risk factors and prevalence may vary geographically and change over time; this chart should be used as a starting point for talking about sexual health and doing your own research.

One unfortunate fact of poly life is that there are a small number of polyamorous people who don't engage in STI testing or prevention at all, because they have fallen victim to conspiracy memes and do not believe that medical conditions like AIDS exist. Fortunately these people are rare, but unfortunately, they are out there. This is another reason why talking to a prospective partner about STI testing, sexual health and sexual history is important.

SHAME AND STIs

STIs and STI testing are often surrounded by stigma and shame. This can play out in poly relationships in many ways. Some sexual health clinics, particularly in small towns, have been known to shame people (women more often than men, from our anecdotal observations) who seek regular STI testing. Many poly people do regular screening, yet there is a perception even among some health care professionals that testing is unnecessary for people in stable relationships. We believe it's important to be open with your health care professional about being polyamorous, but at the same time, we recognize that some people in the medical community are capable of being prejudiced and judgmental about nontraditional relationships.

It's helpful to remember that your doctor works for you. You can always fire him and get another. Wherever possible, if you encounter stigma or shaming from health care professionals, speak up. Say that the behavior is inappropriate. If possible, consider filing a formal complaint, switching health care professionals, or both. The resources section of this book includes information on finding a poly-friendly health professional.

Some people are too embarrassed or ashamed to seek STI testing. Some people see asking others about it, or being asked, as a mark of distrust. But anyone can carry STIs and not know it. Asking for testing doesn't mean you don't trust your partner; it means you recognize that microbes don't care about human values of right and wrong or trust and distrust.

People consider STIs shameful in ways we don't consider other medical conditions shameful. In part this is social conditioning. Shame around STIs, like fear of STIs, can be a component of negative attitudes about sex. As a result, many people who do have STIs, especially herpes, are treated poorly by others—even if, as often happens, the infection was not acquired sexually.

This is, sadly, just as common among poly people as among monogamous people. Many people react with horror to a disclosure that someone has something minor like herpes. We have both heard many people say, "I would never even consider a partner with herpes!" even though, ironically, perhaps half (or more) of the people who say that actually have herpes themselves and just don't know it.* Many of these people are asymptomatic or have one outbreak, easily missed, and never have an outbreak again. A friend of Franklin's, for example, once wanted to start dating a woman who was positive for HSV-2, but his wife objected. Finally, the three agreed to get tested for HSV together—whereupon the wife discovered that she had herpes herself, and had simply never known.

A person with an STI is not dirty or promiscuous. Nor is such a person necessarily a risk. Franklin has had a partner with HSV for more than a decade as of this writing and is tested regularly for it himself, but has never tested positive.

Because so many of us fear STIs, and because protecting sexual health is a legitimate and reasonable concern, fear of STIs can become a "back door" way to control our partners for our own purposes. We might find it difficult to say "I don't want you having sex with Susan because I am jealous of her," but find it easier (more reasonable?) to say "I don't want you to have sex with Susan because I'm concerned about STIs." When we do that, fear of STIs becomes a cover for other concerns we are not addressing honestly.

Such manipulation may not even be intentional. Because of the emotional attachments we have to STIs, a person we don't like may trigger STI fear more than a person we like. This fear can subtly influence the way we feel about a partner's sexual decisions and evaluation of risk. Of course, STI risk does not affect everyone equally. Even relatively non-threatening STIs can be more dangerous to people with compromised immune systems, say, or to expectant mothers. But the same is true of other risks as well. A rational approach to STI risk must include the idea that STI shame is unreasonable.

Speaking of driving cars, isn't it strange that we are willing to risk dismemberment or death by driving over to a lover's house, but we are frequently terrified of STIs that, to most of us, are not nearly as potentially damaging? Deadly STIs exist, but they are rare, especially in poly networks. These are generally the ones that are very preventable with condoms, as the chart on pages 358–59 shows. Common STIs such as herpes (which statistically will affect about 60 percent of the people reading this book) are, for most people, an annoyance at most, far less serious than the possible consequences

---

* *While about 60 percent of North Americans have HSV-1 or HSV-2, between 80 and 90 percent of those are not aware they have it.*

of a car crash. We'll risk gruesome death to visit a partner, yet we are too afraid to express physical intimacy with that partner when we get there. This should not suggest that we, your authors, are cavalier about STIs. We simply believe that research and rational risk management are better than blind fear.

NEGOTIATING RISK TOLERANCE

When talking about safer-sex boundaries and risk tolerance, remember there's no one right answer. Everyone's threshold of acceptable risk is different, and people use different metrics for assessing risk. It might seem like a simple calculus—look at the numbers, decide where your threshold is, act accordingly—but human decisions are never quite this tidy.

We all must decide on the degree of risk we are willing to accept in our sex lives. This decision is an important part of acting with agency. Each of us is responsible for protecting our own sexual health, and that includes making decisions about what risks we will accept. Part of that decision will be emotional, and that's okay.

Just as you have the right to choose your own level of acceptable risk, so do others. Shaming other people for their choices is not good behavior. This includes shaming people for making choices that are not only more conservative than yours, but also less conservative. We've heard people say "So-and-so can't be trusted, because she does things that I think are risky." It's fine to choose not to be sexually involved with someone whose risk threshold is higher than yours, but that doesn't make such a person untrustworthy, reckless or foolish. The degree of risk we're talking about here is relatively small even for someone who has comparatively relaxed boundaries.

SEXUALLY TRANSMITTED INFECTIONS: THE FINE PRINT

We're now going to go into detail about bugs that are considered sexually transmitted infections, their transmission routes, effects and treatment options. The chart on the following two pages sums up the numbers, with the rest of this chapter going into greater detail. The information here is specific to the North American context and assumes you have access to a basic level of medical care (for example, you have access to condoms, testing and antibiotics).

Note that the numbers given here represent averages across the population, but certain subpopulations are at much greater risk than others. For example, in 2010 the U.S. Centers for Disease Control and Prevention estimated that "1.92% (one in 52) of Hispanics/Latinos would receive HIV diagnoses during their lifetimes, compared with an ELR [estimated lifetime risk] for HIV diagnosis of 0.59% (one in 170) for whites and 4.65% (one in 22) for blacks/African Americans." And nationwide, half of HIV diagnoses are in men who have sex with men.

The state of knowledge around many STIs is changing rapidly, and some of the information here is likely to become out-of-date quite soon. Because of all this, we debated whether to include detailed STI information in this book at all. We decided to include it with this disclaimer, because for many people, the level of fear greatly outweighs the access to actual facts. We hope that the information below can help you understand what's out there and get an idea of what your real risk level is.

If there's one thing we'd like you to take away from this information, it's this: STIs are both rarer and more ubiquitous than most people imagine. They are rarer in that the nasties that come to mind when most people think of STIs, such as HIV, are actually much less common and much harder to get than typically believed. Usually minor infections that are a major cause of stigma and shame, such as HSV (herpes), are actually so common that *half the population of North America or more* is infected with oral or genital herpes and doesn't know it. And the most common STI of all, HPV, is one that not very many people are even aware of.

Taken together, we hope that this information, rather than creating fear, will help you understand that some STI risk is both unavoidable and manageable. With reasonable precautions, such as testing, disclosure, vaccinations and the use of barriers, you can protect yourself very well from nearly everything that might cause you serious harm. At the same time, it's a near certainty that an STI will enter your poly network at some point or another. It may be an extremely common one such as HSV, or it may be a less common but still widespread (and completely treatable) infection such as chlamydia. Protect yourself, by all means: be smart and stay safe. But don't freak out about sex, and there's no reason to shame or ostracize people who have contracted an STI.

COMMON SEXUALLY TRANSMITTED INFECTIONS (STIs)

	PREVALENCE IN THE POPULATION (%)	PEOPLE UNAWARE THEY HAVE IT (%)	IS THERE A VACCINE?
CHLAMYDIA	0.5[1] (0.3 in Canada)[2]	NA	No[3]
GONORRHEA	0.1[5] (0.03 in Canada)[2]	NA	No[6]
SYPHILIS	0.005[9] (U.S. and Canada)[2]	NA	No[10]
HIV	0.6 of adults aged 15 to 49[12] (0.2 in Canada; half of cases are among men who have sex with men)[13]	15[14] (25 in Canada)[13]	No[15]
HSV-1	54–62[19, 20]	NA	No[21]
HSV-2	16–22[19, 20, 24]	80–94[25, 26]	No[21]
HPV	27 of women aged 14 to 59 (active infection)[27] (10–33 in Canada)[2]	NA	Yes[28]
HEPATITIS A (acute infections)	0.0004[33] (0.001 in Canada)[34]	NA	Yes[35]
HEPATITIS B (chronic infections)	0.03[36] (0.7–0.9 in Canada)[37]	NA	Yes[38]

All data are for the United States unless otherwise noted. Most data are from 2012, but range from 2008 to 2013. See sources (indicated by superscript numerals) for more details. These are listed after the endnotes, on page 466. NA indicates that data was not available.

IS IT CURABLE?	TYPE(S) OF TEST(S)	TESTING WINDOW (TIME FROM INFECTION TO POSITIVE TEST)
Yes[4]	Swab or urine test[4]	2 to 3 weeks; sometimes up to 6 weeks[4]
Yes, but antibiotic resistance is developing[7]	Swab or urine test[8]	7 days[8]
Yes[11]	Blood test or swab[11]	3 weeks to 3 months[11]
No, but treatable[16]	Blood, oral swab (OraQuick rapid antibody test) [17]	As little as 48 hours; up to 3 months[17] P24 antigen test and quantitative PCR test give earliest results, but may not be available for everyone or in all areas[18]
No, but treatable[22]	Swab or blood[23]	As soon as sores are present for swab, 12 to 16 weeks for blood[23]
No, but treatable[22]	Swab or blood[23]	As soon as sores are present for swab; 12 to 16 weeks for blood[23]
There is no treatment for the virus itself. However, there are treatments for the health problems that HPV can cause.[29]	Visual exam (for genital warts)[30] Pap tests and HPV tests screen for cervical cancer or precancer[31] In Canada, HPV DNA tests have been approved for use in women, but availability is limited[32]	Depends on the test[30]
Yes[35]	Blood test[35]	2 to 7 weeks[30]
Yes[38]	Blood test[38]	4 weeks[38]

THE USUAL SUSPECTS

When people say things like "I've been tested" or "I'm clean," they're usually referring to a specific set of STIs, the ones we'll call "the usual suspects": HIV, chlamydia, syphilis and gonorrhea. These are the infections that most STI clinics will test for as a matter of course when someone goes in for a routine screening. If you say "I've been tested for everything," there's a good chance you haven't: you've probably been tested for these four. They're not the only sexually transmitted infections, and there are some STIs that it's rare to test for. We discuss those others later in the chapter.

Chlamydia. Affecting about a million people in the United States at any given time, chlamydia is a very common sexually transmitted infection, with up to 1 in every 200 people diagnosed each year in the United States. It's caused by a bacterium that infects the mucous membranes. Because it doesn't need to enter the bloodstream, it is easily transmitted through intercourse, shared sex toys or other forms of fluid exchange. Chlamydia can also infect the rectum, throat or eyes through anal or oral sex.

As with most other STIs, most people with chlamydia are asymptomatic, so the only reliable way to know you have it is through testing, which is done by taking swabs from the cervix in women or urethra in men. People who have symptoms may notice an unusual discharge or burning during urination. Chlamydia can remain undetected for months or years, and in women, it can eventually develop into pelvic inflammatory disease, which can cause internal scarring with reproductive effects up to and including infertility.

Chlamydia is generally easily curable with antibiotics. When a person is diagnosed with chlamydia, it's common medical practice to treat all of their sexual partners, without necessarily even testing those partners for chlamydia as well.

Gonorrhea. Another bacterial infection, gonorrhea has been causing trouble to humans since medieval, possibly even biblical times. About 1 in 1,000 people are diagnosed each year in the United States. Gonorrhea is easily transmitted during vaginal and anal sex. It's also possible to get gonorrhea in the throat from oral sex. Condoms are highly effective at preventing transmission.

Gonorrhea is diagnosed with a swab culture. It is treatable with antibiotics, although it has become resistant to many drugs. In recent years, some cases have been found that are resistant to multiple antibiotics, making infections with these strains extremely hard to treat. Half of women who are infected do not have symptoms, but those who do have discharge or vaginal pain. Most infected men will have pain with urination and unusual discharge. Left untreated, gonorrhea can cause pelvic inflammatory disease or spread through the body to affect the joints and heart.

Syphilis. An easily curable bacterial infection, syphilis is rare, at least in high-income countries. That wasn't always the case; syphilis is one of the oldest recognized sexually transmitted infections, and was once a deadly scourge that affected many high-profile people. Symptoms include sores and rashes, progressing, if untreated, to neurological damage and death.

Syphilis is transmitted through oral, anal or vaginal sex, and (rarely) through kissing near a lesion. It is highly transmissible, meaning that if you have sex with someone who has it, you're very likely to become infected yourself. Barriers offer some protection against syphilis, but good data are scarce. Nevertheless, your risk of encountering syphilis is very low (at least if you live in North America). It is diagnosed with a blood test, which is usually—though not always—included as part of routine STI screening.

HIV. The acronym HIV stands for human immunodeficiency virus. For a lot of people (especially if, like us, you came of age in the 1980s), it is the STI that triggers the greatest fear. It is also one you're very unlikely to encounter, at least if you live in North America and unless you're a gay or bi man. (Nearly half of all HIV cases are in men who have sex with men.) HIV is a virus that attacks the human immune system; it is the cause of the disease known as AIDS, which stands for acquired immune-deficiency syndrome. AIDS can kill you, as can many common infections if your immune system is compromised by AIDS. There is no cure for HIV or AIDS, but today there are highly effective treatments (for those who can afford them) to hold it in check. A diagnosis of HIV was once considered a death sentence, but this is no longer the case. Many people with HIV now live out normal life spans with few or no symptoms (though with a heavy drug regimen), and many have lived for years with no detectable viral load.

HIV can be transmitted in body fluids including blood, semen, vaginal fluid and breast milk. In addition to sex, it can be transmitted by hypodermic needles, blood transfusions, pregnancy or breastfeeding. HIV enters the body either directly through the bloodstream (such as with infected needles) or through mucous membranes. Anal sex is substantially riskier than vaginal sex for HIV transmission, and being the receptive partner is riskier than being the penetrative partner. Risk of transmission through oral sex, whether giving or receiving, is extremely low. Condoms are highly effective at preventing HIV transmission.

HIV is detected through a blood test or an oral swab test. Testing is more or less the only way to know whether you have it. Most people with HIV have no symptoms for years before developing AIDS.

HEPATITIS

Paradoxically, most people don't think of hepatitis as an STI, yet it is one of the more common—and also more dangerous—ones. The word *hepatitis* broadly refers to any infection of the liver, but usually people are speaking of hepatitis A, B or C, which are caused by viruses. Hepatitis A is transmitted by consuming infected fecal particles, such as through eating contaminated food or (rarely) through oral sex. Hepatitis B can be transmitted sexually, and both hepatitis B and C can be transmitted through blood. Hepatitis C is not generally considered an STI. All three strains of hepatitis are diagnosed through a blood test. Many STI clinics do test for hepatitis B as a matter of course now, but many still do not.

Most cases of hepatitis A or B in higher-income countries (where people have adequate access to rest, nutrition and clean water) will resolve on their own. Antiviral treatments are sometimes used for hepatitis B. In some cases, though (about 5 percent of infected adults), hepatitis B can become chronic, often leading to cirrhosis and liver failure.

By far the best protection against hepatitis is vaccination. Safe and effective vaccines exist for both hepatitis A and B, and they're covered under many insurance policies. If your family doctor doesn't have it (or you don't have a family doctor), travel medicine clinics—which specialize in preventive medicine for people traveling abroad—are an easy place to get vaccinated.

Now to the common but less serious infections.

HSV (HERPES)

HSV, or herpes simplex virus, is one of the two most common sexually transmitted infections. There are several variants, or strains, of herpes. The two we usually associate with the name *herpes* are herpes 1 and herpes 2, which cause skin lesions that can appear on the face or eyes, around the genitals, or on other parts of the body. Chickenpox is caused by a different strain of the herpes virus, called the herpes varicella zoster virus or herpes 3, which also causes shingles. Mononucleosis is a variant of herpes called herpes Epstein-Barr (EBV) or herpes 4. There are other variants of herpes as well, including cytomegalovirus (herpes 5), a pair of herpes viruses that cause a common childhood disease called roseola (herpes 6 and 7), and a very rare variant usually only found in immunocompromised people that leads to a type of cancer called Kaposi's sarcoma (herpes 8).

Most people think herpes 1 causes cold sores and herpes 2 causes genital herpes, but this isn't accurate; either strain can affect any part of the body. They're incredibly common; according to a recent study, well over half of adults in North America have HSV-1 and one in six North Americans have HSV-2. Most people who have herpes are not aware that they do; another study showed that of people in North America who are seropositive for herpes, less than 20 percent are aware they have it. As mentioned earlier, that means that up to half of all North Americans carry herpes but think they don't.

Part of the reason so few people who have herpes know it is that, for most people, herpes may cause one outbreak and then remain dormant for years or decades. Many people acquire it as a child. Outbreaks, especially of genital herpes, are often so mild they aren't recognized for what they are.

The shame and stigma associated with herpes are far worse than the infection itself. This is particularly ironic when we consider that, statistically, many of the people who loudly proclaim they would never date anyone with herpes actually have herpes and don't know it.

If you've never been specifically tested for herpes, don't assume you don't have it, and don't freak out if a partner or potential partner tells you he does. Don't assume you've been tested for it just because you've had an STI screening. Most clinics don't test for herpes unless you specifically ask them to, and even then a lot of clinics resist testing for it, because it's so common and usually so minor, and the stigma is so great.

There's an idea that having sex with a partner who has herpes is a sure ticket to contracting it yourself, but this is not true. There is no surefire way to guarantee protection, but barriers, antiviral drugs, lysine supplements and even stress reduction all reduce the risk of transmission.

Herpes is very often spread nonsexually; any skin-to-skin contact, including secondary contact, can potentially spread the virus. Many people contract HSV-1 as children through non-sexual contact with other people who have it. Athletes can spread HSV through skin contact; any athlete who engages in contact sports can develop herpes whitlow, a skin infection caused by HSV-1 or HSV-2.

In other words, you can't assume you don't have herpes (if you haven't been tested for it), you can't assume you're guaranteed to get it if your partner has it, and you can't assume you won't get it if you never have a partner who has it. The fear is radically disproportionate to the risk. There's one exception: during childbirth, herpes can be passed to the newborn and have serious effects. An expectant mother having an active herpes outbreak may need a cesarean birth.

Herpes is most transmissible during an active outbreak that causes an open sore. Outbreaks can be prevented or controlled by antivirals such as acyclovir. As we write this book, a vaccine against herpes is entering early clinical trials. Should it prove to be successful, such a vaccine could be on the market within the next decade. This has the potential to drastically alter the landscape of herpes infections. Until such a vaccine is available, the best defense against herpes is knowledge. We believe that many people are unnecessarily stigmatized by herpes, and that we all engage in activities every day that are far more risky than having a partner who has HSV.

HPV

HPV, or human papillomavirus, is the STI you are most likely to encounter. In fact, as many as 80 percent of people will be exposed to HPV over the course of their lives, and anywhere between 10 and 40 percent of people have an active infection right now, with the highest rates of active infection found in people under 25.

HPV is the virus associated with cervical cancer and genital warts, and is now being linked to throat and rectal cancer as well. About 1 in 150 women will develop cervical cancer over their lifetimes, and 1 in 435 will die from it. As scary as this may sound, this is a significantly lower risk than most other kinds of cancer (such as breast cancer, which claims ten times as many lives). And cervical cancer and its precursor condition are very curable if caught early by regular checkups and Pap tests.

Contrary to what many people believe, there is no reliable test for HPV; because it can infect many areas and the infection is localized, false negatives are common. If you're a woman and you've ever had an abnormal Pap smear, you have probably been exposed to HPV. You can be infected with HPV in the rectum and throat as well as parts of the genital area besides the cervix. Most people's bodies clear an HPV infection within one to two years; during that time they can be infectious, but usually not after. Some infections, though, linger. These can cause cancer and infect others years after exposure.

Many people believe that since nearly everyone has been or will be exposed to HPV in their lifetimes, there's no point trying to protect yourself. This is not precisely true. There are hundreds of strains of HPV, dozens of which can cause cancer. Even if you've already been infected with one strain, you can still be infected with another—and there's some evidence that co-infection with more that one strain raises your risk of cancer, though there's no scientific consensus on that point yet.

Vaccines for HPV are available that protect against the most prevalent strains, which together are responsible for 70 percent of cervical cancers and 90 to 95 percent of genital warts cases. Barriers like condoms offer some protection against HPV, but aren't recommended as a reliable risk-reduction strategy. But between barriers and vaccination, you can actually get fairly decent protection. In addition, barriers disproportionately reduce the higher-risk HPV infections: those that are more likely to lead to cervical cancer. You can also purchase latex shorts online; these are worth considering for HPV (or HSV) protection for casual encounters. And women, get Pap smears at the intervals recommended by your doctor—and make sure your doctor knows you have multiple sexual partners.

Many doctors will say that the HPV vaccine is available only to women under age twenty-six. This is untrue. Anyone, of any gender or any age, can get the vaccine; however, you will likely have to pay for it. At the time of writing, the vaccine costs about $150 per dose, and three doses are required over a six-month period. Not all doctors are aware that the vaccine can be given to people over twenty-six; you may have to educate your doctor. In the United States, you can get the vaccine with little difficulty at Planned Parenthood; in Canada, travel medicine clinics are also happy to dispense it.

The number-one controllable risk factor for HPV is the number of sexual partners you have. To reduce their risk of exposure to HPV as well as other STIs, some people choose to limit intercourse to just a few partners over their lives, while engaging in other, non-penetrative sexual activities with other partners. HPV risk is another good reason to understand the sexual histories of people you are considering having sex with, even if they can present test results for the usual suspects (which do not include HPV). The more sexual partners someone has—or has had—the more you may wish to limit the activities you do with them, or have only barriered sex.

We'd be lying if we said there's nothing to be afraid of, or that there's no way to reduce your risk of contracting HPV. But at the same time, we see far too much judgment and fear of people who disclose that they are HPV positive. Most of us will, despite our best efforts, be exposed at least once in our lives, and most of us will never know it. HPV is ubiquitous, and people who have it should not be stigmatized.

For some perspective, remember that most of the countless infectious diseases you are exposed to are not transmitted sexually. If you are not washing your hands when you come in from public places, and using a tissue rather than a finger to clean your eyes and nose, it makes little sense to panic about STIs. In America you have about a 1 in 30 lifetime chance of dying from an infectious disease overall. Compare that to the numbers quoted above. At the same time, of course, death is not the only concern when thinking about STIs: long-term effects such as sterility are also possible. So educate yourself and make the most rational risk assessments you can: but don't live in fear.

QUESTIONS TO ASK YOURSELF

All sex carries risks. There's no way to eliminate those risks entirely, and it's quite difficult for human beings to rationally evaluate risk. The questions below are geared to helping you minimize your risk and determine the level of risk you feel okay with.

- *Do I know my current STI status and that of all my partners? Including HSV (confirmed by testing)?*

- *How do I feel about me or my partner having sex with someone whose STI status is unknown? What do I consider "safer sex" under such circumstances?*

- *How do I feel about me or a partner having sex with someone who has a common STI such as HSV? What do I consider "safer sex" under such circumstances?*

POLY PUZZLES

We can easily be hurt and broken,
and it is good to remember that we can just as easily be the ones
who have done the hurting and the breaking.

DESMOND TUTU

Our experiences with polyamory have taken us nose to nose with some thorny difficulties, some of which we have not yet discovered solutions for. Those puzzles are the topic of this chapter. Some of these problems lack graceful answers. Others seem to lack answers at all. Should you run into one of these, the best advice we can offer is try to keep focused on behaving as ethically as you can, treat those around you with gentleness, and seek to be the best version of yourself. Above all else, use love and compassion as your guiding stars. If you discover a solution to these problems, we'd love to hear from you!

You may see yourself in some of the examples we give. That's okay. We're all still trying to carve trails through this terrain, and some of the dead ends and quagmires along the way look like tempting paths. Our purpose is not to chastise, but rather to alert you to hidden traps that might open unexpectedly beneath your feet.

ENTITLEMENT CREEP

In any relationship, we can become so accustomed to a status quo that it slowly morphs into an entitlement. When this happens in polyamory, the disruption and resource reallocation that a new relationship brings can erupt into anger and conflict if an established partner feels something that is *hers* is being taken away. Entitlement to another's time is the most obvious sort of entitlement creep. Say you have two partners, Linda and Richard. Richard is a busy fellow, so for the past year you've only been able to go on dates with him once a month. This lets you offer more time to Linda, who is used to seeing you three or four times a week. Then Richard's life changes, and he becomes more available to you. So now you see both Linda and Richard twice a week.

Linda might naturally grieve the loss of the more-connected relationship. But she may also have become so accustomed to it that she sees it as a *promise* that you will always spend the same amount of time with her. So when you begin paring back time with Linda, her feelings of sadness or loneliness may be mixed with betrayal or outrage. You've broken a "promise" you never offered. That's entitlement creep.

We've heard this phrased as "He's not respecting my relationship!"— even if the new partner is still receiving less time than the existing ones. Sometimes people do neglect their existing partners in the rush and glow of a new relationship. But "neglect" can be hard to define. New relationships *will* require diversion of resources from somewhere else—if not other relationships, then hobbies, work or even time alone. Not just time but also activities, support and money can be subject to entitlement creep. Communicate explicitly about expectations, rather than assuming that nothing should ever change. As we talk about in "Who owns your time?" on page 285, it's important to recognize the agency of your partners and remember that their time and resources are always their own to give.

This recognition helps clear the way to another part of the solution, which is *gratitude*. If you believe you are getting something by right, it's easy to take it for granted and not recognize its value. Remember that your partner is acting freely, out of love for you and a desire to be with you. Be grateful for what they give, but understand they do not *owe* you the same thing forever.

FATAL CASCADES

When we are afraid of something—losing a partner, say, or being replaced, or not getting a job promotion we feel we deserve—we can act defensively, which can cause exactly the calamity we're trying to prevent. These actions can create cascading feedback loops that are often fatal to a relationship.

Franklin created one of these self-fulfilling prophesies of doom in his relationship with Ruby, described in chapter 8. He felt so threatened when she started dating Newton that he began to act defensively, criticizing her and withdrawing from her, until she broke up with him. He was not originally in danger of being replaced, but his fear of being replaced caused him to destroy the relationship.

When problems arise, look carefully to yourself. Are your actions making the problem worse? Are you blaming a partner for something she hasn't done yet, just because you're afraid she might? Are you actually pushing her toward doing what you don't want? What are the expectations between you? Have you communicated them clearly?

Another version of a destructive feedback loop is what we call the deadly chain. It usually begins simply, perhaps with a compromise that ends up bargaining away something you need to be happy, or with a series of concessions that turn into entitlement creep. Or maybe you've given up some degree of bodily autonomy, like agreeing not to choose a certain type of partner or agreeing not to have certain kinds of sex with new lovers. So now you've agreed to something, and you feel unhappy. Over time your feelings drift from "I'm unhappy that I made that choice," to "I'm unhappy," to "My partner is asking me to be unhappy," to "My partner is making me unhappy," to "I have the right to make my partner unhappy too." Now you're playing the tit-for-tat unhappiness game, where each of you considers your own comfort over the happiness of your partners—descending the deadly chain toward its bitter end.

You can avoid the deadly chain if you are willing to closely examine your priorities, especially as they relate to your happiness. What boundaries can you set to protect your actual needs? How important is your own autonomy? Are you communicating your boundaries and needs? If you have negotiated away something that turns out to be an essential part of your happiness, you always have the right to renegotiate to get it back.

THE CAUCASIAN CHALK CIRCLE

The Caucasian Chalk Circle is a play by Bertolt Brecht, based on the story of the Judgment of Solomon. It involves a young boy whose parentage is disputed: two women claim to be his mother. To decide custody, the judge assigns a test: a circle is drawn on the ground in chalk, and the boy is placed in the middle. The two women stand on either side of the circle, and each take an arm. The judge says that whoever pulls the boy out of the circle gets him. If they pull him apart, they will get part.

You can probably tell how this ends. One of the women refuses to pull hard enough. The judge declares her the true mother, because she is the one who refused to hurt the child. In poly relationships, there are overt cases where two (or more) partners try to pull a pivot person away from the other; the one who cares least about the damage being done to the relationships pulls hardest. And there are plenty of cases where a partner comes right out and says, "You have to choose between him and me." But the tug-of-war is often far subtler than that. Conflicts over scheduling or other commitments, or ongoing struggles with jealousy, or a desire to limit another relationship or to create a relationship structure that makes the other relationships more difficult can create chronic tension, with the pivot feeling pulled in two.

There's no wise judge, of course, to decide who is the more worthy partner. Even following the metaphor of the chalk circle—that the partner who is pulling the least is the more "worthy"—isn't always the best decision. A partner who's demanding that you make a choice might be engaging in valid boundary-setting: "I can no longer remain in a relationship with you if you continue your relationship with Ellen." If you're one of the people "pulling," and you see your partner in pain, it may seem obvious that the thing to do is stop pulling—but that's often harder than it seems. When you see someone else pulling on the other side, it can be terrifying just to let go—because if you do, they'll just go flying out of the circle, into the arms of the other partner. Right?

Of course, in poly relationships, the person in the circle is not a helpless child. She is an adult with agency, capable of making her own choices. To trust enough to stop pulling is to trust your partner to make choices to be with you and nurture your relationship of her own volition. And for the person in the circle, the best survival strategy is firm, clear boundary-setting, such as "I need you to stop pulling on me"—repeated as often as necessary. Make clear and specific commitments about allocating your time, attention and other resources, and then stick to them (see also ping-pong poly on page 280).

One possible coping strategy comes from the original story of the Judgment of Solomon, a solution known as "splitting the baby." In the Judgment of Solomon, the setup is similar: two putative mothers arguing over custody of a child. Solomon commands that the baby be cut in two, with each woman to receive half each. One woman proclaims, "It shall be neither mine nor yours—divide it!" The other woman begs Solomon to spare the child, even if it means giving it to the other woman. Solomon, of course, awards custody to the second woman. In legal parlance, "splitting the baby" has come to refer to splitting the difference in negotiations. In the poly version of this story, "splitting the baby" might be a zero-sum relationship (discussed in chapter 16).

MISMATCHED DESIRE

One of the advantages of polyamory we've talked about is not being dependent on one person to meet your sexual needs. In monogamous relationships, mismatched sexual desire is very common and can become an enormous source of stress; in polyamorous relationships, there's at least the option for a person with the high libido to seek multiple lovers and for the other to have some guilt-free peace.

However, mismatched sexual desire still creates problems in polyamory! Sexual desire is not always general; sometimes a person is drawn to one particular other more than the desire is reciprocated. This can create just as much tension in poly relationships as in monogamous ones. There's no easy solution. All healthy sexual relationships are consensual; we don't believe it's reasonable to expect someone to have sex more often than he wants to. Feelings of guilt or pressure around sex breed resentment, and resentment tends to depress sexual desire even more, creating a self-reinforcing cycle.

Sexual desire isn't necessarily something that can be summoned with the snap of the fingers. If your partner desires you more than you desire him, that doesn't mean there's something wrong with either you or the relationship. It happens. Gentleness with yourself and each other is likely to be much better for your relationship than guilt or blame.

Some positive steps may help rekindle desire. Taking time to be in touch with yourself and your partner without distractions or outside stressors can help set the mood. Spending time touching without an expectation of sex or orgasm at the end can also help. Some couples are happy to grow close by one masturbating while the other cuddles and squeezes. Laurie B. Mintz's book *A Tired Woman's Guide to Passionate Sex* has been found in a peer-reviewed study to help improve the sexual connection in long-term relationships.

But sometimes the only thing that can be done about mismatched desire is to accept that it is what it is, and that a relationship is more than an exchange of sexual gratification.

BAR-RAISERS

Bar-raisers are a specific kind of game changer (see page 248), and they may just be the scariest monster hiding under the poly bed. No one wants to talk about them, yet many—if not all—of the rules and structures imposed on new relationships are designed, at least in part, to protect against them. But they happen, they hurt a lot, and like all game changers, they can't be prevented.

Poly people like to say that one of the advantages of polyamory is we don't have to give up an existing relationship when someone new comes along. That's true, but...sometimes we meet a new person who highlights the flaws in an existing relationship and teaches us that there's truly a better way to live. Or maybe your existing relationship was just fine, but the new partner may show you new things, make you happier, help you realize you can have something you never thought possible, help you see the world in a different light. They may lead you to want more, or they may help you to *be* more. After that you can't quite go home again.

Sometimes a bar-raiser can change what we want from *all* our relationships, or change what we look for in a partner. Sometimes they end up making our other relationships better—though often not until after a fair amount of strife. Sometimes we may decide that other relationships should end. Bar-raisers show us that things we had taken for granted aren't necessarily true. In doing that, they show us paths to happiness we didn't know existed. Suddenly, things we had always accepted don't look so acceptable anymore.

FRANKLIN'S STORY   My relationship with Amber was a bar-raiser. Many of the compromises I had taken for granted as part of polyamory—giving up the freedom to choose my own partners, always having to keep others subordinate to my relationship with Celeste— became too painful to bear with Amber. But more than that, Amber showed me that a different approach was possible: I could have poly relationships without these compromises.

I have also been on the other side of this process. When I started dating my partner Vera, she had three other relationships. Two of those met some, but not all, of her relationship needs. Each offered something she wanted, but with strings and conditions: one was hierarchical, with Vera as a secondary partner, and the other was a good sexual fit but not a good partner fit. Her relationship with me threw the problems into sharp relief, altering those relationships.

The bar-raiser is the worst fear of people in established relationships, because it shows us what's possible. It shows us we don't have to live with compromises we once thought were unavoidable. When your partner lands in a relationship that's at a whole new level of awesome, it can be difficult not to internalize feelings of shame, inadequacy or failure. But doing that can make the problem worse, because when we feel ashamed or inadequate, we're more likely to lash out or be controlling. Feelings of inadequacy create a climate hostile to compassion and understanding.

This is one of those times when compassion begins at home. None of us are perfect. Nobody is so good at relationships that we have nothing new to learn. Good relationships are a journey, not a destination. If someone shows us better ways to do things, *that's okay*. In fact, it's better than okay; it's marvelous! It can truly make our lives better.

Bar-raising relationships aren't exclusive to polyamory. When a person in a monogamous relationship meets someone who raises the bar, the results tend to be catastrophic. People in monogamous relationships are sometimes so fearful of bar-raisers that they don't permit their partners even to have opposite-sex friends. But preventing a poly partner from meeting someone who raises the bar is difficult or impossible. When bar-raisers do happen, they alter the landscape. Scary as it is, we think that's a good thing. Ideally, something great happening to us spurs us to improve all of our existing relationships, revisiting the parts that don't work and building something better in their place.

If you're in a relationship and meet someone who raises the bar for you, be graceful and compassionate. Don't compare your partners to each other. "Why can't you be more like Jordan?" is corrosive to a relationship. Don't rank. Don't blame. Instead, say "We had negotiated this particular arrangement, and it doesn't work for me now. Let's renegotiate. Let's build something stronger. Here are my ideas about how we can do this."

If your partner starts a relationship with someone who raises the bar, you are challenged to rise above your limitations and move with courage toward the best version of yourself. A relationship that raises the bar can, sometimes, be a blessing in disguise: it can show you how to make all your relationships that much better. But not always. Sometimes a new relationship reveals flaws in an existing relationship that can't be fixed. When that happens, there may be no easy way to handle it. The flawed relationship may end.

ABUSE

Some relationships are actively destructive to the people in them, emotionally or physically. Contrary to stereotype, an abusive relationship is often complicated and not always obvious, especially to those inside it. When we think of problematic poly relationships, we tend to focus on the fear that a new partner will be destructive, but often, it's an existing partner that's the problem. After all, longer-lasting relationships have had more time for dysfunctional or toxic patterns to emerge and solidify.

When you're partnered with someone who's in a harmful relationship with someone else, it can be difficult to know what to do. Both of us have found ourselves connected through a partner to an abusive relationship. In

Franklin's case, one of his partners started a new relationship that turned abusive. In Eve's case, she became involved with someone who was already in an abusive relationship. In both cases we felt helpless to protect our partners or intervene in the abusive dynamic.

Abuse often develops slowly, insidiously. It's dangerous to pin your hopes on your partner waking up one day and seeing how bad the situation is. It's more dangerous still to rely on your partner leaving the abusive relationship. Abuse is usually much more obvious to people outside the relationship than those who are in it. And people who do know they are in abusive situations often feel powerless to leave.

If you know or suspect that a partner is in an abusive situation, you may find there is little you can do directly—other than tell him your observations, express your concern, and let him know you're there to support him if and when he decides to try to leave. You cannot rescue your partner, and it can be dangerous to your own mental health to try. In the end, only your partner can rescue himself. Abuse hotlines can offer you more detailed advice—they get many calls from concerned friends and family.

Being in an intimate relationship with someone who is suffering abuse—especially if you fear for their physical safety—can cause you trauma. It's important to set good boundaries for yourself, care for yourself and avoid getting drawn into the abuse dynamic, either as a victim or as a rescuer. Consider talking to a qualified mental health practitioner—not to help you figure out how to save your partner, but for your own sake. In some cases, you may need to protect yourself by limiting your involvement in the relationship or withdrawing from it entirely.

One area where the waters can become very muddy is in hierarchical relationships. We talked more about these relationships in chapter 11. It can be extremely difficult to tease out the warning signs of abuse in hierarchies, because hierarchical relationships can mimic some of the structures of abusive monogamous relationships.

Many primers on abusive relationships list "cuts a person off from other sources of support" as a prime warning sign. Other classic markers include someone making decisions for a partner and expecting her to obey without question, requiring her to check in frequently and report what she is doing, sharing her private information without consent, dismissing or disregarding her feelings, or restricting her access to other people in general. These are ways an abuser creates control, helplessness and isolation.

Each of these red flags sometimes exists in hierarchical poly relationships. In polyamory, limiting a partner's sources of support can play out through restrictions on other relationships, especially rules that prevent a partner from seeing others unless the primary partner is present. Someone who tries to limit a partner's contact with others is not necessarily abusive, but this sure makes abuse easier.

One common element of many hierarchical relationships is that "secondary" partners are not expected—or permitted—to provide certain kinds of support to the "primary" partners. For instance, if a person is sick, there may be a rule that only that person's primary partner is allowed to be a caregiver; secondary partners are not. Other hierarchical relationships may place restrictions on the type of emotional support a secondary partner is permitted to offer, or ask of, a primary partner. Such restrictions too are signs of an unhealthy dynamic.

Many hierarchical structures require that a partner have sex with both members of a couple in order to continue in a relationship with one of them. We believe that requiring that someone have sex with you, and threatening to withhold access to support (such as an intimate relationship with another) if sex is refused, is always coercive and always abusive.

RELATIONSHIP IMPLOSIONS

At some point, you are likely to find yourself involved with someone who has another relationship that's falling apart. This can put you in an extraordinarily difficult position. When your partner's other relationship is disintegrating, you have the difficult balancing act of being supportive without being sucked into the blast radius. It's easy to get emotionally involved when you see your partner hurting. That makes it easy to take sides, seeing the third party only through the lens of your partner's pain. At the same time, you may also become an easy scapegoat for the other relationship's problems.

There's no easy path through this swamp, at least not that we've found. As hard as it is to see someone you love in pain, often you can do little other than be a shoulder to cry on and a place of refuge if needed. This is one of the downsides to polyamory; the odds are good that, sooner or later, someone else will hurt somebody you love, and there's not a lot you can do about it.

One bit of advice we can give is: Do not underestimate how people will hold on to hope for a relationship long after it seems obvious to others that it's over. No matter how much a relationship is hurting your partner, don't assume that eventually he will see this and let go. Don't assume that if your partner is talking about ending it, he actually will. Human hearts have a phenomenal ability to hang on. Sometimes this serves us, but sometimes it doesn't. We often cling to things long after they have stopped bringing us joy.

So for your part, if your partner's harmful or imploding relationship is hurting *you*, don't hang on yourself in the hope that your partner will end it. Until it's over—and sometimes until long after—you're better off assuming that it will continue. *Even if your partner says it won't.* We've seen people go back to unhealthy relationships far too many times, even after leaving or promising to leave. If you know you cannot be in a relationship with your partner if he stays in his damaging relationship, then the best decision might be to leave *now*—before you, too, become too invested in (or damaged by) the situation to be able to leave.

Often you find that in your partner's story, and the story they spread to their social circle, *you* are cast as the villain—particularly if you are relatively new. When a relationship is in crisis, it's easy to blame an "outsider." Again, there's no easy way through this, but we can give you this important truth to help you get through it: It's not you. Even if you're advocating for your needs and that's upsetting your metamour, even if part of the strife in the other relationship is jealousy or fear related to you—it's not you. As long as you act with integrity and recognize your partner's right to make choices, without controlling or manipulating him, you are not responsible for your partner's relationship with his other partners. You are not to blame simply because you have added value to another person's life.

MENTAL HEALTH ISSUES AND POLYAMORY

Mental health issues complicate all relationships. When you add things like anxiety disorders, depression or bipolar disorder to the mix, poly relationship challenges become a lot harder—and in some cases, intractable. A person with a serious psychiatric disorder may also lack the emotional, and in some cases the financial, means to support himself, which can cause him or his partner to feel trapped.

Fully disclosing your known mental health issues is an important part of ethical relationships, because withholding information from anyone about things that affect them erodes informed consent. If you have a mental health issue that is likely to affect those close to you, or if you are partnered with someone whose mental health issues affect your ability to interact with others (for example, if you are a caretaker for someone, or if a partner has a history of violence against herself or others), you are ethically obligated to disclose this information. Unfortunately, the stigma attached to mental health problems can discourage full disclosure. It's our responsibility to treat these disclosures with understanding and compassion, and to make it safe for our partners or potential partners to talk to us.

If you're partnered with someone who has a mental health issue, it can become difficult to treat new people ethically and responsibly. New relationships can be especially triggering to people with some kinds of psychiatric disorders. For example, bipolar disorder is associated with higher rates of divorce and increased substance abuse, and high rates of anxiety can make coping with jealousy or a partner's absences much more challenging. People who have suffered abuse or abandonment may experience uncontrolled anxiety or fear of loss when their partners become involved with other people. This is particularly true if the mental health issues are untreated.

If you're involved with someone who has a partner with mental health issues, and a dysfunctional dynamic exists between your partner and her partner, it can sometimes be difficult to keep yourself from being drawn into that dynamic. It's important to keep a clear distinction between being a partner and being a therapist. Few people are qualified to act as therapists. Even if we are trained for it, therapy usually requires emotional distance—the exact opposite of what we need to nurture romantic relationships.

If you have a mental health issue that affects your ability to engage in ethical relationships, it's also important to take whatever steps you can to mitigate these effects. This might mean therapy, treatment, and making sure you get enough exercise and sleep.

One problem that can arise with some mental health issues is unwillingness to seek treatment, because the issue has become a way to avoid dealing with other problems in a relationship. For example, if you're afraid of your partner spending time with another partner, and you know you can use your mental health issue to require your partner's attention, it can be easy to fall into a pattern where you find you need your partner's support whenever she is about to go on a date.

Similarly, the standard poly advice to "Only add new partners that enhance existing relationships" can, in practice, end up being used to tiptoe around mental health issues. If this policy results in only adding new partners who are okay with a dysfunctional relationship dynamic, or who help enable a person with mental health issues to avoid treatment, we would argue that the policy is not helping anyone.

There are no hard and fast guidelines for relationships involving mental health problems, though setting and communicating clear boundaries is a vital tool. The best advice we can offer is to make choices about what level of involvement is or isn't appropriate for you, and to set your boundaries accordingly.

QUESTIONS TO ASK YOURSELF

Not all problems have solutions. When troubles come up that defy answers, you may find no path out that doesn't involve pain. When that happens, the best you can do is try to reach for the best, kindest, most courageous version of yourself. These questions may help when you're faced with the inevitable poly puzzles:

- *Do the choices I make take me closer to, or further from, the best version of me?*

- *When I am faced with conflict, how do I seek to act with courage?*

- *Are there things I absolutely require in a relationship, and do I communicate those things?*

- *In what ways do I care for myself? How do I care for the people around me?*

- *Can I respond to changes in my relationship with grace?*

- *Do I have problems that make it difficult for my partners to be with me? How do I seek to mitigate those?*

- *Do I let problems in the relationships around me affect me? How do I assert boundaries around problems that aren't mine?*

# RELATIONSHIP
TRANSITIONS

Have enough courage to trust love one more time
and always one more time.

MAYA ANGELOU

People are living, dynamic organisms; you grow or you die. (Actually you die, period; growth is optional.) You will change. Your partner will change. Your relationship will change. This is a fact, something we must accept gracefully. If you fear change, if you cling too tightly to what your relationship is now and insist that this is the way it must always be, you risk breaking it. Yes, sometimes relationships change in ways we do not want, and people grow in ways that take them apart rather than bring them together. That's the risk you accept when you get involved in this messy, complicated business of romantic relationships.

The things you value in your relationship now may not exist in the future. The things you want now, you may not want in the future. The things you see in your partner now may not be there in the future. And that's okay. Adopt a fluid idea about the way your life will look, keep in touch with your changing needs and those of your partners, talk to your partners about these things openly and without fear, and you can build relationships that grow as you grow. If you do not, your relationships can become brittle and shatter.

For example, when your partner starts a new relationship, you will probably have less of her time and attention. Even in the most inclusive group relationships, this can happen. Any relationship is likely to need alone time; no matter how much overlap there is, you're still likely to lose some time and attention. Is that something you can accept? Is your relationship resilient enough? Do you have things in your life other than your partners that enrich it and bring you joy, or is all of your joy dependent on your partners' attention?

Allowing change with grace, without expecting to control how the change happens, is a key skill we have seen in people who create strong, resilient poly relationships. Be clear on what your relationship needs are, be willing to advocate for them, and accept that things are going to change. That way you'll be ready.

RE-EVALUATING RELATIONSHIPS

In long-term relationships, usually a time arrives when the two new people you've become over the years stand there looking at each other and ask, "Whatever we believed or wanted a few years ago, do the people we are now belong in a relationship?" Sometimes the answer is yes: these two new people still want to be together. And then you move forward, perhaps stronger than before.

But sometimes the answer is no, it doesn't make sense anymore. This is normal and okay, and yet somehow we always seem blindsided by this realization. We become angry, and we treat a breakup almost universally in our society as though it shouldn't happen. In fact, people see this realization as a betrayal. Think of the accusation "I don't even know you anymore!" We act as though the ones we love should not be allowed to grow and change or, if they do, it means they love us less.

Since people change all the time, we can debate whether it even makes sense to make lifelong commitments, at least in the way society encourages us to. We're taught that marriage should mean our relationship never changes, rather than meaning we can be family for life but the shape the family takes can change. Instead of the idea of "breaking up," where the presumption is that you'll stay in a relationship until something makes you leave it, perhaps we should sit down every year or few and say, "Okay, who are we now? How is this relationship working? Do we like the way it's going? Should we change something? Do we even still like each other that much? Does it make sense to continue?" If we think of this as renewing the relationship every now and again, then even if the answer to the last question is no, the result does not necessarily have to be a "breaking." To use the widespread poly term, it's a "transition."

Expectations are brittle things. Not only do people change, but every relationship has a natural ebb and flow. Relationships can come and go and come again with the same person. When we acknowledge that, and allow space for changes to happen, we create relationships that can weather almost any storm.

The best way to evaluate whether a relationship is a good one, regardless of what form it takes, is to think about the things you need and want in the relationship, and evaluate whether it gives you those things. It's not the shape of the relationship that's important; it's whether it meets your needs. Another good technique is to interrogate your feelings. When you think about the relationship ending, what is your first response? If it's a sense of relief, maybe it's time for the relationship to end.

Of course, part of the fairy tale that's deeply ingrained in most of us is the idea that relationships only succeed if they last until someone dies. This is, if you think about it, a strange metric for success. If we manage to find one another's company pleasant enough for long enough, someone dies, and then we can claim success. Relationships are often measured in terms of longevity; if they end prior to the death of one of the people, we call them "failures."

In his book *The Commitment: Love, Sex, Marriage and My Family*, columnist Dan Savage described his grandmother's unhappy marriage, which ended in her suicide. He commented:

The instant my grandmother died, her marriage became a success.

Death parted my grandparents, not divorce, and death is the sole measure of a successful marriage. When a marriage ends in divorce, we say that it's failed. The marriage was a failure. Why? Because both parties got out alive. It doesn't matter if the parting is amicable, it doesn't matter if the exes are happier apart, it doesn't matter if two happy marriages take the place of one unhappy marriage. A marriage that ends in divorce failed. *Only a marriage that ends with someone in the cooler down at Maloney's is a success.*

Longevity is a seductive idea, because it can feel like even a joyless, love-less partnership is preferable to being alone. The two of us do not believe that just any relationship, no matter how unhappy, is preferable to no relation-ship. Rather, one of the core beliefs that underlies this book is the idea that only relationships that enrich our lives are worth striving for.

Think about all the measures we use to tell whether or not a relation-ship is successful. How long it lasts? How often they have sex? How many children and grandchildren they have? Perhaps how much money they make? It seems like whenever we try to figure out whether someone else's relationship is successful or not, it rarely occurs to us to ask the people in-volved if *they* believe it's successful.

We have both had relationships end. Almost everyone does. Neither of us would call these relationships "failures," because they contributed to mak-ing us who we are today. We have taken things from those relationships—joy, personal growth, learning, love, laughter—that have enriched our lives. We are better for having had them.

We propose a different metric for the success of a relationship. Relation-ships that make us the best versions of ourselves are successes. Those that don't are not, regardless of how long they last. A ten-year happy relation-ship that ends in friendship is more successful than a lifetime relationship of misery. That doesn't mean we think good relationships are always happy, 100 percent of the time, or that we should bail at the first conflict or trouble. All relationships have their ups and downs; it is not reasonable to expect oth-erwise. On the whole, good relationships promote the long-term happiness and well-being of the people involved; when that no longer becomes possible, and there's no clear path to making it possible, then it might be time for the relationship to end.

RELATIONSHIPS END

A fundamental premise of ethical relationships is that all relationships are con-sensual. That means people are free to enter relationships without coercion, and free to end relationships that are not meeting their needs. An ethical rela-tionship is one where nobody feels compelled to stay against their will.

Coercion can be subtle. Most of us would say, "I would never coerce someone to stay with me against their will," but not all forms of coercion in-volve fists. Coercion takes a thousand forms. One particularly insidious form is the idea that everyone in a poly relationship should be on great terms with, or even be romantic or sexual partners with, everyone else in the relationship. This is an idea that's often given wonderful-sounding names (like "family" or "inclusion"), but there's an ethical trap built into the foundation. Say, for example, that you have a full triad—a relationship with three people who are all sexually and romantically involved with one another. What happens if one of those relationships starts to crumble, or if one of the people no longer wishes to be involved with one of the others? Often an implicit, or even explicit, understanding exists that if that happens, the other relationship will end too.

CHERISE'S STORY Cherise started her exploration of polyamory when she was invited to join a relationship with a married couple, Pam and David. They were new to polyamory themselves, and after many discussions had decided they wanted to find a single bisexual woman who would agree to be with both of them in an exclusive relationship. This, they reasoned, would be a good way to avoid problems with jealousy, and to explore the world of polyamory without going too far outside their comfort zone.

The relationship went well for about six months. After that, things between Cherise and Pam continued to grow, but the relationship between Cherise and David became strained. Eventually, Cherise decided she no longer wanted to be sexually intimate with David.

When that happened, Pam and David became very upset. This wasn't the way they had envisioned things. The idea that one of them might date someone the other was not involved with seemed very threatening. So Pam gave Cherise an ultimatum: "If you end your relationship with David, I will break up with you." Since Cherise was exclusive to them, this meant losing not one but both of her relationships, with all the heartbreak that went along with it.

She reluctantly remained sexually involved with both of them for another few months. Even though she really didn't want to be intimate with David, the discomfort of his unwanted sexual attention seemed smaller than the pain of being dumped by Pam. Eventually the relationship deteriorated to the point where she could no longer stay. Things ended as badly as you might expect. When they did, David and Pam blamed Cherise for the failure; after all, if she had only stuck to the original agreement, nothing bad would have happened!

Attempts to engineer an outcome are almost always thickly sown with the seeds of coercion. If there is only one form a relationship can take, the foundation is laid: play your assigned role or lose my affection. Any situation which dictates in advance how the relationship will develop disempowers the people in it, and disempowerment tends to turn coercive.

Expectations of sexual or emotional intimacy with one person as a price for intimacy with another are an example of this kind of coercion, but it can take other forms. If there is an expectation, for example, that metamours must get along, that implies that if they can't, one or more relationships will end.

And there doesn't even need to be any sort of threat for a relationship to be coercive. Sometimes internal feelings of guilt are sufficient. If you go into a relationship knowing the terms of engagement, and then those terms become hard for you to accept, it's easy to blame yourself: *I knew what I was getting into! I agreed to this! I have nobody to blame but myself! Am I being a home-wrecker by not being able to make this work? Maybe I just need to force myself to be okay with how things are. I went into this with my eyes open, right?*

It has to be okay to end relationships. It has to be okay to end relationships without feeling that our support will be kicked out from under us, or that our other lovers will withdraw their love from us. When it's not okay to end a relationship, consent has left the building.

POLY BREAKUPS

There's a saying among many poly people: "Relationships don't end, they just change." It's a noble idea, and one that society in general could probably benefit from. In monogamous relationships, it's quite common to see ex-partners as potential threats, and many people don't want to maintain friendships with exes (or, more to the point, don't want their partners to maintain friendships with exes). In the poly community, where it's harder to avoid socializing with former partners, there's a greater emphasis on amicable breakups that preserve friendly, or at least civil, interactions.

But relationships do end. Even when friendship continues, the end of a romantic relationship is hard. It's normal to feel hurt. It's also normal to mourn the loss of a partner, and the loss of the shared goals and dreams.

Psychologists say the five stages of grief (denial, anger, bargaining, depression and acceptance) apply to grief over a lost relationship as much as they apply to terminal illness. It takes time to grieve the loss, even when we want to preserve a friendship on the other side. Ending relationships with dignity and grace means knowing the emotional storm is coming and being prepared to weather it.

There's no easy way to deal with the pain experienced when relationships end, at least not that we've discovered. The good news is that the pain eventually ends. It's natural to project our current emotional state into the future, and when pain is our current emotional state, it can be hard to remember that we've ever felt anything else...but pain ends. One thing that can help, at least a little, is to think of it as something to get through, like a bad movie you wish were over already, rather than a part of your identity. "I sometimes feel pain" is very different from "I am a person who has been hurt." When you make pain part of your identity, it's harder to move on from it without suspicion and bitterness. But good relationships require loving as though you had never been hurt before. A guarded heart is a closed heart.

EVE'S STORY   When Peter told me he felt that a breakup with

Clio was coming, I didn't respond the way I expected to. I had seen for a

long time that they had been slipping away from each other, but even so,

I found myself crying. What had once felt like a little family was splitting up, and the situation was entirely outside my control.

It took a few months for their relationship to complete, and I struggled during that time with the lack of clarity. Clio and I had forged a friendship independent of her relationship with Peter; nevertheless, I knew that our relationship would change once she was no longer my metamour—I just wasn't sure how. I felt it wasn't fair to try to hasten a decision just to make the situation easier for me: it wasn't my relationship, after all.

Their relationship officially ended close to what would have been their fourth anniversary. I was traveling when they finally had the conversation; Peter sent me a message when it was over. Again surprising myself, I cried most of the night, looking at old Facebook photos of the two of them—and the three of us—together. I laughed at myself: I was acting like I was the one who had just lost a relationship. In a sense, I had: even though it wasn't mine, Peter and Clio's relationship was an important part of my life. He had grown and changed from it, and so had I.

Poly breakups are both easier and harder than monogamous breakups. They're easier in the sense that when you have more than one partner, you may have more support to help through the loss. It's nice to have people who can understand and empathize with your pain. However, this doesn't actually make the pain go away (though believe it or not, we've both been asked, "If you have two girlfriends and you lose one, it's still okay because you still have a girlfriend, right?" Which is a bit like saying, "If you have two children and one dies, it's still okay because you still have a child, right?") No matter how many relationships you may have, breakups still cause pain.

Poly breakups pose special challenges because the breakups can involve more people, and can create ripples of ambiguity and uncertainty throughout all your relationships. Your partner's breakup may also affect you very seriously, even if you're not dating the same person your partner is. When two people share a partner in common and one of those relationships ends, the pain is greatly magnified.

There can be a lot of strange carryover effects when a poly relationship ends. One common situation arises when a close, nesting partner or primary-style relationship ends—say, for example, a married couple divorces, or a live-in relationship breaks up. People who are less entwined can feel a pull to fill the void, even if they don't want to, and even if the pull is not intentional on the part of the person who broke up. This happened to Franklin when his marriage with Celeste ended. His partner Maryann, who had always been less inclined toward entwined domestic relationships, also backed away; she seemed to feel that his loss created a hole that he might try to fill by scaling up his relationship with her.

Conversely, there can also be an expectation that if a close, domestic relationship ends, the existing relationships are now eligible for "promotion" to a closer, more entwined status, even if that isn't the most natural form for them to take, or if the person experiencing the breakup doesn't want that.

When a relationship ends, it can help to sit down with the remaining partners and talk about what, if anything, that means for those relationships. In a hierarchical relationship that recognizes only one primary, the end of the primary relationship might create an assumption that one of the secondary partners will be promoted to primary, regardless of whether or not that's true (never mind whether the new relationship configuration will still be hierarchical!). When a relationship that formerly occupied a great deal of time and attention ends, there might be an assumption that this time is now available to the remaining partners. Explicitly talking about these expectations is essential.

It's common to see what we call Schrödinger relationships:* relationships that are near-over in practice, but have fallen into a pattern of comfortable non-contact or non-intimacy. It's easy for poly people to let such non-relationships linger a long time, because when you have multiple partners, there's often no incentive to formally end a relationship in order to "move on"—and it can feel easier to drift apart than to have a tough conversation. This can be quite painful, though, if both partners are not aware of what's happening, or are not fully aware of what is happening, and one partner thinks of the relationship as "on" and the other thinks of it as "off."

Other members of the network can suffer too when the two partners involved in the breakup are not clear with each other, or with their other partners, about what is happening. At the very least, metamour relationships can become awkward if you don't know whether you're really relating to a metamour. And as counterintuitive as it may seem, many people need to grieve their partners' lost relationships too. Letting a relationship drift off into the ether without closure can make this process much harder. Clear conversations about relationship transitions can be important for *everyone* affected.

That said, many solo poly people and relationship anarchists do prefer to have much more fluid, undefined relationships that slip between friendship and romance. If this is the case for you, then clarity and "define that relationship" conversations may be much less important for you and your partners. Hopefully, however, you will have had early conversations with them about how the sort of fluidity you prefer in your relationships works for you—and can work for them.

As elsewhere in poly relationships, taking sides is tempting but dangerous during a breakup. It's natural to feel anger toward someone you perceive as causing your partner pain. It also tends to do more harm than good. The poly community is small enough that at some point you're likely to be friends with, or even in a relationship with, someone who is in a relationship with the ex, or knows someone who is. Few breakups involve obvious wrongdoing on one person's side while the other is entirely virtuous in thought and deed. Recognize that relationships end, the reasons for breakups are usually very complicated, and there's not necessarily a villain.

This does not apply, of course, to cases of actual abuse, violence, coercion or assault. Some relationships are genuinely unhealthy by the criteria we set out on pages 91–92, and we believe it's a good idea to end them entirely.

---

* *After the "Schrödinger's cat" thought experiment in which we are asked to imagine a cat that is simultaneously alive and dead.*

In the era of social media, it's incredibly tempting to seek validation on-line. We recommend keeping breakups off social media—even if your former partner doesn't follow this advice. Taking a breakup onto the world stage, especially when you're dealing with the anger part of grief, has a way of backfiring. Remember, the poly community is small, and the people who you make witness to your breakups will probably be your pool of potential partners later.

Children are another special group often affected in poly breakups, since many people find themselves forming close relationships with the children of their partners. As mentioned in chapter 15, it's even common to have mutli-parent live-in households. When a breakup occurs between a child's parent and an adult who's not biologically related to the child, always consider the implications for any children affected. These implications are similar, of course, to those that arise when blended families split up. Even if the adults do not want to continue a friendship with each other, if a child is bonded to nonparental adults, it can be important to find ways to permit an ongoing relationship. This, in turn, makes it all the more vital to strive for amicable breakups. If the two adults find it to painful—at least for a time, as is common—to stay in close contact, metamours who are still connected to the child can often help facilitate a relationship with the former partner.

If there's a happy note on which to end this chapter, maybe it's this. The poly talk of "transitioning" a relationship rather than just "breaking up" is often a correct description, not a euphemism. In monogamous culture, the idea of ending a romance and becoming "just friends" is often treated as a joke. In the poly world, it's often entirely real. It's common for poly folks to be friends with their exes pretty much for life. But resuming contact may take a while; breakups are painful and raw, and a cooling-off period of no contact is often advisable, possibly for months or years. But time mellows all things, and poly exes often eventually find that they can build a lasting friendship.

QUESTIONS TO ASK YOURSELF

The monogamous world offers us few models for relationships that transition into friendships. In the poly community, which can be quite small, staying on friendly terms with exes is a good objective to strive for. Here are some questions that can help in that quest:

- *How do I approach the end of my relationships? What do I want from my former partners?*

- *If a relationship ends, what does that mean for my other partners? Will I try to promote one of them to primary?*

- *When a partner's relationship ends, what can I do to prevent myself from taking sides or being drawn into conflict?*

- *What boundaries do I set around problems within my partners' other relationships?*

- *Have I ever spread bitterness in the community or set people against each other by taking sides or by not keeping confidences?*

PART 5

The Poly Ecosystem

YOUR PARTNERS'
OTHER PARTNERS

No one's family is normal.
Normalcy is a lie invented by advertising agencies
to make the rest of us feel inferior.

CLAIRE LAZEBNIK

Up to now, we've focused on the internal realm—yourself and your feelings—and on your own intimate relationships. In Part 5 we look outward, to your interactions with those around you. Your "poly ecosystem" includes your partners' other partners; your pool of potential new partners; your family, friends and broader social network; and the rest of the world.

Multiple romantic relationships are as old as the human race, but modern polyamory is new in a lot of ways. It's rooted in the modern values of gender equality and self-determination. It places high value on introspection, transparent communication and compassionate treatment of others. But perhaps what sets it apart the most is the opportunity it affords you for connection with your lovers' other lovers. Poly people have invented several terms for them. The most common is *metamours* (from the Greek *meta*, meaning "above" or "beyond," and the French *amour*, "lover"). Some people call them POPs, "partner's other partners," or SOSOs, "significant others' significant others." You might call your metamour your co-lover or even, if you're all a family, your co-husband or co-wife.

How close or distant your relationship is to a metamour can vary enormously. He might be your deeply bonded co-intimate in a group that sleeps together in one big bed, or a guy you've never met. Whatever the case, though, the word *polyamory* carries an implication of goodwill and well-wishing among the people involved—an understanding that "we're all in this together" to some degree or another. Often your metamours become one of the biggest benefits of polyamory.

At least that's the ideal. Good relationships with metamours certainly make polyamory richer, or at least easier. These people can be important sources of insight, aid and support. And yet things get fraught when we try to script in advance what metamour relationships should look like.

BENEFITS OF METAMOURS

The summer before we wrote this book, Eve was in a serious bicycle accident that left her hospitalized for several days and disabled for weeks. At the time Peter was living out of town, getting job experience in a new field while caring for his disabled mother. He happened to be in town when the accident happened, and he spent the weekend in the hospital with Eve, periodically stepping outside to call her other partners with updates. Two days after the accident, he had to head back to the town he was working in. Eve's girlfriend, Paloma, came to the hospital that evening and wheeled her in her wheelchair down the street for a sushi dinner, then brought her back to the hospital room and stayed to cuddle. Later that night, Franklin arrived from Portland. He brought Eve home the next day and provided her with round-the-clock care for another week. In a crisis, everyone pitched in where they were needed and as they were able.

This kind of teamwork—or at least the possibility of it—is one of the things that makes polyamory stand out from other forms of non-monogamy. When they are going well, metamour relationships enrich the lives of everyone in a romantic network. Many people, in fact, see metamour connections as a prime benefit of polyamory. Metamours bring our partners joy, helping them learn and grow in ways they might otherwise not. They provide an extra source of support and strength for our partners, and sometimes for us. They can help negotiate solutions to problems we may not have found an answer for on our own.

Another of polyamory's invented words is *compersion*. This refers to the happy feeling many people experience in seeing their partners take joy from another relationship. Some people use the word *frubbly* to describe this feeling (as a noun: *frubble*). Different people experience it differently: for some it's just a warm glow, while for others, it can be almost as euphoric as being in love. And some people don't experience it at all. It's normal to experience compersion, and it's awesome if you do, but it's also normal never to experience it. Not experiencing it doesn't mean you're broken, or that you can't still benefit from having metamours in your life.

EVE'S STORY   I travel—a lot—and sometimes my travel schedule conflicts with important dates for Peter. A couple of years ago, there was a week when he needed support and I was not able to be there. As we were negotiating our calendars, that weekend was a sticking point. The solution we arrived at, in conjunction with Clio, was for Clio to plan a longer visit for that week. Another time, a few years ago, Peter was in crisis and I was out of town visiting my mother. I called Gwen and offered to pay her costs to take Peter on a nice date, to help him have some downtime.

The ability to make these sorts of arrangements is among the many reasons I love having metamours. (I've jokingly said that it's like having someone you can always rely on to feed the cat.)

I remember the first time I felt compersion. Peter had just been to visit Clio, about three months into their relationship, and she posted a picture on her blog of the two of them. He had an incredibly serene, blissful smile on his face. It was the first time in years I could remember seeing him so happy. I felt a rush that was nearly euphoric—it took me quite by surprise. I'd imagined compersion as a warm, happy feeling but one that was more cerebral—not a visceral, physical emotion like lust or love or rage, which this was for me.

For nearly four years Peter had two other partners, Clio and Gwen. The three of us called ourselves "Team Peter." I loved the idea that we were all on the same team to support (and enjoy) this amazing person we all loved.

The two of us love that we're not the only people who love and support our partners. We love that they have other people to bring joy into their life, and we're immensely grateful for the opportunities our metamours have provided the people we love to grow and change. We adore watching their relationships unfold.

When metamours like or even love each other, it's a wonderful thing for everyone. We've both experienced that blissful place of spending time with two or more of our lovers—or one of them and another of theirs—all of us just enjoying each other's company. That's a good ideal to hope for and even work for, but there can be a trap: We've also seen a craving for that ideal badly fuck up what could have otherwise been some pretty decent situations. If you begin to prize that ideal over the actual needs and personalities of the people involved, you are violating our ethical axiom 1: the people in the relationship are more important than the relationship.

APPROACHES TO METAMOUR RELATIONSHIPS

As you might expect, relationships between metamours are diverse, but they tend to fall into a few broad categories: compartmentalized, networked and polyfamily.

Compartmentalized relationships are treated as very separate. Metamours know of each other, at least in general terms, but don't have any particular relationship with each other beyond dating the same person. Many free-agent and solo poly people have relationships that are largely compartmentalized.

This does not mean that the metamours are *required* to be distant. One nice thing about poly is it allows you to meet other cool people, so even in fairly compartmentalized relationship styles, close cross-friendships sometimes form. There's just no requirement for this to happen. Of course, even in compartmentalized relationships, it's very helpful for everyone to be *friendly* toward one another, even when they are not friends.

Networked relationships are those where metamours enjoy meeting one another and generally get along. Members of the network may plan group outings or events, or a person might invite some or all of her partners to social functions. The people who share a partner set out to build friendships with one another. As you might expect, this doesn't always work out as hoped. Sometimes, despite the best intentions, two people don't get along. People in networked relationships, though, tend to *make an effort* to share friendship. Interconnected networks of friends and lovers who enjoy spending time together are sometimes called "polycules," a play on the poly use of the word *molecule.*

Polyfamily is the word some people use for a network in which the people regard each other, or are expected to regard each other, as "family." A polyfamily is a bit like the Hollywood stereotype of an Italian family: If you marry one person, you're marrying into the whole crowd. All the people who share a common partner are expected to have close ties with one another.

Polyfamilies can happen organically, when the people a person dates happen to quite like one another. Or they can be prescriptive, where there's a stated expectation that dating one person means being part of the family—or in extreme cases, even dating and having sex with that person's other partners. In the prescriptive sense, the polyfamily ideal can seem like a way to short-circuit problems with jealousy, time division or fear of abandonment. Unfortunately, it's hard to mandate that two people must be close to one another just because they fancy the same person. Prescriptive polyfamilies tend to have coercion hiding in their closets, either because they make access to a critical intimate relationship reliant on having a specified relationship with others, or because they make access to the "family" support network contingent on continuing a romantic relationship. In extreme cases, they can dictate "You must be intimate with this person or you will be kicked out of the family completely."

In one way, metamours *are* like the family you grew up in: They are people in your life whom you did not choose. And in that sense, it often *is* useful to think of polycules as being like real families. Not everyone may like each other, but even at worst, you need to be able to sit down to dinner together, smile and make polite conversation at least a couple of times a year.

MEETING METAMOURS

As we discussed in chapter 16, there's no single optimal strategy for when or how (or even if you should) meet your partners' other partners. Ask a dozen poly folks their approach to meeting metamours, and you'll likely get two dozen answers. Some people compartmentalize, not requiring (or necessarily even asking) that their partners meet. Other people have policies that they won't date anyone who hasn't already met all their existing partners. Some polyfamilies require that the "family" vet a potential partner before a relationship begins.

We've seen no policy that clearly gives better results than any other; people's needs and situations are too varied. (For example, Franklin has partners in three countries on two continents. If he were to try to introduce a prospective partner to all his existing partners, the airfare alone would be eye-watering.) That said, some approaches can create problems. When a person *refuses* to meet any of her partner's other partners, for instance, this can point to trouble. Often such a refusal is rooted in insecurity or a desire to pretend the other people don't exist. And it's difficult to build strong relationships when the people involved are in denial about their structure.

When someone has multiple partners who aren't also partnered with each other, she has a certain responsibility to help introduce them—though it is by no means her responsibility alone. We talked about this responsibility quite a bit in chapter 16 (see "Introducing your partners," page 290).

Unless two new metamours already know each other, say because they're part of the same social set (as is common in small poly communities), it's preferable for the pivot to take the initiative in introducing her partners to each other. This is good etiquette to avoid potentially awkward situations, as we've discussed. However, it's certainly acceptable for someone to reach out himself to a new metamour (ideally with the knowledge of the pivot). Either partner is free to do this, of course, but it is especially nice when the established partner reaches out to the newer partner. The established partner is in a more powerful position, and a gesture of welcome to a new metamour—who may be feeling some trepidation about being accepted—can really contribute to putting the newcomer at ease.

Expectation management is key to helping a relationship with a metamour get off to a strong start. Don't expect that because you're both into the same person, the two of you will feel some kind of instant bond. Don't expect immediate intimacy, don't expect to just "get" each other right away, and don't expect instant "family." Your shared partner likes you both because you're *different*, after all, and those differences might make you click, or they may make you feel alien to each other. Accept whatever happens. When meeting any new person, you're best to meet without agenda or expectation.

METAMOURS AND CONSENT

As we hope you have internalized by now, good relationships are always consensual. Part of consent means that people have a fundamental right to choose the level of involvement and intimacy they want with *anyone*, and to revoke consent to intimacy at any time, in any moment.

Many people in poly relationships attempt to solve problems or minimize potential conflict by specifying in advance what role a partner's new partner will play with respect to existing relationships. Sometimes this means requiring that any new partners "add to" or "complement" existing relationships (though what it means to "add to" the relationship is often left nebulous). Other people require that their metamours have certain relationships with them, sometimes up to and including sex.

We are skeptical of such requirements. At best, they treat people as need-fulfillment machines; at worst, they prescribe coercive relationships that make unreasonable demands of intimacy. Some people say, "She can always turn us down, so our requirements are not coercive," but we don't consider this a valid defense. When someone requires you to have an intimate relationship with both of them as the cost of allowing a relationship with one, they've set the stage for coercion. Even if you *want* both relationships at first, what if you change your mind? Requiring both to *continue* as a price for you keeping the one you want, as it grows deeper and more important, builds in a punishment for revoking consent. That's coercion, with creepy overtones of a cult in the making.

When we try to use a relationship with a new partner as a balm to soothe our own fear or jealousy, we are, in effect, using *them*. Treating a relationship as a tool for dealing with our own fears is a covert way of treating people as things. Expecting metamours always to enjoy each other's company—or to screen potential partners based on how well they fit into an existing network—can also create a pocket veto, discussed in chapter 12. We've seen situations where someone who felt threatened by the idea of her partner having other lovers simply found fault with anyone her partner was considering. "I'm just protecting you. You haven't met anyone who meets my standards!" are words we've actually heard. More than once.

Because people tend to assume good intent on the part of their existing partners, while treating new people as possible threats, it can be easy to overlook the pattern and accept that it's the new prospects who are doing something wrong. This can become justification for a screening veto (page 205): "My partner has poor judgment! I have to keep screening out those choices of hers!"

Finally, if dysfunctional patterns such as abuse or codependency exist, a new partner who disrupts those patterns may be a very good thing indeed—but the benefits may not be recognized until much later.

A basic expectation of civility, if not friendliness, is reasonable toward metamours. In any extended family, we all realize that not everyone will get along with everyone else. Being able to get along with people we wouldn't necessarily choose for ourselves is an important life skill, and that goes doubly for polyamory. It is not always possible to see what your partner sees in someone else. Sometimes you have to take it on faith when a partner sees value in another person. Respect for a partner means respect for her choices.

DON'T BE CREEPY

Approaching a partner's other partner can seem like an emotional minefield, where one misstep will lead to explosively unfortunate consequences. And metamour relationships can make or break a relationship, so it's natural that a lot of folks approach them with trepidation.

Remember that if you're in a relationship with someone who starts seeing someone new, you hold a lot of power. You're likely to be more intimidating to that new partner than he is to you. While you see new relationship energy and the excitement of a budding romance, he sees a shared history that is not accessible to him. A new relationship is a time of intense vulnerability for you *and* the new metamour. Treat that vulnerability with kindness and compassion. Forced interaction of any sort, whether it's forced family or forced distance, is still forced.

Part of treating a partner's other partner as a person rather than as a blank slate for your own fears means not being creepy. "Creepy" is a loaded term, but romantic relationships provide ample opportunity for you to be invasive and intrusive. We encourage you not to take advantage of these opportunities. Here is a partial list of things that will likely be seen as creepy or intrusive (all of which we've seen or experienced):

- Spying on your partner or her interactions with your metamours, such as reading her email, monitoring her social media, reading her text messages or listening to her phone calls.
- Eavesdropping on other aspects of your partner's other relationships, for example by checking up on his whereabouts or monitoring his activities.
- Calling, texting or otherwise being needy whenever your partner is on a date. Emergencies happen, and many people like to prearrange check-ins so they know their partners are safe. But beyond that, a habit of constant contact with a partner who's with someone else can quickly become intrusive.
- Oversharing or asking inappropriately intimate questions of a metamour. "Appropriate" is a relative term, and different people have different boundaries around their personal lives. Still, it's good form to pay attention and back off if you're starting to make your metamour uncomfortable.
- Copying a metamour in any way that's not invited or consensual, such as adopting their style of dress, makeup or fragrances, or giving similar gifts, or doing similar activities with a partner (if you're doing it *because* that's what your metamour did, not because that's something you too enjoy).
- Turning up uninvited to places you know your partner will be with your metamour.

- Expecting to be included in all their activities, especially intimate ones.
- Disclosing intimate details of your relationship with your shared partner without establishing whether that's welcome. As we discussed at length previously, everyone has a right to set boundaries around privacy.

As with just about every other part of polyamorous relating, the impulse to deal with the unknown by trying to control the outcome is less likely to succeed than allowing relationships between you and your partners' other partners to take their own course. People, like animals, react poorly to being cornered. Attempting to script how the relationship with a partner's new partner must go is one way to make someone feel cornered. Flexibility in metamour relationships, as in all things poly, is your best approach.

In practical terms, this means seeing your partner's other partner as a person, not a projection of your own fears and hopes. The best approach is the same you might take with a friend of a friend: be open and welcoming, look for shared interests, ask questions. Take the time to get to know them, but without being pushy or intrusive. Make a warm and welcoming space for them, but don't try to force them into it.

TRIANGULATION AND "INTERFERING" METAMOURS

Not getting along with metamours—or having inflated expectations about how excellently you *should* get along—is one of the two biggest pitfalls of metamour relations. The other is triangulation: blaming metamours for your partner's behavior and holding them responsible for your dissatisfaction in your own relationships. No matter how awesome your partner is, how happy he makes you or how head over heels you are, eventually he will do something you don't like. If it's something to do with another of his relationships—investing time in another partner, perhaps, when you would like him to be investing it in you—you can be sorely tempted to misdirect blame onto the other partner.

Why? First, it's easier to be angry with someone we're not involved with. It's less painful to frame an unhappy situation as the fault of a third party than as a problem in our own relationship. It's easier to sit and steam about someone else than to risk the vulnerability of a frank discussion with an intimate partner about our unmet needs.

It's also easy, particularly in conflicts over resource allocation, to see the issue as a conflict between the metamours—one in which the pivot tends to get lost, even though she is the one choosing how to allocate her resources. If Greg is struggling to give enough time to Connor and Paul, it's easy for the conversation to become all about Connor and Paul, no matter who's speaking. The question "What does *Greg* want?" comes up surprisingly less often than you might think. The pivot makes his or her own decisions, and that's where the discussions should be happening. We discussed this in detail in chapters 6 ("Triangular communication," page 99) and 16 ("Who owns your choices?" page 278).

EVE'S STORY   Franklin and I have a long-distance relationship. Each of us lives with another partner and has an active social life. Between our visits, we try to stay connected through frequent Skype and phone calls, "work dates" where we log on to Skype and quietly do our own work (or work on this book), and reading together over the phone.

For about the first six months of our relationship, I had access to Franklin's Google calendar. I found that the pain having this access caused me was greater than any small benefit we got from ease of scheduling, especially since we always arranged our visits through direct negotiation. When I had access to his calendar, I could see everything he was doing when he was *not* with me, including the social events I could not attend, the date nights and camping trips with his nesting partner that collectively exceeded *all* the time he and I had together, and, perhaps most importantly, the things he was choosing to do when he was not available to me.

Eventually, I asked Franklin to remove my access to his calendar. I found that it was far easier for me to feel satisfied in our relationship if I could focus on what I was being given, rather than what I wasn't. Without access to information about his day-to-day life, I am able to practice gratitude for the time Franklin makes for me and cherish the things *we* do together—and pay attention only to my own life the rest of the time.

If we focus on the relationship we're *not* in, it's easy to become invested in what our metamour is getting that we aren't, rather than on what we want and need. Chapter 16 described the monkeys who were happy to get cucumbers until they saw another monkey getting a grape. We humans are not much different. It is much more useful, in creating healthy, fulfilling relationships for ourselves, to focus on what *we* want, what feeds us.

But what if a metamour is just too demanding? What if his demands come not just from trying to get his needs met, but from trying to suck time and energy away from our partner's time with us? What if he's—we've heard this a million times—trying to *interfere* in our relationship? Surely my partner needs to act, doesn't she? Confront him for his destructive behavior? Veto him, if she has that power? In a word, no. Instead, you need to do the same thing as always: work on making your own relationship awesome, advocate for your own needs, set boundaries for how you need to be treated, and let her work out the business with your metamour. Above all, *trust* her to make choices that respect and cherish you. If she's not going to do that, you can't make her.

We've heard people say, "So-and-so broke up my relationship with my ex," but in reality, that's not what happened. Your ex broke up with you herself—because she chose to. Nobody can break up a relationship unless someone in that relationship agrees to it.

WHEN YOUR METAMOURS ARE IN CONFLICT

As you might imagine, in poly relationships there are plenty of configurations in which the urge to take sides can arise: we've already talked about taking sides between partners when you're the pivot, and taking sides during a breakup. But if you're poly long enough, at some point you're likely to have two or more metamours through a single partner who aren't getting along. This will likely cause pain to your shared partner. When that happens, it can be very hard not to want to intervene.

When people we care about are embroiled in conflict, it's tempting to try to mediate. Maybe we think we can offer some special insight, or that we have enough distance to help everyone see everyone else's point of view. If you have rock-solid relationships with everyone involved, and if you are a skilled negotiator—and able to keep your own emotions in check—you may decide to wade into those waters to try to bring peace to your polycule, and you might actually do some good.

However, maybe you're not just an objective mediator; maybe you think someone is right and someone else is wrong. In truth, maybe one person is indeed being unreasonable, even obstinate or manipulative. Maybe your shared partner can't see this. Should you share your observations with your partner, or try to make the unreasonable metamour see the light, or stand by the wronged metamour—taking sides?

We won't say no, but we will say, "Tread very carefully here." Our friend Edward Martin has compared people to the fuel rods and control rods in a nuclear reactor. The control rods are neutron absorbers; they absorb stray neutrons to prevent them from reaching other fuel rods. They are attenuators: they calm things down when things start to go wrong. The fuel rods, on the other hand, are where the runaway chain reactions take place. They're amplifiers: when things go wrong, the fuel rods escalate the problem. When choosing people to include in his life, Edward likes to look for attenuators rather than amplifiers. Faced with conflict, amplifiers escalate the situation—with demands, tantrums, ultimatums and sleep deprivation via all-night processing sessions. Attenuators tend to be flexible, with high emotional intelligence and good conflict-resolution skills.

Taking sides in a conflict between your metamours—or between a metamour and a partner—amplifies rather than attenuates the problem. Your investment in the situation raises the stakes (which may already feel or be quite high), and the metamour you're opposing is likely to become even more entrenched and defensive, lowering the possibilities for a successful resolution. If you are going to be involved at all, it's useful to think about how you can act as an attenuator.

When part of your network is embroiled in a conflict that doesn't directly involve you, probably the most useful thing you can do is listen. We discussed active listening in chapter 7; it's useful here. Offer empathy, without analyzing, fixing or blaming. Many people remain embroiled in conflicts because they desperately need to feel heard. You can help by hearing them. There's also a gotcha here, though. If you're helping your metamours (or partners) by actively listening to them, you may be tempted to start carrying messages between them. After all, they're not hearing each other, right? Maybe they just need some translation help? Nope. No. Uh-uh. Don't do it. If you begin playing messenger, you are likely to *increase* the distance between them rather than decrease it. If they start to rely on you as their interlocutor, it will become harder and harder for them to communicate with each other.

What you *can* do is encourage them to speak directly to one another. If one of them asks for insight about what the other is thinking or feeling, resist the urge to answer, and instead suggest they ask the other person directly. If their conflict is going to be resolved, *they*, not you, will resolve it.

METAMOURS AS THE PRICE OF ADMISSION

In an ideal world, we poly folks could be sure that all our partners would always be thrilled with each other and enjoy spending time together. In such a world, leprechauns frolic with unicorns under trees that blossom with cotton candy. The fact is, sometimes people just don't like each other. Columnist Dan Savage has said that all relationships have a "price of admission." The perfect partner doesn't exist. Everyone has some quirk, habit or trait that becomes annoying once we get involved with them. It might be something as simple as leaving dirty socks on the coffee table. Whatever it is, there's always an annoyance or three that we need to be able to get over if we want to be with someone for long.

In the poly world, sometimes a person's other partner might be that price of admission. Occasionally someone we love very much will love someone very much whom we love not much at all. It's the price of admission for being with that person. Both of us have had the experience of loving people whose partners we care rather less for. The best guidelines we can offer are to behave, to the best of our abilities, like reasonable adults when we're around people we don't particularly like; to understand that these people add value to the lives of those we care about; and to seek to be supportive and compassionate toward those our partners love.

Poly people tend to act as though metamour relationships are free. That is, we invest in relationships with our partners, but don't often think of the investment required to maintain friendships with their partners. In fact, these relationships can require considerable effort to build and maintain, especially for people who tend to be introverted. An expectation of close relationships, or even family, between metamours is a tacit expectation that someone will be willing to invest significant time and emotional energy in us, just to be with us. However amazing we may think we are, that's asking quite a lot.

In open poly networks, an expectation that each person is involved on some level with every metamour, and each of *their* metamours, and each of their metamours, quickly becomes unrealistic. *Dunbar's number*, the number of significant interpersonal relationships that a human is capable of maintaining at once, is generally taken to be around 150. Our own romantic network has occasionally reached more than 80 people, which is more than halfway to Dunbar's number. A serious approach to our whole network as "polyfamily" would require us to neglect many other important relationships in our lives (birth families, relatives, work colleagues, friends, neighbors), just to remain connected to our networks. For an introvert, especially, even the number of first-degree metamours a person might have could exceed her total number of close, lifelong friends.

QUESTIONS TO ASK YOURSELF

Problems between metamours can be as corrosive as problems between partners in poly relationships, so they bear careful thought. Here are some questions to ask yourself about your expectations of metamours:

- *What are my expectations of my metamours?*

- *Do I have to know my metamours? Do I expect to have close relationships with them?*

- *Do my expectations allow space for metamours who might have different expectations?*

- *How do I communicate my expectations?*

- *How and when do I want to meet my metamours?*

- *Do I give my partner space to conduct his relationship with my other partner, without trying to take sides in conflicts or carry messages between them?*

- *What will I do if I don't get along well with a partner's partner? What do I do if one of my partners doesn't get along well with another of my partners?*

FINDING PARTNERS

Each friend represents a world in us,
a world possibly not born until they arrive,
and it is only by this meeting that a new world is born.

ANAÏS NIN

Dating in the poly world is a lot like dating in the monogamous world, with some exceptions. For those of you who are single or solo poly there's not much difference at all, except that you may be openly dating more than one person at once and you need to disclose those other relationships. For people in a close partnership such as a marriage, however, poly dating will likely involve special scheduling or logistical constraints. You might have to work around a partner's schedule or, if you have a nesting partner and you don't live in a large house, you might find it difficult to bring a date home overnight. None of these problems is unique to polyamory, though: monogamous single parents face similar dating challenges.

Still, "How do I find partners?" is one of the top questions we hear about polyamory. And there are certainly unique concerns: finding poly partners, choosing partners who are compatible with you and your poly style, and disclosing your poly relationships are all things to think about.

IT'S NOT ABOUT FATE

The fairy tale of love has a lot to say about finding romantic partners, but most of this info is not very useful to poly folks. A great deal of it has to do with fate and luck and eyes meeting across crowded rooms. We believe luck plays little role in finding partners. Your success or failure at finding good romantic relationships depends on many factors that are within your control. When we have been unsuccessful finding partners, we've found it helpful to look at ourselves, what we're doing, what we're offering and what we're asking for.

Some things consistently make it harder or easier to connect with potential partners. We offer the following guidelines:

- *Try not to make every social encounter about your search for a partner.* The harder you look the more desperate you appear, and the more people will avoid you—except the kind who find desperate-seeming people attractive, and these are often not the kind you'll be able to form a healthy relationship with.
- *Be out, if you can.* You can't say "Poly folks are hard to meet" if you're closeted and nobody knows about you. Although some people have significant barriers to openness, such as concerns over employment or an ongoing child-custody dispute, being closeted will hamper finding poly partners. We discuss coming out in the next chapter.
- *Be casual.* If you treat being poly as if it's a shameful secret, then folks will act as if it's a shameful secret. If you're open and casual about it, then responses are more like "Oh, I have this friend who's poly too. Do you know him? Maybe I should introduce you."
- *Network with other poly folks.* Go to poly groups or events.
- *Don't be afraid to expand your social horizons.* If you don't know any poly folks in your social group, build a new social group. Hang out with other poly people even if you don't want to date them. Become part of the crowd. Get to know people as people before sizing them up as dating material.

SHOULD YOU DATE ONLY POLY PEOPLE?

If you choose only partners who are already polyamorous, as both of us do, a lot of problems are solved right away. However, many people like the opportunity to connect with people who aren't necessarily familiar with polyamory.

Each approach has advantages and disadvantages. Choosing partners who are already poly decreases the chances that, at some point in the future, they'll want a monogamous relationship. It also means they're more likely to have already developed skills to navigate poly. In fact, we know people who won't start a relationship with anyone who doesn't already have at least two partners, on the grounds that dating people with multiple partners allows you to see in advance how well they relate to multiple people.

On the other hand, making this choice really does narrow the dating pool. The poly community in most places is relatively small. Which also means that if you have a bad breakup, everybody will know about it. Then again, maybe that's not a bad thing. Where everyone hears the gossip, there's an incentive to treat people well and keep breakups civil.

If you opt to start a relationship with someone who's new to poly, be prepared for a lot of discussion and negotiation. It can be helpful to read websites, books and other resources about polyamory together. Talk about what polyamory means to each of you, and how your visions of it mesh. Trying to "convert" a person to polyamory is a bit of a mixed bag. Some people take to polyamory naturally as soon as they discover it. Others find that, no matter how hard they try, they can never become happy with it. Starting a relationship with a person who's unsure but willing to "try" may mean painful renegotiations later, and possibly a choice between the end of the relationship and the end of your dreams.

TELLING A PROSPECTIVE PARTNER ABOUT POLYAMORY

So you're on a hot date, maybe with someone you met online or at a party—outside the poly context. Things are looking good, you're feeling chemistry... so when do you talk about polyamory?

EVE'S STORY It was the year before I started my first poly relationship, with Ray. Peter and I had formally opened our relationship three years before, but we'd had only a few mediocre dates with people we met online, and a few awkward and ill-fated attempts at initiating interest with people in our social circle.

I met Hugh at a concert by a folksinger who happened to be openly polyamorous. I naively assumed that Hugh would be aware of and comfortable with poly. The two of us hit it off, flirting throughout the concert, and at the end of it, we exchanged numbers. A few days later, we met for dinner and a political lecture (you know, just your routine leftist-intellectual first date).

I knew I had to bring up polyamory—and Peter—with Hugh, but had no idea how. So I looked for an opening in the conversation. Hugh started talking about his union involvement. *Aha! My opening. Peter was in a union too!* The words came out all at once. "Oh yeah, my husband is in a union and is really involved in it and oh, by the way, we're polyamorous and oh, you don't know what polyamory is?"

A look of shock and betrayal briefly crossed Hugh's face—but I thought to myself, *Of course, I never actually told him I wasn't married, right?* To his credit, he recovered quickly and gracefully. We went to the lecture and politely said our goodbyes. There was no second date.

Ask people in the poly community when to bring up polyamory and many will say, "Before the first date," though a few will hold out. "Not until you're sure you want a relationship."

We are definitely in the "Before the first date—if not earlier" camp. You might avoid bringing up the subject early for fear of "scaring off" a prospective partner. However, we find this logic faulty. If someone isn't okay with polyamory, you *want* to know right away so you don't waste each other's time.

Putting off the conversation too long will make an incompatible partner feel like you pulled a bait and switch; you deprived him of the chance to give informed consent to being on a date with you at all. Our policy is unapologetic openness: If one of us is on a first date with someone, that person is *already* well aware we are polyamorous.

Being forthright is much easier when you hold the abundance model of relationships. Wanting to put off disclosure about polyamory reveals a scarcity model: an idea that relationship opportunities are so rare that every opportunity must be pursued, even a wrong one. When it comes to bringing up polyamory, simple and direct is usually most successful, especially if you are already partnered. Hiding or talking obliquely about your partner or spouse is really not going to impress your date—at least not in a good way.

Treating polyamory like bad news that needs to be broken gently also isn't a great approach. People take their cues about how to respond to something from the way you present it. If you treat polyamory as if it's an unfortunate medical condition or a guilty secret, that's how they'll see it. If you treat it as a bold philosophy that you're proud to share with the world, they may be impressed by your avant-garde amazingness.

Start simply. "I'm polyamorous." Explain what that means to you. "I believe in open relationships with the knowledge and approval of everybody, and maybe multiple interconnections if everything clicks for the people." Ask questions, such as "Are you open to polyamory?" or (if you know your prospective partner is poly) "What kind of poly do you practice? What kind are you most interested in?" Approaching a potential new partner with integrity means being transparent about your relationship expectations.

WHERE ARE POLY PEOPLE?

If you're shopping for bread, you'll have more success in a bakery than in a hardware store. If you're looking for poly people, you're more likely to find them among openly poly people than among people who prefer traditional relationships. A quick online search may turn up poly groups wherever you are. Check Modern Poly's *Polyamory Group Registry* (polygroups.com), and also search Meetup.com and Facebook for groups in your area.

If no real-life groups are near you, the major social media have many poly communities, and there are web forums and dating sites for poly people.

Huge numbers of poly people are on the free dating site OkCupid.com. There, answering lots of personality questions (hundreds) and marking poly-related ones as "mandatory" will help you zero in on your peers, as will listing "polyamory" as an interest in your profile. At the time of writing, a new poly social networking site called K-Tango was in beta testing; this looks like a site worth watching. The two of us met each other through Twitter: Eve was following Franklin, who tweeted about an astronomy lecture. Eve, who happened to be in Portland for a conference, attended—and the rest is...well, this book.

It's a lot harder to find poly people if you're not open about being polyamorous. Imagine a cocktail party with ten poly people there, none of them open. All ten might end up thinking, *I wonder where I can go to meet poly people? Not here!* We've had multiple people at a single conference or workplace quietly come up and confide in us that they're poly, but don't want anyone else to know about it. Of course, because polyamory is such a vast umbrella term for so many different styles of relationships, someone who says "I'm poly!" may mean something different by it than what you do. Get them talking about what they mean.

THE IMPORTANCE OF PARTNER SELECTION

The notion that we don't choose our relationships is surprisingly widespread. Compatibility, shared vision, mutually negotiated relationships—none of these things matter in the face of True Love, says the fairy tale. When we fall in love, we are obligated to start a relationship. And once we're in it, the love is the fuel that makes it go. As long as we're in love, we will be happy. Many grown-ups believe this.

FRANKLIN'S STORY   A few years back, I was speaking about alternative relationship models at a convention. One of my fellow panelists, a writer, was complaining that he'd never been able to find a partner who understood his writing habits; his partners tended to complain when he got an idea in the middle of the night and got up to write, or when he would lock himself in his office through dinner because he had a burst of inspiration and was too absorbed to stop and eat.

I suggested the solution to this problem was to choose partners up front who understood the way he worked and were okay with it. The man was quite shocked at this idea. "You don't choose partners!" he insisted. "Relationships just happen. You don't screen lovers the way you would look for an employee at a business!"

If we, like Franklin's fellow panelist, accept the idea that we do not choose our partners, we tend to wake up and find ourselves in relationships by default, not design. We may end up, as the writer at the panel did, with partners who are a poor match, because we don't apply good partner selection criteria. We don't think to ask questions that might tell us how well matched we are.

We do have choices about our romantic lives. You can skip right over vast quantities of relationship problems by exercising good partner selection skills at the outset—and yes, partner selection is a skill. Part of it is recognizing the choices we make, and part of recognizing our choices is acknowledging that while we may not always have control over our feelings, we have control over whom we are in relationships with. Love, of and by itself, is not enough to guarantee a good relationship. Good relationships grow by careful tending, but they start with good selection. (Or as gardeners like to say: "Right plant, right place.")

One part of the skill of partner selection is knowing our "deal-breakers" —what would make a partner a poor choice for us. Sexual incompatibility is one common deal-breaker; drug or alcohol abuse is another. So is a history of violence against past romantic partners. But many others are more subtle, such as, in the case of the writer at the conference, disrespect for work habits that are really important to you.

When selecting a partner, there's a strange state of limbo you can end up in: a person doesn't display any particular red flags or deal-breakers, but you also don't feel really enthusiastic about her, either. If we make choices based on whether or not someone hits any of our deal-breakers, we might plow ahead with a relationship without considering whether or not that person has the qualities we *want* in a partner.

One good policy for partner selection is "'Fuck yes' or no." This policy, first articulated by writer Mark Manson, is based on the idea that it makes no sense to invest time and romantic energy with someone you're not that excited to be with, or who isn't excited to be with you. If the idea of dating someone doesn't prompt an enthusiastic "Fuck yes!" then the answer is no. Ambivalence has little place in romance.

The approach we recommend relies more on asking ourselves questions about what this person has to offer, rather than asking whether this person has disagreeable traits. Franklin likes to use questions such as these:

- Does this person have wisdom I find attractive?
- Has she done something that shows me she is likely, when faced with a difficult decision, to choose the path of greatest courage?
- Has she done something that shows me that, when faced by a personal fear or insecurity, she is dedicated to dealing with it with grace, and to investing in the effort it takes to confront, understand and grow beyond it?
- Does she show intellectual curiosity, intellectual rigor and intellectual growth?
- Has she dealt with past relationships, including relationships that have failed, with dignity and compassion?
- Is she a joyful person? Does she value personal happiness? Does she make me feel joy?
- Does she seem to have a continuing commitment to understanding herself?
- Does she value self-determinism?
- Does she approach things with energy and enthusiasm? Does she engage the world?
- Does she demonstrate personal integrity?
- Is she open, honest, enthusiastic and exploratory about sex?
- Does she communicate openly, even when it's uncomfortable to do so?

The previous chapter talked about the idea of amplifiers versus attenuators: people whose response to stress tends to make things worse vs. people who tend to make things better. This idea applies to partner selection. When you're considering dating someone, ask yourself: "Does this person have a history of leaving their social circle better or worse than they found it?"

One factor that can be very revealing is how a prospective partner talks about ex-partners. Are they monsters? Is every story about an ex a tale of woe, in which the ex plays the Big Bad Wolf? This could mean that if you become romantically attached, you'll have the starring role in a future monster story. In contrast, when someone is on generally good terms with former partners, that speaks volumes.

Look at a date's current relationships, if any. Do they seem turbulent or generally smooth? Do you like the way this person treats his current partners? Does he speak positively and respectfully about them? If so, he will likely do the same about you.

POLY DATING AND CHILDREN

Poly dating with kids in the picture is in many ways similar to monogamous dating for single or divorced parents. In chapter 13 we told the story of Clara and Elijah, a polyamorous couple with two young children. Many of the strategies they employed represent general best practices for dating with children. Clara chose a partner, Ramon, who had children of his own, and the adults all worked out supportive scheduling strategies around the kids' needs. Not every dating partner would want to do that.

You might seek partners who like being around children, though not everyone considers this a requirement. It can certainly be easier for parents when their partners are kid-oriented people. At minimum, you at least want to feel like your kids are *safe* around your partners.

As with metamours, a time will eventually come when you will want your partners to meet your children. Most parents we've spoken to prefer not to introduce new partners to their children until the relationship is fairly well established. This serves two purposes: ensuring that *you* are comfortable with and trust the new partner, and not having your child become attached to someone you're not sure is going to stick around. Of course, the right time to introduce a new partner to a child will probably need to be decided by all the child's parents.

Some people believe having children provides a good rationale for a screening veto, as discussed in chapter 12. Our answer is: sort of. Certainly, when two (or more) parents share custody and caretaking of a child, particularly a very young child, *all* of them need to be on board regarding who else is allowed into the child's space. This doesn't necessarily mean, however, that all parents need to have veto over new relationships. It might mean that certain partners don't meet the children or come to the home. That will, of course, restrict a relationship in many ways, but choices about how those restrictions will then play out can be left to the people in the relationship.

Finally, remember that your relationship with your child is *a relationship*, and a very high-maintenance one. And you need to care for that relationship when you are in the throes of a new romance. Just as your partners may feel insecure and scared, so might your children. They too may need reassurance that they are still special, still loved, still irreplaceable. It can be very helpful, as Clara did, to schedule special alone time with your children the way you would schedule "date nights" with your partners: one-on-one time where they have your undivided attention and do something fun with you, so they see that you are still committed to them.

MISMATCHED SUCCESS

It's common to see poly relationships in which one partner has much more success meeting new people than another. This can create resentment, guilt and anxiety all around. Some highly sociable people try to scout up dates for their more introverted partners. This rarely succeeds. It can feel a bit awkward to be approached by someone who says, "Hey, would you like to date my boyfriend?" or "How'd you like to go out with my wife?"

In reality, we are responsible for our own dating experiences. It's not your job to provide your partner with new dates. Different people find it easier or harder to meet people, but if you're the one who meets people easily, you're not doing anything wrong. If your partner finds it harder, that's not your fault. Unless you're a professional marriage broker, your ability to find partners for another person is limited (and your responsibility for it, nonexistent).

What strategies work when one person in a couple finds it easier to date than the other? An introvert may need to practice pushing his comfort zone a bit; he might ask an extroverted partner to help bring him into new situations. Different people succeed in different social settings. A person who doesn't meet people easily might have more success in "closed" settings—for example, among friends and acquaintances—than in "open" settings, such as parties or bars. Some people prefer looking online; a web search can turn up guides for how to use OkCupid to find poly people successfully. As mentioned, specifically poly dating sites are springing up all the time.

Social networking through our partners can be another powerful way to meet people, as long as you don't burden your partner with expectations or let your partner run the show. Peter's partner Gwen is someone Eve originally met on OkCupid. They had a four-way date with Gwen and her live-in partner, Finn, and while there was no chemistry between Eve and Finn, Gwen and Peter hit it off. And Clio knew Eve online for about six months before she started dating Peter; her acquaintanceship with Eve was a key factor in her accepting Peter's request to come to her town for a visit.

KITTYCAT LESSONS

A "kittycat lesson" is what we call a situation where we generalize poorly from our experiences or learn a lesson that works against us.

FRANKLIN'S STORY   For many years, my mother had a fluffy white cat that might reasonably have been called obstinate. It's not that she was incapable of learning. Far from it. She was a very bright cat; she just tended to learn the wrong lesson. For example, whenever my mother opened the refrigerator door, the cat, realizing that the fridge was the source of all goodness, would try to dart inside.

My mom tried to teach the cat not to do that by closing the door on her nose. The cat learned the lesson quickly—not "I shouldn't try to get into the refrigerator," but rather "I should dash in the instant I can before the door hits my nose."

One kittycat lesson we have both seen many times involves strategies for finding new partners. People who feel threatened by polyamory often try to manage risk by placing rigid limitations on new partners. Yet people with experience in poly often avoid restrictive relationships. So the people who get into such relationships tend to have little poly experience and few skills. When problems happen and the relationships end, the people who placed the restrictions may decide they were not restrictive *enough,* and then try to limit new partners even more. So, in a variant of the cascading self-fulfilling prophesy of doom, people with poly experience avoid them even more, which increases the likelihood they will only find partners with limited poly experience, which increases the odds of trouble.

If you require your relationships to take a specific shape, finding someone who will fit that exact shape is especially difficult, as described in chapter 17. Looking instead for good *people,* not for good role-fillers, leaves you open to connection even if it takes a form you didn't expect. If you truly are open to only one specific form of poly relationship, then it's helpful to think in terms of *what you're offering* and *what you expect.* The more you expect, the more valuable your offer had better be. Would *you* take it, if someone like you offered it to you right now?

SIGNING ON TO THE RULES

Consent to a relationship must be informed. It's difficult, when the butterflies are fluttering in your tummy, to make a level-headed analysis of the relationship opportunity in front of you. It can be difficult, if your new partner has butterflies fluttering in *his* tummy, for him to be completely honest with you about things that might put you off—problems in his other relationship that might spill into yours, say, or constraints you might not appreciate.

Any time you start a relationship with a person who is already partnered, there will probably be responsibilities, expectations and commitments already in play. Learn them. Don't go into a relationship blind.

Talk directly to your partner about what effects her other relationships may have on you. What time constraints will affect you? Is your partner out or closeted? Will you be allowed to talk about your relationships? Will you be expected to act as a secondary partner? Are there veto arrangements? What expectations, if any, will there be with respect to your metamours? Will you be allowed (or expected) to meet them? Will your new partner expect to have input into—or veto over—other relationships you might want to start in the future? Are there any other stipulations you'll be subject to?

Franklin prefers to start new relationships only with people who have at least one and preferably two other relationships already. A great way to see what might be in store is to watch how your new partner interacts with his existing partners. What do those relationships look like? What expectations does your new partner have of them? What limitations does he place on those relationships? Every relationship is unique, of course, but patterns can still be revealing. If your partner is kind, compassionate and considerate in his other relationships, he will probably be kind, compassionate and considerate with you. If he seems controlling or demanding of other partners, you can expect the same.

As difficult as it is to consider these things in the giddy rush of a new relationship, it's better to find things out at the start, rather than after you've become more deeply invested emotionally.

A CAUTIONARY NOTE ON COUPLE-CENTRISM

When two people have only each other as partners, they naturally fall into a pattern of sharing everything, committing all time and resources to the relationship. So when one decides to open her heart and life to a new person, the other often feels that she is losing something—time, focus, energy—and often she is.

Imagine you have planted an oak tree in your garden and tended exclusively to that tree for many years. The tree grows big and strong, forming a beautiful canopy that expands over the entire garden, shading everything beneath it. You love that tree and the shade it gives and have spent many long summer days beneath it, looking up into its branches.

Then one day you find a tiny plant. It intrigues you. You don't know what it's going to grow into, but you want to find out. You want to plant it in your garden...but you don't have any sunny spot left. Your beloved oak tree is shading everything. You don't want to harm your oak tree, so you just plant the new thing in a shady spot, thinking, *Maybe it will be something, a nice fern perhaps, that likes the shade.* Sometimes that's what happens. The relationship that gets planted beneath the old relationship naturally thrives in the shade. But when that happens, it's sheer luck.

Most romantic relationships do not naturally stay small and inconspicuous. Eventually, there will be a conflict: either the new relationship will wither, or the older relationship must be trimmed a bit to allow sunlight for the new one to grow. Many couples go through this process, and many survive it with healthier relationships as a result. But it can be painful, particularly for the partner being "pruned." Often the new partner ends up taking the brunt of the conflict, shouldering shame and blame as the interloper, the "other." For this reason, many experienced poly people approach people in long-term couples with caution.

Many closely coupled people are indeed available for deep intimacy with others, maintain autonomy over their relationship decisions, and gracefully make room in their lives to honor both their existing commitments and new ones. How do you identify such people? If you're the newcomer, take some time to get to know the couple and observe whether they have strong, independent identities apart from each other or appear completely enmeshed. Here are some signs to look for:

- Do they always appear at events together, or do they sometimes attend separately?
- If one is invited, do both always attend?
- When they are at events together, do they mingle separately or are they always side by side?
- Do all their pictures on social media show them together, or do they appear with a variety of friends and family members?
- Do they have separate close friendships, or are all their friends shared?
- If they are closeted about polyamory, are they closeted because of genuine risk one of them faces (for instance, a custody dispute or a teaching job) or because they do not want to lose the status and privileges afforded to a couple?
- Can they schedule their own time, or do they always need to check with each other first?

The poly community is, unfortunately, filled with people who have been terribly hurt by well-meaning but inexperienced couples. As Eve's girlfriend, Paloma, has said, "I'm not critical of couples, I'm critical of bad behavior"—and people often use being part of a couple as an excuse for bad behavior. As we've discussed, be especially careful about becoming involved with a member of a couple who doesn't give you a voice in what your relationship will look like. That can lead to all sorts of mischief. A common scenario is that when the couple's relationship changes—which it almost certainly will—

you may find yourself unceremoniously dumped...often with a heaping helping of blame for whatever changes happened in the couple's relationship.

We shouldn't need to say this, but you don't have to go into a relationship as a secondary partner if you don't want to. And if you do, you do not
have to simply accept what's offered. You can still advocate for your needs,
both at the beginning and later on as things move along.

QUESTIONS TO ASK YOURSELF

When you're interested in a new person, considering these questions may
help you decide whether they are a good choice for you as a partner:

- *Am I excited by the prospect of being with this person? Is he a "Fuck
  yes!"?*

- *Does this person have relationship values similar to mine?*

- *Do I understand and agree to any rules that will apply to my
  relationship?*

- *Am I being asked to give up anything to be in this relationship? If so,
  do I feel that what I will get in return is worth the price?*

- *Is this person available to give me what I think I want in the
  relationship—in terms of time, emotional intimacy, and freedom for
  the relationship to grow?*

- *Is there anything about this person I'm hoping will change?*

- *Does this person help me be the best version of myself?*

Asking the following questions of a potential partner can help you figure out
whether your values and approaches will mesh well in a relationship:

- *How do you feel about polyamory? Do you have experience with poly
  relationships, and what does that look like for you?*

- *What are your goals in a poly relationship?*

- *What restrictions, if any, do you (or your partners) put on other partners?*

- *Will I be expected to have a particular kind of relationship with your other partners?*

- *What does polyamory mean to you?*

- *Do you have any expectations about the role I will be expected to play in your life?*

THE REST OF
THE WORLD

Our stories may be singular,
but our destination is shared.

BARACK OBAMA

When Franklin first began to live non-monogamously, there was no such thing as a "poly community." Since then the landscape has changed radically. Organized poly groups are still relatively young: only a handful predate the 1990s, and most started after the turn of the century. They have proliferated in recent years, in part because community is such an essential part of healthy poly relationships. By the time Eve and Peter opened up, they were able to find poly groups and other poly people, though they had to move to a big city to do so. Nowadays, poly discussion, support and social groups exist all over North America and western Europe and are beginning to pop up elsewhere. Nearly every city in the United States has at least one. The Internet is filled with them; it's hard to find social media sites without large, active poly forums. Poly-related dating sites are appearing so quickly it's hard to keep track of them.

Having a social network that understands who we are is important on a number of levels. Simply knowing that we are not alone, that there are others like us, is tremendously empowering. Franklin receives many emails from people expressing how validating it is just to know they aren't alone in wanting a life of happy multiple relationships. A support network also helps provide reality checks. No one can do this alone. When we can talk to other people about the problems we're having, hear their stories and gain their insights, it equips and empowers us to build better relationships ourselves. Having a community of peers who won't repeat the monogamous scripts—that problems in a poly relationship happen because we haven't found The One yet, that poly relationships aren't "real," and so forth—liberates us and helps us find solutions that work.

It's hard to overstate how important this is. Most of us have deeply internalized messages about what's okay in relationships. Polyamory requires us to uproot and discard many of those messages. This becomes a lot harder if the people we turn to for support reinforce those messages whenever we confide in them. "Well, what do you expect?" "That's what you get for cheating." "Why are you letting her do this to you?" "You must have low self-esteem." "He's just using you for sex." No matter how bold or resilient you feel starting out in the world of polyamory, believe us, this kind of thing will wear you down—and when your relationships are struggling and you need emotional support, the lack of empathy can be downright devastating.

One common example is what happens when a couple agrees to be polyamorous, then breaks up. If the members of the couple are primarily tapped in to monogamous culture, the story that will get traction will be the standard cheating narrative. This will be doubly true if it appears that one person left her partner for someone else. It can be very easy for the partner who was "left behind" to enlist the support of his community in vilifying his ex and her new partner. The shaming this can entail can be extremely destructive if you have even a trace of those monogamous scripts left in your own internal self-evaluation process. We have seen this happen many, many times.

You need poly friends. Just take our word for it. A poly social network is also important for something we talked about in chapter 4: self-efficacy (page 61). Recall that self-efficacy is a belief that you can do something, even if you have never done it before. That's awfully hard if you have no role models who have succeeded at what you're trying to do.

It's common for the people in a monogamous relationship to become each other's main or even only social support structure. Many monogamous couples do almost everything, including nearly all of their socializing, together. They may share the same friends, spend most or all of their leisure time together, even have the same hobbies. There's nothing wrong with this, but polyamory creates a potential complication. If your partner is on a date with another partner, you may feel adrift, without any activities you're accustomed to doing alone. There's not a great deal of social support for just one member of a relationship.

Building a social network of polyamorous and poly-friendly friends is a huge benefit. Developing individual hobbies and interests, social circles who don't expect you will always be with your partner, and activities you can do on your own all benefit you—not only when your partner is off on a date with someone else, but also in making you happier and more resilient.

FINDING YOUR COMMUNITY

Where are poly people? The short answer is "everywhere." We have met polyamorous people just about everywhere you can think of, including at fast-food restaurants. The number and size of the organized communities hints at the number of people interested. We have spoken to polyamorous people from Ghana, South Africa, Norway, Sweden, Germany, Ukraine, and just about everywhere else. For every person who's part of a poly discussion group, there are many more who are polyamorous without being part of a community.

The easiest way to find poly people is to be open about being polyamorous yourself. The more open you are, the easier it gets. When you treat polyamory as something normal and casual, you create a safe place for others to open up to you.

FRANKLIN'S STORY   One day several years ago, I was at a printing company waiting to meet with someone about a print job. It was a Monday afternoon, and the receptionist asked, "Did you do anything interesting this weekend?"

"Yes," I said. "My girlfriend and I went to see *The Happening* on Saturday. After that, her other boyfriend and his other girlfriend and I went out to dinner. We had a great time, but the movie was pretty mediocre. I don't recommend it."

"Oh, you're polyamorous!" she replied. "So am I! Besides my boyfriends, I don't know many other poly people."

Franklin's is just one of many, many similar experiences we have had as openly poly people. When you're new to polyamory, meeting other poly people can feel impossible. Creating a safe place for other people to be open with you requires courage, but often the rewards are more than worth the risk. To find poly-related discussion and support groups, Google, social media sites, Meetup.com and polygroups.com are your friends. Do a search for "polyamory" and the name of the closest city or large town, and see what turns up.

There's a lot of overlap between poly and kink communities. The organized BDSM world is older and more established than the organized poly community, so towns that don't have a poly presence will still often have gatherings of kinky people. Even if you're not that interested in kink, you can sometimes find poly people by attending BDSM munches, which are social events where kinky folks get together in low-pressure public spaces to chat and socialize. You don't need to be kinky to attend a munch. If kink isn't your thing, fear not; once you've connected with a few poly people, you'll find it easier to meet more.

If you can't find a poly community where you are, create one! This can be as simple as starting a meetup on a site like Meetup.com. Decide on a schedule and a venue (lots of poly social meetups happen in restaurants or cafes), and commit to being there every month. You might get only one or two people showing, or even nobody at all the first few times, but that's okay. Perseverance pays off. The women's discussion group that Eve helps organize went more than a year with only two or three people showing up before it took off; today meetings often fill to capacity within a few hours of being announced.

If you'd rather have a focused discussion, with topics and moderation, find online poly communities (social networking sites are valuable for this) and announce your intentions. Set a time and a place, maybe your home if you like (it's quieter and more sociable than a restaurant). Create a website or social media page if you can, and list it on polygroups.com. Again, you may not get many people at first, but these things tend to gather steam over time. If your interests are more in building a social network, host poly movie nights or have poly outings to events such as movies or shows.

POLYAMORY AND LGBTQ COMMUNITIES
The intersection of polyamory with lesbian, gay, bi, trans and queer communities has been complex and sometimes turbulent. Well before the polyamory movement got rolling in the late 1980s and 1990s, many gay and lesbian communities had already established their own cultural norms around non-monogamy. For example, *The Ethical Slut* was written against a backdrop of queer and kinky community, and it only briefly mentioned polyamory in its first edition. A great deal of polyamorous thought was pioneered by queer women such as Janet Hardy, Dossie Easton and Tristan Taormino.

While poly communities and discussion groups tend to be very accepting of LGBTQ people, most people in them tend to come from a cisgender and largely heteronormative background, and these groups can still have subtle problems with homophobia and transphobia. Cis hetero people may not be able to identify with the issues that gay, lesbian and trans people live daily. So it's no surprise that self-identified queer, gay, lesbian and trans people are not always comfortable in poly communities. Bisexual women, on the other hand, make up a large proportion of many poly groups, although bisexual men tend to be rare, absent or invisible. In some areas so many women in poly communities identify as bisexual that many people seem to assume it by default.

Unfortunately, the gay and lesbian communities have not always been accepting of bisexuality. (Franklin's partner Amber used to identify as lesbian and felt that she could not express her attraction to men without being ostracized.) The emergence of the poly community offered a place for bisexual-identified people, and later trans people, to find acceptance among people interested in non-monogamy. This may explain in part why poly groups today often have a relatively high percentage of bisexual and trans members.

Some people who identify as gay, lesbian or queer express concerns that polyamory is politically problematic. The fear is that polyamory harms efforts by gay, lesbian and trans activists to portray gay relationships as non-threatening, or that polyamory may pander to stereotypes that non-straight people, particularly gay men, are sexually promiscuous. Because members of sexual minorities are subject to social censure already, there can be pressure on people in same-sex relationships to be "model citizens" by promoting relationship ideals that are as socially acceptable as possible.

Other complaints leveled at polyamory have included the idea that it spreads STIs; that the gay community needs people willing to model successful, long-term monogamous relationships; that polyamory damages efforts toward legal same-sex marriage; and that in the context of gay and lesbian subcultures, it distracts attention away from the civil rights struggles of gay people. Even activists who support polyamory can express the idea that gays and lesbians should focus their attention on matters of basic civil rights first, rather than spend time and effort promoting acceptance of polyamory.

It doesn't help that media portrayals of polyamory tend to focus on straight cis people. This means that LGBTQ people or groups may view poly as something straight people do, or as something that reinforces conventional gender roles and power inequities.

Some poly lesbians find it especially difficult to come out in their communities, because lesbian couples have fought so hard to gain social recognition that they are wary of anything that seems to risk undermining that recognition. The small size of such communities can make it difficult for some gays and lesbians to have the same freedom of choice and expectations of privacy that cisgender, heterosexual people enjoy. ("Anyone can know except my softball team!" is something we've heard more than once—really!—and on opposite sides of North America.) We've also heard from trans people who have been told that polyamory "de-legitimizes" them by preventing them from finding "true" intimacy. Franklin has heard people say polyamory is something that trans people settle for when they can't find "real" relationships of their own.

Resistance to polyamory and bisexuality is by no means the case everywhere, though at one time it was common. What appears to be the oldest continuously running in-person poly discussion group in the world was founded in 1997 by a lesbian triad who encountered animosity toward polyamory from other gays and lesbians. And what resistance remains is diminishing. Since about 2000 the landscape seems to have changed greatly, with much greater acceptance of polyamory in gay and lesbian communities. In some places it's now accepted very widely, and many pride parades regularly include a poly presence. Discussion groups are cropping up just for LGBTQ polys—you name it, there's probably a Facebook group for it.

The result of all this is that your experience will vary depending on which of the letters you identify with, where you live and the particular communities you have access to. It's a good bet, though, that you will encounter more ignorance than hostility, and you will likely need to spend time educating both the straight/cis poly people you connect with and any LGBTQ communities you're a part of.

THE POLY CLOSET

How and whether to come out, and to whom, is a major topic of conversation throughout the poly world. Many people believe being open isn't an option for them. Deciding whether to be out is something all people in poly relationships eventually need to address. The decision is a personal one. There is no "right" answer. As among gays, everyone has the right to decide for themselves whether and how much to be open about their life.

There are many advantages to being out. You cease to live in fear of exposure. Being out makes finding partners far easier, you can more easily identify your enemies, and your allies can find you.

There absolutely are costs to being out. Polyamory is not a protected status; people can lose their housing or their jobs if they have a hostile landlord or boss. If you are divorced and not on good terms with your ex, custody of your children may be at stake; Franklin has seen at least one person lose custody of her children because of her involvement in polyamory, though she was later able to win custody back. In the U.S. military, Article 134, paragraph 62 of the Uniform Code of Military Justice prohibits adultery if the conduct prejudices "good order and discipline" or is "of a nature to bring discredit upon the Armed Forces." In practice, whether you will be targeted depends on whether someone is out to get you. Prosecutions are quite rare, but in theory servicemen in adulterous relationships may be disciplined, dishonorably discharged and even imprisoned, regardless of whether the arrangement is consensual. While we can't find any examples of military prosecution for polyamory, many servicemen and women cite fear of prosecution as a reason to be closeted.

Even without specific concerns about child custody, housing, employment or military service, many choose to remain closeted because they don't want friends or family to find out. But there are costs to remaining closeted too. And these costs may not be borne equally by all the people involved with the closeted person. Often he or she is already in a socially approved relationship of some sort, such as a marriage. A couple in a recognized relationship gets to claim the benefits of social approval and validation, while many of the drawbacks for their being closeted fall on their other partners, who may chafe under the demand for secrecy.

For example, when a couple is closeted, it's a pretty sure bet that any third or fourth person will have to steer clear of all their social functions, from family holidays to company picnics. If they do come, the relationship will likely be downplayed or not acknowledged at all. In extreme cases, the non-sanctioned partner may even be presented as an employee, such as a nanny or personal assistant.

A closeted person may have no social support network to call on in hard times. Problems in the relationship may thus stay under wraps, festering quietly. It can also be difficult to feel secure in the relationship when your partner is always saying "No, we're just friends," or even "She works for us." This is likely to make the "secret" partner feel like a source of shame, that she's being forced to compromise her integrity, or both.

For that reason, if you're building a relationship with someone who is closeted, especially if she is already in a socially approved relationship, it's important to discuss what that means. What does she gain from being closeted, and at what cost to you? Will it be okay if your relationship is never acknowledged for what it is? What happens if there is an accidental disclosure? Is there a benefit to you of remaining closeted? How important is it to you to be able to talk freely about your relationship? If you are never able to be seen in public with your partner, will that become a hardship on you? Under what conditions, if any, can these restrictions be revisited? Has the cost of coming out been balanced against the cost of remaining in the closet?

THE RISKS OF BEING OUT

When we talk to people who are closeted, the most common concerns we hear about being out are worry over disapproval from close family members or friends, fear of being seen as "weird" or "strange" (or worse, as a victim), fear of being excluded from social or church groups, and fear of the effect their being out will have on children (for example, many poly people say that other parents won't allow their children to play with the children of openly poly people).

All these things can happen. Poly people have been cut off by family members, had their children's friends (or even their children) snatched away, and been told they aren't welcome in church groups because they're poly. Sometimes the reaction is based on an idea that polyamory is inherently immoral—that it's little more than sanctioned cheating. Some people even find poly more objectionable than cheating, which is something that mainstream culture at least understands. Sometimes the reaction is driven by feelings closer to home. We have spoken to many people who, upon coming out to monogamous friends, are told, in essence, "You are a danger to our relationship. I don't want you near my spouse." Eve has lost several close male friends after coming out as poly. As a married woman, she had not been seen as a threat.

FRANKLIN'S STORY   Many years ago, when I first started dating Maryann, my new relationship caused conflict between my business partner at the time and his girlfriend. His girlfriend believed that Maryann was his "type," so when she and I started dating, his girlfriend became convinced that he would follow my lead and want a poly relationship too.

They argued about it for almost a week, in spite of the fact that my business partner had never expressed any interest in polyamory generally or in Maryann specifically.

We call this particular response "fear of the polyamorous possibility," a term coined by Dr. Elisabeth Sheff. Sometimes it is expressed as fear that poly people are always on the prowl. At its root, it's the fear that polyamory *offers an attractive option*—for your partner, and maybe for you. About all you can do when faced with this reaction is to explain that you're not interested in people in monogamous relationships. Don't expect that always to work, though. Sometimes you have to accept that you will lose friends.

EVE'S STORY   My very first coming-out story is a perfect horror story of what to avoid. Peter and I had made the decision to be poly the year before, but we were clueless in how to talk about it, or to whom, or how to meet people. I had a crush on his friend Justin, who was married to an acquaintance of mine, Jeanne. We decided it would be a good idea to come out to them by having Peter talk to Justin about our open relationship and my interest in Justin.

Their conversation went well, but Justin said that Jeanne would never accept an open relationship, and Peter and I considered the matter closed. Except that a few weeks later, Justin told Jeanne about the conversation. The next day, Jeanne sent me two of the most vitriolic, angry emails I have ever received, before or since. She had decided that my entire relationship with her had been a ploy to get to Justin, that I had been implementing a long-term master plan to manipulate her, or perhaps even go behind her back. She accused me of taking a desperate grasp at a fantasy and told me, "I will warn you to keep your eyes and your mind off my husband." I asked her to meet me to talk face-to-face, but she refused to see me.

This experience was the first time I realized just how far Peter and I really were from mainstream society: by the traditional script, I was clearly in the wrong, and Jeanne was absolutely right to hate and fear me. Until then, I had imagined we might be selling our friends short by not telling them, but with this, I began to doubt myself—and them.

Eve and Peter lost many friends besides Justin and Jeanne, even after learning the (rather obvious to them now) lesson that it's better to find out how people feel about polyamory—and you being poly—*before* you disclose an interest in them. This kind of rejection never happened again quite so dramatically, but many people gradually distanced themselves, stopped returning calls, changed the subject when we'd mention our other partners. Usually it didn't seem to be judgment that created the distance, only discomfort—a feeling that they were somehow no longer the same, that their friends couldn't relate to them. And to be fair, the experience was so chilling that they may have pulled away from other friends in the small community they lived in—which they left shortly thereafter, to move to a large city—purely out of self-defense.

COMING OUT POLY

Being open has a lot of personal advantages. It relieves what is for many a constant sense of tension and dread about what will happen if someone says the wrong thing or lets the wrong information slip. It's easier to be authentic to yourself when you don't need to hide who you are. It's easier to act with integrity when you're authentic to yourself. Not expecting partners to be closeted, and being willing to acknowledge partners as partners, helps promote strong, secure relationships.

EVE'S STORY   During the four years that Peter and I explored the idea of opening our relationship, without being sure what that would look like, we didn't talk to any of our friends or family about it.

Even when we bought a house with another family, we didn't come out to them. We saw it as part of our private sex lives, no one's business.

That all changed when I fell in love with Ray.

Ray was very quickly becoming an important part of my life, but one I couldn't mention. I would censor myself when I talked to my friends, and I realized that that wasn't okay. And falling for Ray was changing everything for me: who I was, what I wanted, what my marriage would look like from then on. If my friends were going to know me, they needed to know about Ray.

So I made a list of all the most important people in my life. And one by one, coffee after coffee, I came out to each one of them. For the most part, my friends lived up to the trust I'd given them. Though some fell by the wayside or pulled back, most were not only supportive of my choices, but have done their best to learn and understand, to ask questions and not make assumptions. They've been willing to spend time with my other partners and with Peter's other partners.

Then I came to the last name on the list. My mom. I'd always felt my mom held up my relationship with Peter as some kind of personal romantic ideal. When we separated, four years into our relationship, we never told her; we were too afraid of the pain the disappointment would cause. So it was pretty darn scary to tell her about being poly, that we weren't that romantic ideal and never would be.

Peter and I drove to meet my mom for dinner one evening and agreed that was when we'd tell her. On the drive there, I began to panic. Peter took my hand and asked me if I'd like him to do the talking; I said yes.

That may sound cowardly, but it turned out to be important. It's not just that Peter is a good talker. Hearing about my relationship with Ray in Peter's own words allowed my mother to see that he was on board with it, a full participant in our decision to be poly, and supportive of my relationship with Ray. If she hadn't heard it from Peter, she could have easily imagined that I was just cheating and we were trying to put a positive spin on it, or that I was taking advantage of Peter.

So you're ready to come out. How do you do it? Every person may have a different preferred approach. That said, some approaches succeed more often than others. You probably don't want to sit down at the Thanksgiving table and say, "Mom, Dad, I want you to know I'm having sex with a bunch of people. Pass the cranberry sauce?" Holidays can be stressful under the best of circumstances, with everyone hoping Uncle Bill won't repeat last year's incident with the lampshade and the toaster. Plus, coming out means revealing something deeply personal about yourself, and that usually works better as part of a private conversation.

A more successful approach might be "You know my friend Marcel, right? Who I spend a lot of time with? Marcel and I are in a romantic relationship. There's nothing wrong between Ambrose and me. Our relationship is excellent, and I'm grateful to have his support as I explore my relationship with Marcel. We're very happy together. I love you, and it's important for me to be authentic with you." Focus on the positive, without apology or evasion. You're here to share yourself, not to apologize for being who you are. Talk about how polyamory is a part of your life that makes you happy. Above all, remember the people you're talking to are people you want to share authenticity with.

It certainly helps to have your partners right there, or at least your socially recognized partner, as with Eve and Peter. This shows, in a way that can't be ignored, that your partners really are in on it and okay with it. Otherwise your listeners may sometimes assume you're not telling them the real story, or that you are deluded. Allow them time to process what they're hearing. The people who love you want what's best for you, even if they think what's best for you comes from a rigid social script. If someone reacts negatively, you may be tempted to respond defensively. Try not to do that. Be polite and cordial. Say "I would be happy to discuss this with you more, if you like." Be willing, if the other person is interested, to share what it is about your relationships that brings you joy. And then be prepared to give people space! It can take time for friends and family to come around to understanding that you're not a terrible cheater stepping out on your long-suffering partner or taking advantage of a string of lovers.

Being polyamorous is still not as well understood as, for example, being gay or bisexual. So it's likely that the people you come out to will have a lot of questions about what it means. It helps to have a short spiel about what polyamory is. You can explain the basics: It's a form of romantic relationship where you have more than one romantic partner at the same time with everybody's knowledge and consent. It's not a form of cheating, sanctioned or otherwise. The focus of polyamory is different from the focus in swinging, which tends to be more concerned with recreational sex rather than romantic relationships. It's not the same as polygamy, which is the practice of having multiple spouses. It's not about collecting a harem, as polyamory tends to give all the people involved freedom to be involved in more than one relationship at once. It doesn't mean that your existing relationship, if you have one, is in trouble.

It helps to start by telling people who are more likely to be supportive. Sometimes, if you have one family member you are sure will be a problem, coming out to more accepting friends or family first is useful, because they can act as allies when you talk to others. Even if they try to be supportive, people can also be unintentionally hurtful when they first learn about polyamory. If someone says, "Oh, I thought you and Olivia were happy," that doesn't necessarily mean they're trying to disparage your relationship. It may simply indicate an assumption that polyamory means you're dissatisfied with your partner. A simple, upbeat "Oh, we are! We love being together!" is a good way to address this response. Again, focus on the positive. Don't let the other person get under your skin.

Coming out doesn't have to involve a deep, serious conversation. Sometimes the easiest way is to let it arise naturally in a conversation.

"What did you do last night?"

"My boyfriend and I went out dancing with his wife and her girlfriend. We had a great time! There's a new place downtown that's really nice, though the band was only so-so."

Answer questions that come up, but don't feel compelled to share more information than the person you're talking to seems interested in hearing.

People take their cues for how to respond from the way you present something. If you're open and casual about coming out, people will tend to react like it's not a big deal. If you act like it's shameful or embarrassing, people will think it is. Anxiety about being out makes it more difficult to act casual, so the more you're worried about the way someone will respond, the more likely you'll receive a negative response, which increases your anxiety about coming out, which makes it more likely people will respond poorly...and so on.

Remember that coming out is a process, not something that happens in an instant. You might choose to come out to some people first, then gradually expand the circle.

Women coming out as polyamorous sometimes face greater social pushback than men do, because of the double standard that men with multiple partners are "studs" while women with multiple partners are "sluts." This double standard can result in much harsher judgment for women. It can be tempting to counter accusations of promiscuity by saying, "No, I'm not promiscuous, I'm very selective," or "I'm polyfidelitous," but that ends up reinforcing the double standard. It's a way of tacitly saying, "Yes, promiscuity is bad, but I'm not that way."

We don't know of any thirty-second elevator speech that effectively counters this ingrained social attitude. The best advice we can offer is to meet it with confidence and self-assurance. Keep your cool, respond calmly that a woman's value doesn't depend on her sex life or being opposed to sex, and above all, avoid internalizing this kind of judgment.

COMING OUT AND CHILDREN

One question nearly every poly parent has is when and how to explain things to children, and how much to disclose to them. The best guideline we know of, repeated to us over the years by dozens of poly parents, is to be open, within age-appropriate boundaries. For you to answer questions honestly as they arise may be all many children need or want; you may never need to have a serious sit-down talk about your lifestyle (although your child may some-day want to initiate one). The healthiest poly homes we know of are the ones where the parents are open about their partners.

Trying to conceal relationships from children is unlikely to work and may lead them to feel that your relationships are somehow shameful or dirty. At the same time, there's rarely a need to disclose *anything* about your sex life to your kids, except—perhaps—when it's time to have the safety talk with them about their own sex lives. "You know how Mom's boyfriend has two other girlfriends? Well, here's how we keep that safe." In between, well...your three-year-old probably doesn't need to know that your good buddy Brian is anything other than a friend who loves Daddy. Your six-year-old is likely to pick up that Brian is pretty special to Dad, and by eight years old, she'll have probably figured out that Brian is Daddy's boyfriend.

The situation is a little different if you have older kids and decide to open your relationship. Your children won't have grown up accustomed to having other partners around. Then you probably will need to have the Talk. You will likely find it easier to come out to them once you actually have a new partner, or at least when someone's on the horizon. Again, you don't need to disclose more than is appropriate for your child's age. A younger child may just need to know that the new person is important; an older one should be told that they are a partner. You may or may not choose to go into the word *polyamory*.

Your child will need many of the same reassurances as adults: That your being poly doesn't mean the parents don't love each other anymore. That it doesn't mean you're going to have a string of strangers parading through the house. That you are committed to keeping them safe and happy, and that you want to know about any concerns they have about any partner of yours.

When Franklin's partner Vera came out to her daughter Angelica, who was six, Angelica asked for veto power over Vera's partners. Vera told her no, but said that she could always talk about a concern, that she had a right to get to know Vera's partners, and that she had a right to continue to see Vera's partners even after Vera was no longer involved with them, if she wanted.

Be prepared for the possibility that your children, particularly preteens or teenagers, will reject your polyamory outright. It may take them years to understand and accept. In fact, polyamory may become part of the focus of their teenage rebellion. They may hurl toxic judgments at you, as happens to lots of parents with teenagers; you've just given them a special target. The fact that it's to be expected—and ultimately not about you—doesn't mean it won't hurt. Have faith that by the time they are adults, they are likely to come around.

Children also complicate whether to be out publicly. Depending on where you live, you and your kids may experience stigma, and you may even face legal threats. Particularly in some conservative areas of the United States, polyamory can be and is used as a powerful weapon in custody battles. (In most parts of Canada, where polyamory has been recognized by the courts as legal, evidence of polyamory is very hard to admit into child custody or child protection cases.) Teachers and other parents may react badly to your lifestyle and end up taking it out on the kids. These are all considerations in the decision whether to be out.

Many poly parents are out in their wider communities, and—sometimes after a period of adjustment—many find that it presents little difficulty. (Your mileage may vary, of course: this is very location-specific.) Even if you live in a fairly accepting community, you may find that your kids feel embarrassed about not having a "normal" family. It's a good idea to think about how to balance your own need to be out against your kids' needs or desires for privacy, especially as they get older.

COMING OUT TO THERAPISTS AND HEALTH CARE PROFESSIONALS

We believe it's very important to be honest about polyamory with certain people. As Franklin's mom says, "Never lie to your doctor or your lawyer. They can't help you if they don't know the truth." Most doctors will probably assume, if not told otherwise, that their patients are straight, cisgender and monogamous. Being polyamorous is not the STI risk that some people believe it to be, but it does raise your risk profile. Some doctors are reluctant to give STI tests to patients who are married or in long-term relationships, for example, because they assume the tests are unnecessary.

With therapists or counselors, being out is arguably even more important. Being able to talk freely to your therapist is essential to effective therapy. More to the point, if your therapist judges you or tries to pin whatever problems you have on polyamory, you have a bad therapist. You want to discover that so you can get a different one.

Coming out to a health care professional means, as with anyone else, overcoming your fear of judgment or disapproval. But remember that your doctor and your therapist are your employees. You're paying them to render a professional service. Professional ethics require them to conduct themselves appropriately, regardless of their personal beliefs about relationships.

If you're not out to others, you may be concerned that a health care professional might out you to family members, your employer or other people. In most cases this is a violation of professional ethics, may be against the law and may give you grounds to sue. Patient confidentiality is an important part of the health care system; without it, people can't be expected to open up about important things. Nevertheless, some doctors and, slightly more often, therapists do behave unethically, so the risk of you being out to them is not zero.

Franklin has a speech he uses with any new medical professional that goes something like this: "If you and I are going to work together, there are some things you need to know about me. One is that I am polyamorous. I have multiple sexual partners, with the knowledge of everyone involved. I am aware of STI risks and I take care to talk to all my partners about our health boundaries. We take safer-sex measures as appropriate. I am also involved in consensual BDSM activities with some of my partners. This means there may be times when there are marks on my body. This does not indicate I am in an abusive relationship. If you have any questions or concerns, please ask me now, and I would be happy to talk to you about them. If you have a problem with this, please let me know, as I don't believe we will be a good fit for each other."

There are booklets and resources on the Web for therapists and other professionals explaining what they need to know about polyamorous relationships. If you're concerned that your therapist won't know how to talk to you about your romantic life, see the links to these at the end of this book. It pays to ask other poly folks for referrals to doctors or other professionals. Finding a poly-aware professional can save you a lot of stress, and you shouldn't have to teach a professional about polyamory on your dime. If you can't get a referral, you can try a Web search for "poly-aware professionals," though that's more likely to succeed in or near a large North American city. Directories of queer-friendly or kink-friendly professionals can also be quite helpful, as these people tend to also be poly-aware or at least not sex-negative.

There's a special pitfall in working with a health care professional who is herself part of an alternative community: you may end up meeting them in a social context. Handling this overlap requires impeccable boundaries and integrity on the part of the professional. We've seen it handled very badly, with serious negative consequences. The person you're working with should normally be covered by some sort of licensing board or professional association, which will usually have a code of ethics. Such codes normally discourage social contact outside the professional relationship.

LETTING YOUR LOVED ONES LOVE YOU

Accepting you as poly may be a big step for the people close to you. They may feel they don't know you as well as they thought they did, or that you're a different person than they thought you were. Over time, most will come to see that you are still the same person they've always cared about. The truth is that most people—though certainly not all—will eventually adjust their worldview a bit to make it big enough to fit someone they love, rather than become permanently estranged from a close friend or family member. Coming to terms with you being poly may force them to confront inner demons of their own. This can take time.

EVE'S STORY   It took time for my mother to come to terms with my polyamory. I gave her books, which she read. She had occasional "Where did I go wrong?" moments. At first she resisted meeting Ray, though eventually she did. That helped: she was able to see him as a real person, and our relationship as a real thing, and see how much we cared about each other. About a month later she sent me this email, with a request to share it with Peter and Ray:

My Dearest Eve, Peter, and Ray,

I began reading the books you lent me on polyamory, starting with the Wendy-O Matik book because it looked like it would be quick and easy to read, and that resulted in quite an epiphany when I found myself reading the same things I thought, believed in, and forgot decades ago.

Years ago, before I met any of you, I figured out about love and loving and being loved. I believed it and preached it, and when I had an opportunity to actually do it, guess what? I totally fucked it up! And by that, I mean I not only failed to make it work by not even beginning to practice what I'd been loudly and vehemently preaching to anybody with the patience to listen, but I did as much damage as I possibly could to as many people as possible (including, but unfortunately by no means limited to, myself), and emerged feeling aggrieved and self-righteous about it all.

So you might think that, when you told me you had decided polyamory was right for you, I reacted with anxiety and defensiveness because I'd had such a devastating experience myself, but you would be wrong. I reacted that way because I sensed something really ugly was lurking beneath the surface of my integrity with which, whether I chose to or not, I was about to come face to face.

I'm guessing the point of dredging all this up now is that maybe it will leave me free to love all of you, and the other friends and lovers that will come into your lives, respect the choices you have made, and be proud of your courage, independence, and ability to love in ways for which you will find very little support and much discouragement. Anyway, that's my hope.

I'm entirely supportive of the way you have determined to live your lives and delighted that my daughter has two such wonderful men in her life.

Much, much love,

Mom

When we make ourselves vulnerable to others, we do more than show them how we value their friendship. We show that we trust them and are willing to be seen by them. We choose to let them show us the best of themselves. This is, perhaps, the best reason to come out to those we love.

QUESTIONS TO ASK YOURSELF

It's important to consider whether you have an adequate social support system when you begin polyamorous relationships. It's also important to carefully consider why you choose to remain closeted or to come out, and the effects that this decision will have on you and those close to you. Here are some things to think about:

*   *Do I have access to a social support system that is friendly to and knowledgeable about polyamory?*

- *Do I feel like I have friends I can discuss relationship problems with who will not blame polyamory as the problem?*

- *Who in my life is important for me to be able to talk to about my relationships? Whom do I think it's important for my partners to meet?*

- *If I am thinking about staying closeted, how will I feel about concealing my important relationships from people who are close to me?*

- *What risks do I face—including personal, professional or physical—in being public about my polyamorous relationships? Are these risks I can afford to take?*

- *If I am thinking of staying closeted, is it because I face genuine and serious risks, or am I concerned about being inconvenienced or losing status?*

- *Who else is affected by my decision to be out or closeted? Do I understand the effects my decision will have on them?*

LAST WORDS:
LOVE MORE, BE AWESOME

He loved her, of course,
but better than that,
he chose her, day after day.
Choice: that was the thing.

SHERMAN ALEXIE

Amid all the boundary-setting and agreement-making, the time management and the emotional processing, the balancing of needs and desires and the realities of life, it's easy to lose the thread of *why* we're doing this at all. Why are we poly? Hell, why do we have any relationships?

It's important, and useful, to come back often to the root of polyamory: love. We have relationships because we, as human beings, are wired to love. And without love as the core of our relationships, and as the principle we come back to in everything we do in those relationships, the other principles—as indispensable as they are—aren't going to get us anywhere. Love is the great clarifier of values. Without it, whatever framework we create will remain hollow and, ultimately, lifeless.

For a surprising number of problems, the solution is in fact *more love.* The principle of more love can cut through many dilemmas in relationships. Listen. Cherish your partners. Cherish *yourself.* Trust your partners. Be trustworthy. Honor others' feelings and your own. Seek joy for everyone involved.

As we researched this book and collected people's stories, we were struck by how often it seemed like the people who were able to navigate their way through poly situations that would have devastated others did so by *being awesome*. They did the hard work, they cared about each other, they didn't give in, they reasoned with their overpowering emotions. They set compassionate boundaries. They honored their loves' agency even when they were afraid of losing what they valued most. They faced their own deepest fears for the sake of themselves and the people they cared about. Being awesome is such a valuable skill to cultivate that we offer it here, along with more love, as a key takeaway from this book. When faced with a challenging situation, the simple pledge to yourself to be awesome will carry you and your relationships very far indeed.

In the end, a recipe for successful relationships might look like this:

Be flexible. Be compassionate. Rules can never cure insecurity. Integrity matters. Never try to script what your relationships will look like. Love is abundant. Compatibility matters. You cannot sacrifice your happiness for that of another. Own your own shit. Admit when you fuck up. Forgive when others fuck up. Don't try to find people to stuff into the empty spaces in your life; instead, make spaces for the people in your life. If you need a relationship to complete you, get a dog. It is almost impossible to be loving or compassionate when all you feel is fear of loss. Trust that your partners want to be with you, and that if given the freedom to do anything they please, they will choose to cherish and support you. Most relationship problems can be avoided by good partner selection. Nobody can give you security or self-esteem; you have to build that yourself.

And if you remember nothing else from this book, remember this: Love more and be awesome.

GLOSSARY

You'll find a more comprehensive glossary of terms related to polyamory and other forms of open relationships at *morethantwo.com*.

ANCHOR PARTNER. A partner with whom you share a close, long-term, committed connection. May be a live-in partner with financial entanglements; relationship may include an expectation of a significant time commitment.

ASEXUALITY. A lack of sexual interest in other people, or a lack of interest in sexual activity. A person who is not sexually attracted to others may identify as asexual.

BISEXUAL. Used to describe someone who is sexually attracted to or sexually active with partners of both sexes, though not necessarily equally.

CHEATING. In a relationship, any activity that violates the rules or agreements of that relationship.

CISGENDER. A person who identifies as the same gender that was assigned to them at birth.

CLOSED GROUP MARRIAGE. A polyfidelitous relationship in which all the members consider themselves to be married.

CLOSED RELATIONSHIP. Any romantic relationship, such as a conventional monogamous relationship or a polyfidelitous relationship, that specifically excludes the possibility of sexual or romantic connections with others.

COMPERSION. A feeling of joy experienced when a partner takes pleasure from another romantic or sexual relationship.

CONDOM COMPACT. An agreement within a group to use barriers for sex with people outside the group, but not with others in the group.

COUPLE PRIVILEGE. External social structures or internal assumptions that consciously or unconsciously place a couple at the center of a relationship hierarchy or grant special advantages to a couple.

COWBOY, COWGIRL. A monogamous person who engages in a relationship with a polyamorous partner with the hope or intention of separating the poly partner from any other partners and bringing him or her into a monogamous relationship.

DEMISEXUAL. Used to describe a person who is largely asexual but may develop sexual attraction after a stable emotional connection is established.

DON'T ASK, DON'T TELL. A relationship structure in which a person who is partnered is permitted to have additional sexual or romantic relationships on the condition that his or her partner does not know anything about those additional relationships and does not meet any of those other people.

DYAD. The relationship between any two people, distinct from the connections either person has with anyone else.

EXCLUSIVE RELATIONSHIP. See closed relationship.

FLUID BONDING. 1. Practices that involve the exchange of bodily fluids from the genitals, such as barrier-free sex. 2. A set of boundaries, agreements or rules between two or more people who are engaging in unbarriered sex designed to protect the fluid-bonded status.

FRUBBLE, FRUBBLY (BRITISH). See compersion.

GROUP MARRIAGE. See closed group marriage, polyfidelity.

HETERONORMATIVE. Assumptions and presumed social roles that promote the idea of heterosexual relationships as the norm and that equate biological sex, gender identity and gender roles.

HIERARCHY, HIERARCHICAL RELATIONSHIP. An arrangement in which one relationship is subject to control or rule-making by participants in another relationship. Usually involves veto; may also involve restrictions on activities, commitment, entanglement, time or emotions.

INTIMATE NETWORK. *See* romantic network.

LIFE PARTNER. A partner, usually a romantic and/or sexual partner, with whom one has the intent of a long-lasting and intertwined committed relationship.

METAMOUR. A partner's other partner.

MOLECULE. Used to describe a set or subset of polyamorous relationships, such as a triad, vee or quad, or a complete *romantic network*. *See also* polycule.

MONOGAMY. The state or practice of having only one sexual partner or romantic relationship at a time.

MONO/POLY. A relationship between someone who self-identifies as polyamorous and someone who self-identifies as monogamous.

NEW RELATIONSHIP ENERGY (NRE). A strong, almost giddy feeling of excitement and infatuation common in the beginning of any new romantic relationship, which usually lasts for a few months but can last as long as several years.

ONE-PENIS POLICY. An arrangement in which a man is allowed to have multiple female partners, each of whom is allowed to have sex with other women but may not have any other male partners.

OPEN MARRIAGE. Any marriage whose structures or arrangements permit one or both of the members involved to have other sexual relationships, romantic relationships, or both. The term *open marriage* is a catchall for marriages that are not emotionally or sexually monogamous, and may include such activities as polyamory or swinging.

OPEN NETWORK. A relationship structure in which the people involved are free to add new partners as they choose.

OPEN RELATIONSHIP. 1. Any relationship that is not sexually monogamous. 2. A relationship that permits "outside" sexual entanglements, but not loving or romantic relationships.

OTHER SIGNIFICANT OTHER (OSO). 1. A partner's other partner. 2. A person's partner when that person has more than one partner: *Bob is my husband, and Joe is my other significant other.*

PIVOT. The person "in the middle," with two or more partners.

POLY. Something that is polyamorous or about polyamory: a poly relationship, a poly person, a poly discussion group.

POLYANDRY. One woman with multiple husbands, the less common type of polygamy.

POLYCULE. A *romantic network,* or a particular subset of relationships within a *romantic network,* whose members are closely connected. Also used to describe a sketch or visualization of a *romantic network,* as these drawings often resemble the depiction of molecules used in organic chemistry.

POLYFAMILY. 1. A set of polyamorous people who live together and identify as part of the same family. 2. A polyamorous group whose members consider one another to be family, regardless of whether or not they share a home.

POLYFIDELITY. A group of people who are romantically or sexually involved with one another, but whose agreements do not permit them to seek additional partners, at least without the approval and consent of everyone in the group.

POLYGAMY. Having multiple wedded spouses at the same time, regardless of the gender of those spouses. *Polygyny*—one man with multiple wives—is the most common form of polygamy in societies that permit multiple spouses. For that reason, many people confuse the two.

POLYSATURATED. Describes someone who is polyamorous, but not currently open to new relationships or new partners because of the number of existing partners, or because of time constraints that might make new relationships difficult.

PRIMARY/SECONDARY. A hierarchical relationship structure in which the partners who are higher in the hierarchy are referred to as "primary" and other partners are referred to as "secondary." Sometimes used to describe a non-hierarchical relationship structure in partners are not equal to one another in terms of interconnection, emotional intensity or entwinement in practical or financial matters. (We discourage the latter use, which is becoming less common among poly people.)

QUAD. A polyamorous arrangement involving four people, each of whom may or may not be sexually or emotionally involved with all the other members. This arrangement often begins with two couples. Quads may also be part of a larger *romantic network*.

RELATIONSHIP ANARCHY (RA). A philosophy or practice in which people are seen as free to engage in any relationships they choose, spontaneity and freedom are valued, no relationship is entered into or restricted from a sense of duty or obligation, and any relationship choice is considered allowable. Relationship anarchists often do not make a clear distinction between "partner" and "non-partner."

RELATIONSHIP ESCALATOR. The default set of social assumptions concerning the "normal" course of a relationship, usually proceeding from dating to moving in together to getting married and having children.

ROMANTIC NETWORK. The sum total of a person's partners, those partners' partners, and so on. Usually used to describe an open network. Usually includes smaller molecules such as vees, triads or quads.

SECONDARY. *See* primary/secondary.

SWINGING. The practice of having multiple sexual partners outside of an existing romantic relationship, most often engaged in by couples as an organized activity, and with the understanding that the focus of those relationships is primarily sexual rather than romantic or emotionally intimate.

TRIAD. A polyamorous arrangement in which three people are involved with one another. Occasionally applied to vees. Triads may also be part of a larger *romantic network.*

TRIGGER. A specific thought, action, sight or event that sets off an emotion that is usually linked to past traumatic events and may not actually be related to the current, triggering situation.

UNICORN. A hypothetical woman who is willing to be involved with both members of an existing couple, to have no relationships other than with the members of the couple, to not be sexually involved with one member of the couple unless the other member of the couple is also there, and usually to move in with the couple.

VEE. A polyamorous arrangement involving three people, in which one person is romantically or sexually involved with two partners who are not romantically or sexually involved with each other. Vees may also be part of a larger romantic network.

VETO. A relationship agreement, most common in prescriptive primary/secondary relationships, which gives one person the power to end another person's additional relationships, or in some cases to disallow some specific activity.

WIBBLE, WIBBLY (BRITISH). A feeling of insecurity, typically temporary or fleeting, when seeing a partner being affectionate with someone else. Sometimes used to describe minor pangs of jealousy.

NOTES

2   THE MANY FORMS OF LOVE

27   **Statistics**   Barry W. McCarthy and Maria Thestrup, "Couple Therapy and the Treatment of Sexual Dysfunction," in *Clinical Handbook of Couple Therapy,* 4th ed., ed. Alan S. Gurman, 591–617 (New York: Guilford Press, 2009), 593.

27–28   **Celibacy**   Kinsey Institute, "Frequency of Sex," *Frequently Asked Sexuality Questions to the Kinsey Institute,* http://www.kinseyinstitute.org/resources/FAQ. html#frequency (last updated July 21, 2012; accessed November 12, 2013).

9   BOUNDARIES

157   **"Tests" a predator gives**   Gavin de Becker, *The Gift of Fear: Survival Signals That Protect Us from Violence* (New York: Dell, 1998).

10   RULES AND AGREEMENTS

169–170   **An inverse relationship to trust**   Andrea Zanin, "The Problem with Polynormativity," Sex Geek [Blog] (January 24, 2013), http://sexgeek.wordpress.com/2013/01/24/theproblemwithpolynormativity.

12   VETO ARRANGEMENTS

205–6   **Starting the feedback**   Mistress Matisse, "Poly Power of Veto," Control Tower [Column], *The Stranger* (September 13, 2007), http://www.thestranger.com/seattle/control-tower-and-kink-calendar/ Content?oid=316814.

14   PRACTICAL POLY AGREEMENTS

236   **Novel situations**   See, for example, Timothy D. Wilson and Daniel T. Gilbert, "Affective Forecasting," *Advances in Experimental Social Psychology* 35 (2003): 345–411.

236   **I will limit you**   Zanin, "Problem with Polynormativity."

15   HOW POLY RELATIONSHIPS ARE DIFFERENT

259   **Phenylethylamine**   H. Sabelli and J. Javaid, "Phenylethylamine Modulation of Affect: Therapeutic and Diagnostic Implications," *Journal of Neuropsychiatry and Clinical Neuroscience* 7 (1995): 6–14; D. Marazziti and D. Canale, "Hormonal Changes When Falling in Love," *Psychoneuroendocrinology* 29 (2004): 931–36.

260   **Limerence**   Dorothy Tennov, *Love and Limerence: The Experience of Being in Love,* 2nd ed. (Lanham, MD: Scarborough House, 1998).

268   **Long-term outcomes for kids**   Elisabeth Sheff, *The Polyamorists Next Door: Inside Multiple-Partner Relationships and Families* (Lanham, MD: Rowman & Littlefield, 2013).

269–70   **Parental shaming**   Sheryl Sandberg, *Lean In: Women, Work, and the Will to Lead* (New York: Alfred A. Knopf, 2013): 134–39.

269   **Guilt management**   Ibid., 137.

16   IN THE MIDDLE

280   **Ping-pong poly**   Ferret Steinmetz, "Failure Patterns in Poly: The Ping-Pong Partner," The Ferret [blog] (December 16, 2013), http://www.theferrett.com/ferrettworks/2013/12/failure-patterns-in-poly-the-ping-pong-partner.

288–90   **Monkeys and cucumbers**   Frans de Waal (Director), *Moral Behavior in Animals* (TEDxPeachtree, Atlanta, GA, November 2011), video, http://www.ted.com/talks/frans_de_waal_do_animals_have_morals.

17   OPENING FROM A COUPLE

297   **Swinging chapter**   Dan Savage, *Skipping Towards Gomorrah: The Seven Deadly Sins and the Pursuit of Happiness in America* (New York: Penguin, 2003).

18   MONO/POLY RELATIONSHIPS

314   **Column on cowboys**   Mistress Matisse, "Cowboys and Injuries: When Monogamists Pursue the Polyamorous," Control Tower [Column], *The Stranger* (July 29, 2010), http://www.thestranger.com/seattle/control-tower/Content?oid=4555764.

19   SEX AND LAUNDRY

343   **Survey**   Kinsey Institute, "Frequency of Sex," see note for pages 27–28.

Sources for chapter 20 begin on the next page.

21   POLY PUZZLES

379   **Bipolar disorder**   Jules Angst, "The Emerging Epidemiology of Hypomania and Bipolar II Disorder," *Journal of Affective Disorders* 50, no. 2 (September 1998): 143–51.

22   RELATIONSHIP TRANSITIONS

384   **Grandmother's unhappy marriage**   Dan Savage, *The Commitment: Love, Sex, Marriage, and My Family* (New York: Penguin, 2005): 113.

24   FINDING PARTNERS

419   **"Fuck yes" or no**   Mark Manson, "'Fuck Yes' or No," Mark Manson [blog] (July 8, 2013), http://markmanson.net/fuck-yes.

20   SEXUAL HEALTH

All online sources in this list and the chart sources, unless otherwise indicated, were accessed March 2014.

348   **Several studies**   See, for example, L. J. Bauman and R. Berman, "Adolescent Relationships and Condom Use: Trust, Love and Commitment," *AIDS and Behavior* 9, no. 2 (2005): 211–22; W. Glauser, "How to Talk to Patients about STI Screening," *Medical Post* 47, no. 7 (2011): 24; and M. P. Bolton, A. McKay, and M. Schneider, "Relational Influences on Condom Use Discontinuation: A Qualitative Study of Young Adult Women in Dating Relationships," *Canadian Journal of Human Sexuality* 19, no. 3 (2010): 91–104.

348   **Risk of STI infection**   T. D. Conley et al., "Unfaithful Individuals Are Less Likely to Practice Safer Sex Than Openly Nonmonogamous Individuals," *Journal of Sexual Medicine* 9 (2012): 1559–65.

350   **Antiretroviral drugs**   Jared M. Baeten et al., "Antiretroviral Prophylaxis for HIV Prevention in Heterosexual Men and Women," *New England Journal of Medicine* 367 (2012): 399–410; Robert M. Grant et al., "Preexposure Chemoprophylaxis for HIV Prevention in Men Who Have Sex with Men," *New England Journal of Medicine* (2010): 363: 2587–99.

351   **Effectiveness of barriers**   L. E. Manhart and L. A. Koutsky, "Do Condoms Prevent Genital HPV Infection, External Genital Warts, or Cervical Neoplasia? A Meta-analysis," *Sexually Transmitted Diseases* 29 (2002): 725–35; Emily T. Martin et al., "A Pooled Analysis of the Effect of Condoms in Preventing HSV-2 Acquisition," *Archives of Internal Medicine* 169, no. 13 (July 13, 2009): 1233–40.

351–52   **Assessment of risk**   W. M. Klein and Z. Kunda, "Exaggerated Self-Assessments and the Preference for Controllable Risks," *Organizational Behavior and Human Decision Processes* 59 (1994): 410–27.

352   **Win the lottery**   Mike Orkin, *Can You Win? The Real Odds for Casino Gambling, Sports Betting and Lotteries* (New York: W. H. Freeman & Co., 1991).

352   **Perception of risk**   Mehdi Moussaïd, "Opinion Formation and the Collective Dynamics of Risk Perception," *PLOS ONE* 8, no. 12 (December 30, 2013): e84592, doi:10.1371/journal.pone.0084592.

352   **No direct benefit**   Paul Slovic and Ellen Peters, "Risk Perception and Affect," *Current Directions in Psychological Science* 15 (2006): 322.

352   **Herpes 1**   Richard P. Usatine and Rochelle Tinitigan, "Nongenital Herpes Simplex Virus," *American Family Physician* 82, no. 9 (November 1, 2010): 1075–82.

355   **Have herpes themselves**   L. Newson, "Clinical: The Basics—Herpes Infections," *GP*, 34 (June 19, 2009), http://go.galegroup.com/ps/i.do?id=GALE%7CA202043631&v=2.1&u=ubcol umbia&it=r&p=HRCA&sw=w&asid=7083d653cc68ce0be1722e49d0f622fa; R. Gupta, T. Warren, and A. Wald, "Genital Herpes," *Lancet* 307 (2007): 2127–37; "An estimated 13.6% of Canadians (2.9 million) tested positive for HSV-2"; "Among those who tested positive for HSV-2, 6% reported having been diagnosed

with the infection; 94% were unaware that they were infected." M. Rotermann et al., "Prevalence of Chlamydia Trachomatis and Herpes Simplex Virus Type 2: Results from the 2009 to 2011 Canadian Health Measures Survey," *Health Reports* 24, no. 4 (April 2013): 13, 12. http://www.statcan.gc.ca/pub/82-003-x/2013004/article/11777-eng.pdf.

355   **Herpes statistics**   H. A. Beydoun et al., "Socio-demographic and Behavioral Correlates of Herpes Simplex Virus Type 1 and 2 Infections and Co-infections Among Adults in the USA," *International Journal of Infectious Diseases* 14S (2010): 154–60, doi:10.1016/j.ijid.2009.12.007; M. Gilbert, et al., "Using Centralized Laboratory Data to Monitor Trends in Herpes Simplex Virus Type 1 and 2 Infection in British Columbia and the Changing Etiology of Genital Herpes," *Canadian Journal of Public Health* 102, no. 3 (2011): 225–29.

355–56   **Possible consequences**   The United States has more than 10 million car crashes each year, killing more than 30,000 people. Your lifetime odds of dying in a car crash in the United States are 1 in 108. If HSV and HPV are included, most people will encounter an STI in their lifetime, but very few of those will suffer serious, let alone fatal, consequences. For example, although about 80 percent of unvaccinated people will have an HPV infection in their lifetimes, only 1 in 435 women will die of cervical cancer—and other avoidable risk factors, such as smoking and failing to have Pap tests, also affect that number. Car crash statistics: National Safety Council, "Lifetime Odds of Death for Selected Causes, United States, 2009a," *Injury Facts* (2013), http://www.nsc.org/news_resources/injury_and_death_statistics/Documents/Injury_Facts_43.pdf.; Deaths from cervical cancer: American Cancer Society, Cancer.org, "Lifetime Risk of Developing or Dying from Cancer," http://www.cancer.org/cancer/cancerbasics/lifetime-probability-of-developing-or-dying-from-cancer (last updated September 5, 2013).

356–57   **Subpopulations at greater risk**   U.S. Centers for Disease Control and Prevention (hereafter CDC), "Estimated Lifetime Risk for Diagnosis of HIV Infection Among Hispanics/Latinos—37 States and Puerto Rico, 2007," *Morbidity and Mortality Weekly Report* 59, no. 40 (October 15, 2010): 1297–1301, http://www.cdc.gov/mmwr/preview/mmwrhtml/mm5940a2.htm.

357   **Men who have sex with men**   CDC, "Trends in HIV/AIDS Diagnoses Among Men Who Have Sex with Men—33 States, 2001–2006," *Morbidity and Mortality Weekly Report* 57, no. 25 (June 27, 2008): 681–86.

360   **Chlamydia statistics**   CDC, "Chlamydia—CDC Fact Sheet," http://www.cdc.gov/std/Chlamydia/STDFact-Chlamydia.htm (last updated March 13, 2014); CDC, "2012 Sexually Transmitted Diseases Surveillance: Chlamydia," http://www.cdc.gov/std/stats12/chlamydia.htm (last updated January 7, 2014).

360   **Chlamydia transmssion**   U.K. National Health Service, "Chlamydia—Symptoms," http://www.nhs.uk/Conditions/Chlamydia/Pages/Symptoms.aspx (last updated August 28, 2013).

360   **Treatment of partners**   H. Hunter Handsfield et al., *Expedited Partner Therapy in the Management of Sexually Transmitted Diseases* (Atlanta, GA: U.S. Department of Health and Human Services, 2006).

361   **Gonorrhea strains**   CDC, "Sexually Transmitted Diseases (STDs): Antibiotic-Resistant Gonorrhea Basic Information," http://www.cdc.gov/std/Gonorrhea/arg/basic.htm (last updated November 18, 2013).

361   **Syphilis transmission**   K. Eccleston, L. Collins, and S. P. Higgins, "Primary Syphilis," *International Journal of STD & AIDS* 19, no. 3 (March 2008): 145–51, doi:10.1258/ijsa.2007.007258; C. A. Koss, E. F. Dunne, and L. Warner, "A Systematic Review of Epidemiologic Studies Assessing Condom Use and Risk of Syphilis," *Sexually Transmitted Diseases* 36, no. 7 (July 2009): 401–5, doi:10.1097/OLQ.0b013e3181a396eb.

361   **HIV statistics**   Public Health Agency of Canada, "Summary: Estimates of HIV Prevalence and Incidence in Canada, 2011" (2012), http://webqa.phac-aspc.gc.ca/aids-sida/publication/survreport/estimat2011-eng.php.

361–62   **HIV transmission**   Canadian AIDS Society, *HIV Transmission: Factors that Affect Biological Risk* (2013); Richard Crosby and Sarah Bounse, "Condom Effectiveness: Where Are We Now?" *Sexual Health* 9, no. 1 (2012): 10–17, http://dx.doi.org/10.1071/SH11036; S. C. Weller and K. Davis-Beaty, "Condom Effectiveness in Reducing Heterosexual HIV Transmission (Review)," *Cochrane Collaboration* 4 (2007): 1–22, http://www.cdnaids.ca/home.nsf/ad7c054e653c96438525721a0050fd60/4d4cf1 6b70a7247f0525732500678839/$FILE/HIV_Transmission_Factors_that_Affect_ Biological_Risk.pdf.

362   **Hepatitis C**   CDC, "Viral Hepatitis" http://www.cdc.gov/Hepatitis (last updated March 20, 2014).

363   **Herpes statistics**   Fujie Xu et al., "Trends in Herpes Simplex Virus Type 1 and Type 2 Seroprevalence in the United States," *JAMA: Journal of the American Medical Association* 296, no. 8 (2006): 964–73, doi:10.1001/jama.296.8.964; Fujie Xu et al., "Seroprevalence of Herpes Simplex Virus Type 2 Among Persons Aged 14–49 Years—United States, 2005–2008," *Morbidity and Mortality Weekly Report* 59, no. 15 (April 23, 2010): 456–59.

364   **Herpes transmission**   American College of Nurse-Midwives, "Genital Herpes," *Journal of Midwifery & Women's Health* 58, no. 5 (2013): 597–98, doi:10.1111/jmwh.12062.

364   **HPV exposure**   Public Health Agency of Canada, "Human Papillomavirus (HPV)," http://www.phac-aspc.gc.ca/std-mts/hpv-vph/fact-faits-eng.php (last updated June 7, 2012); National Cancer Institute, "Understanding Cancer Series: HPV," http://www.cancer.gov/cancertopics/understandingcancer/HPV-vaccine/AllPages.

364   **HPV rates of infection**   HPVinfo.ca, "Incidence and Prevalence of HPV in Canada" (2007), http://www.hpvinfo.ca/health-care-professionals/what-is-hpv/incidence-and-prevalence-of-hpv-in-canada/.

365   **Cancer risks**   Cancer.org, "Lifetime Risk of Developing or Dying from Cancer," http://www.cancer.org/cancer/cancerbasics/lifetime-probability-of-developing-or-dying-from-cancer (last updated September 5, 2013).

365   **HPV infection**   L. Raphaelidis, "Making Sense of HPV," *Journal for Nurse Practitioners* 2, no.5 (May 2006): 329–32, doi:10.1016/j.nurpra.2006.04.012; CDC, "Incidence, Prevalence, and Cost of Sexually Transmitted Infections in the United States—CDC Fact Sheet" (February 2013), http://www.cdc.gov/std/stats/STI-Estimates-Fact-Sheet-Feb-2013.pdf.

365   **Co-infection**   H. Trottier et al., "Human Papillomavirus Infections with Multiple Types and Risk of Cervical Neoplasia," *Cancer Epidemiology, Biomarkers & Prevention* 15 (2006): 1274–80, doi:10.1158/1055-9965.EPI-06-0129; A. K. Chaturvedi et al., "Human Papillomavirus Infection with Multiple Types: Pattern of Coinfection and Risk of Cervical Disease," Journal of Infectious Diseases 20 (2011): 910–20, doi:10.1093/infdis/jiq139.

365   **Vaccines for HPV**   Public Health Agency of Canada, "Human Papillomavirus (HPV) Prevention and HPV Vaccines: Questions and Answers," http://www.phac-aspc.gc.ca/std-mts/hpv-vph/hpv-vph-vaccine-eng.php (last updated March 31, 2011). See also the Gardasil website, www.gardasil.com.

365   **Condoms and HPV**   S. Richards, "An Overview of Genital Warts," *Nursing Standard* 28, no. 24 (2014): 46–50, http://dx.doi.org/10.7748/ns2014.02.28.24.46.e8344; R. L. Winer et al., "Condom Use and the Risk of Genital Human Papillomavirus Infection in Young Women," *New England Journal of Medicine* 354, no. 25 (2006): 2645–54; K. K. Holmes, R. Levine, and M. Weaver, "Effectiveness of Condoms in Preventing Sexually Transmitted Infections," *Bulletin of the World Health Organization* 82, no. 6 (June 2004): 454–61.

365   **Higher-risk HPV infections**   Raphaelidis, "Making Sense of HPV," see note 2 for page 365.

365   **Controllable risk factor**   Eileen F. Dunne et al., "Prevalence of HPV Infection Among Females in the United States," *JAMA: Journal of the American Medical Association* 297 (2007): 813–19.

366   **Infectious disease statistics**   "List of Preventable Causes of Death," Wikipedia, note 5, citing A. H. Mokdad et al., "Actual Causes of Death in the United States, 2000," *JAMA: Journal of the American Medical Association* 291, no. 10 (March 2004): 1238–45, doi:10.1001/jama.291.10.1238, http://en.wikipedia.org/wiki/List_of_preventable_causes_of_death#cite_note-JAMA2000-5.

Sources for the chart on pages 358-59 are listed at the end of this section.

SOURCES FOR CHART, COMMON SEXUALLY TRANSMITTED INFECTIONS (STIs) (PAGES 358–59)

1   U.S. Centers for Disease Control and Prevention (CDC), "Chlamydia," *2012 Sexually Transmitted Diseases Surveillance,* http://www.cdc.gov/std/stats12/chlamydia.htm (last updated January 7, 2014).

2   Public Health Agency of Canada, *Report on Sexually Transmitted Infections in Canada 2010* (Centre for Communicable Diseases and Infection Control, Infectious Disease Prevention and Control Branch, 2012), http://publications.gc.ca/collections/collection_2013/aspc-phac/HP37-10-2010-eng.pdf.

3   Genome British Columbia, "BC Researcher Closing in on Chlamydia Vaccine," *News Releases* (February 25, 2014), http://www.genomebc.ca/index.php?cID=1478.

4   Smart Sex Resource, "Chlamydia," *A–Z Topics* (2012), http://smartsexresource.com/topics/chlamydia.

5   CDC, "Gonorrhea," *2012 Sexually Transmitted Diseases Surveillance,* http://www.cdc.gov/std/stats12/gonorrhea.htm (last updated January 7, 2014).

6   A. E. Jerse, M. C. Bash, and M. W. Russell, "Vaccines against Gonorrhea: Current Status and Future Challenges," *Vaccine* 32, no. 14 (2014): 1579–87, doi:10.1016/j.vaccine.2013.08.067.

7   CDC, "Gonorrhea—CDC Fact Sheet (Detailed Version)," *Gonorrhea,* http://www.cdc.gov/std/Gonorrhea/STDFact-gonorrhea-detailed.htm (last updated January 7, 2014).

8   Smart Sex Resource, "Gonorrhea," A–Z Topics (2012), http://smartsexresource.com/topics/gonorrhea.

9   CDC, "Syphilis," *2012 Sexually Transmitted Diseases Surveillance,* http://www.cdc.gov/std/stats12/syphilis.htm (last updated January 7, 2014).

10   C. E. Cameron and S. A. Lukehart, "Current Status of Syphilis Vaccine Development: Need, Challenges, Prospects," *Vaccine* 32, no. 14 (2014): 1602–09, doi:10.1016/j.vaccine.2013.09.053.

11   Smart Sex Resource, "Syphilis," *A–Z Topics* (2012), http://smartsexresource.com/topics/syphilis.

12   Central Intelligence Agency, "Country Comparison: HIV/AIDS—Adult Prevalence Rate," *The World Factbook,* https://www.cia.gov/library/publications/the-world-factbook/rankorder/2155rank.html.

13   Public Health Agency of Canada, "Summary: Estimates of HIV Prevalence and Incidence in Canada, 2011" (Centre for Communicable Diseases and Infection Control, Infectious Disease Prevention and Control Branch, 2012), http://www.phac-aspc.gc.ca/aids-sida/publication/survreport/estimat2011-eng.php.

14   CDC, "HIV in the United States: At a Glance," *HIV/AIDS,* http://www.cdc.gov/hiv/statistics/basics/ataglance.html (last updated December 3, 2013).

15 World Health Organization, "HIV Vaccines," *HIV/AIDS*, http://www.who.int/hiv/topics/vaccines/Vaccines/en/.

16 Ibid., "HIV/AIDS," *Online Q&A*, http://www.who.int/features/qa/71/en/ (last updated October 2013).

17 BC Centre for Disease Control, "Tests and Diagnosis," *HIV/AIDS Overview*, http://www.bccdc.ca/dis-cond/a-z/_h/HIVAIDS/overview/default. htm#heading5 (last updated November 18, 2013).

18 AIDSmeds, "Am I Infected? (A Guide to Testing for HIV)," http://www.aidsmeds.com/articles/HIVtests_4717.shtml (last updated June 4, 2013).

19 H. Bradley et al., "Seroprevalence of Herpes Simplex Virus Types 1 and 2—United States, 1999–2010," *Journal of Infectious Diseases* 209 (2014): 325–33, doi:10.1093/infdis/jit458.

20 Xu et al., "Trends in Herpes Simplex Virus," see note for page 363.

21 CDC, "Genital Herpes—CDC Fact Sheet (Detailed Version)," *Herpes*, http://www.cdc.gov/std/herpes/stdfact-herpes-detailed.htm (last updated February 13, 2013).

22 Ibid., "Genital Herpes—CDC Fact Sheet," *Herpes*, http://www.cdc.gov/std/herpes/stdfact-herpes.htm (last updated March 20, 2014).

23 Smart Sex Resource, "Herpes Simplex Virus," *A–Z Topics*, http://smartsexresource.com/topics/herpes-simplex-virus.

24 L. Corey and H. H. Handsfield, "Genital Herpes and Public Health: Addressing a Global Problem," *Journal of the American Medical Association* 283, no. 6 (2000): 791–94, doi:10.1001/jama.283.6.791.

25 L. Newson, "Clinical: The Basics—Herpes Infections," *GP* (June 19, 2009): 34, http://go.galegroup.com/ps/i.do?id=GALE%7CA202043631&v=2.1&u=ubcolum bia&it=r&p=HRCA&sw=w&asid=7083d653cc68ce0be1722e49d0f622fa.

26 Rotermann et al., "Prevalence of Chlamydia Trachomatis and Herpes Simplex Virus Type 2," 10–15, see note for page 355.

27 E. F. Dunne et al., "Prevalence of HPV Infection Among Females in the United States," *Journal of the American Medical Association* 297, no. 8 (2007): 813–19, doi:10.1001/jama.297.8.813.

28 CDC, "Other Sexually Transmitted Diseases," *2012 Sexually Transmitted Diseases Surveillance*, http://www.cdc.gov/std/stats12/other.htm (last updated January 7, 2014).

29 Ibid., "Genital HPV Infection—Fact Sheet," *Human Papilloma Virus (HPV)*, http://www.cdc.gov/std/hpv/stdfact-hpv.htm (last updated March 20, 2014).

30 Smart Sex Resource, "Types of STIs," *About STIs* (2012), http://smartsexresource.com/about-stis/types-stis.

31 Ibid., "Screening," *Human Papilloma Virus (HPV)*, http://www.cdc.gov/hpv/screening.html (last updated February 5, 2013).

32 Public Health Agency of Canada, "What Everyone Should Know about Human Papillomavirus (HPV): Questions and Answers," http://www.phac-aspc.gc.ca/std-mts/hpv-vph/hpv-vph-qaqr-eng.php (last updated October 9, 2012).

33   CDC, "Table 2.1 Reported Cases of Acute Hepatitis A, by State—United States, 2007–2011," *Viral Hepatitis Statistics & Surveillance,* http://www.cdc.gov/hepatitis/Statistics/2011Surveillance/Table2.1.htm (last updated August 19, 2013).

34   Public Health Agency of Canada, "Hepatitis A Vaccine," *Canadian Immunization Guide,* http://www.phac-aspc.gc.ca/publicat/cig-gci/p04-hepa-eng.php (last updated November 30, 2012).

35   Smart Sex Resource, "Hepatitis A," *A–Z Topics* (2012), http://smartsexresource.com/topics/hepatitis.

36   CDC, "Table 3.4: Reported Cases of Laboratory-Confirmed, Chronic Hepatitis B Virus (HBV) Infection, by Sex, Race/Ethnicity, Age Group, Place of Birth and Case Criteria—Emerging Infections Program (EIP) Hepatitis Surveillance Demonstration Sites, 2011," *Viral Hepatitis Statistics & Surveillance,* http://www.cdc.gov/hepatitis/Statistics/2011Surveillance/Table3.4.htm (last updated August 19, 2013).

37   Public Health Agency of Canada, "What You Need to Know: You Can Have It and Not Know It," *Hepatitis B—Get the Facts,* http://www.phac-aspc.gc.ca/hcai-iamss/bbp-pts/hepatitis/hep_b-eng.php (last updated August 21, 2010).

38   Smart Sex Resource, "Hepatitis B," *A–Z Topics* (2012), http://smartsexresource.com/topics/hepatitis-b.

RESOURCES

There's a lot out there on polyamory, as well as the skills—such as communication and cultivating healthy self-esteem—that are useful in creating happy poly relationships. With the list below, we've tried to present a few of the standouts in each category.

RELATIONSHIPS

The Dance of Intimacy: A Woman's Guide to Courageous Acts of Change in Key Relationships, Harriet Lerner (Harper Perennial, 1989). A classic book, geared at women but useful for everyone, on maintaining clear boundaries and a strong self while building intimacy in relationships. Harriet Lerner also maintains an excellent (though monogamy-focused) blog on the *Psychology Today* website.

Daring Greatly: How the Courage to Be Vulnerable Transforms the Way We Live, Love, Parent, and Lead, Brené Brown (Penguin, 2012). About expressing courage in all our relationships and throughout our lives by daring to be our most authentic selves.

Emotional Blackmail: When the People in Your Life Use Fear, Obligation, and Guilt to Manipulate You, Susan Forward and Donna Frazier (William Morrow, 1998). A primer on recognizing and dealing with emotional manipulation and blackmail in romantic relationships.

SELF

The Gifts of Imperfection: Let Go of Who You Think You're Supposed to Be and Embrace Who You Are, Brené Brown (Hazelden, 2010). A small but life-changing, evidence-based book on confronting insecurity, believing in our own worthiness and living what Brown calls "wholehearted" lives. Brown also writes a blog at *brenebrown.com.*

The How of Happiness: A New Approach to Getting the Life You Want, Sonja Lyubomirsky (Penguin, 2007). Another research-based book that delves into the factors in personal happiness that are within our control.

COMMUNICATION AND CONFLICT

The Dance of Connection: How to Talk to Someone When You're Mad, Hurt, Scared, Frustrated, Insulted, Betrayed, or Desperate, Harriet Lerner (HarperCollins, 2009). Excellent techniques for high-stakes communication in any kind of relationship and emotionally charged situations.

Nonviolent Communication: A Language of Life: Life-Changing Tools for Healthy Relationships, Marshall Rosenberg and Arun Gandhi (Puddledancer Press, 2008). A guidebook for clear, compassionate communication that teaches the foundations of authentic communication without bullying.

The Joy of Conflict Resolution: Transforming Victims, Villains and Heroes in the Workplace and at Home, Gary Harper (New Society Publishers, 2009, available direct from newsociety.com). On the "drama triangle" in conflict and how to find a path out of it through curiosity and compassion.

Messages: The Communication Skills Book, Matthew McKay, Martha Davis and Patrick Fanning (New Harbinger Publications, 2009). A workbook containing practical exercises for improving personal communication skills in personal and professional life.

SEX

The best, most current information on STI prevention and testing can be found at the websites of the U.S. Centers for Disease Control and Prevention (cdc.gov) and Planned Parenthood (plannedparenthood.org).

The Ethical Slut: A Practical Guide to Polyamory, Open Relationships and Other Adventures, Dossie Easton and Janet W. Hardy (Greenery Press, 2nd ed., 2011). The landmark book on non-monogamy, first published in 1997.

A Tired Woman's Guide to Passionate Sex: Reclaim Your Desire and Reignite Your Relationship, Laurie B. Mintz (Adams Media, 2009). A book aimed at heterosexual women with the goal of rekindling desire in long-term relationships, with success that has been supported by peer-reviewed research.

POLYAMORY

Redefining Our Relationships: Guidelines for Responsible Open Relationships, Wendy-O Matik (Defiant Times Press, 2002). A tiny manifesto on abandoning the relationship escalator and creating intentional, ethically non-monogamous relationships.

The Polyamorists Next Door: Inside Multiple-Partner Relationships and Families, Elisabeth Sheff (Rowman & Littlefield Publishers, 2013). An in-depth, inside view of polyamorous families based on over a decade of research.

The Polyamory on Purpose Guide to Poly and Pregnancy, Jessica Burde (CreateSpace, 2013). A complete guide to pregnancy in poly relationships, covering topics including planned pregnancy, unintended pregnancy, custody and child care.

The Jealousy Workbook: Exercises and Insights for Managing Open Relationships, Kathy Labriola (Greenery Press, 2013). Forty-two practical exercises that can be completed solo, with a partner or with the help of a therapist.

BLOGS AND WEBSITES

More Than Two, morethantwo.com. Franklin's own website, maintained since 1997, with a wealth of information on managing poly relationships. He and Eve also maintain a blog at morethantwo.com/blog.

Solopoly, solopoly.net. An excellent blog from a solo poly perspective, covering everything from the politics to the practicalities of solo polyamory.

The Polyamorous Misanthrope, polyamorousmisanthrope.com. A long-running blog that's a gold mine of supremely practical poly advice, all written with a good dose of humor.

The Radical Poly Agenda, radicalpoly.wordpress.com. A blog that takes on the political and ideological implications of polyamory from a feminist, anarchic perspective.

Sex Geek, sexgeek.wordpress.com. Andrea Zanin's blog on polyamory, sex positivity, kink, and all things sexy and geeky. Pragmatic poly advice that goes beyond the couple-focused, heterosexual, monogamy-plus model.

Polyamory in the News, polyinthemedia.blogspot.ca. A site that reviews global media coverage of polyamory and also contains comprehensive lists of worldwide poly events, poly groups and poly books.

Polyamory Weekly, polyweekly.com. A weekly, down-to-Earth podcast by Cunning Minx, covering poly issues with a good dose of compassion and humor.

MEMOIR
Open: Love, Sex and Life in an Open Marriage, Jenny Block (Seal Press, 2009). A personal memoir of suburban polyamory that narrates Block's exploration beyond her monogamous relationship.

The Husband Swap, Louisa Leontiades (CreateSpace, 2012). An emotionally raw and deeply vulnerable memoir of Leontiades's entry into polyamory when she and her husband began a cross-coupled quad. Likely to resonate with many couples who are in the early stages of opening their relationship.

INDEX

The letter "n" after a page number indicates a footnote and the letter "t" a table. **Boldface** page numbers indicate definitions in the glossary.

Made in the USA
Middletown, DE
11 December 2014